THE BIG BOOK OF UFOS

THE BIG BOOK OF

UFOs

Chris A. Rutkowski

DUNDURN PRESS
TORONTO

Copy Editor: Matt Baker
Design: Jesse Hooper
Printer: Transcontinental

Library and Archives Canada Cataloguing in Publication

Rutkowski, Chris
        The big book of UFOs / by Chris A. Rutkowski.

Issued also in an electronic format.
ISBN 978-1-55488-760-6

        1. Unidentified flying objects. 2. Unidentified flying objects--
Sightings and encounters. I. Title.

TL789.R785 2010   001.942   C2010-902408-7

1 2 3 4 5   14 13 12 11 10

We acknowledge the support of the **Canada Council for the Arts** and the **Ontario Arts Council** for our publishing program. We also acknowledge the financial support of the **Government of Canada** through the **Canada Book Fund** and **The Association for the Export of Canadian Books**, and the **Government of Ontario** through the **Ontario Book Publishers Tax Credit program**, and the **Ontario Media Development Corporation**.

Care has been taken to trace the ownership of copyright material used in this book. The author and the publisher welcome any information enabling them to rectify any references or credits in subsequent editions.

                                                                J. Kirk Howard, President

www.dundurn.com

Dundurn Press	Gazelle Book Services Limited	Dundurn Press
3 Church Street, Suite 500	White Cross Mills	2250 Military Road
Toronto, Ontario, Canada	High Town, Lancaster, England	Tonawanda, NY
M5E 1M2	LA1 4XS	U.S.A. 14150

To Nu

CONTENTS

PART THREE: CONTACT: ABDUCTIONS, CREATURES, AND THE SEARCH FOR PROOF

Acknowledgements

To produce a Big Book, one must have friends and colleagues with Big Hearts. I certainly have many of these.

In terms of writing and encouragement, I must thank my writers' group, Off The Wall, including Evelyn Woodward, Susan Rocan, Kevin Russell, Sam Courcelles, K.C. Oliver, Katherine Lovejoy, and Barbara Lange.

My publisher, Dundurn Press, has helped me refine and craft my manuscript into readable form, particularly their staff: Matt Baker, Margaret Bryant, Tammy Mavroudi, Karen McMullin, Michael Carroll, Jennifer Scott, and especially Beth Bruder.

For assistance with scanning and artwork, I would like to thank Pat Goss and Stacey Archer, as well as Jennifer Wang, Susan Birdwise, Vladimir Simosko, Zachary Rutkowski, Erwin Dirks, and Billy Booth.

For moral support and for sharing views, news, and ideas about UFOs, I would like to thank Alan and Cindy Anderson, Geoff Currier, Geoff Dittman, John Danakas, Grant Cameron, Sue St. Clair, Terry Groff, Linda and Don Percy, Dave Trimble, Stanton Friedman, Nicholas Roesler, Vladimir Simosko, Francois Bourbeau, Errol Bruce-Knapp, and Chris Reid.

Finally, it goes without saying, but I will anyway: a special thank you to my wife Donna, who kept the house going while I was hiding in the study. Her support and inspiration are what keep me going. Not only that, she's pretty.

Thanks also to Vicki and Zach, who told me they helped her around the house with chores and other duties as assigned.

THE METRIC SYSTEM

Throughout this book, you'll find measurements in metric units. If you find this at all confusing, it may help to reference this handy chart:

1 centimetre = 0.3937 inches

1 metre   = 3.281 feet

1 kilometre   = 0.6214 miles

OR

1 inch   is roughly   2.5 centimetres

1 metre   is roughly   3 feet (a little more)

1 kilometre   is just over   half a mile

For temperatures, weights, and complicated conversions, you can find several free conversion sites online.

Introduction

This is a big book about UFOs.

I've been writing about the UFO phenomenon for almost 35 years, having investigated hundreds of UFO sightings, interviewed thousands of witnesses, and conducted research since the mid-1970s. I've heard it all: from pilots' eyewitness accounts of encounters with craft that seemed to defy physics, to the befuddlement of professionals who insist that aliens visited them in their bedrooms.

I have travelled across Canada on investigative expeditions, and driven through the Midwestern United States to interview witnesses in many counties. I have sat throughout the night in some popular UFO haunts, but never saw anything that defied explanation, much to the chagrin of my guides and companions.

As an astronomer, I spent many hours with my eye frozen to a telescope eye-piece at brutal temperatures — my record is -42 degrees Celsius at 3:30 a.m. — watching the Moon's terminator plunge a small crater's rim into darkness. I have shown eager kids and their parents Saturn's rings through a small scope at public star parties, and I have presented papers at astronomical conferences.

I'm fascinated with space and astronomy. I was taught by brilliant minds such as cosmologist Dr. Martin Clutton-Brock and "pure astronomer" Dr. Richard Bochonko, for whom spherical astronomy and orbital dynamics came naturally. But not me.

I've always had a sense of wonder about the universe. Growing up, my most common question was, "Why?" Now I know the most appropriate answer is not, "Because," but, "Why not?"

At a young age I wondered if there was other life out there, somewhere. It was a sensible enough question. After all, we're here, so why shouldn't there be other beings on other planets, wondering the same thing?

After more than 35 years of investigation and research — and wondering — I still don't know. Why has the UFO phenomenon been so persistent? Why do people still report seeing unidentified objects in the sky, despite the best efforts of scientists to assure them there is nothing of concern? Why do we persist in wondering?

I've written several books, published dozens of research papers and reports, and over the past decade posted many blog entries and tweeted about the UFO phenomenon.

This Big Book of UFOs contains some of the most interesting stories and cases from my files, some of which have appeared in my other books, but many which were researched and are described here for the first time. I don't think any non-believers will be convinced, nor do I expect ardent UFO fans will doubt some of the more popular UFO tales.

The idea behind this book is to inform and entertain, and make you wonder.

As I still do.

LIFE IN THE UNIVERSE

1
THE UFO QUESTION

BY THE NUMBERS

Ten percent of all North Americans have seen UFOs.

This is not a number picked frivolously out of thin air (pardon the pun), but a statistic based on polls and surveys in the United States and Canada, done by various independent polling organizations and groups.

When asked the question, "Have you ever seen a UFO?" one in every 10 people will say, "Yes."

DID YOU KNOW?

Only one out of every 10 UFO sightings is actually reported.

This number is significant. In 2009, according to Statistics Canada, there were 33.8 million people in Canada and 303.8 million people in the United States. Ten percent of these are 3.3 million people for Canada and 30.3 million for the U.S. — definitely a lot of UFO witnesses. The percentage is the same in other developed countries such as Mexico and Britain.

The significance of this data is that according to 2009 data published by Statistics Canada, only slightly fewer people have asthma (2.3 million) as have seen UFOs, although more have high blood pressure (4.6 million). By way of comparison, seven million children are afflicted with asthma in the United States, and 46 million people in America have been diagnosed with arthritis (about one in five adults). Depression affects 17 million Americans.

Credit: Jennifer Wang.

The importance of these comparative statistics is that there is great concern about the large number of people with high blood pressure, arthritis, depression, and other diseases, and this has resulted in national programs to educate the public about prevention and treatment of these conditions. However, more than three million Canadians and 30 million Americans believe they have seen UFOs, and yet this does not seem to be of concern to educators, politicians, or the scientific community.

If, as some suggest, people who see UFOs are imagining them or simply seeing things, should this not be cause for some worry, since one in 10 people cannot trust their own eyes? Or if, as others believe, people are seeing spaceships from other planets, would an armada of three million vessels not cause some anxiety for military strategists?

WHAT ARE UFOS?

Of course, these statistics need some expansion and interpretation. The term *UFO* is very ambiguous, being simply an abbreviation of the phrase *unidentified flying object*. In popular culture, it has come to mean "alien spacecraft," but that is not necessarily what has been observed or reported.

Ufology Research, an independent and unfunded group that has been studying UFO reports in Canada for more than 30 years, has published the Canadian UFO Survey, compiling case data and an annual analysis of UFO sightings reported officially in Canada. In 2008, a record 1,004 UFO cases were examined. In 2009, the total was only 801 cases.

In general, since the yearly analyses began in the 1980s, the number of UFO sightings reported in Canada steadily increased overall, until the drop in 2009. This is in direct contradiction to news stories and skeptical UFO TV shows which have stated throughout the past 25 years that the number of UFO reports was decreasing.

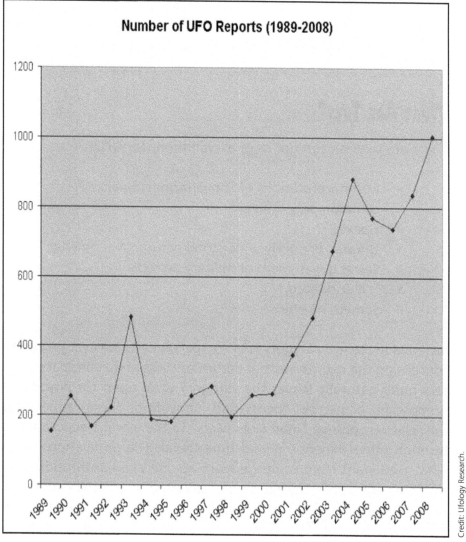

The number of UFOs reported in Canada during 1989 to 2008.

Comparisons with other databases, such as the National UFO Reporting Center in the U.S., show a general increase in the number of reported UFOs over the past several years. Why the public is being told that UFOs are on the decline is not clear.

Remember, however, that this number of UFO reports is raw UFO cases, and many turn out to be aircraft or satellites. Still, there are dozens of high-quality unknowns each year.

When someone asks, "Do UFOs really exist?" do you answer with a yes or a no? This is actually a trick question, because the question itself is not phrased correctly.

UFOs are, quite simply, Unidentified Flying Objects, and they certainly exist! There are thousands of reports of unusual objects filed every year with various organizations by people who did not know what it was they were seeing. To them, they were definitely *unidentified* objects, mostly seen flying in the sky.

WHAT ARE THEY?

There are six basic categories of explanations for UFOs:

- Misinterpretations of conventional objects or common phenomena;
- Hoaxes;
- Unusual or poorly understood natural phenomena;
- Secret government or military projects;
- Hallucinations;
- Something else.

Included in the last category is every speculative idea ever proposed concerning the extraterrestrial nature of UFOs and alien spacecraft. This quite naturally leaves the category wide open for anyone to propose his or her pet theory and innovation. These range from the relatively passive "man from Mars" to the extragalactic, and on through other dimensions and time travel. The motivations as to what they want from us range from benign alien anthropologists watching our daily routines to preparation for insidious oppression, colonization, or slavery.

UFOs are merely objects in the sky that defy explanation by an observer. Obviously, such objects exist. Some stimulus was in the sky to affect an observation, and thus cause a UFO sighting.

The question that was probably intended is: "Do flying saucers from other planets exist?" The answer to this question is one that has led many skeptics and believers to go at each others' throats in vicious arguments.

WHAT DO THE PEOPLE SAY?

Polls have been conducted regarding people's belief in UFOs as alien spacecraft. As early as 1957, a poll found that 25 percent of Americans thought there was a possibility that flying saucers were from outer space. The first Gallup Poll on the subject in 1966 found that about 5 percent of the population had seen a UFO and 46 percent believed UFOs were real objects and not imaginary.

In 1971, a survey of engineers and academics found that 54 percent believed UFOs were real and that 32 percent thought they were from outer space.

By the time of the next Gallup Poll in 1973, numbers had changed somewhat. About 11 percent of the population believed they had seen UFOs and 51 percent thought UFOs were real. A Canadian Gallup Poll in 1974 found Canadians were a bit more skeptical: 36 percent said UFOs were real, and 8 percent said they had seen a UFO.

A Roper Poll in 1974 showed 40 percent of Americans "believed in UFOs," and a Canadian Gallup Poll in 1978 found that 46 percent thought UFOs were real and 10 percent had seen one. An American Gallup Poll in 1978 found 9 percent had seen a UFO and 57 percent thought they were real. Almost 10 years later, in 1987, the same number said they had seen UFOs, while slightly less, about 49 percent, thought UFOs were real.

Among the intellectual elite, it seems that UFOs are a given commodity. A 1975 poll of the French branch of Mensa — the international group for which you need to have an IQ in the top 98 percent of the population — found that almost all (93 percent) believed in UFOs, 52 percent thought they were from outer space, and 49 percent had seen one. A survey of American Mensa members found lower but still significant results: 64 percent thought they were space-ships from other planets and 16 percent had seen UFOs. In 1984, the magazine *Psychology Today* polled its readers and found that about half of them "believed" in UFOs.

A Scripps News Service Poll in 1995 found that 50 percent "believed" in

UFOs while a *Newsweek* magazine poll found only 48 percent believed "reports of UFOs are real."

In 2002 the Sci Fi Channel enlisted Roper to poll Americans about UFOs and found that about 48 percent believed aliens have visited Earth and 14 percent said they or someone they know had a "close encounter" with a UFO.

Finally, in 2008, Scripps News Service polled Americans about their belief in UFOs. They found that 8 percent of the population had seen a UFO but 20 percent know someone who has seen a UFO. About 30 percent believe aliens from space have visited Earth.

All these polls show that about half the population believes UFOs are real, although what that means is a matter of debate. More significantly, about 10 percent of all North Americans believe they have seen a UFO.

The term *flying saucer* is very liberally applied to UFOs by news media and most laypeople. The term was first coined in 1947 when pilot Kenneth Arnold claimed he had seen silver disc-like objects flying near Mt. Rainier in Washington State. When asked by a reporter to describe what he had seen, Arnold replied that the appearance of the objects' flight was that they moved as if they were plates or saucers skimming across water. A headline writer quickly took the analogy as *flying saucers*, and the name stuck in the public mind.

Arnold's objects were in a special category of what are called today *daylight discs*. These are in the minority when compared with the bulk of UFO reports; most UFO sightings are of objects known as *nocturnal lights*. Such objects are simply lights in the night sky that behave in ways that seem mysterious to their observers. Many of these turn out to have explanations such as an aircraft, satellite, star, planet or meteor.

What kind of people see UFOs? While some skeptics might answer that UFO witnesses are delusional, gullible, or uneducated, the reality is that the demographics of UFO witnesses cuts across all ages, socioeconomic statuses, educational backgrounds, occupations, and cultures. Furthermore, many witnesses are people with significant training in observation and judgment. Unfortunately, many UFO witnesses are reluctant to tell others of their sightings for fear of being ridiculed by skeptics. This attitude is changing, thankfully, and it appears that society as a whole is becoming more accepting of those who have had remarkable experiences.

Did You Know?

UFOs have
been reported by astronomers, pilots,
and air traffic controllers.

2
BEYOND OUR SOLAR SYSTEM

A MODEL OF THE NEARBY STARS

Let's start with the sun, but let's make it a bit smaller. Imagine that it is the size of a pea held in the palm of your hand. On this scale, the Earth is actually invisible, but would be about 1.2 metres away from the pea. But where would the *next nearest* pea be? That is, where, using this scale model of size and distance in our local astronomical neighbourhood, would the next nearest star be located? In front of your home, a block away? Farther downtown?

The answer is that if our star, the sun, was as small as a pea in your hand, the next nearest pea (Proxima Centuari) would be almost 320 kilometres away.

That's how vast the space between stars is, and how far away we are from even the *nearest* one. However, the nearest star may not harbour life. In fact, statistics tell us that intelligent life and extraterrestrial civilizations may be relatively rare in our universe. Some astronomers believe that we are completely unique in our Solar System, although most think that there are other civilizations out there, somewhere.

Most readers will have grown up with science fiction TV shows such as *Star Trek* and movies like *Star Wars*, in which interstellar travel is commonplace and apparently simple. We live in the Steven Spielberg generation, in which science fiction concepts are accepted as reality or at least seem probable. But while present-day science is making advances in these areas, we're still a long way from even sending manned spacecraft to other planets within our own local Solar System. The fastest space vehicle launched from Earth to date will take thousands of years to reach the distance of even the nearest star.

The first spacecraft to leave our Solar System was Pioneer 10. It was launched in 1972 and reached the orbit of Jupiter in 1973, after which it continued on, but stopped transmitting signals to Earth in 2003 when its power source stopped functioning. It is heading in the direction of the constellation Taurus and will pass close to the star Aldebaran in about two million years.

Did You Know?

The belief
that life exists elsewhere in the universe
can be traced back to the Greek philosopher Anaxagoras, who
in the fifth century B.C. wrote that the universe is teeming with life.
He coined the term *panspermia*, which literally means
"seeds of life everywhere."

Pioneer 10's twin is Pioneer 11. It made a flyby of Saturn in 1979 and is heading in a different direction, this time for the constellation Aquila. It will reach it in about four million years. Both Pioneer 10 and Pioneer 11 had plaques attached to their sides upon which was inscribed a message to anyone or anything that might find the spacecraft some day. The plaques have pictures of a man and a woman, the Pioneer spacecraft, and instructions on how to find Earth based on navigating between pulsars in our galaxy.

Two spacecraft that were launched after the Pioneers but which will reach nearby stars sooner are Voyager 1 and Voyager 2. The first also went by Jupiter and is heading towards the constellation Camelopardalis, which it will reach in 300,000 years. Its twin, Voyager 2, is going in the direction of Sirius, the Dog Star, and will get there in "only" 150,000 years.

The fastest moving of these four spacecraft is Voyager 1, which is travelling at about 63,000 kilometres per hour. If you could drive a car that fast, you could go around the entire Earth in 45 minutes, assuming that someone built a road around the equator.

Despite what may seem to be a pessimistic view of travel times in outer space, it's theoretically possible for us to build spacecraft today that could reach a planet orbiting a nearby star within the lifetime of an astronaut on board. Einstein showed that a spacecraft moving fast enough would have time slow down on board the spacecraft while to an observer, on Earth, time would pass normally and it would seem that the spaceship was gone a very long time, perhaps many decades. To the astronaut, time would move more quickly and he or she would age at a much slower rate, reaching the destination in only a relative handful of years.

This is still a long way from "Warp Factor Three," but it shows that space travel is possible even with our present technology. But here's the single fact that could change science fiction into science fact: *not all stars are the same.*

THE STAR FACTOR

The Milky Way has about 100 billion stars. Some are hotter than our Sun; some are cooler than our Sun. Some are larger; some are smaller. Some are younger; some are older. In fact, some are *much* older — even billions of years older. What this means is that some stars with planets that can support life have had much longer to nurture and advance the life into highly evolved and technological civilizations. It is reasonable to think that some of these civilizations may have advanced so far technologically that they have discovered a way to travel between the stars like in the TV show *Star Trek* or at least have lifetimes that allow long journeys between stars. Maybe they have found ways to use sleep chambers to prevent aging on long voyages.

At any rate, the possibility that some alien civilizations are much more advanced than us is very good. If so, perhaps they have visited the Earth during our history or are doing so now. Just because we have no incontrovertible evidence they are doing so is not proof they are not doing so.

By definition, aliens will think and act in alien ways, beyond our comprehension and understanding. Maybe we simply cannot detect their existence because of some peculiar characteristic of their spacecraft.

OUR NEAREST NEIGHBOURS

There is a great deal of modern scientific research and brilliant deductive studies in the emerging field of *exobiology*: life outside of the Earth. Hardly a month goes by without more analyses being completed on another sample of Martian soil or rock in a quest for evidence of extraterrestrial organisms. The duplication of amino acid formation in the early stages of Earth's history has convinced many scientists that life would likely arise on other planets and produce creatures somewhat similar to ourselves.

We know with a high degree of certainty that other human-like creatures do not exist elsewhere in our Solar System. Speculation is rampant that primitive lichens and bacteria may exist on Mars, in Venus' atmosphere or perhaps even on a large moon of Jupiter or Saturn. Regardless, our local star system has been more or less

UFOs and Aliens in Literature

The term *Martian* conjures up images of bug-eyed monsters, many-tentacled monsters and evil aliens, all intent on doing us in, but also a black-headed cartoon character who battled Bugs Bunny in several shorts and features. As well, Edgar Rice Burroughs, creator of Tarzan, wrote a series of space romance novels in the early 1900s in which American John Carter travelled to Mars and battled many strange creatures, often necessary to rescue maidens in distress.

eliminated for extraterrestrial life, based on our knowledge of what conditions are necessary for life to be viable, such as heat, light, water, etc. Where else might it occur?

On a clear night, you can see only about 5,000 of the billions of stars in the universe. The rest are too far away and their light is too dim to be seen by us here on Earth. Some of these stars are physically very close to us and can be called our neighbours, even though they are still trillions of kilometres away!

The nearest star system to us is the Centauri triplet of stars right next door, only 40,621,000,000,000 kilometres away! That's about 4.3 light years in astronomical terms; it takes light waves more than four years just to reach us from those stars.

The nearest of all other stars is Proxima Centauri. It's a dim, red star that orbits

What is a Light Year?

Distances in space are measured not in miles or kilometres, but in light years. One light year is the distance that light travels in one year. Although light seems instantaneous, it actually takes time for it to travel great distances. The speed of light is 300,000 kilometres per second.

For example, since the Moon is about 376,000 kilometres away from the Earth, light takes a little over one second to travel between the Earth and Moon. The sun is much farther away, and light takes about eight minutes to reach us from its surface. But other stars and galaxies are much farther away, and light takes many years to travel that far.

the pair of stars known as Alpha Centauri A and Alpha Centauri B. These three stars perform a kind of cosmic waltz with one another, with Proxima dancing by itself while revolving around the two others of the trio. Proxima is about 4.2 light years from us, while its companions are 4.3 light years away. Alpha Centauri A is the same colour as our Sun, which means it is about the same temperature as the Sun. All things being equal, it might be able to support planets like Earth and sustain life.

However, with three stars orbiting around one another, the mechanics of planetary formation are complicated, so stable orbits for small planets may be difficult. But the two main stars of this system are a considerable distance apart, about the same as the distance between Earth and Uranus, so there may be stable orbits for planets close in to their stars.

In the movie *Avatar*, this is exactly what has happened, and one of the large gas giant planets orbiting Alpha Centauri A has a moon named Pandora that is inhabited by the mysterious blue creatures named *Na'vi*.

Next out is Barnard's Star, named for Edward Barnard of Lick Observatory in California, who discovered it in 1916. It is a dim, cool star like Proxima Centauri and is the closest nearby star that can be seen from the northern hemisphere, in the constellation Ophiuchus. Although it is about six light years away, it's getting closer to us, zipping through the galaxy at such a rate that it will come closer than Proxima Centauri in about 11,000 years, then move off again into deep space!

Wolf 359 is yet another small red star, this time in the constellation Leo. German astronomer Max Wolf measured its movement and listed it in a catalogue in 1917.

Our Nearest Neighbours

1. Proxima Centauri
2. Alpha Centauri A
3. Alpha Centauri B
4. Barnard's Star
5. Wolf 359
6. Lalande 21185
7. Sirius A
8. Sirius B
9. Luyten 726-8 A
10. Luyten 726-8 B
11. Ross 154

Credit: NASA.

Other planetary systems may have more than one sun in the sky. This artist's conception shows what the sky might look like on a planet orbiting within a three-star system. Could such a planet support life?

More than seven light years away, it's very faint and is actually one of the coolest stars known. Any planet orbiting this star would have to be very close to it in order to get enough heat and light to support any kind of life.

Lalande 21185 is in Ursa Major, better known as the Big Dipper. It was first catalogued by French astronomer Jerome Lalande in 1801. Although it's much brighter and hotter than the previous few stars in our list, it's not as warm as our Sun. Even though it is a bit more than eight light years away, astronomers have been able to detect a planet around it and it may have more. Could life have formed here?

Sirius, the Dog Star, is in the constellation Canis Major, more than eight-and-a-half light years from us. It is the brightest star in our sky, blue-white in colour and very noticeable when it is shining in the night, often casting shadows on Earth. It's about twice the size of our sun but much, much hotter. It might be possible for life to form on a planet in orbit around it, but it would complicated by Sirius' companion star, Sirius B, which is a much smaller star — a dwarf star — that is only about the size of Earth but is made of very dense matter. A milk jug filled with this kind of matter would weigh as much as a four-story building on Earth. Could life form in this two-star system?

Luyten 726-8 A and B are two small stars in the constellation Cetus, and are nearly nine light years away from Earth. They were discovered by Willem

UFOs and Aliens in Literature

One of the first stories to describe an alien visiting Earth is the classic literary work *Micromegas*, by the French satirist Voltaire. Written in 1752, the story tells of how someone from a planet orbiting Sirius travelled to Earth in the company of a Saturnian. These beings were supreme in many ways, least of all their size; one was 120,000 feet tall! The story was essentially a way to poke fun at French society at the time, so was quite fanciful, with the giants plucking ships out of the water and scorning the little Earthmen who thought themselves superior to others. In the story, the alien visitors marveled at our primitive and illogical society.

Luyten, a Dutch astronomer, in 1948. They are also "red dwarf" stars but have a distinctive characteristic that may make them unfit for sustaining life: they flare up occasionally, sending streams of energy into space. These flares are similar to those that shoot out from our own Sun, sometimes causing electrical blackouts on Earth. However, the flares on the Luyten stars are much more powerful and have greater energy.

Ross 154 is another red dwarf star in the constellation Sagittarius, and is more than nine light years from Earth. It also flares, with outbursts every few days.

Some other relatively nearby stars, such as Tau Ceti and Epsilon Eridani, were the targets of an attempt to establish radio contact with extraterrestrial beings in the 1960s. Our messages apparently were not answered, so they don't feel like answering, they weren't listening, or they're not there to begin with.

The nearest star that is most like the sun is Tau Ceti, in the constellation Cetus. It's only 12 light years away and does not exhibit flaring like other near stars, so it has a better likelihood of having planets with life. This is why it has been the target of searches for extraterrestrial life. No planets have been located in orbit around it, although Tau Ceti is known to have a disc of debris surrounding it, meaning that any planets there would have been bombarded with asteroids, perhaps wiping out life that may have started to form. Still, it may be one of the best local prospects for our finding alien life. No radio signals have been detected emanating from the Tau Ceti system, but scientists have not given up hope. Tau Ceti is one of five "best bets" that are being considered for new searches by dedicated instruments looking for signs of extraterrestrial life.

Another one of the "best bets" is Epsilon Eridani, a star similar in composition to the Sun. It's less than 11 light years away from Earth, but because it is relatively close, some direct astronomical measurements of it are possible, and it is known to have at least one large planet plus a ring of rocky debris. As long ago as 1960, a radio listening program called Project Ozma targeted both Tau Ceti and Epsilon Eridani, with no success. Recent observations have likewise not yielded any signs of life. However, because its temperature and size are like the Sun, it is the nearest star thought to be capable of having planets that could have life.

For this reason, many science fiction works have involved Epsilon Eridani: the space station *Babylon 5* orbited a planet around Epsilon Eridani; Isaac Asimov's *Foundation* series is set partly in the Epsilon Eridani system; and the popular video game *Halo* has the planet Reach as a military base that saw much fighting over two game visualizations, with other planets of Epsilon Eridani part of the action as well.

OTHER PLANETS

Recently, astronomical techniques and imaging have advanced so much, it has been possible to detect planets around some stars. More than 400 extrasolar planets have been found using high-powered telescopes and spectral analyses of starlight. Because of their incredible distances, nearly all of these planets are much bigger than Earth, and in many cases, far bigger than Jupiter, the largest planet in our own Solar System.

In January 2010, astronomers discovered a planet only about four times as massive as Earth. What's more, it is only about 80 light years away from us, in the constellation Hercules. However, this relatively small exoplanet is very close to its star (named HD156668) and is therefore far too hot to sustain life as we know it.

In 2004, astronomers detected a large planet orbiting the star Gliese 436, a dim red dwarf only 33 light years from Earth. It is about the size of Neptune, smaller than Jupiter but much larger than Earth. In 2008, astronomers announced they had found a second planet inside the orbit of the first one, possibly less than twice the size of Earth. This very hot planet zips very quickly around its parent star, only a fraction of the distance from it that Mercury orbits our Sun, and we know that the surface of Mercury is hot enough to melt lead! In addition, other astronomers believe there may be other planets in this same system. This is exciting news, because it adds support to the theory than most stars will have a system of planets, similar to our own Sun. What's more, one of these planets orbiting Gliese 436 is not much bigger than Earth, possibly Earth's own twin. Could it possibly harbour life, too? And it's practically our next-door neighbour, only 33 light years away; if an alien civilization existed there, maybe its inhabitants are curious about Earth!

SUPPOSE ...

Let us suppose that there *are* sentient beings somewhat like ourselves (with whatever degree of sentience we have) on a planet circling a relatively nearby star, perhaps Tau Ceti. For some reason, these beings decide to visit us and launch a rocket ship (or flying saucer) towards us with a select group of space travelers on board.

If they travel with a top speed of the fastest space vehicle Earth engineers have themselves launched in various directions, the one-way trip to Earth from Tau Ceti would take approximately 50,000 years. This is because although Tau Ceti is 11 light years away from us, light travels at 300,000 kilometres per second, a speed which we can barely consider, let alone achieve.

In Their Own Words

Thousands of UFO sightings are reported each year. Throughout this book, examples of actual, unedited letters from UFO witnesses will show how the phenomenon is observed and how it its interpreted. In all cases, the names of witnesses have been removed for their privacy.

Talkeetna, Alaska
December 21, 1994

I sat in the outhouse about midnight with the front opening to the northwest. I looked up about due north and saw bright strobes of red and green, thinking it was a jet en route from Anchorage to Fairbanks. (Talkeetna is in the Anchorage-Fairbanks air corridor.) I looked up again and the lights had not moved any appreciable distance like jets do. I noticed that one of the blinking lights appeared to be purple and blue, unlike any aircraft markings. The lights appeared about 40 degrees off the horizon almost due north and did not appear to move. The strobes were quite bright for what seemed to be an object quite far away.

My wife joined me in the observation and saw the same red, green and blue strobe-type lights, but did not see purple. I put the binoculars on the lights and could make out no shape, but the colored light flashes appeared to come from the top and bottom. I got out my daughters telescope and tried to find the object but only found a luminescent sphere somewhat like the moon except without dark areas. Since it was near zero with a bit of wind, I had trouble stabilizing this small telescope, and am not sure I focused on the object I saw with the binoculars. I did not see any other bright objects in that part of the sky.

We continued to observe the colorful strobe lights for more than an hour and a half, during which time it travelled a few degrees to the east and became increasingly distant. I've observed planes and satellites, but never anything like this. The night was so clear that anyone for many miles around could have observed the same thing.

I spoke about it on the radio to a neighbor a few miles away the following night, and she said she had seen a similar thing about this time of year some years ago. There are military operation areas nearby, and maybe there is some sort of super slow satellite or some extremely high helicopter, but I am curious to know what it might have been.

Reported by Anonymous
Source: Ufology Research

It would be a long voyage, even if the Tau Cetians are placed in some sort of cryogenic suspension or stasis, or if they are extremely long-lived. There is no guarantee that their equipment would continue to function properly over such a long period of time. Not only that, as they travel, their home planet and the Earth itself will age in normal time; drastic geological and biological changes will occur in the course of 50,000 years. We (or their kin) may not be here. Our technology and society may have advanced to an unbelievable level, or perhaps not.

It is the technology that may be the important factor. A possible scenario would be the following:

IF their star began its planet-forming process before our own sun did, then they may very well be far in advance of us technologically; and

IF they are more advanced than us, they may have been able to design spacecraft that can attain velocities far in excess of our own capabilities, perhaps even speeds a significant fraction of light; and

IF they can obtain such velocities, then a 50,000 year journey could be condensed into a much shorter time span, perhaps only a few years or months; and

IF they decided that a trip was warranted, they might choose to visit Earth; then

IF they are visiting us, their means of transportation here could be observed by us as UFOs.

Did You Know?

The Outer Space Treaty, drafted by the United Nations in 1967 and signed by the United States, United Kingdom, and Soviet Union, holds that if any extraterrestrial life is discovered, the secretary-general of the U.N. must be notified. (Part Two, Section A, Article 5, Point 3.)

SETI

The Search for Extra-Terrestrial Intelligence (SETI) is the name of scientific studies of distant objects in the universe in the expectation that extraterrestrial life exists and can be detected. Some SETI projects search for electromagnetic transmissions like radio signals from civilizations on distant planets, while others are more passive and involve the search for extrasolar planets. Some SETI projects have been government funded, while others, especially recent research, have been primarily funded by private sources.

In 1960, Cornell University astronomer Frank Drake used a radio telescope at Green Bank, West Virginia, to examine the stars Tau Ceti and Epsilon Eridani for radio signals that might be from alien civilizations. His experiment was called

10 REPORTED SHAPES OF UFOs

1. Saucer
2. Sphere
3. Cigar
4. Egg
5. Boomerang
6. Triangle
7. "Fuzzy"
8. Fireball
9. Starlike
10. Blob

"Project Ozma," after the Queen of Oz in L. Frank Baum's books about the *Wizard of Oz*. However, Drake did not detect anything out of the ordinary.

In 1971, NASA funded a program called Project Cyclops that proposed the construction of hundreds of small radio telescopes linked together so that they could act as one huge eye to look for signals from other civilizations in the galaxy. It was never built, largely because the price tag in the 1970s was more than $10 billion.

In 1974, an experiment at the Arecibo radio observatory in Puerto Rico sent a signal into space towards the globular cluster M13 in the constellation Hercules, about 25,000 light years from Earth. The signal contained a detailed message from we Earthlings, giving our location in the Solar System, information on our planet, and what we look like. Of course, since the message will take 25,000 years to reach its destination, even if aliens there received our message and replied right away, we wouldn't know for another 50,000 years!

The 1970s saw many astronomers scanning the skies for possible indications of life in the universe. And, in 1977, something remarkable may have been detected. On August 15, a researcher monitoring space for radio signals using the Big Ear radio telescope of Ohio State University noticed a strange signal that was not manmade. It was called the "Wow!" signal because it may have been from aliens across the galaxy! Wow!

Other SETI programs have included SERENDIP, META and BETA, each becoming more and more efficient and powerful at scanning more and more radio frequencies for possible signals from extraterrestrial civilizations.

In 1999, the University of California created SETI@Home, a user-based system for sifting through a vast amount of radio signals recorded by a SERENDIP radio telescope. Its concept was as ingenious as it was simple. Rather than using one expensive and massive computer to look for alien signals within a mass of data, the SETI@Home project invited anyone with a home computer to download a program along with small collections of data and run the analysis during the personal computer's downtime. With almost 200,000 volunteers, the result is a combined effort that is more powerful than that of one large computer.

However, not everyone is a fan of the SETI program. In 2009, Brad Niesluchowski, an information technologist at Higley Unified School District in Mesa, Arizona, resigned after an audit of schools' computers found that he had installed the SETI@Home program on many of them in 2000. It was claimed that the program had slowed down the schools' computers and interfered with other operations. It was estimated that it would cost about one million dollars to bring the computers back into normal operation. Even though Niesluchowski's intentions were purely scientific, his passion ended up costing him his job.

UFOs and Aliens in Movies

The Day the Earth Stood Still (1951) is a classic even beyond ufology, turning the alien invasion theme on its head. When the alien Klaatu's saucer hovers over Washington, it creates absolute chaos, despite his good intentions. When he tries to give humans some gifts and wisdom, the response is less than warm. This is a story of hope and peace dashed by our inherent xenophobia, and the inappropriate and unwise use of military force when faced with what we might perceive as a threat to ourselves and society. How will we react when an alien spaceship does land on Earth?

UFO SIGHTINGS, FROM FROM PAST TO PRESENT

1
UFOs Before 1900

SIGHTINGS OF OLD

Throughout recorded history, people have seen unusual objects in the sky that they could not explain or understand. The earliest ancestors of humans may have looked up and seen a multitude of bright lights that hung motionless in the sky or zipped quickly across the bowl of night. The Milky Way — our galaxy — would have been visible as a bright patch of white that extended from horizon to horizon. Some ancient peoples called it the "Backbone of Night" (as noted by astronomy popularizer Carl Sagan).

A few objects in the sky were different, however. The brightest one was blinding in its intensity, and at certain times of the year, it gave a pleasing warmth. Another, about the same size, illuminated the ground and allowed seeing things when the brighter one had fled below the horizon or fell into the ocean, but didn't offer any heat at all.

Some of the lights in the sky were brighter than others, and some had different colours. A few were bright enough to cast shadows. It wasn't until much later in the evolution of our civilization that some humans began systematically observing the objects in the sky and noticing patterns and periodicity to their movements. The movement of the brighter ones could be predicted over time, and they found that using a tree or stone marker to indicate the rising of a particular bright light could help determine the coming and going of seasons. This was important for knowing when to plant crops for growing food and learning the migration patterns of wild animals that were hunted for their furs.

It became very important to study the objects in the sky. Soon, some people became experts at doing it and were looked upon as wise counselors, advising kings and leaders when to go on journeys, when to get slaves working in the fields, and when to go to war.

These early astronomers were astrologers who tracked the changes in the sky and came up with imaginative explanations for the comings and goings up above. Gods were playing with us, blessing us or reprimanding us as they saw fit, and humans had very little control over their own destiny. The best that could be hoped for was to try and please the gods or at least keep them from punishing us in some way.

But who were these gods? They obviously were not human, for they had powers of flight, control of weather, and doled out heat and light when they saw fit. They were, by definition, extraterrestrial; they were truly alien beings about whom we knew very little. Did they reside in ornate palaces held high in the air? Were there other worlds like our own?

It wasn't until Galileo demonstrated that some of the brighter lights in the sky were planets like our own, with smaller objects revolving around them, that it was realized that gods or other creatures might live on worlds other than Earth. But if so, how did they travel between there and here?

Some writers thought that such travel was done with large balloons. Others thought that giant birds could carry people between worlds. One Jules Verne story had humans travelling through the Solar System after accidentally being plucked from the air by a comet. Others suggested astral or soul travel was the way to explore the universe.

But that's how *we* would get from here to there. How would aliens on other planets travel between the stars? Would they use the same methods and technology? Would we even recognize them if they were here?

This last point is one that has led to some interesting speculation. Suppose, for example, that aliens visited Earth at some point in our history, rather than contacting us right now. What would our ancestors have thought of them?

The answer is that it depends on when they came for their visit. If an alien race came to Earth before recorded history, we would of course have no way of knowing they had been here. Or would we?

ANCIENT ASTRONAUTS

Statistically, it is more likely that aliens have visited Earth in the past than they are visiting right now. This is because given the billions of years since Earth was formed, if there are any aliens out there, the window of opportunity for them to happen to be in our neighbourhood is billions of years in length. It would allow for many visits or many different aliens to visit, even allowing for the alien civilizations themselves to evolve and develop space travel over the course of hundreds or thousands or

In Their Own Words

Channel Islands, California
February 13, 1995

Before I state what I saw I would like to clarify that I am using UFO in the very literal sense. I, and four of my friends saw something that we cannot explain. Here's the story.

At about 11:00 p.m. PST last night my friend called me over to his room. His room looks out on the Channel Islands and is on the 7th floor, giving it an excellent view. On the horizon I saw a line of lights. After summoning two more friends and getting a pair of binoculars was able to see it somewhat more clearly. The lights were arranged symmetrically around the axis perpendicular to us.

I will describe the lights as I saw them from left to right. The first light was slightly above the others, after a small space there was a group of four lights close together in a straight line, after another space was a single light, a larger space separated it from a pair lights in the centre, another equally large space lead to another single light, a smaller space separated this single light from a another straight line of four lights, at the end was another light above the rest at the same level as the first.

Through the Binoculars it appeared that the object was actually curved. At this point we left the dorm and went down to the beach to get a better view. As we watched we noticed it moved from East to West (The Ocean in Santa Barbara is actually to the South so it was moving from our left to our right) at differing speeds. It would go very fast for a short time and then stop. At one point I saw it bob down and then resume moving. My friend saw it tilt along the perpendicular axis as well while looking through binoculars.

We have no explanation for what it was. It disappeared behind one of the islands and did not reappear. The Islands are about 26 miles away and the thing appeared to be about an inch long from our perspective, for the distance then it must have been very large. This would rule out aircraft since 747s on approach into LA appear to be about an 1/8 of an inch and would be at roughly the same distance, if not closer. It also covered an incredible amount of space in a very short time, faster than we have seen other ships travel. Therefore we are at a loss. We have speculated that it might have something to do with Pt. Magu which is a Navy Training area S of here.

Reported by Doug A.
Source: Ufology Research

millions of years. On Earth, we're just now starting to take our first few hesitant steps into space.

Suppose a race of spacefaring aliens visited Earth just as the first primitive life forms began evolving in the ocean. They might have considered making a note to visit in another million years or so, to see how we were making out.

Suppose they came back when apelike creatures were just developing an early kind of structured society. Would they interfere? Would they decide we were too aggressive and wipe us out so that we could start again? Would they recognize that we had reached a particular stage in evolution and just needed more time to progress?

What if the aliens arrived just when humans were in an early age of technological development, say, 5,000 years ago. We had fire and some rudimentary smelting of ore into metal by about 3000 B.C., but before that we were in the Stone Age. Our understanding of the world was limited at this time, and there were many competing mythologies to explain the forces of nature. Tribal warfare was the global pastime, and we lived in small feudal communities that were ruled by strong warriors. (Not that this has changed all that much....)

Imagine what would have happened if an alien spaceship (let's say it was a flying saucer) landed just outside a small village and the occupants got out to say hello. What would be the reaction of the humans to these visitors?

Some humans would have viewed the visitors as interlopers, threatening their territory. Perhaps they would try to attack the people from the sky.

Some would have been terrified, for early mythologies understood the gods who controlled the heavens to be powerful and not to be crossed. They might have venerated the aliens as gods, realizing they had powers and abilities far beyond the Earthly technology of the time.

From the aliens' perspective, however, what would they have thought of the Earthlings standing before them? They may have been amused at the reaction. They may have been prepared for the humans' response, as they likely would have considered the various possibilities as they prepared to land.

UFOs and Aliens on TV

ALF was about an Alien Life Form who crashes on Earth into a suburban neighbourhood. He is harboured by the Tanner family, who take him in as an eccentric houseguest. The little, annoying, furry creature was from the planet Melmac, which was destroyed during a nuclear war, and he wants to ensure that the same doesn't happen to Earth. The series lasted from 1986 to 1990 and was followed by a TV movie.

Indeed, why would they land and contact humans at all? In the fictional world of *Star Trek*, we are told of the "Prime Directive," Starfleet's General Order Number One, which forbids any interference with the normal and healthy development of alien life and culture. In particular, a developing society is not to be given any knowledge or technology that is beyond its ability. Although this is a fictional law, it does make sense, as natural development should be preferred over outside intervention.

In another fictional story, Olaf Stapleton's book *Star Maker*, primitive people are not told of the alien race observing them to keep their "independence of mind."

But these laws are fictional. It would not be surprising to find that an alien race might have different ideas about interference with a planet's development. They might view their assistance as essential to our development. Perhaps their evolution was similarly boosted.

If aliens visiting Earth were not bound by such a non-interference law, they might show themselves openly and perhaps even share technology with the

UFOs and Aliens in Literature

In 1657, Cyrano de Bergerac had written the "Comical History" of his *Voyage to the Moon*, where he met beautiful creatures living in lush palaces in Edenlike surroundings. This was also true of the first real science fiction story, "The Diamond Lens" by Fitzjames O'Brien, published in 1858. In this story, a man uses a powerful microscope to see and communicate with a tiny female creature "of perfect beauty." In other words, early stories about aliens pictured them as basically people like ourselves, but with remarkable powers and wisdom that surpassed our own abilities and knowledge.

primitives. They might give the chief of the tribe special weapons to defeat enemies or show the people how to smelt metals into utensils and other things. Aliens might use their own devices to help manufacture items for use in the village, or provide food when hunting is unsuccessful and crops fail.

If any of these scenarios happened in the past, there might be evidence of alien intervention still on the Earth. Some artefacts might exist in museums or are still buried in archaeological sites, waiting to be discovered. The premise of Arthur C. Clarke's classic *2001: A Space Odyssey* is that after nudging our evolutionary development in primitive times, aliens left an artefact on the Moon, waiting for us to travel into space and eventually find it.

If aliens visited Earth during the Bronze or Iron Age, they would have been here during Biblical times. How would they have been viewed by Mesopotamian peoples?

Many books have been written about the concept of alien intervention in early human history. Barry Downing, whose book *The Bible and Flying Saucers* set the tone for many later authors, built upon ideas from earlier writers. Some, such as Robert Charroux, wrote extensively about ancient artefacts that puzzled historians and were thought by some to have alien origins. Downing's thesis can be summarized in the following passage:

> ... if beings from another world came to Earth with the intention of molding a specific religious perspective on a group of people — chosen people, the Jews — and if these beings in their UFO caused the parting of the Red Sea, provided manna in the wilderness, put

on a display of power at Mount Sinai while giving Moses various instructions, and finally led Israel through the wilderness to the Promised Land, hovering night and day over the Tent of Meeting, then I dare say that the people involved in this sequence, the people who were under the influence of the beings in the UFO, might very well record the events in which they were involved.

Downing's interpretation of biblical events as being caused or designed by extraterrestrial aliens is not unique, and the idea has been explored in depth by numerous others.

One explicit work about direct alien intervention was that of Josef Blumrich, *The Spaceships of Ezekiel*, a detailed analysis of the "wheels" seen by Ezekiel in a vision. He believed these were actually part of a landing module similar to the one that NASA sent to the Moon. This wasn't surprising, since Blumrich was the chief of a NASA department at the time.

The most popular writer on the theme of ancient astronauts was Erich Von Daniken, whose wildly popular book, *Chariots of the Gods?*, was published in 1968. It took the world by storm when it was translated into English and became easily accessible. It led to several sequels, a storm of controversy, skeptical analysis, and even the creation of a tourist theme park in Europe which has now been closed.

Von Daniken himself was preceded by several authors, including Morris K. Jessup, whose much earlier work *UFOs and the Bible* (1956) suggested that holy book "is a treasure house of UFO data." Modern UFO-related books continue the theme of aliens as our ancestors and the reason for our development of civilization. Many authors are of the belief that the pyramids and other ancient monuments were either built by aliens or with their assistance. Similar claims are made about Stonehenge in England and the large ornate cities of the Aztecs in Central America.

In Peru, unusual linear markings adorn the seacoast and interior desert. These Nazca lines, as they are most often called, were created in about 1,000 B.C. by the agricultural society that was inhabiting the area at the time. Why they produced the lines and shapes is not known, but what is known is that the designs were made by removing a dark layer of surface rocks to expose lighter sand. Some of the designs include monkeys, hummingbirds, and fish, but also simple geometric shapes. In addition, the lines in some cases are several kilometres long, spanning valleys and rugged areas along the coast.

Since the largest of the designs is almost 200 metres across, it has been suggested that the designs and figures are best seen from the air, leading to speculation that they were made for aerial visitors' benefit. In 1955, writer James Moseley suggested that the Nazca lines were markings to direct space visitors towards specific places on Earth.

Von Daniken took this a step further and suggested that the lines were actually airstrips for alien navigation and vectoring in for contact. However, because the lines run across very uneven ground this is unlikely. Would alien interstellar space-craft even need runways?

One thing is certain with regard to monuments and other ancient artefacts preserved over the centuries. Ancient peoples, once thought to be uneducated and unaware of basic principles of science, possessed a better understanding of mechanics and astronomy than previously thought. There is evidence that many buildings and monuments seem to be aligned with celestial phenomena such as the sun and planets, and some temples show an advanced knowledge of engineering and construction. While this may suggest to some that aliens helped humans in their early development, perhaps it just shows that humans are at least a bit smarter than we give them credit for.

MORE EARLY UFOS

If we look beyond the possibility of visitation by alien civilizations in prehistory, there are many intriguing records of observations of aerial objects in documents dating back hundreds or thousands of years. Some people believe that these recorded observations are indications that aliens have been visiting Earth during relatively recent periods in history.

- Well within recorded history, the classical Chinese poet Chi Yuan, who lived around 300 B.C., wrote that one day after he had just finished visiting the grave of an emperor, a large jade "chariot" pulled by four fearsome dragons came down from the sky and landed near him. Chi Yuan climbed onto the miraculous vehicle and soon found himself being carried far to the west towards the holy Kun-Lun Mountains.

- Somewhat later, during Roman times, historian Pliny the Elder noted that in 66 B.C., a "spark" fell from a star and descended towards the Earth, grew as large as the Moon, then shank back to a small size and returned to the heavens.

- In 564 A.D., St. Gregory, Bishop of Tours in France, wrote that "golden globes" were seen flashing quickly across the sky.

- More than 500 years later in Switzerland, in 1104, objects described as "burning torches, fiery darts and flying fire" were seen in the air, along with "swarms of butterflies and little fiery worms" that "took away the light of the sun."

- From 1211, there is a story that during Sunday mass in Kent, England, the congregation watched in amazement as an anchor dropped from the sky and caught on a tombstone. They looked up to see a strange ship hanging in the sky, with odd people looking over its side. One of these people jumped overboard and seemed to float downward as if swimming in water. When the churchgoers ran to grab him, he swam back up to the boat, cut the anchor rope and flew away. The anchor left behind was said to have been taken by a blacksmith and turned into scrollwork on the church pulpit.

- In November and December of 1388, historian Henry Knighton recorded that in Leicester, a "burning and revolving wheel" was seen moving in the sky.

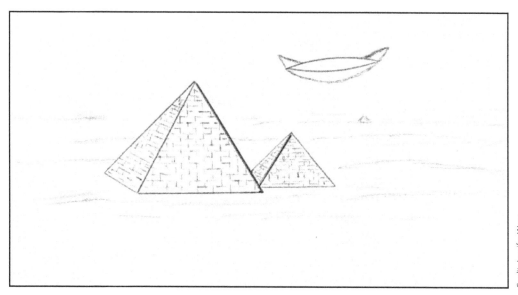

Credit: Jennifer Wang.

Flying wheels are said to have been seen over the pyramids in ancient times.

- Strange lights and objects were seen by many residents of Nuremburg on April 4, 1561 — about 450 years ago. Records of the event suggest that a veritable "invasion" by a plethora of lighted objects created fear and trembling among peasants and lords alike. What actually was seen is impossible to guess at this late date.

Credit: Jennifer Wang.

Observations of fiery shields are recorded in historical documents.

- Only five years later over Basel, Switzerland, one morning the sky filled with black globes that danced about and became flame-red. They seemed to burn up and disappear before the eyes of many amazed residents.

- In Sheffield, England, on December 9, 1731, a "dark red cloud" appeared around 5:00 p.m. Underneath it was a second object, but this one was very bright and gave off bright rays of light. The rays moved about the sky and emitted a great amount of heat, forcing one observer to take off his shirt even though it was the middle of winter.

- When was the first flying saucer seen? On January 2, 1878, farmer John Martin was doing some hunting outside of Denison, Texas, when he saw a round, dark object hanging in the bright blue sky. He watched as the baseball-sized object grew larger as it approached him, then looked away to rest his eyes. When he looked up again, the object was overhead, still continuing on its way, but was now, in his words, the size of a large "saucer" at a considerable height. It flew on and away from him until it was lost to sight.

- On July 30, 1880, a large bright object flew over St. Petersburg, moving in a triangular formation with two smaller objects. They moved together, without making any sound, across the city, remaining in view for three minutes.

UFOs AND ALIENS IN LITERATURE

War of the Worlds (1898) may be the best-known alien invasion story, depicting profoundly alien aliens bent on conquering Earth. Orson Welles' radio broadcast of it in 1938 sent people running panicked into the streets, and the several movie versions of it have done reasonably well in the cinema. The technologically superior Martians are defeated not by humans, but by something unexpected: the invaders all die when their immune systems fail to protect them from Earth bacteria and viruses, from which the Martians had no protection.

THE GREAT AIRSHIP WAVE

North America experienced what has come to be known as *The Great Airship Wave* between about 1896 and 1898. Many unusual aerial objects were reported floating or hovering in the skies, usually with accompanying descriptions of airships or gondolas suspended underneath large balloons. The reports were well-documented, with many articles and some books devoted to the phenomenon.

Accounts of observations of these objects appeared in literally hundreds of small-town newspapers across the continent. Some of the stories included personal narratives of meetings with the occupants or inventors of the vehicles. The strange craft often had bright lights or "headlights" that dazzled their observers, noiselessly sailing overhead and leaving as mysteriously as they came. Many of the stories were eventually determined to have been hoaxes written by newspaper editors in an attempt to boost circulation.

The first sightings considered part of the wave were reported in the fall of 1896. The *Sacramento Bee* carried a story on November 17, 1896, that a bright light was seen by hundreds of people. The light was too distant for most observers to distinguish its shape, other than that it resembled a globe and travelled on an undulating course through the sky, against the prevailing wind, "like a ship through water." Other witnesses described an oblong or ovoid shape with propellers or a fan with a moveable light that swung back and forth, playing on the ground below. The witnesses were divided on whether the passenger cabin was on top or beneath the craft. Whatever it was, the strange craft remained visible for nearly half an hour. Embellishments and speculation abounded, with some people claiming they heard voices coming from the craft, either laughing or giving orders to whoever was at the controls. The builder of the aerial vehicle was thought to be an inventor who lived in the Sacramento or San Francisco area and was highly secretive about his remarkable machine because his device had not yet been patented.

The Decatur *Daily Republican* of April 16, 1897, noted that on the previous night, an airship landed near Springfield, Illinois. Farmhand John Halley and local vineyard owner Adolf Wenke said that it landed five kilometres west of the city along the Jefferson Street road. They said a long-bearded man then emerged and inquired what town he was near. Halley noted: "Inside the car was seated another man and also the scientist's wife." He said they usually rested during the daytime in remote parts of the country in order to conceal the vessel's huge wings. When they asked the scientist his name, "he smiled and pointed to the letter M., which was painted on the side car." After bidding the farmers farewell, he pressed a button and the ship flew off.

The *Chicago Times-Herald* for Tuesday, March 30, 1897, noted:

> The mysterious air ship was seen again last night by a number of Omaha people. It hovered in sight about the time church services were over and in half an hour had disappeared.
>
> This time the "air ship" came into view in the southeastern portion of the horizon. It was in the shape of a big bright light, too big for a balloon, and glowed steadily.
>
> It sailed over the city to the northwest and there disappeared

behind the houses and bluffs. It moved very slowly and seemed to be quite near the earth. Nothing but the light was visible. A big crowd at Twenty-fourth and Lake Streets watched the trip of the visitor.

Did You Know?

Before he was president, Jimmy Carter saw a UFO on January 6, 1969. He and 10 other people were in Leary, Georgia, when they all saw a light moving in the sky at about 7:15 p.m., flashing red and green. Skeptics have dismissed the UFO as Venus, but Carter has not conceded it was an ordinary object.

In Winnipeg, Canada, on July 1, 1896, at about 6:00 p.m., many residents observed an odd "balloon" come from the west and make a "rapid journey some thousands of feet above the Earth." It was said to have been larger than a child's toy balloon, but the same size as those used for "ascensions at River Park." Tethered balloon rides were a popular attraction and novelty in 1896.

Canada was invaded by more American-style airships in 1897, when on April 14, a "specter" with attached lights "as large as the Moon" flew from North Dakota towards Glenboro, Manitoba, at an estimated speed of "365 miles per hour." Then on May 1, "the light of the strange vessel came into view about nine o'clock on the eastern horizon, near the St. Boniface Hospital in Winnipeg." It moved over the city, then headed northwest, towards Stony Mountain.

The witness reported: "Only the bare outline of some dark object could be seen besides the strange, heavenly light, evidently from the 'masthead' of the aerial craft." This time, the strange vehicle was seen by many reputable citizens, including the lieutenant governor of the province, the Honorable James Colebrooke Patterson, who curiously enough had just completed a term as federal minister of militia and defence.

Sightings were reported across the country. On August 14, 1897, the *Vancouver Daily World* prodded its readers:

Have You Seen the Light in the Heavens? If Not You Are Not up to Date!

It has been hovering in the skies above Vancouver almost every night this week, and has been viewed by many. It was last seen on Friday evening and may be on view tonight, and again it may not. Last night the strange object in the skies was noticed to the north of the city across the city travelling in an easterly direction. The luminous ball of fire or airship as some call it was closely watched. It approached with great swiftness, paused in midair, then surrounded itself with flashes of color and moved towards the northeast.

The newspaper added, "N. C. Schon of Burnaby saw the luminous body while on the steamer Rithet on Monday night. He states that it moved parallel to the sea far below the star line and looked like a bright red star surrounded by a luminous halo. It was cigar shaped and seemed to travel slowly and occasionally there seemed to drop a shower of sparks like the sputtering of an arc light."

The *Victoria Daily Colonist* of August 7, 1897, informed its readers: "That strange aerial curiosity the fire balloon that has been completely mystifying people of the northwest during the past two or three months is evidently becoming bolder or more people are keeping late hours than formerly and in consequence have had the good fortune to catch a glimpse of it. What it is, or where it comes from or where it goes to, and who or what manner of men are responsible for its movements, remains just as much as a puzzle as when the bright light first made its appearance in the sky a few months ago."

The *Colonist* also noted that some firemen had watched the light for a considerable length of time:

For upwards of two and a half hours Firemen North and Swain of the city brigade had opportunity to inspect the erratic visitor yesterday morning. However when it was finally lost to sight in the morning air they were completely mystified as to all its character as when they first sighted it ... It had no discernible form, balloon shape or otherwise, it was just a great light as large from the distance it was viewed as a drum from one of the hose reels, and brighter far, according to the two firemen than an electric light.

... Until four o'clock the brilliant body remained suspended in mid air passing slowly from east to west and back again three times and only disappearing with the coming of the day. At one time the firemen believed they saw a dark body outlined behind the circle of intense light but they could not identify it positively.

Its editors speculated, "The favourite theory is that some local inventor is trying the product of his daring in the privacy of the night, preparatory to giving his secret to the world. It must be a fact that the inventor is the most successful keeper of a secret to appear on the scene for quite some time and yet this seems the most rational explanation put forward. Too many have seen the mid night visitor for people of common sense to doubt the presence of a mysterious something ..."

Sightings of odd aerial vehicles and lights continued through that summer.

Many airship reports were fuelled by news stories of the announcement of a Swedish engineer, Salomon Andrée, that he would attempt a balloon flight over the North Pole from Scandinavia into Canada. In July 1897, Andrée's aerial expedition left the island of North Spitzbergen in a large, well-equipped balloon. Some carrier pigeons were received from the explorers early into the voyage, and then nothing.

Credit: Ufology Research.

Airship sightings were so common in the late 1890s that newspapers used them in their advertisements to sell products.

In Their Own Words

Oklahoma City, Oklahoma
July 2, 1953

On July 2, 1953, I saw an object. It was round as a balloon or a dish. As high as it was, it would be hard to say whether it would be metal because anything would reflect the sunlight.

It seemed to stand still, but when I looked through the glasses it seemed to be moving back and forth within a short radius. I couldn't see anything hanging on it at all. When it left it seemed to go straight up; it did not go sideways. If it had been a balloon it would have burst. There was no sound.

I saw this object between 1830 and 1900; I think about 1845. I watched it for approximately 10 or 15 minutes and it was out of sight. I stayed 10 or 15 minutes longer to see whether or not it would come back. It went out of sight about 1900.

I observed this object through 7x50 binoculars from the ground.

The object was about 5 degrees SW from directly overhead Tinker Air Force Base.

I have had quite a bit of experience observing aircraft in the air; I was in the Air Force for four years and have worked three years on the Guard Force at Tinker Air Force Base. I see quite a bit of aircraft while on duty.

The weather was clear. There was a blue sky background.

The object was 40,000 to 50,000 feet high.

Reported by Robert M.
Source: Project Blue Book Archive, MAXW-PBB19-100

On August 9, the *Manitoba Free Press* carried a story that described lights in the sky across Canada over British Columbia and Manitoba, wondering if Andrée's airship was off course and wandering throughout the North. It printed a letter from a reader who advised them:

Douglas (Manitoba), Aug. 6, 1897. / To the Editor of the *Free Press.*

Sir, In case some of your numerous readers may have noticed something similar at some other point I would draw your attention to a peculiar matter noticed on the night of the 5th. About 11 p.m., just before retiring, a something that at first looked like a falling star appeared directly north of the residence of Mr. John Kyle, some four miles east of here. The person first to notice the strange object was led to call the attention of all in the house to the matter. For over half an hour we watched the strange visitor, as it seemed to rise and fall and sway from east to west, but gradually travelling further and further northward, until about 11:45, it disappeared from view. At times several of those watching the peculiar object, which all the while shone brightly, thought they could discern the shape of a massive balloon just above the bright light. It would be interesting to know if the circumstance was noticed by any others, and if so, what the impressions conveyed were.   R.M. SCOTT

The editor then noted, "Any who have noticed similar objects are asked to inform the *Free Press*. If Andrée persists in floating about Manitoba barn yards let us find him."

Similarly, the *Manitoba Morning Free Press* for September 14, 1897, printed a letter from a correspondent in Scotland who explained that on August 5, 2005, a large light assumed to be a balloon passed over Prince Albert shortly after 6:00 p.m., heading west-north-west. To compound the mystery, the same paper on September 18 carried another account of a sighting:

Was it Prof. Andrée?

St. Petersburg, Sept. 17th. A telegraphic message was received here from Krasnoyarsk, in the interior of Siberia, which says on September

14, the inhabitants of the village of Antzifiroskoje, in the district of Veniselsk, Arctic Russia, saw a balloon, which is believed to be that of Prof. Andrée, the Swedish aeronaut, who left the island of Tromsoe shortly before 2:30 p.m., July 11, in an attempt to cross the Polar region. The balloon, it is added, was in sight for five minutes.

Over the next several months, people around the globe reported seeing Andrée's aerial expedition flying through the sky, but no actual trace of him or his companions was ever found.

Then, in 1939, the remains of the frozen bodies of the crew were discovered on a small island in the Arctic Ocean north of Spitzbergen. Investigators concluded that not long after they launched, the balloon had become covered in ice and they were forced to make a crash landing on the rocky outcrop. Therefore, none of the sightings thought to be Andrée's balloon could have been that craft, despite speculations to that effect. The sightings could not have been fireballs or *bolides*, the proper name for cometary debris burning up in the atmosphere, because the durations were usually many minutes, too long for astronomical objects. On the other hand, the objects moved too swiftly for misidentified stars or planets.

What had everyone seen?

Comments made in the press in 1897 and later during the early part of the 1900s bear a strong resemblance to those made regarding modern-day UFO reports. Doubt was expressed over the veracity of the witnesses. Many people were unwilling to use their names in reports.

Skywatchers speculated about craft built by secret organizations, and many people were outright skeptical and simply didn't believe that the objects were anything other than meteors. However, those who had witnessed an airship were adamant and insisted they had definitely seen the thing, in the same way that UFO witnesses today insist that what they observed was really there.

Researchers have found that, although the idea of awkward and mechanical flying machines in the late 1800s is fanciful, the reality is that dozens of patents were issued to inventors of "aerial cars" and "flying gyrators" as far back as 1844, with many more in the years following 1880. It is quite possible that some airship reports were of experimental vehicles, although there is no question that many simple observations of lights in the night sky were misidentifications of stars and planets, exactly as today.

At the time airship stories were in circulation, the world was going through a rapid boom in economy, technological development, exploration, settlement, and communication. The atmosphere was rife for wild speculation about wonders in the skies. There was some skepticism, but there was also a wide range of speculation as to their origin and mechanisms. The press noted that the objects brought puzzlement and wonder at the strange sights in the heavens.

A certain amount of ridicule was present, and there were satirical pokes at the witnesses by various institutions. The airships sold newspapers and products through their depiction in broadsheets and posters. Eventually, the sightings decreased in number (or, at least, the media lost interest), and reports slowly ceased being recorded.

The airship wave of the closing years of the 19th century subsided, and the next era of strange sky wonders began.

Did You Know?

The modern era of flying saucers began on June 24, 1947, when pilot Kenneth Arnold saw several metallic disc-like objects flying near Mt. Rainier.

2
1900–1947

COMETS, METEORS, OR SOMETHING ELSE?

The most written-about case of a strange flying object in historical Russia took place on June 30, 1908, over Siberia. Early in the morning of that day, hundreds of people in and around the Tunguska region reported seeing an oval fireball passing overhead, changing direction and speed, with a luminous trail behind it. A massive explosion was felt throughout the continent, with seismic stations in Irkutsk and Tashkent registering tremors. The sky glowed so brightly that people could read newspapers at midnight in Moscow, Paris, and even in London.

It was not until 1927 that an expedition funded by the Soviet Academy of Sciences managed to visit the swampy wilderness area, and what they reported was more astounding than anyone had imagined. A wind-driven firestorm had swept the area, uprooting and charring trees in a region measuring thousands of square kilometres in diameter.

Many theories have been proposed to explain the event, ranging from an asteroid impact, a comet, black hole, nuclear blast, and even an alien spaceship. Most scientists now favour a cometary impact as the most likely explanation. If it had been a relatively small asteroid, like the object that created the Barringer Meteor Crater in Arizona, there would be some evidence of a well-defined gouge on the landscape.

At about 9:05 p.m. EST on the night of February 9, 1913, a strange phenomenon was seen in the skies over much of Canada and the United States. Beginning in Saskatchewan and heading to the east, a "procession" of brilliant lights made their way slowly and majestically overhead. Some witnesses described the sight as a red object with a long, fiery tail. Others saw two, three or more sources of light travelling one behind the other, each with separate trails of sparks. As soon as these were out of sight, dozens of smaller lights in groups of twos, threes, and fours again passed overhead on the same apparent path from northwest to southeast, all with glowing tails. There were even reports of the strange phenomenon as far east as Bermuda.

Estimates of the total number of objects in the procession ranged as high as 1,000 or more, although the best approximation was that 10 or 15 objects, each possibly composed of a number of smaller bodies, were seen over a 4,000 kilometre path over the entire continent. The duration of the event was said to be as long as three and a half minutes.

Astronomer Dr. Clarence Chant presented a very detailed analysis of the meteor train including many reports from eyewitnesses. He noted, "The front portion of the body appears to have been somewhat brighter than the rest, but the general colour was a fiery red or golden yellow. To some the tail seemed like the glare from the open door of a furnace in which is a fierce fire; to others, it was like the illumination from a 'search light'; to others, like the stream of sparks blown away from a burning chimney by strong wind. Gradually the bodies became smaller, until the last ones were but red sparks, some of which were snuffed out before they reached their destination. Several report that near the middle of the great procession was a fine large star without a tail, and that a similar body brought up the rear."

The spread of reports was very remarkable. Chant noted that the place farthest west from which a report has been received was Mortlach, about 105 kilometres west of Regina, Saskatchewan, where they were described as travelling from west to east. However, in Ontario, the meteors were described as travelling generally from northwest to southeast, and there were enough observations reported to allow triangulation and calculate their true path.

Credit: NASA.

The Barringer meteor crater in Arizona was formed 50,000 years ago when a large chunk of rock hit the Earth, creating a hole more than 150 metres deep and over a kilometre wide.

UID YOU KNOW?

UFOs have
been reported from every continent on
Earth, including Antarctica.

From Campbellville, Ontario, the meteors passed directly overhead, travelling from northwest to southeast, and over Hespeler, they "seemed to go right over our heads," in a line about 15 degrees to the west of the zenith.

Chant calculated that based on the elevation angles and triangulation that the meteors were at a height of about 40 kilometres, just within the Earth's atmosphere, and travelling at a speed of somewhat less than 15 kilometres per second. However, these values were debated among the astronomical community and a much higher altitude of about 70 to 80 kilometres was later accepted.

The procession also made its presence known through noise. Chant noted that at Niagara-on-the-Lake the windows rattled, and at St. David's, Rev. G. Munro heard the sound but looked in vain up in the sky to see the cause of it.

Similarly, near Sand Hill, Ontario, a witness reported, "Some had tails and some seemed to shoot a red vapor which threw a beautiful red glow. They came in bunches or groups. I counted 10 in one group and I think there were 20 groups. As they disappeared in the east there was a loud report like rolling thunder, and then another sound like thunder, and a tremor of the earth."

And in Shelburne, Chant noted, "There must have been an earthquake the night before, that the vibration was quite perceptible, and the noise was like a series of blasts going off. In the *Shelburne Economist* it is stated that a man living 12 miles west of the town was awakened from sleep and thought that his horses were wrecking the stable. On investigating, however, he found the horses perfectly quiet."

Other sample observations included:

> Fort Frances, Ontario: "I saw them come slowly from the northwest; first, a string like candles, about forty of them; then, after 5 minutes, another string in the same line and about eight in number. They made

the snow red quite a while after they had disappeared in the east. There was no sound, and they were lower than the stars. They went slow. A big one led the first string. I am sure you will hear something. *It must be the end of the world*. It was about 9 p.m. They did not pass overhead, but north of us."

Peterborough, Ontario: "The appearance was like that of an express train lighted up at night. The elevation was about 25 degrees. Movement was slow and the duration about 3 minutes. In the first section there seemed to be from six to nine lights, with slightly spreading ends. Then, in succession, some three or four not so brilliant sections passed. The most striking feature to me was the regular movement in an even plane. There appeared to be no curve whatever. No noise was heard. It was the grandest display I have ever seen."

Beyond the objects seen that night, there were also scores of other sightings recorded across North America on the days just before and just after the procession, and in some cases minutes or hours before or after. Chant also noted a daylight sighting that may or may not have had anything to do with the sightings on February 9:

I shall refer to a curious observation reported in *The Toronto Daily Star* for Monday, February 10. At about 2 p.m. on that date some of the occupants of a tall building near the lake front saw some strange objects moving out over the lake and passing to the east. They were not seen clearly enough to determine their nature, but they did not seem to be clouds, or birds, or smoke, and it was suggested at the time that, perhaps, they were airships cruising over the city. Afterwards it was surmised that they may have been of the nature of meteors moving in much the game path as these seen the night before.

Many years later, the identity of the meteors in the procession was still being debated. In the journal *Popular Astronomy*, Vol. XLVII, No. 6, June-July, 1939, astronomer C.C. Wylie argued that the procession was not a series of meteors in a long train. He stated that "the popular explanation of the phenomenon is that a cluster of fire balls travelled from Saskatchewan across North America, and over the Atlantic to the equator, a distance of some 5,700 miles. Several considerations, of which we will mention four, make this explanation untenable."

Wylie's chronology of events was that:

1. A detonating meteor fell over Ontario on February 9 at 9:06 p.m., Ontario time.

2. A shadow-casting meteor was observed from Ann Arbor, Michigan at 10:15 p.m., CST. (11:15 p.m. Ontario time.)

3. A spectacular fireball was observed from Bermuda at 10:00 p.m. Atlantic time (9:00 p.m., Ontario time.)

4. A shadow-casting meteor observed in Ontario on February 10 at 1:25 p.m.

In addition to these spectacular meteors, several groups of shooting stars were observed, among them the ones over Fort Frances at 9:00 p.m. CST. A string of 40 or so meteors, followed after five minutes by a string of eight, passed north overhead. Meteors were also observed over Pense and Morllach, Saskatchewan ("Must have been hundreds") and even as far afield as Watchung, New Jersey.

UFOs and Aliens in Movies

Earth Versus the Flying Saucers (1956) was one of the best saucer movies of the 50s, with excellent special effects for its time, including the now-classic but cliché stock footage of plastic model saucers flying over Washington, D.C. The malevolent aliens were clearly here to take over the planet, with displays of force such as blowing up buildings and automobiles. The film conveyed the fear and panic that many people expressed regarding the "invasion" of saucers over the U.S. in the 1950s, when a flurry of UFO sightings over Washington was actually reported, and the resultant military response to the alien menace.

Charles Fort, the chronicler and collector of news reports of unusual phenomena, and for whom the field of Fortean research is named, questioned the meteor explanation. Indeed, if he had still been active when Wylie disputed Chant's conclusions, Fort would have certainly had some cynical comments to offer. In his book *New Lands*, Fort noted:

> It is questionable that the same spectacle was seen in Bermuda, this night. The supposed long flight from the Saskatchewan to Bermuda might indicate something of a meteoric nature, but the meteor-explanation must take into consideration that these objects were so close to this earth that sounds from them were heard, and that, without succumbing to gravitation, they followed the curvature of this earth at a relatively low velocity that can not compare with the velocity of ordinary meteors.

Fort's belief was that alien civilizations were possible, and that some observations of aerial objects were undoubtedly due to their appearance.

THE 1915 INVASION OF CANADA

The headline of the *Toronto Globe* on February 15, 1915, read: "Ottawa in Darkness Awaits Aeroplane Raid." Call-outs in the body of the article warned: "Several Aeroplanes Make a Raid into the Dominion of Canada," and "Entire City of Ottawa in Darkness, Fearing Bomb Droppers."

One alarming series of headlines and secondary headlines told readers: "Machines Crossed St Lawrence River, Passing over Brockville — Two over Ganonoque — Seen by Many Citizens, Heading for the Capital — One Was Equipped with Powerful Searchlights — Fire Balls Dropped." To anyone reading the latest news from the country's capital, it appeared as though Canada was about to enter the war on its own home front.

The excitement began on the night of February 14, about 9:15 p.m., when many people in Brockville were startled to see the lights of unknown aircraft crossing over the St. Lawrence River and heading for Ottawa. The lights were even seen by the mayor and three city constables. The unidentified craft flying rapidly overhead was said to have made "unmistakable sounds of the whirring motor."

A second flying machine was heard as it crossed the St. Lawrence River from the direction of Morristown, New York. As it passed overhead, three balls of fire were seen to drop into the St. Lawrence. Some observers thought these might have been bombs, while others worried they could have been flares used by enemy pilots to find their way across the border or over the ocean to the Canadian interior. Two more aerial invaders were reported to have passed over the east and west ends of Brockville, raising further fears.

The mayor said he also had seen a bright beam of light, like a searchlight, flash out from the aerial craft, lighting up an entire city block. The police chief, facing numerous inquiries from nervous citizens, called the mayor for instructions of what to do. He then relayed information to the mayor and police chief of Ottawa, advising them of the approaching aircraft.

At approximately 9:30 p.m., the mayor of Gananoque contacted the Brockville police chief with the news that two invisible aircraft were heard quite distinctly passing overhead there. With so much activity over the seat of government, it was not long before advisors met with Prime Minister Robert Borden and evaluated intelligence information about the mysterious fliers. Borden and his caucus were concerned that the lights of Parliament Hill would make it an easy target for any invasion, and ordered them to be turned off.

Under direct orders by the government, Parliament Hill went dark at about 11:15 p.m., and the entire city of Ottawa followed suit at approximately 11:20 p.m., including Rideau Hall and the Royal Mint. Shutters were secured and windows were darkened throughout the Capital region. Military and police marksmen climbed to the roofs of government buildings in Ottawa and were given orders to shoot down any hostile aircraft. This was the first blackout and air raid in Canadian history, only one month after the first raid on Britain.

Ottawa was not the only target of an "aerial invasion" that night. Early in the morning of February 15, people living in a Toronto suburb notified police of a "strange aeroplane" hovering over their homes. Later in the morning, a man in Guelph saw "three moving lights passing over the agricultural college." He called out to other residents in his boarding house who also watched the silent lights until dawn.

Meanwhile, far to the west, three people returning home from a late-night game of curling in Morden, Manitoba, heard a peculiar noise in the sky and looked up to see a bright light moving to the northwest. They, too, described it as an "aeroplane" travelling swiftly through the night sky.

It is important to note that there may have been an explanation for at least some of the objects seen in the skies over Ontario that night. It was reported that the hysteria in Ottawa was the result of a prank by a few jokers in Morristown. Supposedly, three fire balloons with fireworks attached were sent aloft in celebration of the 100th anniversary of the end of the War of 1812. The explanation went on to say that the fireworks created the impression of aircraft lights and engines, falling balls of fire and the beam of light seen over Brockville.

In Their Own Words

West Springfield, Massachusetts
September 1, 1994

This summer on Labor Day weekend in West Springfield, Massachusetts. My wife and myself saw what appeared to be a green fireball. We observed it for approx. 6–7 seconds before it disappeared over the horizon. I checked with the local science museum and the astronomer in charge of the planetarium said she saw it too. However she said she would check with Boston Observatory and they told her nothing was reported to them. How odd us three were the only ones that saw it and reported it.

Reported by T.T.
Source: Ufology Research

At first, the government and its citizens refused to believe this. Even the profoundly skeptical Dominion Observatory rejected the explanation, noting that prevailing winds were from the east and would not have taken the balloons northeast towards Ottawa from Morristown. However, on February 15, a Brockville policeman found a paper balloon near Eastern Hospital, and a second paper balloon was later found along the river. This seemed to validate the explanation of fireworks, and afternoon media took advantage of the discoveries to poke fun at the morning dailies that had been quick to fall victim to hysteria. Nevertheless, the next night, the lights of Ottawa were again turned out and guns were set up on rooftops.

Later research showed that at the time of these observations, only a handful of aircraft in the United States were actually capable of making the flight from the border to Ottawa, and none of these were capable of carrying searchlights.

TWO CASES IN THE 1930s

Elsewhere in the world, an early report of an unidentified object occurred in 1930, in an area southwest of Rio de Janeiro called Jacarepagua, long before any modern development. A couple was asleep in their small cottage one night, situated in a large expanse of primitive grassland. They were awakened to light streaming into their bedroom through the slats in the blinds, a very unusual thing because there were no others living near them and no roads or railroads near their homestead at that time.

When they opened the window to look out, they were shocked to see a large craft, "a white rounded object with two monstrous 'eyes'" and a leg or column coming down from it. The eyes were square, brick-shaped holes in its body, and they likened it to a man-made "ghost" constructed to frighten them for some reason. The husband took out his pistol and fired several shots in its direction, but the object was unaffected.

The object crossed the lawn in front of them, moving slowly up and down as if it was walking. It then rose up and headed for a dam some distance away, but paused and rotated back to "look" at the couple several more times before it was lost in the distance. The next day, the wife broke out in a rash of some kind, but it cleared up after a few days. Another apparent physical effect was that the grass on their lawn had turned from a lush green to a dead grey.

On June 10, 1931, pioneer aviator Francis Chichester (later knighted for his courage) was flying solo between Australia and Norfolk Island across the Tasman Sea when he saw flashes of light that he assumed were from other nearby aircraft. He noted that a "dull, gray-white shape of an airship" like an "oblong pearl" was heading towards his plane. He was momentarily distracted by more flashes beside him, and when he looked ahead the airship was gone.

Soon, however, another such craft emerged from the clouds on the opposite side of his airplane. He wrote in his diary that the object "drew steadily closer until perhaps a mile away when ... it suddenly vanished." The odd object reappeared near where it had been obscured from sight and flew closer to Chichester's path. He could

UFOs and Aliens in Literature

Buck Rogers and Flash Gordon started beating up bad guys in space in the 1920s and 1930s.

see a dim glow of light on its leading edge and rear section as it approached, but to his astonishment, the object seemed to be shrinking in size instead to getting bigger. Before his eyes, the object faded and "became its own ghost," leaving behind a small cloud in the shape of an airship.

THE BATTLE FOR LOS ANGELES

In parallel to the fireballs over the Canadian Parliament, a similar military scare occurred over Los Angeles in 1942. Known as the "Battle of Los Angeles," many people witnessed odd lights and objects, some flying in formations of 10 or more, on the night of February 24 to 25. Because of the war raging at the time, and since this was only a few months after Pearl Harbor, the reports led to antiaircraft artillery fire being shot into the sky.

Because of war jitters, people were anxious about a possible attack from across the Pacific. They were somewhat justified, as just the night before, on February 23, 1942, a Japanese submarine surfaced about a mile offshore and shelled an oil refinery near Santa Barbara. Around 7:15 p.m., almost 20 shells were shot at the shore, yet little damage was actually done. Some shells landed well off target, but the bold attack created a fear of an invasion along the west coast of North America. Eyewitness reports suggested the sub may have been heading further south, towards Los Angeles.

So, when unidentified lights were reported over Los Angeles the next night, air raid sirens sounded throughout Los Angeles County and the entire area was blacked out. At 3:16 a.m. on February 25, the 37th Coast Artillery Brigade began firing more than 1,400 anti-aircraft shells into the air at the lights. The "battle" lasted more than an hour.

One witness noted: "I could clearly see a V formation of about 25 silvery planes overhead... they were moving slowly across the sky toward Long Beach." An experienced Navy observer watched with powerful binoculars and said he could count nine silver aircraft when they passed into the beam of a searchlight.

The objects flew in and out of view as searchlights played across the sky, all the while under fire from the big anti-aircraft guns, which unfortunately were so loud no one could tell if the aerial objects were making any engine noise. Gunners were certain that their shells must have hit their targets, although there was no evidence that this was so. An "all clear" was finally sounded at 7:21 a.m.

Although the supposed enemy aircraft didn't fire on any targets, there was some damage — from friendly fire! Several buildings were hit by stray American shells, and three civilians were killed! Three other people died of heart attacks because of the stress of watching the battle rage in Los Angeles' skies.

While it was assumed that the unidentified aircraft were Japanese bombers or perhaps kamikaze pilots, it was learned after the war that the Japanese had not been able to stage an attack on American mainland until some time later when they reached Alaska in mid-1942. It was possible that this was simply a case of war nerves, although enough witnesses thought they had actually seen something.

One suggestion put forth in later years was that the Los Angeles "incursion" was caused by some Japanese fire balloons. It is known that in 1944 and 1945, the Japanese army had launched more than 9,000 incendiary balloons, knowing that they would be carried eastward to North America via the jet stream. The idea was that they would reach land and set fire to buildings, crops and forests, disrupting American livelihood. It is estimated that approximately 300 of these fire balloons did reach America, but they had much less of an effect than was expected. A few people died when their curiosity got the better of them and they examined a landed balloon too closely, and one forest fire was thought to have been caused directly by one of the balloons. It is thought that at least some of the balloons made it as far inland as North Dakota and Saskatchewan.

The prevailing opinion of historians as to the cause of the Battle of Los Angeles was that it was a weather balloon that had gone astray. However, some writers on the subject of UFOs have suggested that the objects were extraterrestrial craft of some kind.

GHOST ROCKETS

European ufological history began before Kenneth Arnold saw his crescent-shaped objects over Washington in the United States in 1947. Starting early in 1946, residents of Scandinavian countries reported seeing strange "ghost rockets" zooming and flashing through the skies. Many of these were fireballs, bolides, and large meteors, but others were seemingly of more unusual objects.

An interesting CIA document dated April 9, 1947, was located by researchers investigating early UFO accounts. It listed several reports of "rockets and guided missiles" seen over Norway and Sweden. It noted: "A strange object flying through

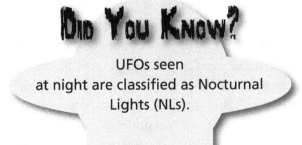

Did You Know?

UFOs seen
at night are classified as Nocturnal
Lights (NLs).

the air was observed at noon today (July 13, 1946) by workmen in Stockholm. The object was round, and appeared to be rather small. It sent out a strong blue-green light, but no sound could be heard." Another citation reads: "It is reported from Hudiksvall that railway workers this morning saw an object a few meters long and with backward-sloping wings flying towards the north at a height of about 150 meters. They heard a sound resembling that of an outboard motor."

Some of the ghost rockets flying over Scandinavia were said to have been detected on radar, and there was speculation that they were of Russian origin. Certainly, the Russian base at Peenemünde could be considered suspect in this regard, except that these odd missiles were said to also have been mystifying the Russians as well. Indeed, even after British bombing of that base in 1943, a V-2 from Peenemünde crashed in Sweden in June 1944 and was appropriated by the British.

In December 1944, work on a winged version of the V-2 rocket was underway and there was a successful flight on January 24, 1945, reaching an altitude of about 80 kilometres. In May 1945, at the war's end, the Soviet Army occupied the base but very little was found to indicate it had been in operation. Later, at least one historical record noted: "Western intelligence is convinced that the Soviets conducted missile tests from Peenemünde in the late 1940s (the Scandinavian 'ghost rockets'). But Russian historical sources available after the downfall of the Soviet Union do not support this belief."

A CRASH BEFORE ROSWELL?

On August 16, 1945, Jose Padillo and his friend Remigio Baca were riding their horses near Walnut Creek in a remote area of New Mexico. Although Jose was nine and his friend was only seven years old, they were very comfortable in the saddle. Both had been riding horses from the time they were barely able to run, and growing up on ranches, they were used to being out on the range. They had been sent out in the morning to look for a cow that had wandered away from the Padillo Ranch.

Only a month earlier, the first atomic bomb had been detonated at Trinity Site in New Mexico. In a matter of weeks, bombs were dropped on Hiroshima. But something else happened not that far from Trinity Site, and Padillo and Baca were witnesses to it. They kept quiet about what they had seen for decades as they lost track of one another as they grew up and apart. Then, after a chance meeting, they renewed their friendship that had been tested back in 1945 and finally came forward with their story in 2003. They described a bizarre event.

The two boys had entered some uneven ground along a dry creek bed, and the horses were having difficulty — their hooves were not able to get a good foothold on the rough chunks of mud. They decided to leave the horses and proceed on foot. Padillo tied up his horse on a cactus branch and his friend did the same with his own animal.

UFOs and Aliens in Literature

In 1934, a landmark story titled "A Martian Odyssey" (there's that Martian theme again!) by Stanley Weinbaum featured an encounter with an ostrich-like creature called Tweel, who was sentient and able to communicate with visiting astronauts on its home planet. In other words, Tweel was an alien who wasn't out to destroy the Earth, nor was it something to be overcome. It was truly alien in the sense it didn't look or act human, yet possessed qualities that we would recognize as intelligent and civilized. This trend in science fiction stories would continue in the 1930s and 1940s.

Off in the distance, Padillo had seen a mesquite thicket, a good place for a cow to hide. They went in its direction, clambering over sharp rocks and cacti with large thorns. Storm clouds formed as they slowly made progress towards their destination. By the time they neared the thicket, a loud "Boom!" announced the arrival of the rain.

The boys quickly ducked under a ledge to get shelter from the storm and its possible lightning bolts. They waited out the cloudburst as it sent torrents of water down onto the creek bed and lightning flashed around them. Such storms were common, but always short-lived.

Padillo and Baca talked for a while, watching the downpour turn the dry creek bed briefly into a fast-moving river. In a matter of minutes, however, the rain stopped and most of the water had sunk into the ground out of sight. Soon, the clouds lifted and the sun came out again.

They came out into the open and began travelling again towards the patch of mesquite. Suddenly, the ground quaked and they were startled by more light, but it did not seem like lightning. They assumed it was something involving the nearby army base.

Nearing the mesquite bushes, they were able to hear the sounds of a cow from inside. Sure enough, as they approached, they could see the cow — and a baby calf. They decided to have lunch while the cow dried off its calf.

While they ate, Jose happened to glance up, looking further along the creek bed. A wisp of smoke was rising from somewhere just over a rise in the desert scrub. He thought that lightning from the sudden storm had started a brushfire. They put their lunches down and left the cow to tend to its calf while they went exploring in the direction of the smoke.

As they made it over a ridge, they stopped and gaped at a strange sight. There was a long groove dug into the ground, as long as a railroad train. And at its end, almost hidden by smoke, was a bowl-shaped object the colour of tarnished metal. They assumed a stray rocket had crashed.

They moved in to the crash scene, but found that the ground was very hot, as if there had been a great fire. As they walked among the smoldering greasewood trees, they had difficulty breathing because the smell was bad and the air was unbelievably hot and humid.

Baca noticed the ground was covered in patches of small pieces of shiny metal, but very thin, like the paper inside a cigarette package. He picked up one that was jammed between two rocks, and as he did, it unfolded by itself! Baca crumpled it together in his palm and let it go again. Sure enough, the curious piece of metal opened up and flattened out, without any help.

Easing their way over boulders and broken rock, they were eventually able to get within three to five metres of the object.

Padillo looked into a jagged hole in the side of the large, circular thing, and saw some people inside, moving around. But he was shocked to see they were not human. Instead, they were small

UFOs and Aliens in Literature

Of course, the most popular alien of all time looks and acts very humanlike. In 1938, the first Superman comic strip appeared, about an alien who was not only friendly towards Earth people, but who vowed to protect them as well.

creatures that had the general shape of people. These strange beings moved back and forth inside the object so fast they seemed to blur their features. They were barely bigger than the two boys, with no hair on their heads, and skinny arms and legs. The scene and the creatures' appearance seemed somehow unreal.

Baca was very afraid at seeing these creatures, and began to run away. Padillo was more curious and didn't share his friend's concern, but he decided to go with him so they would not be separated.

They both went back the way they came, leaving the gouge in the Earth and its occupants behind. They passed right by the cow and her calf, finally reached their horses, then quickly untied them, mounted, and galloped away.

When they made it back to their ranch, it was already dusk. They found Jose's father, Faustino Padillo, who asked them right away about the lost cow.

The boys explained what had happened and what they had seen. Jose's father was surprised at their story, but was more surprised at how they were acting. However, he reassured them that what they had seen was likely only some army operation. He decided he would go with them to check on the area in a few days. He called a friend who was a police officer and invited him out to their ranch to come along when he went with the boys to look into the discovery.

Two days later, the four of them drove out in two trucks as close as they could get to the mesquite thicket, then hiked in to where the boys had found the gouge in the Earth and the strange craft with the little creatures. But when they got there, Padillo and Baca were surprised not to see any sign of a disturbance or a metallic craft. They went farther down the canyon and noticed that the ground was covered in shallow lines or grooves, as if someone had used a giant rake to even out the debris and rocks. Suddenly, they came upon the metallic craft, although it was now resting at a different angle than when the boys saw it, and it was almost completely covered in dirt and branches.

The two men climbed on top of the large saucer-shaped object and looked inside. There was no sign of any life at all. They came back out, puzzled by what they had seen.

Padillo's father wondered what to do, but the police officer pointed out that the ranch was on federal land and that Padillo was paid by the National Wildlife Refuge for tending the land. Furthermore, Baca's father worked for the government as well, and they worried that the army would be concerned if they knew the boys had been to this area. They decided to do nothing about their discovery, and told the boys that the object was probably a new kind of weather balloon, and they were not to tell anyone else about it. The small creatures were just figments of their imaginations.

With that, they walked back to the trucks and drove home.

The young Padillo and Baca were a bit disappointed. They were sure that they had stumbled across something very important, but Padillo's father was right. Maybe it was nothing at all.

They were even more surprised when, a few days later, some soldiers showed up at the ranch. They explained that a balloon did in fact come down in the creek bed, and to recover it and its payload, the Army needed to build a road over the desert scrub so that military vehicles could drive there safely.

"But don't tell anyone we are doing this," the soldiers directed. "It is a military secret."

The boys watched the military transports and jeeps come and go over the next several weeks. They wondered what really had crashed into the desert.

Many years later, when they were grown up men, they remembered the events of that night.

"I am sure it was a flying saucer that crashed there," Padillo told investigators. "Just like the one that crashed at Roswell two years later."

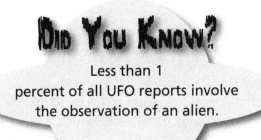

Did You Know?

Less than 1 percent of all UFO reports involve the observation of an alien.

Almost everyone has heard the story of the flying saucer that was said to crash near Roswell, New Mexico, in 1947. Some witnesses insisted that they saw pieces of the craft being carted away by the U.S. Army, and that a cover-up of the event has been in place ever since. According to some versions, bodies of small creatures were found in the wreckage, and they are being kept at a top secret laboratory, perhaps in a place known as Area 51 in Nevada.

But Padillo and Baca may have seen an even earlier crash, of a different spaceship.

"I don't know what we saw," Padillo says today, "but I will never forget it."

KENNETH ARNOLD: THE MAN WHO STARTED IT ALL

At 2:00 p.m. on June 24, 1947, Kenneth Arnold finished his work as a fire control engineer at the Central Air Service in Chehalis, Washington. He took off from the Chehalis airport in his own Callair aircraft for a short trip to Yakima, but he decided to assist in the search for a marine transport plane that had gone down somewhere near Mt. Rainier, not far away.

He flew around the area, then turned and began flying east towards Yakima. His altitude was about 2,800 metres. He noted the sky was "crystal clear" and that it was a perfect day for flying. He saw a DC-4 in the air about 24 kilometres away from him, but at a much higher altitude.

Suddenly, a bright flash attracted his attention. He looked around for the source and eventually saw nine "peculiar" aircraft flying south at about the same altitude as his own plane. He noted they were flying very fast, approaching the mountain, and he thought they were jets. The flashes recurred as they would occasionally dip and adjust their flight slightly, catching the Sun.

Arnold couldn't tell what kind of aircraft they were because they were initially very far away, but he soon got closer as they drew nearer the mountain, and he could see them against the snow. He was surprised to see that they didn't have tails or stabilizers like jets would. He timed their speed with the clock on his dash and a distant reference point. They were indeed going very fast, as fast as or faster than some military planes.

To make sure that he was not seeing a mirage or reflection, Arnold opened the cockpit window and watched them through the clear high air. After almost three minutes, the formation of odd objects had passed behind a distant ridge of mountains out of sight. But Arnold had a good enough look at the objects as they wobbled in flight that he could determine they were roughly disc-shaped, with a missing chord at their trailing edges that made them look like chubby crescents.

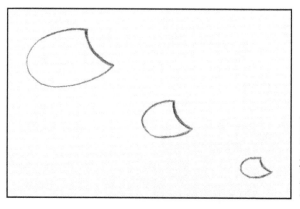

In 1947, pilot Kenneth Arnold saw a formation of disc-like objects flying over mountains in the Pacific Northwest. These were the first reported flying saucers.

Credit: Ufology Research.

When Arnold landed at Yakima, he told his story to the ground crew there. A helicopter pilot told Arnold the discs were probably just a flight of guided missiles from a nearby military base. Arnold then flew to Pendleton, Oregon, but wasn't aware that someone from the Yakima airport had called ahead to let them know a pilot on his way there had seen some very unusual objects. Pendleton was in the midst of an air show, and when Arnold landed there, many people wanted to hear his story.

The next day, although he had been told by some skeptics he had just seen guided missiles, Arnold was certain he had seen something more unusual, and he went to Pendleton's newspaper office to speak with reporters there. The result was a wire service news story written by reporter Bill Bequette, which read:

> Pendleton, Ore., June 25 (AP) — Nine bright saucer-like objects flying at "incredible speed" at 10,000 feet altitude were reported here today by Kenneth Arnold, Boise, Idaho, [a] pilot who said he could not hazard a guess as to what they were.
>
> Arnold, a United States Forest Service employee engaged in searching for a missing plane, said he sighted the mysterious objects yesterday at three pm. They were flying between Mount Rainier and Mount Adams, in Washington State, he said, and appeared to weave in and out of formation. Arnold said he clocked and estimated their speed at 1200 miles an hour.

Although it is sometimes noted that Bequette was the one who first coined the term *flying saucer*, that term does not actually appear in his news story. What likely happened is that as the wire story went out to newspapers across the continent, headline writers composing the story in their local papers created the phrase from a quick reading of the news copy. The result was that many newspapers carried the Bequette story under a headline that contained the now-familiar term *flying saucer*, even though neither Arnold nor Bequette actually called the objects that at all.

Several explanations for Arnold's sighting have been put forth over the years by skeptics and debunkers, all of which are inadequate. An example is that suggested by Harvard University astronomer Dr. Donald Menzel, who in 1977 proposed that the discs Arnold observed were actually raindrops on the Callair aircraft's windows. This, of course, makes no sense when Arnold's own testimony is read, which clearly indicates he had thought of such an explanation himself and opened the window to rule this possibility out.

If one was to propose a more reasonable explanation for Arnold's sighting, it is more likely that what he saw was a group of secret military test vehicles, perhaps missiles with their fins and/or ailerons rendered invisible by the bright sunlight reflecting off their surfaces. However, no evidence uncovered through any investigation of the case has been offered which would support this contention.

We are left with a sighting of nine saucer-like objects that sparked the popular imagination and impressed the image of flying saucers indelibly on our collective memories.

THE ROSWELL UFO CRASH

Strictly speaking, the famous (or infamous, if you prefer) case involving a crash of a flying saucer near the town of Roswell, New Mexico, in 1947, is not a very "good" UFO report. In fact, were it not for a series of events that followed the sighting of an unusual bright object, the case might have remained lost to history. But this incident has become possibly the best-known UFO case in the annals of ufology, spawning books, movies, TV series, and achieving legendary status among hard-core believers and the general public.

On July 2, 1947, business owner Dan Wilmot and his wife were sitting outside on their porch, enjoying the summer evening. At about 9:50 p.m., they saw a bright, disc-shaped object with glowing lights flying northwest very rapidly. To a reporter from the *Roswell Daily Record*, Wilmot described the object as shaped like "two inverted saucers mouth to mouth" and an estimated six to eight metres in diameter.

Over the next few days, sightings of unusual objects were reported in the general area. Most were of bright fireballs, such as one on July 4 described as a "brilliant light" plunging to Earth, similar to an aircraft on fire and falling from the sky.

This handful of sightings was hardly remarkable. In fact, the cases have characteristics of astronomical phenomena known as *bolides* — pieces of comets or planetary debris which impact the Earth's atmosphere at high speeds and immediately burn up, leaving a trail of light that is often blue, green, or orange. Each year, many of these objects are seen and reported as UFOs, but later assigned an "explained" or "possibly explained" status by investigators and researchers.

If the Roswell case rested solely on these relatively unexciting reports, it would have faded into obscurity. However, on July 4, rancher Mac Brazel had been watching the skies during a severe lightning storm and heard a large boom that didn't sound like thunder.

The next day, July 5, 1947, he was riding his horse through a pasture when he came upon a large mass of debris unlike anything he had seen before. Scattered throughout an area 400 metres long by hundreds of metres wide were numerous metallic strips that looked like dark tinfoil. Examining it in some detail, he said that as he crumpled it in his hand then released it, a strip would assume its original shape and could not be bent or wrinkled. As well, he found sticks of lightweight material like balsa wood, upon which were inscribed odd writings like hieroglyphics.

Brazel collected some of the pieces and took them home. He showed them to his family and to some neighbours, who all marvelled at the unusual quality of the material. Brazel notified the local Sheriff, George Wilcox, who in turn contacted the nearby Roswell Army Air Field, since the two thought the debris had come from a military operation of some kind.

Major Jesse Marcel, Intelligence Officer of the 509th Bomb Group, drove from the base to Wilcox's office, where he interviewed Brazel and examined some of the debris he had brought into town. Upon hearing the details of Brazel's find, Marcel believed the crash to be that of an aircraft and decided to travel to the site along with Captain Sheridan Cavitt, a counterintelligence officer from the Roswell base. Driving in separate vehicles, they arrived at the location too late to be able to do an extensive search, so Marcel and Cavitt decided to sleep overnight there in the desert.

In the morning, they explored the area in detail and found material scattered throughout a large crash site over a kilometre long and almost 300 metres wide. They also found pieces of debris that resembled tinfoil and several lengths of light rods like balsa wood. However, unlike balsa wood, the rods could not seem to be bent or broken.

Cavitt left in the middle of the afternoon, while Marcel stayed and loaded much of the remaining material into the trunk of his car. He finally headed towards home late in the evening, stopping there in the early hours of the morning before going to the base. He woke up his wife and his 11-year-old son Jesse to show them what he found in the desert. He told his family that he had found the remnants of a crashed flying saucer. Later, his son Jesse told investigators about the strange metallic "I-beams" that had lettering like hieroglyphics on them, and that his father had been very excited about what he had seen.

Marcel returned to the airfield and informed his superiors of the discovery. The 509th's press officer, Walter Haut, was ordered by his commander, Colonel William Blanchard, to send out a press release to the effect that a flying saucer had been captured.

On July 8, the *Roswell Daily Record* ran the headline: "RAAF Captures Flying Saucer On Ranch In Roswell Region," announcing the recovery of something by the Roswell Army Air Field. Soon, media were calling the base and Sheriff Wilcox's office for the real story of what had been found.

The debris was shipped to Brigadier General Roger Ramey of the 8th Air Force at Fort Worth, Texas. There, Ramey called the local media and told them the debris was not of a flying saucer but a weather balloon. The sticks and metallic pieces were actually part of a radar reflector.

On July 9, the newspaper ran a story under the headline "General Ramey Empties Roswell Saucer," essentially retracting the earlier story. It also ran a story about Brazel, indicating he was mistaken and that he was sorry ever to have caused such a commotion. That seemed to end the affair, and the incident was brushed aside.

After the fact, researchers found evidence that military personnel had visited radio and newspaper offices in the Roswell area, requesting the original copies of the first, erroneous release about the flying saucer. Complicating the story and adding further intrigue, some military personnel later claimed that they witnessed or they themselves loaded very unusual wreckage onto flatbed trucks or transport aircraft destined for Los Alamos or Fort Worth or other classified locations.

It was many years later before anything more was learned about Roswell.

In February 1978, Stanton Friedman, a nuclear physicist and outspoken advocate for the reality of flying saucers from outer space, was in Baton Rouge, Louisiana, for a TV interview. While he was waiting to go on, he was told that a man living not far away was a former Air Force officer who had seen and touched some debris from a crashed flying saucer. Friedman was curious and looked him up: Jesse Marcel, who was then in Houma, Louisiana. Friedman interviewed him at length and learned that there was much more to the story than most people knew.

Friedman reopened the case and found additional witnesses and others who seemed to be able to corroborate the amazing story that an unknown craft of some kind had indeed crashed in the New Mexico desert. His investigations became the basis for a book authored by Charles Berlitz and William Moore, *The Roswell Incident* (1980).

In October 1978, Friedman was at Bemiji State University lecturing about UFOs and met a couple who told him that a friend of theirs named Barney Barnett, who had since passed away, had described seeing a crashed flying saucer in New Mexico sometime in the 1940s. Barnett was an engineer working for the government, and was deemed very reliable. His story seemed to match that of Marcel, with one added feature: he had seen several small bodies near the crash debris.

While in Minnesota, Friedman talked about this story with William Moore, a high school teacher with a strong interest in UFOs. He suggested to Moore that he research the Barnett story and see if it had any merit. A few months later, Moore discovered newspaper clippings that told the Roswell story. The investigation of the Roswell crash began in earnest.

In Their Own Words

Weyauwega, Wisconsin
February 2003

My son and I were visiting a friend of mine in Weyauwega. My boy was sledding in the snow and I was taking pictures.

It was in the evening and was starting to get dark pretty quickly. My son pointed up to the sky and we noticed some lights coming in from what I believe is the south west. At that point I just pointed the camera up and took the shots. The object really gave me the impression of a balloon — except for the lights. They seemed to cycle all different patterns.

The object passed almost directly overhead and then headed south towards the train tracks. As the object passed I could make out more of a disk shape than a balloon shape. I just remember my son asking me over and over what it was and I didn't have a clue.

Reported by Anonymous
Source: UFOCasebook.com

Speculation about the incident flourished during the next decade. Friedman found additional witnesses, and in 1988 the Center for UFO Studies (CUFOS) sponsored a team to locate the crash site. In 1991, author Kevin Randle and CUFOS investigator Don Schmitt published their book *UFO Crash at Roswell*, claiming that the government had retrieved the debris, cleaned up the site and was covering up its possession of several alien bodies.

One of the new witnesses located was mortician Glenn Dennis. He said he was working in a funeral home in 1947, when he got a call from the base about whether small, child-size coffins were available. As well, he said that when he had been at the base hospital one day in July, he had been ordered to leave after speaking with a nurse who told him she had assisted on autopsies on weird, tiny, childlike bodies.

After the TV show *Unsolved Mysteries* aired an episode in 1989 about the Roswell incident, a Missouri man named Gerald Anderson called in to say he was rock hunting with his family in New Mexico in 1947, and had also seen the crashed flying saucer. What's more, he later told investigators that he had seen three alien bodies underneath the hull of the saucer, with a fourth tending to his injured crewmates. But he said military personnel showed up and ordered the rockhounds to go away and never tell anyone what they had seen.

Anderson's story seemed to be corroborated by another independent witness, Frank Kaufman, who said he was part of a military search party that had found a crashed saucer some distance away from Brazel's debris site. He too said he had seen a large craft half-buried in sand, as well as a number of small humanoid bodies.

In 1992, another book by Friedman and co-author Don Berliner came out with a new theory — that two crashed saucers were actually recovered in 1947, along with their alien crews. *Crash at Corona* explained why Anderson's story was inconsistent with the Brazel discovery: one saucer exploded in midair, leaving only debris, while the other crashed almost intact.

What really happened at Roswell? The case and its numerous investigations have taken on lives of their own, with researchers debating one another on TV shows and in books and magazines. Even those whose new evidence seems to support another writer or investigator seem to be at odds with others' statements. It is a confusing quagmire of facts, anecdotes, and, very likely, fiction.

FLAPS AND WAVES

Ufologists recognize several periods in history during which there were significant increases in the numbers of UFO reports either throughout the world or in several countries at the same time. These are called *UFO waves*. These were in the years 1896–1897, 1947, 1952, 1957, 1966–1967, 1973–1975, 1988–1989, 1993, 1996–1997, 2004 and 2009.

In addition, there are localized or regional increases of UFO reports during short periods of time, usually over a few weeks or months, called *UFO flaps*. A good example of this was the Stephenville, Texas, UFO flap of 2008, when hundreds of people reported seeing UFOs near this small town over a matter of weeks.

It's no wonder, then, that skeptics and debunkers have had fun with the Roswell case. The late Philip Klass, who made a name for himself as a UFO arch-skeptic, took great delight in pointing out inconsistencies and problems with various theories. For example, in 1994, when the U.S. Air Force released a report on an internal investigation into the Roswell claims, the controversy reached a new plateau. They claimed that in 1947, a secret program called Project Mogul was conducted by scientist Charles Moore in the Roswell area.

Moore supervised the launching of balloons with equipment for monitoring Soviet nuclear tests. Each balloon had reflective materials that allowed radar tracking for easy retrieval. According to Air Force records, one of the Mogul balloon arrays was launched on June 4 and was lost by radar tracking near the Brazel debris site a few weeks later. What seemed to clinch the case was the fact that some of the balloon package material was balsa wood held together with glue and packing tape, some of which was emblazoned with abstract designs and lettering that could have been mistaken for hieroglyphics.

But in June 1997, the Air Force came up with a different explanation for the Roswell debris. An internal study discovered that shortly after 1947 a military project was underway, involving the dropping of mannequins from high-altitude balloons to help understand the injuries sustained by pilots and crew who fell from their aircraft. According to the Air Force, it was these three- and four-foot hairless mannequins that were seen by Roswell witnesses and interpreted as aliens.

Needless to say, this explanation hasn't sat well with investigators and researchers. Some point out that the mannequins were not deployed until long after the Roswell debris discovery. This is countered by the detail that eyewitness accounts of alien bodies did not emerge until decades after the fact, allowing the possibility of confusion in witnesses' memories about the year of their observations. The alien bodies story became even more confounding with the publication of a new theory in 2005 that the small bodies with large heads were actually human victims of progenia or other malformations who had been subjects in Air Force experiments.

The problem with coming up with a viable and coherent explanation for all the Roswell evidence and claims is that first the Air Force denied there was any event at all. Then it suggested that the crash was Mogul balloons and later added the mannequin explanation. This sounds suspiciously like arm-waving exercises — trying to make the data fit the theory, and not the other way around. Pro-UFO researchers are probably justified in looking askance at these explanations, which seemed to change as newer information was discovered by researchers.

In fact, since part of the Roswell legend is the switching of newspaper stories to comply with military demands, the accusation of a cover-up may be valid. Even if the truth behind the Roswell crash stories is something militarily terrestrial, there is enough evidence to suggest a cover-up of some kind is involved. But was an alien spaceship behind it all, or a top secret military accident?

Researchers note that the air base near Roswell was the only one with nuclear capability in 1947. Furthermore, the area was home to former Nazi rocket scientists spirited out of Europe following the end of the Second World War as part of Operation Paperclip, an attempt to obtain secrets of rocketry and nuclear science. Certainly some experiments would have resulted in at least a few "accidents" which would have been highly classified.

One argument in defense of an apparent cover-up is that with all the secret projects underway in the area in the late 1940s, and with compartmentalization of knowledge in a typical military approach, it is indeed possible that some high-ranking (and most low-ranking) military personnel would not have had knowledge of certain experiments taking place literally right under their noses.

The most vexing issue is that of time. We are well past the sixtieth anniversary of the Roswell case. Most firsthand witnesses are dead. All relevant official documents may have crumbled out of existence long ago, or been accidentally (or purposefully) destroyed.

In 2007, the publication of the contents of an affidavit signed by Walter Haut, the 509th's press officer responsible for the initial report that a UFO had been found, created a considerable stir within ufology. It was supposedly written in 2002 and sealed until his death. Throughout his lifetime, Haut maintained that he had never seen any wreckage, and even stated this explicitly on the Larry King show on CNN in 2003.

However, in the affidavit, Haut stated that he not only had seen it but handled wreckage from the crash site. He wrote that it was "unlike any material I had or have ever seen in my life." Further, he was later taken to a hangar where he was shown an object "12 to 15 feet in length, not quite as wide, about 6 feet high, and more of an egg shape." And, most astonishingly, "from a distance, I was able to see a couple of bodies under a canvas tarpaulin." Later in his post-mortem confession, he stated: "I am convinced that what I personally observed was some type of craft and its crew from outer space."

Skeptics have charged that there is no evidence Haut actually drafted the affidavit himself, as he was already becoming frail and feeble at the time it was written. Indeed, on that same CNN program in 2003 he did appear confused and did not even stay through the entire planned interview. Yet, one ufologist insisted that when Haut was interviewed in 2001, he was clear of thought and knew precisely what he was talking about.

UFOs and Aliens on TV

A TV series based entirely on the UFO mythology surrounding this incident is *Roswell*, which ran from 1999–2001. The premise was that some aliens did survive the crash of a craft at Roswell in 1947 and hatched in 1989 as young aliens with the physical appearance of humans. They are unaware of their heritage and powers but learn them over time as they are hunted by the FBI and other factions who want to capture them. Essentially a teenage romance series, the TV show was based on a series of popular young adult literature novels.

As for the change of heart about seeing the wreckage, while Haut was alive, there was no way that he would have admitted seeing it as he would still have been liable for prosecution. In order to protect himself, he could be on record to admit his falsehood only after his death.

Despite the excitement within ufological circles about this testimony, even a signed affidavit by a key witness to the Roswell incident does not offer proof that the crash really occurred. Furthermore, the Roswell crash is only one of several alleged cases where an alien spacecraft has been said to have impacted Earth. Other crashed-saucer cases have been cited and discussed elsewhere in the world, including Kecksburg, Pennsylvania, in 1965; Johannesburg, South Africa, in 1953; and Moriches Bay, New York, in 1989.

If any alien debris was recovered by military personnel near Roswell, it has long since been hidden or disposed of. The public debates among believers and non-believers (or other believers with opposing theories) have contributed to a cover-up of the true nature of the original event. In short, we may never get to the bottom of what occurred in the New Mexico desert in 1947.

The Roswell case goes far beyond the debate as to whether or not an alien spacecraft crashed into the desert. Roswell has taken on a life of its own, with an annual celebration and series of UFO conventions in the area. There are tours of the crash site, souvenir stands, museums, and yearly re-enactments of the incident. The town has had parades, costume contests, and even a commissioned musical theatre show to commemorate the event.

It's almost as if the Roswell story did not have to be true anymore.

3

THE BEGINNING OF THE FLYING SAUCER ERA

HARMON FIELD

Following the sighting of metallic disc-like objects by Kenneth Arnold, many more people reported seeing unusual objects in the sky.

On July 10, 1947, at about 5:30 p.m., two Pan American Airways mechanics and a third witness were driving up a mountain road about 10 kilometres south of Harmon Field, an American Air Force Base near Stephenville, Newfoundland.

J.E. Woodruff, J.N. Mehrman, and A.R. Leidy reported seeing a silver, disc-shaped object flying high overhead at an estimated altitude of about 3,000 metres. The object was flying in a horizontal arc over the base and towards the north-northeast. Its size was comparable to a C-54 transport aircraft. As it flew past, it left behind a bluish-black trail about 24 kilometres long. One of the witnesses (not specified in the report but thought to be Woodruff) had a camera with him and managed to take two Kodachrome pictures of the trail.

Copies of these photos are part of the official Project Blue Book files. Although very poor reproductions, they nevertheless show the odd smoke trail in the sky. Weather records confirmed there were scattered clouds between 2,400 to 3,000 metres that supported the original altitude estimate.

This case was investigated by Army Air Force Intelligence and was of particular concern to military officials because of a perceived threat that the Soviets may have been behind the appearances of flying saucers. If this was the case, then it was obvious that in order to spy on the U.S., flights from the U.S.S.R. would have to pass over Canada. The initial report was filed by Harmon base intelligence officers on July 16, with a more detailed report received at the Pentagon on July 21.

Air Force Brigadier General George F. Schulgen, then chief, Air Intelligence Requirements Division, Office of the Assistant Chief of Staff, A-2 (Intelligence) ordered intelligence officers at Wright Field in Dayton to go to Harmon Field to assess the situation and report directly to the Pentagon. The Wright T-2 chief, Colonel Howard M. McCoy, dispatched a team by July 30.

The T-2 investigation report on the Harmon Field case noted: "The bluish-black trail seems to indicate ordinary combustion from a turbo-jet engine, athodyd motor, or some combination of these types of power plants. The absence of noise and apparent dissolving of the clouds to form a clear path indicates a relatively large mass flow of a rectangular cross-section containing a considerable amount of heat."

The report did not consider that a meteor or fireball had made the trail, even though this explanation was the official conclusion on the case file. However, Blue Book documents showed that the Pentagon was still focused on a Soviet connection. As noted in a report on the case, "Wright Field investigators spoke with the commander of Harmon Field and others to make sure that no British or Canadian aircraft had been in the area at the time. And since they knew no American aircraft were to blame, they privately concluded something of 'foreign origin' made that curious split in the clouds over Newfoundland."

What we are left with is a well-witnessed and intensely investigated UFO case, reported long before the term *UFO* was coined by the American military. In the early years of the Cold War, the Soviets were suspected, since the object seen was not "friendly." The photographs show a very strange rocket-like exhaust trail or contrail, proving that something definitely was seen by a number of qualified observers that day. It was one the first photographs of an unidentified flying object reported in North America.

Credit: Ufology Research.

In 1947, an unusual object was seen over a U.S. air force base in Newfoundland. Photographs were taken of the smoke trail it left behind.

In Their Own Words

San Francisco, California
November 3, 2004

An airline transport pilot with 14 years' experience in commercial aviation can't quite explain what he saw at 11 p.m., November 3, 2004. His aircraft was approaching the city from the east, passing just north of Stockton, when he received instructions from the tower to descend from 35,000 to 24,000 feet [10,500 to 7,200 meters].

"While approaching San Francisco from the east, an orange dot began to glow and seemed to flash higher up to the west of us. I thought that it was a planet. It then changed color from orange to white. Again, I thought a planet could be illuminated through a [local] atmosphere that would explain the color change.

"It then began to move in a northeasterly direction. Once again, being in an airplane, it is very easy to think an object is moving, from small corrections the autopilot makes. I found a handful of stars to serve as a reference point and verified that the object was slowly moving north.

"It moved about 30 degrees and then stopped. Then, it made a slight tangent to the right and continued moving for about 20 more degrees. It stopped and turned again to the right and continued for 10 degrees, then stopped again and disappeared.

"The whole sighting ran about two minutes or so from start to finish. It was difficult to judge the actual distance and speed. When I talk about 'moving in degrees and turning,' I am talking about my [cockpit] viewpoint and compass degrees. The UFOs size was very small, about the size of the stars and planets you see in the sky.

"We had initially been at 35,000 feet [10,500 meters] but had descended to 24,000 feet [7,200 meters] when we saw the object. We were above the clouds with a clear view, and there was a crescent moon behind us. The weather in San Francisco was partly cloudy skies and light rain.

"There were two of us in the cockpit, and we both witnessed the same thing. We were both in awe. I have been flying for 14 years have never witnessed something like this before."

Reported by Anonymous
Source: UFOCasebook.com

A UFO CASUALTY

The first death due to a UFO took place on January 7, 1948. Captain Thomas Mantell, a veteran pilot who had flown in the battle of Normandy in 1944, was scrambled with three other pilots in response to reports of an unidentified object over Marysville, Kentucky. The sightings started at about 1:20 p.m., with many area residents reporting something in the sky, and at 1:45 p.m. an object looking like a white umbrella was seen by an airport tower operator and the commanding officer at Fort Knox.

Mantell, flying an F-51, climbed dangerously high in order to get closer to the object, reaching an altitude of more than 6,000 metres, without his oxygen mask. On his radio, he described the object as "metallic" and "of tremendous size." He continued to fly upward, but the other pilots decided to break off the pursuit. Radio contact was lost with Mantell as he reached 6,900 metres. The wreckage of his plane was found near Franklin, Kentucky.

News reports announced that an air force pilot died while chasing a flying saucer. However, after a lengthy investigation, the object was identified as a Navy Skyhook balloon, a secret high-altitude experiment — information not shared with the air force. Mantell had died because of military compartmentalization: only those involved in the Skyhook program knew of its existence, and the air force did not know it was a military operation. He was not shot down by a flying saucer; he had climbed too high and his engine likely stalled, leading to the unfortunate crash.

FOUR MORE SAUCERS

- During the afternoon of April 5, 1948, several researchers at a geophysics laboratory on Holloman Air Force Base in New Mexico all saw two unusual dish-shaped objects, white or grey in colour, about 30 metres in diameter, and high up in the sky. One object moved upward, then moved sharply to one side, dropped and made a loop in the air and vanished. The other flew rapidly to the west, made a similar loop and vanished as well.

- On May 7, 1948, at 3:00 p.m., three people in Memphis, Tennessee, saw as many as 50 shiny objects flying at high speed across the sky. Although most were travelling all in a straight line, a few seemed to occasionally deviate from the line and weave in and out. They did not make any noise, even though a few seemed to have whitish tails that were thought to be exhaust. A check with a meteorological office showed that only one balloon had been launched that day, and there had not been any military aircraft flying in the vicinity that afternoon. The suggestion that the witnesses had seen a train of daytime meteors was rejected. The incident was listed by Project Blue Book as "unknown."

- On June 30, 1948, the ship *Llandovery Castle* had left Kenya bound for Cape Town. At 11:00 p.m. on July 1, it was going through the Straits of Madagascar when the lookout and some passengers saw a light high in the sky heading in their direction. As they watched, it descended until it was only about 15 metres above the water and began travelling alongside the ship. As it flew, it shone a beam of light like a searchlight down onto the water, then the beam and its lights were extinguished. The crew and passengers of the ship were then able to see that the object was a cigar-shaped metallic craft, with its rear section cut off. It did not have any windows or portholes and seemed to be 300 metres in length. It kept pace with the ship for approximately a minute, then it ascended to about 300 metres in altitude, flames came out of its tail section and it shot ahead becoming lost to sight quickly.

- On August 20, 1949, astronomer Clyde Tombaugh was casually observing the sky one night near Las Cruces, New Mexico, with his wife and mother-in-law beside him. In February 1930, he had been comparing sets of photographic plates taken of the night sky when he noted one star seemed to have moved from one night to the next; he had discovered the planet Pluto. But on this night, nearly 20 years later, he and his family saw something completely different that left him perplexed. They saw a half-dozen rectangles of greenish light, moving together in a line from the northwest to the southeast. It was as if they were windows on a long, cylindrical object, moving about 35 degrees in altitude, making no sound as they sped rapidly across the sky and vanished within three or four seconds.

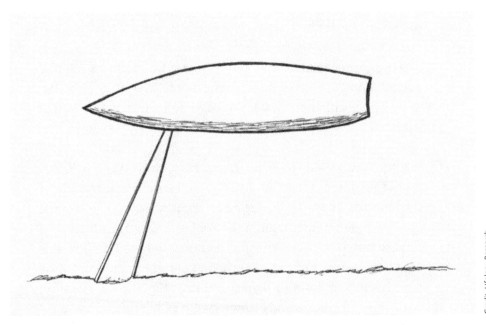

On June 30, 1948, a cigar-shaped object flew by a cargo ship, shining a light on the water as it passed by.

Credit: Ufology Research.

GOOSE BAY

In 1941, the United States built an Air Force Base at Goose Bay in the heart of Labrador, a strategic location, leading to the ocean. It facilitated anti-submarine exercises and staging of aircraft on overseas flights. A set of Distant Early Warning (DEW) Line sites was constructed in Labrador during the Cold War and monitored at a NORAD site at Goose Bay beginning in 1953. The 641 Aircraft Warning and Control Squadron was based there and began flying missions for "surveillance, identification, and interceptor control."

Given this mandate, when the flying saucer phenomenon began spreading in the 1940s and unidentified aircraft were being reported, Goose Bay seemed to be a major hotspot. It was not surprising that an American airbase on Canadian soil might be the site of many saucer sightings, just like so many other bases worldwide.

What is perhaps a bit surprising, however, is that there were so *many* saucer sightings at Goose Bay. In the 1940s and 1950s, there were 20 known reports, a considerable number for such a remote base. Most people were unaware of what was being seen and reported by pilots and other military personnel, although rumours of events persisted over the years.

The first known sighting near Goose Bay took place in the summer of 1948 and was described by a military witness who came forward much after the fact, relating his story to UFO investigators. He provided few details but painted a picture that can be easily visualized, showing the reaction of the intelligence community and the command chain.

Major Edwin A. Jerome, USAF (Ret.), stated that in the summer of 1948, a high-ranking inspection team was visiting the base's radar facilities as part of a tour looking at refuelling and servicing capabilities for all military and civilian aircraft on North Atlantic air routes. During the generals' inspection of the USAF radar shack, the operator painted a high-speed target on his scope going from

UFOs and Aliens in Literature

In 1938 C.S. Lewis published *Out of the Silent Planet*, the first of a trilogy of books in which people from Earth travel to Mars (here called Malacandra) where they encounter a race of intelligent seal-like creatures called *hrossa* and others. However, the caretaker of the planet is Oyarsa, an angelic being who belongs to a race that oversees intelligent life. Unfortunately, the being in charge of the Earth has become evil, and as a result we have fallen from grace.

the northeast to the southwest with a calculated speed of about 15,000 kilometres per hour. This caused considerable concern since the base personnel wanted to look good in front of the inspection team, and such a calculation must have been an error.

Jerome noted: "The poor airman technician was brought to task for his apparent miscalculation." However, when the target appeared a second time, the brass saw the target on the screen themselves. They dismissed it as poorly calibrated American equipment. They then went to the Canadian side of the base to inspect the RCAF facility and learned that the equipment there had also just tracked the same or similar object. The inspecting officers branded the incident a coincidence. The anomalous target on both scopes had been moving at speeds faster than anything known to be possible.

Jerome was an intelligence officer at the base and was ordered to make a report on the incident. It had been suggested that the object was a meteor, but when he interviewed radar operators on both sides of the base, he found the object was tracked as it maintained an altitude of 18,000 metres throughout its flight and he believed this ruled out a meteor as a possibility. While conducting his investigation, he was shocked to learn that the very next day, both radars again reported an anomalous object, this time moving slowly over the base at about 16 kilometres per hour at 14,000 metres. This time, the anomaly was explained as "high-flying seagulls."

Remember, this case occurred long before rockets and jet aircraft were capable of such speeds or high-altitude helicopters were possible. The consternation of the inspectors and the embarrassment of the radar technicians must have been considerable, and was something that was talked about in the mess hall for many weeks.

If a radar case is explained as being due to faulty equipment, technicians point out that the same equipment is used to track known military operations without malfunctions. You can't really have it both ways; either the equipment was working or it wasn't.

Through the rest of the decade, there were four more known sightings at Goose Bay. Three of these were October 29, 31, and November 1, 1948, with little information available on the first two other than that they were noted in Project Blue Book. But Donald Keyhoe, a noted journalist and author of several UFO books, described the cases this way, citing the third case as well:

> One of the first cases, involving three separate incidents, took place in Labrador, at Goose Bay Air Force Base. About 3 a.m. on October 29, 1948, an unidentified object in slow level flight was tracked by tower radar men. Two days later, the same thing happened again.

But the following night, on November 1, radar men got a jolt. Some strange object making 600 mph was tracked for four minutes before it raced off on a southwest course. At the time, weather conditions were considered as a possible answer. But ... this obviously must be ruled out.

A fourth Labrador sighting took place on September 9, 1949, when a military aircraft pilot saw an egg-shaped object disappear into a cloud at a high speed.

4

THE FIFTIES

GOOSE BAY REDUX

In the 1950s, UFOs were again plaguing the Goose Bay air force base. On September 14, 1951, at 9:30 p.m., another sighting there was recorded in Blue Book case files, listed as *No. 969*.

Technical Sergeant W. B. Maupin and Corporal J.W. Green were witnesses when two objects were tracked on radar on a collision course. One of the radar operators attempted to warn the objects of the imminent collision and was surprised to watch one avoid danger by moving to the right. A third unidentified track then joined the first two. The entire incident lasted more than 15 minutes. No aircraft were known to be in the area.

It's difficult to say what might have happened in the radar booth that night. It's likely that someone there remembered the unfortunate incident with the visiting dignitaries just three years earlier and wanted to avoid another reprimand. So, he logically decided that the unknown objects were aircraft and handled them as unidentified traffic, vectoring them to safety. It appears rather unlikely, however, that two spacecraft from another planet would need assistance from a terrestrial radar operator for flight directions.

The next year, another weird "something" was reported over Goose Bay. Edward Ruppelt, former head of Project Blue Book said that one night early in 1952, the pilot of an Air Force C-54, about 320 kilometres southwest of Goose Bay, contacted the tower to report a large "fireball" had buzzed his airplane. It had come from behind and had not been seen it until it was "just off the left wing," only an estimated 30 or 60 hundred metres away.

The base officer-of-the-day, also a pilot, was in the flight operations office and overheard the report. He went outside and saw a light coming from the southwest. In the blink of an eye, it flew over the airfield, increasing to the size of a "golf ball at arm's length," looking like a "ball of fire." The object seemed so low and close that the officer and the driver of his command car dropped to the ground and hid under the car because they were sure it was going to hit the ground nearby. But as they watched, the fireball made a 90-degree turn over the airfield and flew off to the northwest. In the control tower, the technicians saw the object make its right-angle turn and were certain it was not a meteor.

Unidentified Flying Hat

A photographic UFO case, in McMinnville, Oregon, has been debated since it was reported in 1950. On June 8 of that year, Paul Trent and his wife watched a dark, hat-shaped object flying over their property and some clear photos were taken. Skeptics and believers have traded insults about the case for more than 60 years, focusing on shadows on buildings in the foreground, density of the image on the negative, and so forth. There's no question that something was captured on film, and if the witnesses were truthful, an unidentified flying object did pass over a small farm that day.

This incident was discussed during a briefing Ruppelt had some time later in the Pentagon with General Samford, the Director of Intelligence, some members of his staff, two Navy captains from the Office of Naval Intelligence, and other officials. He was describing some outstanding *Unknown* UFO reports he had investigated and noted they were increasing in number. Even though the reports were detailed and contained a great deal of good data, he noted they still had no proof that UFOs were "real." An officer used the Goose Bay sighting as an example of an unexplained case, and said it, too, could not be accepted as proof of alien spacecraft. Ruppelt noted: "I said that our philosophy was that the 'fireball' could have been two meteors: one that buzzed the C-54 and another that streaked across the airfield at Goose AFB. Granted a meteor doesn't come within feet of an airplane or make a 90 degree turn, but these could have been optical illusions of some kind."

The colonel asked, "What are the chances of having two extremely spectacular meteors in the same area, traveling the same direction, only five minutes apart?"

Ruppelt's response was that he "didn't know the exact mathematical probability, but it was rather small ..."

The colonel went on:

Why not assume a point that is more easily proved? ... Why not assume that the C-54 crew, the OD, his driver, and the tower operators did know what they were talking about? Maybe they had seen spectacular meteors during the hundreds of hours that they had flown at night and the many nights that they had been on duty in the tower. Maybe the ball of fire had made a 90 degree turn. Maybe it was some kind of an intelligently controlled craft that had streaked northeast across the Gulf of St. Lawrence and Quebec Province at 2,400 miles an hour.

"Why not just simply believe that most people know what they saw?" the colonel said with no small amount of sarcasm in his voice.

Also in 1952, on June 1, a cargo ship was anchored at Port Gentil, Gabon, when at 2:40 a.m. the first mate notified the Master Seaman that a bright object was passing directly overhead. He said he had watched it come from the shore, stop, turn and continue on its course out to sea, once again making an erratic move as it flew near the ship. The Master held up his binoculars and saw a bright, "phosphorescent orange light, circular in shape and moving at great speed in a seemingly straight-line course." He followed the light for three minutes as it headed out to sea and was lost to sight. He confirmed that there were no planes in the air near there at the time.

Far to the north but only a handful of weeks later on July 15, 1952, two bakers in Boukanefis, Algeria, were outside their shop at 11:00 p.m. when they saw an object shaped like a "plate," flying through the sky and giving off a greenish smoke. It kept a constant course as it headed south across the desert and out of sight. That year, UFOs were reported in many towns across Algeria and Oran, including Lamorciere, Mostaganem, Algiers and Marrakech, but also far to the south in the Belgian Congo near its uranium mines.

On June 19, 1952, yet another radar and visual saucer-sighting occurred at Goose Bay AFB. It was described in a number of sources with slightly differing details, but the substance of the case remains interesting throughout the varying citations.

At 2:37 a.m. that morning, Second Lieutenant Agostino and an unidentified radar operator saw a red light that turned white and seemed to wobble. Radar tracked a stationary target that quickly grew then returned to its previous size, possibly a disc rotating to present a wider reflective surface.

Did You Know?

The United States Air Force began
using the term *UFO* instead of *Flying Saucer* in 1952,
because they didn't want people to assume that aliens
were piloting the craft.

Journalist Donald Keyhoe had his own version of the story:

On the night of June 19, 1952, Goose Bay Air Force Base, in Labrador, came in for a brief observation. Just as radar men picked up a UFO track, ground men outside saw a strange, red-lighted object come in over the field. The radar blip suddenly enlarged, as if the device had banked, exposing a larger surface to the radar beam. At the same moment the watching airmen saw the red light wobble or flutter. After a moment the light turned white and quickly disappeared. Apparently the unknown craft had gone into a steep climb ...

Keyhoe noted his source was a USAF intelligence report, although which one is unclear. He commented on this case again in an article in *True Magazine*:

On June 19, 1952, a new incident occurred at Goose Bay Air Force Base — the fourth to date. Just after midnight, a weird red light appeared, holding a southwest course. At the same time, tower radar men caught it on their scope. After hovering briefly at 4,000 feet, the light suddenly turned white. At about this instant, the blip on the scope "brightened." This effect, familiar to operators, is seen when a plane banks, the larger surface exposed to the radar beam causing a sharper return.

There are some obvious inconsistencies in the stories, however. Was the radar blip stationary or moving? If it was stationary, it could not have been the red object that "came in" over the airfield.

However, this meagre information perhaps does not give justice to what actually happened. In a fascinating account published on the Internet, a former radar operator related the situation in a fascinating narrative style, his memory vague about the date but full of details surrounding the incident. He posted the information on a website devoted to military reminiscences, hoping to find answers to some of his questions from more than half a century ago.

Bob Jones was stationed at Goose Bay AFB during 1952–53, and was the radar maintenance technician on duty at the American radar site when the encounter occurred. He said that in late December 1952 or early January 1953, a severe winter storm was raging and winds were gusting up to 110 kilometres per hour. The storm was so intense that all of the F-94 jet interceptors were tied down to prevent them from being damaged by the high winds. No air traffic had been detected by the radar through the storm, which brought heavy snow and reduced visibility to less than 23 metres. Jones noted the radar at Goose Bay was manufactured during the Second World War and could not cancel out ground clutter, preventing the accurate tracking of objects within about 32 to 64 kilometres from the antenna.

Around 11:00 p.m. a target appeared on the radar screen, about 145 kilometres to the north and approaching the base at about 145 kilometres per hour, and the radar could not determine its altitude. Jones noted that "the fact that the target was approaching from due north (0 degrees on the radar screen) was very unusual since no military or civilian airfields were located in that direction. Its slow speed of travel was equally strange. Most aircraft that approached Goose Bay from a northerly direction were flights coming in from Thule, Greenland, where the United States was building an air base and radar site."

The object proceeded south at a constant speed and heading and was classified "Unknown." Despite the weather, the F-94 interceptors were ordered to scramble. Because they were all tied down, it took 45 minutes to get airborne and by that time the object had entered the ground clutter and tracking was lost.

However, only a few minutes later, two more objects appeared on the radar screen, at the same range but this time on a bearing of 45 degrees. The radar operators directed the F-94s to intercept them. Although the aircraft had nose-mounted radar, they normally could locate their targets using their own radar and home in on them. None of the jets were able to detect a target, but the ground radar controller was able to track all six targets on his screen. At one point the ground controller guided one pilot toward a target so that the jet and the target merged on the screen, yet the pilot could neither see it visually nor on radar. The interception exercise seemed fruitless.

About an hour later, the three unknown targets reappeared on the ground radar screens. They were in formation and heading southeast towards Newfoundland. Jones figured that Goose Bay was a rendezvous point for the objects.

Another attempt was made to intercept the unknown objects. This time six F-94s were scrambled and flew throughout the area looking for any aircraft, without success. The targets continued on, oblivious to the frenzied search underway, and eventually disappeared 160 kilometres southeast of Goose Bay. The jets were recalled to the base, although the pilots' frustration was evident from radio chatter in which they complained the ground radar operators needed to clean their radar screens.

This was not unexpected, since the pilots had been scrambled to fly in dangerous weather conditions and had been even directed to fly into locations where other aircraft might have been flying.

Jones noted, "There was definitely something in the sky that night that was under intelligent control ... Their slow speed and how they navigated in such terrible weather remains a mystery."

A number of other cases occurred over Goose Bay over the next few years. On April 6, 1953, at 7:00 p.m. between Goose Bay and Sondestrom AFB in Greenland, a USAF transport pilot and his co-pilot saw a white light at 4,500 metres on a steady course, descending in a shallow turn.

Then, on May 1, 1953, at 11:35 p.m., the pilot and radar operator of a USAF F-94 jet interceptor, as well as a control tower operator, saw a white light that evaded interception by scrambled jets. The sighting apparently lasted for 30

UFOs and Aliens in Literature

In 1944, during the World War II, a short story was published about a soldier of the future who encounters an alien under mysterious circumstances. It was written to question our human tendencies to fight against our enemies rather than work with them towards solutions. The story was "Arena," by Frederic Brown. In this time period, Earth is at war with the Outsiders, creatures that look like large red beach balls with tentacles. But a third, supremely powerful race intervenes and pits one man against one Outsider in a contest to determine which civilization will be allowed to continue.

minutes, during which time some kind of triangulation was attempted on the object. There were four more incidents at Goose Bay in 1953: on May 2, May 12, June 11, and June 22. On this last date, at 2:10 a.m., for five minutes the pilot and radar operator of yet another USAF F-94 observed a red light flying at 1,900 kilometres per hour, eluding pursuit by the jet, which has a top speed of only 1,000 kilometres per hour.

Another Canadian case that received relatively little attention took place on April 16, 1953, near Chatham, New Brunswick. At 3:34 p.m., an airline pilot formerly with the air force was flying at 2,750 metres with his co-pilot on a routine flight when they saw a disc-like metallic object approaching them from directly ahead, but flying about 450 metres below their altitude. The object was estimated to be about five to eight kilometres away when they first saw it, and it approached at about 275 kilometres per hour and "passed beneath and behind" their plane. At its closest point, they could see it was definitely not an aircraft, and was about 7.5 metres in diameter, leaving no trail or exhaust.

The official report filed with Project Second Storey, the Canadian Government's official UFO study, read: "Both observers are quite definite in stating that the object was *not* a balloon. The object passed nearly over Chatham but has not been reported by any other witnesses." (Emphasis in original.) And, in the "Interrogator's opinion," the file noted the observer to be "very reliable."

Several months later, on December 16, 1953, Kelly Johnson, one of the developers of the infamous U2 spyplane, reported seeing an anomalous object while at his ranch near Agoura, California. Around 5:00 p.m., he and his wife watched a dark, saucer-shaped object hanging low in the sky. It remained stationary for several minutes, then began to move away from him and against the direction of movement of other clouds in the sky. He guessed that it was about 60 metres in length but couldn't reconcile it as any known aircraft. He maintained it was mysterious and not a conventional vehicle. In addition, two of Johnson's test pilots also observed the same object while flying near Long Beach, California. Skeptics have argued that pilots are not perfect observers and frequently make errors of observation, but one would hope that their observational skills with regard to telling the difference between a conventional aircraft and something else would be better than that.

CONFIDENTIAL OFFICIAL USE ONLY

S940-105

PROJECT SECOND STOREY

Sighting Report

(A Separate form is to be used for each observer) UNCLASSIFIED

DIRECTORATE OF OPERATIONS

JUL 3 1953

A. Details of observer.

1. Name of observer:

   Surname:.................Initials...........

2. Address of observer:

   C/o Maratime Central Airways   Moncton
   Number   Street   City

   New Brunswick
   Province

3. Occupation and previous relevant experience:

   .... is a Government Inspector flying with
   Maratime Central. He is an experienced 'bush' and
   'RCAF' transport pilot.

4. Age Group:.....................Unknown..................

5. Has observer seen "flying objects" before, and if so, briefly,
   when, where, and circumstances:

                        Unknown

   ....

   ....

6. Was observer wearing glasses?

                        Unknown
   ....

B. Details of Observation

7. Date and local time:

                    16 April 53   1534 AST
   ....

8. Position of observer as accurately as possible:
        Pilot of aircraft flying at 9000' over Chatham.
        Speed 170 knots - heading 009.

   ....

9. General description of sighting:
   .... sighted the object some 3 to 5 miles
   ahead at an estimated altitude of 7500'. Object
   approached at approximately 150 knots and passed beneath
   and behind the observers aircraft.

   ....

   ....

CONFIDENTIAL

- 2 -

UNCLASSIFIED

10. Number of objects:.........One..

11.Length of time observed......30 seconds...................................

12.Position in which first seen:

Bearing:....................North. 3 to 5 miles..(See para. 8)...

Elevation.....................7800'.................................

....

....

13. Position in which last seen:

Bearing...................(See Para. 9)..............................

....

Elevation..

....

14. General description of any changes in the direction of motion.

........................NIL..

....

15. Detailed description of apparent shape:

.....................Round and disc-like............................

....

....

....

16. Detailed description of apparent brightness:

....

.........................Unknown....................................

....

....

17. Detailed description of colour.

..Initially a metallic shine, changing on closer view......

...to a more dull metal shade.....................................

....

18. Apparent size (e.g. angle subtended)

....

................Estimated to be 25' in diameter.................

....

- 3 -

CONFIDENTIAL

UNCLASSIFIED

19. Description of exhaust or vapour trails, if any.
............No trail or exhaust.............................
....
....

20. Description of noise, if any:
..............................Unknown........................
....

21. Weather conditions:

    (a) Clouds..3500 Scatter 25000 Scatter........

    (b) Visibility...........15 plus................

    (c) Precipitation:..........Nil.................

    (d) General remarks:.Wnd at 5000!.- 300/12......
          Wnd at 7000! - 320/20 Surface Wnd - XNE 4

22. Was the object flying above, below or in and out of cloud?
..................Between cloud layers...................

23. Did anyone else see the object? If so, names and addresses:
.......Yes, Co-Pilot of same aircraft.................
.......Name unknown - Maratime Central Moncton NB....
....
....

24. Is there other contributory evidence:
    (Photographic, or electronic, etc.)
....
..............................NO.............................
....

25. Any other details: (including sketch if possible)
....Both observers are quite definite in stating that...
....the object was NOT a balloon. The object passed....
....nearly over Chatham but has not been reported by....
....any other witnesses.
....
....

Documents from Project Second Storey, the Canadian equivalent of Project Blue Book, show that on April 16, 1953, a metallic disc flew by an aircraft at close range.

Perhaps the most cited UFO incident over Labrador occurred on June 30, 1954. This involved not just a military aircraft, but also a commercial airliner with many passengers who witnessed the object as well. Eleven crew members and the pilot of a BOAC Stratocruiser all shared the experience, and the pilot was driven to write about it at length in his in his routine flight report.

Captain James Howard was flying the airliner, approaching Goose Bay just after sunset at around 9:00 p.m. local time, on an otherwise uneventful New York to London flight. Suddenly, he saw a large black object "like an inverted pear suspended in the sky." There were six additional objects in formation ahead and behind the main UFO, all "keeping station not less than five miles away."

Radioing the Goose Bay tower, he was told that there were no other aircraft in the area. As he watched with his co-pilot, the primary object changed its shape into a "flying arrow — an enormous delta-winged plane turning in to close with us." It paced the airliner for more than 15 minutes and about 130 kilometres of flight, during which time other crew members and passengers also observed the strange phenomena.

Goose Bay, as in the other cases, again scrambled a jet fighter to intercept the odd formation, but as the fighter approached, the objects "appeared to return to their base ship." Shortly thereafter, the cluster of objects simply "faded away." The objects had no vapour trails or lights. At no time did any of them appear on radar.

James McDonald, an astronomer who studied UFO cases in depth, believed the BOAC case to be one of the strongest on record, with no satisfying explanation. In his analysis he noted that "no meteorological optical phenomenon could reasonably account for the reported phenomena ... To suggest that a natural plasmoid (ball lightning) could keep pace with an aircraft at that speed and distance seems entirely unreasonable. The speed and motions rule out meteors. The peculiar maneuvering of the smaller objects and the curious shape changes of the larger object suggest no conventional explanation."

Interestingly, Blue Book does not have an entry for this case, even though it was reported that a Goose Bay aircraft was vectored to give chase. It is not clear how this could be possible, given the rather thorough listings of Blue Book cases that are now available.

Martin Shough, a British UFO researcher, has produced a remarkably detailed analysis of this case, more than 65 years after the incident occurred. Using witness testimony, weather information and other data, he suggests the objects seen were caused by a mirage, making the witnesses think they were looking at a structured craft when in fact they were simply observing an atmospheric refraction.

Finally, two other sightings are recorded for Goose Bay during the rest of the 1950s. On February 12, 1956, at 11:25 p.m., for one minute, an F-89 pilot and a radar operator both saw a green-and-red object rapidly circling the jet, which was tracked on radar. No further details are available. Three years later, on August 10, 1959, on the Goose Bay AFB at 1:28 a.m., RCAF pilot Flight Lieutenant M.S. Mowat watched a large, star-like light crossing 53 degrees of sky in 25 minutes.

KELLY–HOPKINSVILLE

The Kelly–Hopkinsville case is a classic of UFO literature that has puzzled both believers and debunkers alike. Dr. J. Allen Hynek, the leading UFO researcher of the early days of ufology, said the Kelly–Hopkinsville case seemed "preposterous" and offensive to "common sense." Despite this, the case as a whole is interesting and many investigators consider it a solid example of a close encounter of the third kind.

Did You Know?

A close encounter with a UFO in which creatures or entities are seen is classified as a *close encounter of the third kind.*

At around 7:00 p.m. on Sunday, August 21, 1955, the Sutton and Taylor families were enjoying an evening together in their home near the towns of Kelly and Hopkinsville, Kentucky. Billy Ray Taylor went outside to the well to get some water and saw a flying saucer soar through the sky and drop down into a gully along the farmyard. He ran back inside the farmhouse to tell everyone, but they just thought he had seen a shooting star and weren't that interested.

That is, until about an hour later when their dog started barking loudly just outside the door. Billy Ray and Lucky Sutton opened the door just in time to see the frightened dog claw its way under the house. It seemed to be running from a short, strange, silver-suited creature that was approaching from the field. It looked like a monkey about a metre tall, with a large head, bulbous glowing eyes, pointy ears, and clawed hands on the end of long arms that were raised over its head.

The men reached inside for their guns and shot at the creature, which apparently was hit because it did a backwards flip but righted itself again. The sound of the buckshot and bullets striking the creature was hollow and metallic, "just like I'd shot into a bucket." The men went inside when they saw it clamber up the side of the house. Soon, it or a similar creature appeared at a window, and the men shot it point-blank through the screen. It flipped again and dropped out of sight.

Billy Ray went outside, and everyone watching his exit saw a clawed hand grasp at his head from the roof overhang. Another family member ran past him and shot the creature on the roof from the yard, causing the strange being to flip over again and end up on the other side of the house. Then they saw another creature up in a tree on a branch, and when it was shot it floated gently down to the ground and scampered off. Throughout the next hour, creatures seemed to scurry in the shadows around the house, dashing around trees and outbuildings. The family heard scraping noises on their roof, as if clawed feet were moving around up there.

Finally, after about three hours of being trapped in their own house by these strange creatures, the family had enough and made a dash for it, getting into their two vehicles and speeding to the sheriff's office in Hopkinsville, 11 kilometres away. They explained breathlessly what had happened and the police officers went with them back to their farm, but there was no sign of the intruders. The police left around 2:00 a.m. and the family nervously went to bed. Alas, the creatures seemed to return when the coast was clear, and family members saw them again, poking heads in windows and darting around the outside of the house. Come morning, there was no sign of any "invasion" from the night before.

The seven adult witnesses and later their children were interviewed by reporters several times over the next few days. Skeptics simply assumed that the witnesses had been drunk or hallucinating, leading the family to stop granting interviews after a short while. Another theory offered was that the family had seen monkeys that had escaped from a zoo, but the witnesses insisted they had been close enough to see if the creatures were animals.

Under questioning, a clearer picture of the creatures unfolded. Their bodies were thin, like "a formless straight figure," with arms almost twice as long as the legs, but their hands were "huge, bulky looking things." Their heads were round and completely bald; their eyes were large saucers, set about 15 centimetres apart and seemed to wrap around the side of the face. The mouth was "not much more than a straight line across the face." Each of the seven witnesses gave identical stories of the events that transpired that night, and virtually identical descriptions of the odd creatures.

Once the word got out about their experience, the family was subject to a great deal of ridicule and negative publicity. They soon refused to discuss the matter with anyone, understandably. One investigator noted: "The Suttons seem never to have been tempted to recant and get back into the good graces of society," and that "neither adults nor children so much as hinted at the possibility of a lie or mistake — in public or to relatives; there was no trace of retraction."

So, either the Suttons either made up a story so fantastic that no one would believe them, or something unusual happened at their farm that night. It's easy to dismiss the case simply as a fantasy, but the Suttons were adamant that what they claimed to have happened really happened, and not one of them ever changed their story.

THE LAKENHEATH INCIDENT

On the night of August 13–14, 1956, two military bases in the east of England tracked several fast-moving objects. Two aircraft were sent up to intercept them, and the pilots were to visually track them as they manoeuvred at high altitude. Official U.S. Air Force reports showed that the sightings could not be explained as radar malfunctions or as unusual weather phenomena.

Did You Know?

The band Foo Fighters took their name from UFOs! A *foo fighter* was the name given to unusual lights and objects seen by Allied and Axis pilots during the Second World War.

At 9:30 p.m. the U.S. Air Force operations at RAF Bentwaters tracked a UFO on radar. According to records, it flew 80 kilometres from east to west in only 30 seconds. Calculations showed it must have been travelling between 8,000 and 10,000 kilometres per hour.

A few minutes later 12 to 15 more objects were tracked moving over the base, after which they seemed to merge into one very large object. And, according to the size of the image painted on the radar scope, the object was much larger than the largest known aircraft flying at that time. While under observation, the large target on the radar scope stopped occasionally then flew out of range.

At 10:00 p.m., another target was tracked over the air base, flying at a high speed that was calculated to be an incredible 19,300 kilometres per hour.

Less than an hour later the radar picked up a target going east to west, but this time calculated to be practically a slowpoke, flying "only" 3,200 kilometres per hour. However, an operator in the control tower noticed something visually: a bright light flying overhead from east to west that could have been the object on radar, and it was less than two kilometres above the ground. The object may have been seen by another witness, too: the pilot of a military transport plane flying near the base reported seeing a bright light that was streaking underneath his plane at high speed, also following the object's east to west course.

While the airmen and control tower operators were comparing notes and puzzling over what had just transpired, radar operators at both Bentwaters and Lakenheath detected a stationary object only 30 to 40 kilometres southwest of Lakenheath. As they watched their screens, the object began moving north towards them at a moderate speed, about 650 to 1,000 kilometres per hour. The object behaved very strangely for an airplane, making sudden changes in direction without slowing down for turns.

Determined to solve the mystery, the air force decided to scramble a Venom jet to intercept whatever was flying over the air bases. According to a teletype from the airbase at Lakenheath to Air Defence Command in Colorado:

> The aircraft flew over RAF station Lakenheath and was vectored toward a target on radar 6 miles east of the field. Pilot advised he had a bright white light in sight and would investigate. At thirteen miles west he reported loss of target and white light. Lakenheath RATCC vectored him to a target 10 miles east of Lakenheath and pilot advised target was on radar and he was "locking on." Pilot reported he had lost target on his radar. Lakenheath RATCC reports that as the Venom passed the target on radar, the target began a tail chase of the friendly fighter. RATCC requested pilot acknowledge this chase. Pilot acknowledged and stated he would try to circle and get behind the target.

As noted in the Condon Report, the USAF study of UFOs by the University of Colorado, the pilot was unnerved at the situation:

> The interceptor pilot continued to try and shake the UFO for about ten minutes ... He continued to comment occasionally and we could tell from the tonal quality he was getting worried, excited and also pretty scared.
>
> He finally said, "I'm returning to Station ... Let me know if he follows me. I'm getting low on petrol." The target (UFO) followed him only a short distance, as he headed south southwest, and the UFO stopped and remained stationary. We advised the interceptor that the UFO target had stopped following and was now stationary about 10 miles south ... He rogered this message and almost immediately the second interceptor called us on the same frequency. We replied and told him we would advise him when we had a radar target, so we could establish radar contact with his aircraft ...
>
> The number two interceptor called the number one interceptor ... and asked him, "Did you see anything?" Number one replied, "I saw something, but I'll be damned if I know what it was." Number two said, "What happened?" Number one said, "He (or it) got behind me and I did everything I could to get behind him and I couldn't. It's the damnedest thing I've ever seen."

The 1969 report by the Air Force-funded study reported, "In summary, this is the most puzzling and unusual case in the radar-visual files. The apparent rational, intelligent behavior of the UFO suggests a mechanical device of unknown origin as the most probable explanation of this sighting. However, in view of the inevitable fallibility of witnesses, more conventional explanations of this report cannot be entirely ruled out." Finally, the study concluded that "although conventional or natural explanations certainly cannot be ruled out, the probability of such seems low in this case and the probability that at least one genuine UFO was involved appears to be fairly high."

A similar case, often considered one of the best on record, is the encounter of an American crew of an RB-47 aircraft on July 17, 1957, over the continental U.S. Their plane was followed by an unidentified object that was apparently also tracked on radar, by ground as well as onboard instruments. The argument for the high quality of this case is based in part on the fact that all personnel were highly qualified and highly trained, yet were unable to solve the mystery of their pursuer.

UFOs and Aliens in Literature

In 1950, a series of stories was written by Ray Bradbury, collectively called *The Martian Chronicles*. The stories are about human exploration of Mars, which we learn is a dying race that is physically very similar in appearance to Earthlings. The stories are also about our human failings, and the eventual extinction of the human race. In a reversal of what happened in *War of the Worlds*, it is humans who bring disease to the Martians, who then die out on their own world.

The Condon Committee, which studied UFO reports for the United States Air Force, made the following statement about the case: "If the report is accurate, it describes an unusual, intriguing, and puzzling phenomenon, which, in the absence of additional information, must be listed as unidentified." However, its director then stated: "... it may be assumed that radar 'chaff' and a temperature inversion may have been factors in the incident." This is contradicted later in the same study, when an in-depth analysis of the case offers three hypotheses: a radio-optical mirage of another plane seen through an inversion layer in the atmosphere; anomalous propagation echoes on the radar screens; and a light on the ground that was mistaken for a flying object. The analysis concludes that "there are many unexplained aspects to this sighting, however, and a solution such as given above, although possible, does not seem highly probable ... From a propagation standpoint, this sighting must be tentatively classified as unknown."

THE SATURN-SHAPED SAUCERS

Trindade Island is a small dot on the map, off the east coast of Brazil. (Not to be confused with Trinidad, which is in the Caribbean.) During the International Geophysical Year of 1958, scientists around the world gathered data throughout the world on changes in the world's climate, as they all did again recently.

Brazilian scientists working with that country's Navy selected Trindade Island as a site to gather samples and launch weather balloons with instrument packages. A base was set up and several ships were anchored offshore to facilitate research activities. The balloons were tracked by personnel onboard the Navy ships and retrieved in order to collect the data. Curiously, some of the researchers reported seeing odd lights and other objects near the balloons at high altitude, but could not identify them.

On the morning of January 6, 1958, Commander Carlos Bacellar, chief officer at the scientific base, watched the launching of a weather balloon with an attached instrument package. It was fitted with a radio transmitter that sent out signals as it ascended, allowing easy tracking. However, as he monitored the receiver inside the base hut, the signals faded and then stopped unexpectedly. This occasionally happened in high winds and stormy conditions, but the day was clear with few clouds.

Bacellar went outside to see what might have happened to the balloon and found it well within sight, gaining altitude and nearing a cloud. As he watched, the balloon and its package were suddenly drawn upward into the cloud, and after 10 minutes it reappeared over the cloud but without its package. Then, using binoculars, Bacellar watched as a silver crescent-shaped object moved from behind the cloud and moved off. A technician with Bacellar also saw the object through his theodolite. As puzzling as this was, what happened next was more remarkable.

Not far away, off the coast of Trindade Island, the Brazilian Navy ship *Almirante Saldanha* was anchored as scientists were packing up their experiments to return home. Among the crew and passenger contingent of 48 was Almiro Barauna, a civilian with expertise in underwater photography. At 12:15 p.m., he was on deck with some of his camera gear when a retired Brazilian Air Force officer called to him, drawing his attention to a bright object in the sky over the island.

As he looked in the direction the officer was pointing, another officer ran towards them, also gesturing skyward. Barauna saw the object flashing in the sunlight, moving towards the island, and watched as it passed in front of a cloud. He quickly took two photographs of the object before it flew behind a mountain. It reappeared on the other side, apparently closer to the witnesses because it seemed larger in angular size. It was metallic grey, looking like the planet Saturn — that is, an oval with a ring. Barauna took one more photo but was being jostled by the excited group of witnesses on board and couldn't get any more clear shots off. The object flew off across the ocean away from the ship and was lost to sight.

Once it was gone, Barauna took the film out of the camera and entered into the animated discussions on deck about the object. It was an hour later that he took the film into the ship's darkroom with a Brazilian air force officer, and developed the photos. There was no photographic paper available, so he couldn't print the negatives, but these were examined and seen to have images of the object.

When Barauna got back to his home in Rio de Janeiro, he printed the negatives and took them to the Navy office. A few days later, he was called to the office and was interviewed about the circumstances surrounding the photographs. Over the next

Credit: Ademar Gevaerd.

In 1958, civilian and military personnel watched a Saturn-shaped object fly over Trindade Island, off the Brazilian coast. Several photographs were taken as it flew rapidly over the island and out to sea. The first photograph of the object.

Credit: Ademar Gevaerd.

Close-up from the first photograph.

Credit: Ademar Gevaerd.

The second photograph.

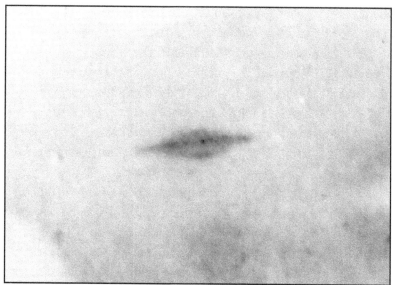

Credit: Ademar Gevaerd.

Close-up from the second photograph.

several days, officials discussed the case at length, then eventually decided to release the photographs to the media. This caused a sensation; newspapers and their reporters worked hard to get additional witnesses' testimonies, and politicians argued about the incident in Brazil's parliament.

The Brazilian Navy issued a carefully worded news release stating that "this Ministry cannot make any statement about the object sighted over the island of Trindade, for the photographs do not constitute enough evidence for such a purpose." It was noted, however, that the object was not a weather balloon or a stray missile. Another statement noted that "there are indications of the existence of unidentified aerial objects."

Originally, the photos were explained by debunkers as being of an aircraft viewed head-on, giving the impression of an egg-shaped body bisected by a line that was the "ring." Later, it was said that Barauna had simply faked the photos in collusion with one or more people on the ship. However, this ignores the fact that several witnesses had given testimony about seeing the object flying overhead, although the Navy failed to get official statements from any of them except Barauna! Finally, one critic discovered that Barauna had demonstrated trick photography in exposing a previously photographed UFO in Brazil, publishing his work in a magazine. The implication is that he learned from his subject and created a hoax that would stand up to scrutiny.

Debunker Donald Menzel described how Barauna did it, in his opinion: "In the privacy of his home the photographer had snapped a series of pictures of a model UFO against a black background. He then reloaded the camera with the same film and took pictures of the scenery in the ordinary fashion. When the film was developed, there was the saucer hanging in the sky."

Supporters have countered that no such model ever turned up in Barauna's possession, although this in itself isn't enough to dismiss the allegations. Menzel did, however, state that only Barauna and one other person actually said they saw the object, at odds with statements by investigators, who listed several witnesses of the event. Menzel may have had a good explanation for the photos, but his investigation was otherwise weak.

Recently, this issue of the photographic trickery was again raised among ufologists discussing important cases. The magazine in which Barauna's expertise at faking flying saucer photos was made available in the original Portuguese but with translation into English for a broader readership and greater accessibility. In fact, the Trindade photos were placed side by side with some of his "fake" saucer photos for comparison, and there is no question that they do look similar.

Brazilian ufologist A.J. Gevaerd defended Barauna in a detailed rebuttal to skeptics in 2008, pointing out that his photographic experience and the published article on fake UFO photos was well known; he never denied it. Gevaerd also noted that Barauna was not the only witness to the sighting — in the same magazine that published the "fake" saucer photos, there was an article about the Trindade case, noting the many witnesses to the passage of the object over the ship.

Gevaerd argued in favour of Barauna's veracity, stating: "I can tell you that no one has ever caught him in any kind of dishonesty or even in a small lie. On the contrary, he is still remembered by everyone as a serious, reputable and decent person."

In Their Own Words

Kamuela, Hawaii
February 5, 1995

Last night I saw an unusual but explainable bright light in the sky. About 10:45 p.m., I was returning to my home from walking my dog when I noticed a noctilucent cloud (one which is illuminated by sunlight after dark because of its extreme altitude). The cloud was not unusual but was interesting to look at. After a few minutes, a pin point of yellow light in the middle of the cloud became brighter and brighter until it was about half as bright as our street lights which are the same yellow color. I watched the light for 30 sec. to 60 sec. until it dimmed the same as it had brightened. Then I watched the cloud until the sun finally set on it.

I would have dismissed this light as just the head light of an airplane which turned toward me for 30–60 sec. and then away. Even the unusual yellow color could have been from the atmosphere which causes our colored sunsets, setting moon, planets and stars.

However, tonight, I learned from the Honolulu news that yellow/orange lights had been observed in the skies over windward (east) Oahu for the last week. Many lights together were observed by many different people at different times and different locations. All descriptions were of yellow lights. Those who live on windward Oahu are accustomed to seeing the many aircraft (airliners and military) and I believe they would not have reported this unless it was very unusual.

The news report included an official statement by agents of MUFON that this was a hoax employing bag & candle hot air balloons. I can honestly tell you that what I saw was no hot air balloon. It looked more like the head light of a jumbo jet. It would seem to be quite a coincidence that anomalous yellow lights are being seen to the east of Oahu and to the west of Hawaii (200 miles apart) at the same time and are not caused by the same phenomenon. It would also seem unlikely that the Oahu sightings were all airplanes flying directly at the observers simultaneously.

Reported by R.C.
Source: Ufology Research

In 2008, Gevaerd made public an English translation of an interview with Amilar Viera Filho, a witness to the Trindade UFO who was on board the Brazilian Navy vessel and was president of the Icarai Underwater Fishing Club at the time. Filho was not interested in UFOs and was on board the ship to deliver supplies from the mainland. He said that Brazilian Air Force Reserve Captain Jose Viegas saw the object first and called out to Baruana, who began photographing it. By the time Filho saw it, the object had already moved from over the ocean and was over the island. He described seeing "a gray object which turned bright then went away slowly then increased speed until it disappeared on the horizon." Filho insisted: "that object was really in the sky. I can assure that because I saw it and I'm saying that I'm sure!" He noted: "The Brazilian Navy also asked us not to disclose anything."

What makes this case most interesting is that it continues to spark discussion and controversy. More details about the sighting continue to emerge and are becoming accessible to ufologists. Was it a hoax?

Several months after the Trindade incident, in August 1958 in Russia, a silver craft was seen on the side of Tsarina's Mountain near Leningrad. Members of a topographical survey were doing some work there when one of them called the others' attention to a strange object moving noiselessly through the sky. It was a cigar-shaped object, like an airplane fuselage, with a shiny metallic surface but no doors, windows, or stabilizers. It veered unexpectedly and flew out of sight rapidly. There were no rocket ranges in the area, and the scientists could not explain the event.

Although not over Russian soil, a few years earlier, in 1956, famous Soviet pilot Valentin Akkuratov was with a crew on a mission in the far north near Greenland when his plane descended through clouds into clear sky and saw an object flying parallel not far away. It was lens-shaped, off-white, with "pulsating edges," with no wings, windows, or visible exhaust. Since the Soviet crew believed it to be an American craft, they ascended again into the cloudbank. After flying for 40 minutes, they came out of the clouds and were surprised to see the same object, still pacing them. They decided to approach the craft and altered their course to intercept it, but it turned as well and continued to maintain a constant position relative to their aircraft. After 15 minutes of this game, the object increased its forward velocity, flying away and then up higher in the atmosphere.

WAVING AT THE ALIENS

In 1958, Father William Booth Gill was an Anglican priest working as a missionary in Papua New Guinea. He had heard of reports of odd lights in the sky over the large island in Oceania, but was not sure of what to make of them. He and other missionaries in the region had been discussing such reports in their correspondence, but Gill was skeptical. In fact, when one of his friends reported a sighting in October 1958, he believed that what was actually seen was the Soviet satellite Sputnik, which had been launched recently.

On April 9, 1959, Gill was at his mission near the town of Boianai when he saw a light on the side of a mountain some distance away. The light vanished, but then appeared 10 minutes later on the other side of the mountain, which would have been impossible had anyone been carrying a lamp or torch across that difficult terrain. He was even more curious when his assistant Stephen Gill Moi reported to him that a saucer-shaped object had been seen in the air over the mission a few months later on June 21. Gill puzzled over the incidents but remained skeptical about the notion of flying saucers.

That is — until June 26 at 6:45 p.m., when he was standing outside the mission and saw a bright light in the northwest. He noted that this bright object was above the planet Venus in the dusky sky, which he had been watching the past few nights. He called to some of the other missionaries so they could see it as well. As they watched, more villagers joined them until three dozen people were all looking at the sparkling object. It grew larger as it seemed to approach them until it was hovering nearly overhead and was resolved to a disc-shaped object with four legs on its underside. On its sides were several panels or portholes, as they were variously described by witnesses. Gill estimated the size of the craft to be about 10 metres across, and only about 100 metres away in the sky, although without reference points, he admitted this was only an estimate.

On the upper surface of the saucer, four humanoid figures could be seen through the glare of the light emanating from the object. They seemed to be doing some chore, moving around, and occasionally moving out of sight. A "shaft of blue light" seemed to be shining up from the object into the sky, illuminating the figures on the deck. After about 45 minutes, the object was obscured by clouds and was lost to sight. It reappeared in another hour, accompanied by several smaller lights, then vanished into the clouds again after a few more hours. Gill had the wherewithal to have many of the crowd sign a written account of their observations, an indication of his awareness of the scientific and investigative process.

The next evening at 6:00 p.m., the strange craft returned, with its crew again clearly visible on its upper deck. Two smaller objects flanked the larger "mother ship." On its upper deck, two figures could be seen, bending over and moving their arms as if they were adjusting something. After a while, Gill noticed that one of them appeared to have turned and was looking down at him, leaning over the side of the saucer with its hands on a guard rail.

Father Gill decided to wave at the "man," holding his arm over his head, and was surprised when he received a response in kind. A native man watching with him joined the fun and waved at the figure on board; not only him, but a second figure on board waved back as well. Then Gill waved with his companion and all the figures on the craft waved back. "There seemed to be no doubt that our movements were answered," he noted.

UFOs and Aliens in Literature

Although most people have heard of the movie *2001: A Space Odyssey*, few have heard of "The Sentinel," a short story written by Arthur C. Clarke, published in 1951. In the story, a highly advanced race is discovered to have left a beacon on the Moon, and when humans interrupt it, it is realized that the aliens now know we have evolved and ventured into space.

Gill realized that a purposeful communication was possible with the craft's occupants, so as it was getting dark, he sent for a flashlight to be brought to him. When it arrived, he shone it in the direction of the craft, turning it on and off repeatedly as a signal. In response, the entire craft swayed back and forth in a pendulum motion, which Gill interpreted as a good sign. They continued to alternately wave and shine the flashlight, and the figures or craft responded with movement. Then the creatures moved out of sight on the object and the two-way communication ceased by about 6:25 p.m. However, a blue "searchlight beam" shone out of the craft a few times, but Gill and the other observers did not know if it was in response to their actions.

At 6:30 p.m. Gill left his observing and went inside the mission to have dinner. This fact alone suggested to skeptics that this entire story was a hoax, for what reason could there be for anyone to stop watching a flying saucer from another planet hovering over your head? Gill addressed this very question and others during an interview nearly 20 years later. He explained that since he had watched the apparently same object for four hours the night before, and since he believed it was actually just an American hovercraft staffed by military personnel, he didn't think it was all that unusual. He said he did pop his head outside the door at about 7:00 p.m. and noted that the object was still in the sky, but had moved away slightly. When he checked again at 7:45 p.m., the sky was completely overcast and the strange craft was lost to sight.

The UFOs were back the following night, at 6:45 p.m., when as many as eight objects formed a line across the sky over the mission, but they were not near enough this time that any figures could be seen on board. Gill and the villagers watched the lights intermittently until about 11:30 p.m., when he went inside to bed. Just before he did, there was a loud metallic "bang" on the roof of the mission, as if something heavy had been dropped down onto it, but nothing was found the next day when the roof was examined, not even a dent.

The observations of Father Gill, his colleagues, and the townspeople have been debated among ufologists and debunkers for over 50 years. In 1960, the Department of Air, Commonwealth of Australia, issued a statement which noted that although it could not come to a definite conclusion, it nevertheless explained the case as "reflections on a cloud." Furthermore, the Royal Australian Air Force later concluded three of the lights seen were Jupiter, Saturn, and Mars, implying that explained the entire series of observations.

Harvard astronomer Donald Menzel, known for debunking UFO reports, stated that Gill's saucer was likely the planet Venus, since Gill "never mentions it as a point of reference." In fact, as noted earlier, Gill described both Venus and the strange craft in his account, completely negating this explanation. Later, Menzel stated that Gill's observation of creatures on board the craft was likely due to his not wearing glasses, since Gill suffered from astigmatism. But when questioned about this, Gill told an investigator that he always wore his glasses, and that other witnesses who had good eyesight saw the creatures as well. Yet another debunker suggested that Gill simply made up the UFO stories to entertain his colleagues. Again, this ignores testimony from the dozens of other witnesses and the dozens of other UFO sightings reported in the area about that time.

Did You Know?

A close encounter with a UFO in which the UFO interacts with the environment by leaving traces, affects radio reception, and makes animals upset is classified as a *close encounter of the second kind*.

5
THE SIXTIES

FROM ALIEN PANCAKES TO FLYING CONES: A TIMELINE

June 22, 1960

During the summer of this year, something unusual fell from the sky into Clan Lake of the Northwest Territories in Canada. The incident was investigated by the RCMP and RCAF, but is still unresolved. It may have been Canada's first UFO crash.

Around 6:00 p.m., two men from Yellowknife were dropped off by a floatplane on the shore of Clan Lake, about 50 kilometres north of the city. After the aircraft took off, they began preparing their camp, when they heard a rumbling sound as if there was a large airplane somewhere in the distance — something unlike the floatplane. The noise grew louder over the next 20 minutes and the two men searched the sky for any sign of what was causing the noise.

Suddenly, they heard a loud splash, and turned to see "some object with arms or spokes rotating in the water" about 520 metres away on the opposite shore. The object was estimated to be about 1.2 to 1.8 metres wide, and was spinning rapidly, throwing water. After a few minutes, the object "spun down," stopped its movement and settled out of sight. The object did not seem to have been giving off any steam or smoke. After it was stationary, the backwash from its agitation of the water reached the edge of the lake where the two men were standing.

The men took a canoe and paddled over to where the object had been in the water. Grass about half a metre high along the shore appeared to have been burned, and an adjacent area of grass about five by 20 metres was cut and the blades scattered.

The men used paddles and a pole to explore the bottom of the lake near the shore where the object had been. They discovered a channel that had been gouged into the silt beneath the water, roughly corresponding to the patch of reeds and grass that had been cut. The underwater groove was about a third of a metre deeper at one end and a metre deeper than the normal lake bottom.

It was almost a month later, on July 18, 1960, that the witness made it back to civilization and had an opportunity to report his experience to the Royal Canadian Mounted Police. The following day, the RCMP sent a plane to fly to the area. They noted: "it would appear that an object did land on the east side of Clan Lake," but nothing was found during their preliminary investigation. The RCMP found "a space approximately twelve feet wide and forty feet long where the reeds are completely gone and the water in this space [is] slightly deeper."

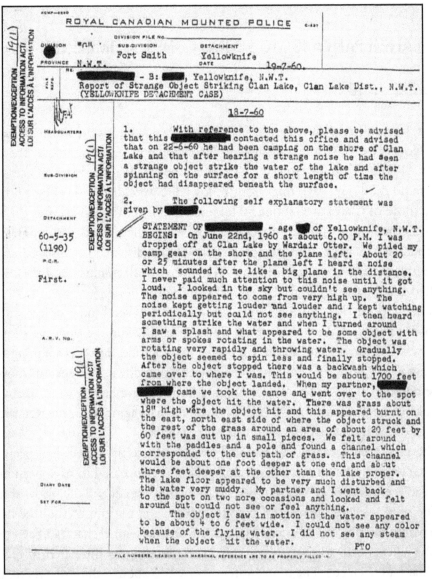

In 1960, something crashed into Clan Lake in the Northwest Territories. The RCMP investigated, but nothing could be found under the water.

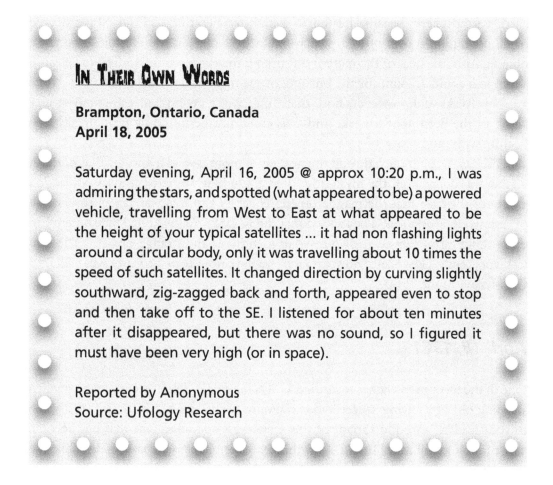

The RCMP thought about canoeing in, but it was considered too difficult a journey, through many long portages. Arrangements were made to fly in a second time with a Geiger counter to check for radiation, and they did so on August 15, 1960. By this time, the lake level had lowered and it was possible to wade through only about a third of a metre of water at the site. They probed the black silt lake bottom with metal rods but could not find anything. No significant radiation was detected. Before leaving the site, it was marked for locating in the winter after freeze-up, thinking that they would return then with a magnetometer.

On August 16, 1960, the RCMP passed the case along to the Royal Canadian Air Force, since they thought the object was "worthy of the attention of someone such as the RCAF." However, on September 23, 1960, the RCAF sent the RCMP a confidential missive, noting that "space tracking agencies in both Canada and the U.S." did not track anything in the area.

The RCAF also offered its explanation for the event. In their opinion, the object that fell into the lake "was a meteorite which, in the process of descent through the earth's atmosphere, became heated to a high temperature ... [and] some degree of disintegration was in process which might have created the illusion of rotating objects. Also, the heat of the meteor on striking the earth would undoubtedly cause steam and could account for the burning of the reeds and grass."

The RCAF did, however, note that "the object penetrated the compact clay layer" of the bottom of the lake and thus could not be found by probing the lake bottom with metal rods.

The case was left open during the next eight months, and it appears that nothing further was done about the mysterious object. On May 16, 1961, the RCMP added a note to their file that the magnetometer check of the area was cancelled because of various circumstances. They added that the RCMP "Yellowknife Detachment can do nothing further on their own towards identifying the strange object." The case was, apparently, closed, and 50 years later, we have no way of knowing what fell into Clan Lake in June 1960.

April 18, 1961

One of the most tired clichés regarding UFOs in popular literature is that of an alien stepping out of its flying saucer and exclaiming to the amazed witnesses, "Take me to your leader!" An odd variant of this scenario is a strange case that has become part of ufology folklore. In effect, in this case, the aliens may have said, "Take me to your kitchen!"

Just before lunch, farmer Joe Simonton heard an odd noise outside his home and ran outside in time to see a silver, egg-shaped object land in his yard. It was about four metres high and nine metres across, and Simonton saw that it was more hovering over the ground than actually resting upon it. He bravely walked over to it as a hatch opened, and inside he could see three "men," with dark complexions and dark hair, "like Italians." They wore uniforms consisting of a kind of turtleneck sweater and close-fitting headgear. Simonton could hear a whining sound, as if from a generator, and observed that the interior of the craft was like black wrought-iron.

One of the men saw Simonton and held up a silvery jug with a handle and motioned to him in a way that Simonton understood that he wanted it filled with water. The unflustered farmer quickly stepped up to do his hospitality, taking the jug and going inside his house to fill it from a tap.

When he returned with the desired supply of water, Simonton saw that one of the men was sitting at a flat counter, apparently cooking something as if on a stovetop. The farmer, being no slouch in the cooking department himself, gestured at the chef and conveyed his curiosity about what was on the grill. In reply, one of the men passed Simonton three "pancakes" — small, flat, cookie-like things with numerous holes.

As Simonton examined the mysterious products, one of the men attached a cord or harness to the inside of the hatch, and pulled it closed from the inside, leaving no visible seam. Within a matter of seconds, the craft had risen about six metres, rotated slightly, then emitted a blast of gas from exhaust tubes on its outside and flew away at high speed.

Credit: Susan Birdwise.

In 1961, Joe Simonton saw an egg-shaped UFO land in his yard. The creatures inside gave him some pancakes that they had been cooking on their stove inside their craft.

Remarkably, there may have been another witness to the event. Investigators noted that around the time of Simonton's encounter, an insurance agent named Savino Borgo was driving along Highway 70, about a kilometre and a half from Simonton's farm. He reported seeing "a saucer rising diagonally into the air and then flying parallel with the highway."

When the local Sheriff investigated, there was of course no physical evidence to prove that such a craft had been there, except for the pancakes. One of these was eventually given to the U.S. Air Force for studying, another went to a civilian UFO group, and Simonton attempted to eat the other. He noted that it tasted like cardboard.

The USAF directed the Food and Drug Laboratory of the U.S. Department of Health, Education and Welfare to test its sample, and later reported: "The cake was composed of hydrogenated fat, starch, buckwheat hulls, soya bean hulls and wheat bran ... [and] the material was an ordinary pancake of terrestrial origin."

Perhaps it was terrestrial, but definitely from a decidedly healthy organic recipe. The aliens were health nuts!

The case received wide publicity, mostly because it was so fantastic. The National Investigations Committee on Aerial Phenomena (NICAP) made public statements about their investigation of the case, but some ufologists noted that "when the press interest died, NICAP dropped the whole thing."

Simonton was more supported by the Aerial Phenomena Research Organization (APRO), whose investigators were more impressed with his veracity. When one debunker suggested Simonton had simply been hypnotized (although the better term would have been entranced), APRO representative Cecile Hess scoffed at the suggestion, saying, "If I ever saw a sincere and honest man, it was Simonton."

Nevertheless, Simonton faced enough ridicule that he was fed up with the accusations about him. He told a UPI reporter some time later: "If it happened again, I don't think I'd tell anybody about it."

October 1963

Passengers and crew on a Chinese airliner flying from Kuangtung to Wuhan all saw three luminous objects that chased the plane for 15 minutes. The pilots were in radio contact with civil aviation authorities during the entire encounter, and when they landed the crew was interrogated and the passengers were told not to speak about what they saw.

A few months later, residents of Shanghai watched as a large cigar-shaped object flew slowly through the sky. Chinese fighter jets were scrambled but were unable to get near the object. It was later reported by the Chinese news agency that it had been an American missile. The military also were involved in chasing a spherical object that had risen from behind a rocky ridge near Dingxian City in Hubei Province in September 1971.

June 1965

Farmer Maurice Masse was concerned when patches of lavender he grew in his fields for the French perfume industry were missing, and he suspected vandals were at work.

At 5:45 a.m. on July 1, 1965, he was sitting on his tractor preparing for the day's work and smoking a cigarette when he heard an odd whistling noise. Military helicopters had landed in his fields before and since he didn't want another one to damage his lavender, he walked towards where the noise was coming from.

But instead of a helicopter, Masse saw there was a strange, egg-shaped craft resting on six legs, about 90 metres away. It was about the size of an automobile and had a small dome on its top. Beside it were two small figures that he at first thought were young boys who might be responsible for the vandalism, so he walked towards them to grab them. However, as soon as he got near, he saw that they were beings more than a metre tall in green, tight-fitting coveralls. They had large bald heads, pointed chins, slanted catlike eyes, and their skin was a ghastly white.

When he was about 15 or 20 metres from the beings, one turned to face him and reached for a small tube that was hanging on a belt at its side. A beam of light shot out the tube, striking Masse. He was suddenly paralyzed, unable to move, although he could still breathe and watch what was going on. The two creatures talked with one another in low sounds and then they went into the craft through a door that slid open for them to pass. Soon, the craft rose and vanished, disappearing as if it went through some kind of doorway in the sky.

UFOs and Aliens in Literature

Another story by Clarke, titled "The Star," raised some interesting questions when it was published in 1958. In this case, the aliens were never actually encountered, but it is realized by a space-faring priest that the Star of Bethlehem was the visible sign of a star which exploded, wiping out an entire race on a planet in orbit around it.

The paralysis wore off after about 15 minutes, and Masse walked over to where the craft had been and saw depressions in the lavender from its legs. He went into town and told a café owner what he had seen, and the news soon made it to the local police. The tale was the talk of the town and many people visited with Masse and went to the site. Ufologists eventually investigated and took soil samples, finding only that the spots where the lavender had been affected were hard and highly calcified. Lavender would not grow there for several years.

Following his experience, Masse was very tired for three days, sleeping for over 12 hours each night. He also told investigators that there was some additional aspect of the incident that he did not want to reveal to anyone. "Nobody will make me tell it," he stated.

June/July 1965

British, Argentine, and Chilean personnel stationed on Deception Island in Antarctica reported seeing odd, coloured lights moving over their base for periods of up to 30 minutes. On July 3, 1965, at 7:20 p.m., nine scientists and technicians at Aquirre Cerda, the Chilean Antarctic base on Deception Island, watched a stationary light moving east to west in the sky, low on the horizon. It was of "solid appearance like a celestial body," flying on a "trajectory with oscillations," eventually disappearing into the clouds. Twenty minutes later, seven personnel saw another object, this time oval shaped, with intensity brighter than a first magnitude star. They watched it for more than an hour as it was stationary sometimes, then moving "above the stratus," all the while flashing different colours. It too was low on the horizon, estimated at about eight to 16 kilometres away. While it was in sight, instruments on board an Argentine Navy ship were affected by some kind of magnetic field.

An official report from the officers insisted that the object was not a hallucination and that the testimonies of the personnel were valid. The commander of the Chilean base stated: "It is rash to say that we all saw a flying saucer, like those in science fiction. But nevertheless it was something real, an object traveling at a staggering speed ..." He concluded: "As far as I am concerned it is a celestial object that I am unable to identify. That it could be an aircraft constructed on this Earth, I do not believe possible."

It would be so easy to dismiss this case as that of refracted observations of a star or planet, despite the scientists' testimony. Yet, one can wonder why scientists trained in their field, especially meteorologists like those at the base who saw these lights, were unable to reduce their observations to sightings of common astronomical objects. Surely someone on board a long-term oceanic mission would have been familiar enough with the night sky from hours of sky-watching that the possibility of the object being a star or planet would have occurred to him or her?

August 14, 1965

A man was driving from Itabira to Belo Horizonte in the state of Minas Gerais, Brazil. At around 8:00 p.m. he saw a glow in the distance beside the road, and puzzled over what it was because there were no houses or buildings there at the time. When he got close enough, he stopped his car and turned off his lights to get a better look. He saw a bright white patch shaped like a trapezoid, and he decided to get out and walk closer to see what it was. When he was only about 30 metres from it, he "felt the presence" of a huge disc-shaped object. It was at least 90 metres in diameter and 15 metres in height, hovering motionless only a metre above the pavement. He could see a dome of some sort on top, but he did not see any windows or other openings or protuberances.

The object was completely black, making no sound, and was visible only because of the bright light streaming out its underside. The man watched in awe for several minutes until the object began moving slowly away from the road down into a depression that led to a field and corral. The witness noted the bright light that it shone on the ground was so intense, "one could have seen an insect creeping there." When the disc was about 450 metres away, the beam of light decreased in diameter and it then began rising until it was at the height of the road again. It rose up more quickly and disappeared into the sky.

The witness noted: "I was under the impression that there were beings aboard it though I cannot explain what gave me this impression." He wrote: "After it was lost from sight, I went on standing there for some time, motionless, before I decided to proceed on my journey."

December 9, 1965

Around 4:45 p.m., something unusual was seen dropping from the sky over Kecksburg, Pennsylvania. There were many eyewitnesses, including pilots who reported a shock wave as a strange, fiery object whizzed past their aircraft. The UFO was moving relatively slowly, unlike a meteor, and took about six minutes to fly from the north to the south over rural Pennsylvania, leaving a smoke or condensation trail hanging in the air. What's most strange is that eyewitnesses insisted that the object changed direction in mid-air, turning east before it finally fell to earth.

Did You Know?

A UFO seen within 150 metres is classified as a *close encounter of the first kind*.

Two young children rushed into their home and told their mother that a star had fallen into the nearby trees and had started a fire. She called the police and fire station thinking her children must have seen a plane crash, since she saw a column of smoke rising from the trees in that area. When she was led back to the site by her children, she found that the army was already there and had sealed off the area. However, the army told the local police and media that nothing had been recovered from the crash site and that the case was closed.

Years later, investigators learned that civilian firemen had seen blue lights where the object had fallen and noted that the tops of trees in the area had been broken as if something had smashed through them on the way down. In addition, some local residents insisted that they had seen a military flatbed transport leaving the crash site with a large, tarpaulin-covered object. One witness even claimed he had seen the army loading a weird, acorn-shaped object onto the flatbed trailer.

A note in Blue Book files reports that military investigators went to the site to retrieve the object that started the brush fire. This, of course, is completely contradictory to the official statement that *nothing* was located at the site.

One explanation for the incident is that an ordinary meteorite fell from the sky. However, if so, why is the meteorite not catalogued and listed with other such rocks by geologists? This seems to be a case where something odd has been covered up by military personnel. A more reasonable explanation is that it was a crashed satellite or rocket booster, likely Russian in origin, hence the secrecy.

January 19, 1966

Probably the best-known historical UFO case in Australia is that of the Tully saucer "nests." A possible precursor to the famed crop circles of England in the 1980s and 1990s, the Tully incident occurred in a remote area in north Queensland. However, the Tully case has marked differences with what was reported in England decades later, including some possible meteorological explanations and the likelihood that hoaxers were not involved.

Around 9:00 a.m. on a clear and warm summer morning near Horseshoe Lagoon, banana farmer George Pedley was driving his tractor along an access road on the property of a neighbour when he heard an odd hissing sound. Thinking that one of his tires had sprung a leak, he stopped and climbed down to look at them. Walking around the tractor, he was surprised to see a grey, football-shaped object, like two saucers glued rim to rim. It was rising from the ground about 25 to 30 metres up the road. It seemed to be about eight metres in diameter and slightly less than three metres in thickness, and it appeared to be spinning.

The UFO was already about 10 metres in the air and was ascending above the trees very quickly. In about 15 seconds, it had reached close to 20 metres in the air and then flew off towards the southwest.

When it had gone, Pedley travelled up the road towards where the object seemed to have been. He found a circular area that had been swept clean of reeds and the water inside was rotating slowly, in approximately the same estimated dimensions as the object. When he returned a few hours later for another look, he found marsh grass swirled in a clockwise direction, with no scorching or evidence of burning. The grass initially appeared green when newly fallen but turned brown quickly.

He went to tell the marsh's owner, Albert Pennisi, who noted that his dog had been in a frenzy and barking in the direction of the marsh that morning. Furthermore, he told Pedley that he had been having odd dreams about a UFO landing on his property. He went with Pedley to visit the area, taking photographs and even wading into the swamp and diving underneath the floating mat of reeds to discover their roots had all been cut away.

That evening, Pedley reported his experience to Tully police, and an officer visited the site the next morning. The nearby Royal Australian Air Force base was contacted, and two days later the military office there asked the Tully police to file a formal UFO report and take samples of grass from the affected area. It was a full week after the incident that the report was filed, and RAAF records confirmed that there were no aircraft in the area at the time of the sighting. Despite this, the police investigator was of the opinion that the swirled patch in the grass had been caused by a small helicopter and that Pedley had mistaken sunlight gleaming on the rotating blades for a disc-shaped craft.

Other explanations were offered, including that of a waterspout that sucked up water in the swamp and uprooted the marsh grass into a circular pattern. It was also suggested that there was nothing really unusual about the "nest" at all, and that a strong downdraft during a severe thunderstorm could have caused the *lodging* of the grass — a common occurrence whereby standing grass or wheat is blown flat by the force of wind. However, it was recognized that these explanations did not account for the object Pedley claimed to have observed.

During the next month, several other nests were discovered, all nearby the original discovery. Cane farmer Tom Warren and a schoolteacher named Hank Penning had found two more nests, only about 25 metres from the Tully one. They were only three metres in diameter — considerably smaller than the original. This time, one mass of reeds was swirled clockwise, while the other was counterclockwise. Three more were found within a week, by yet another cane farmer. Two were three and a half metres in diameter, while the other was the smallest: two and a half metres across. These were speculated to be further visitations, more whirlwinds, or copycat hoaxes.

Queensland and Brisbane Universities and the Royal Australian Air Force all conducted some studies on the affected reeds but could not come to any conclusion as to what had caused the circles in the swamp.

June 19, 1966

A remarkable multiple-witness UFO case in occurred in Vietnam, during the time American soldiers were heavily engaged in the conflict there. The case received very little attention at the time, even though there were hundreds if not thousands of military UFO witnesses, since Nha Trang was a heavily defended coastal base in South Vietnam, with more than 40,000 troops and about 2,000 American personnel. A civilian UFO group, the National Investigations Group on Aerial Phenomena (NICAP), investigated the incident and managed to interview one of the military eyewitnesses.

The Nha Trang base was in a valley, on a south-facing beach along the ocean. On the night of the incident, bulldozers were clearing roads west of the base, small aircraft were being readied for flight on an airstrip to the east, and a Shell Oil tanker was anchored in the bay to the southwest. At 8:00 p.m., many of the troops had gathered in an open area of the base to watch an outdoor movie, the projector run by a diesel-powered generator.

At around 9:45 p.m., a very bright light like a flare suddenly appeared north of the base. Since flares were often deployed, this wasn't particularly surprising, but this light was moving erratically. According to a witness: "It dropped right towards us and stopped dead about 300 to 500 feet up. It made this little valley and the mountains around look like it was the middle of the day."

As the mass of soldiers watched, the object began moving again and rose swiftly out of sight within a few seconds. But while it was over the base, the soldier reported that their "generator stopped and everything was black and at the Air Force Base about ½ mile from here all generators stopped." Even the engines stopped on the aircraft at the airfield nearby. The witness noted: "There wasn't a car, truck, plane or anything that ran for about four minutes." Even the ship anchored offshore experienced the same power blackout. Later, checks of all the generators and engines at the base could not find anything wrong with them.

The soldier further noted that "a whole plane load of big shots from Washington got here this afternoon to investigate." Apparently, news of the incident was broadcast widely on military radio stations, but nothing was ever reported in the stateside media. The case would certainly have created cause for concern, since it temporarily crippled a major military base during a period of operations in an intense conflict.

Top Five Reasons Why UFOs May Not be Alien Spacecraft

5. There may not be any life elsewhere in the universe.
4. If aliens were visiting Earth, scientists would know about it.
3. The USAF says there is no evidence that UFOs are alien spacecraft.
2. The distance between stars is too great to allow interstellar travel.
1. Most UFO reports can be explained as ordinary objects.

April 28, 1967

At 11:30 a.m., coast guards at Brixham, Devon, reported seeing a large cone-shaped object that they believed was hovering at an altitude of 4,500 metres. They watched it through a set of high-powered binoculars mounted on a tripod, and were able to determine that the object seemed to be revolving. It was shaped "like a cone with the sharp end pointing upward," appearing to shine as if it was made of glass or metal. Towards the bottom of the object was a small opening like a door, with a white rim that was reflecting sunlight as well. The bottom itself was crinkled and "seemed to consist of strips of metal hanging down."

The object drifted slowly northwest over the next hour, rising in altitude. As they watched, an aircraft making a vapour trail approached the object from the northeast, flew above it then dived and came around to approach it from below. The trail faded, the aircraft disappeared from view, and the object also disappeared into clouds. They later learned that no Royal Air Force aircraft was in the area at the time. The Ministry of Defense suggested that the object was "something like the reflection of car headlights or some sort of meteorological phenomena."

October 26, 1967

Several months after the event at Brixham, another dramatic incident occurred for which the Ministry of Defense had an absurd explanation. Angus Brooks, a retired British intelligence officer and British Airways employee, was walking his dogs one morning near Ringstead Bay, Dorset. He was pausing to recover his breath because of the Force 8 gale that had been blowing across the field. His attention was caught by an aerial craft that descended quickly into view and slowed to a stop, despite the wind, about 400 metres away and about 60 metres in the air. The oddly structured vehicle had a central chamber of about eight metres in diameter, and four fuselages at its front and rear. These cigar-shaped protuberances shifted their position when the object came to a hover, so that they were evenly spaced around the middle of the craft. Including the four shafts sticking out, the craft measured approximately 50 metres from tip to tip, and seemed to be made of a translucent material. After some time, two of the cigar-shaped appendages shifted again to combine with a third, and the craft ascended into the sky and was lost to sight.

Investigators noted that the object was hovering at a strategic location centred between an atomic energy station, an underwater weapons base, and a USAF communications base. Checks with the various bases did not show any unusual activity at the time. The witness was interviewed a few months later by officers from the British Ministry of Defense, and in their report they concluded that what he had seen was a "vitreous floater" in his eyeball, and also that he had perhaps fallen asleep while resting and imagined the rest. However, as the witness himself noted, it would have been nearly impossible to fall asleep while sitting in such a strong wind.

March 16, 1967

A remarkable incident took place at Malmstrom Air Force Base near Lewiston, Montana, after a UFO was reported directly over one of the E-Flight missile silos. At 8:45 a.m., an alarm sounded and each one of the Minuteman missiles was suddenly indicating a "No Go" status. Military witnesses admitted that while unidentified lights were seen in the area of the base, power interruptions occurred and the launch capability of the silos were completely disabled. If that wasn't of grave concern to the U.S. Air Force, it should have been. There was never a satisfactory official explanation for the events that night. In fact, the only way that the event was replicated was through sending a strong electromagnetic pulse through the shielded missile system from an outside source.

UFOs AND ALIENS ON TV

In the first episode of *The Invaders* (1967–1968), architect David Vincent accidentally learns that aliens have begun invading Earth and tries to warn the world. However, people don't believe him, and the aliens find out about his plan so they try to eradicate him. Vincent is on the run from the aliens but travels across the United States trying to convince people of the danger among them. Vincent eventually enlists some people to help him, but is essentially on his own. The Invaders are not human in appearance but take on human form as disguise. However, the disguise process is not perfect; unless given periodic "boosts" they are in danger of reverting back to their true form. When killed, the aliens glowed red and evaporated, leaving no evidence of their existence. The paranoia displayed in this show certainly influenced writers of the *X-Files*, which carried it to the extreme.

A CASE STUDY: THE FALCON LAKE INCIDENT

On May 20, 1967, Stefan Michalak left the Falcon Lake Motel in Eastern Manitoba very early in the morning and headed north into the bush, intending to indulge in his hobby of amateur prospecting. Around 9:00 a.m., he found a quartz vein near a marshy area, close to a small stream, and began inspecting the rock formation. At 12:15 p.m., Michalak was startled by the sounds of some geese nearby, agitated by something. He looked up and saw two cigar-shaped objects with bumps on their upper surfaces. They were about forty-five degrees in elevation, glowing bright red and descending in his direction. As they approached, these strange objects seemed to become more oval and then disc-shaped.

The farthest one of the pair stopped its advance and hovered in mid-air, while the other drew nearer, dropped down and appeared to land on a large, flat rock about 45 metres away. The one in the air stayed for a short while, then departed, changing colour from red to orange to grey as it flew into the west, where it disappeared behind the clouds.

In 1967, Stefan Michalak encountered a disc-shaped flying saucer in a rugged area of the Canadian Shield.

The craft on the ground started changing colour too, from red to grey, until it finally was the colour of "hot stainless steel" and surrounded by a golden glow. As he watched the craft with fascination, Michalak knelt behind a rock outcropping, trying to remain hidden from sight. For the next half-hour, he stayed there, making a sketch of the object and noting waves of warm air radiating from the craft, the smell of sulphur, the whirring of a fast electric motor, and a hissing as if air were being expelled or taken in by the craft. Because he had been chipping away at the rock before the arrival of the craft, he was still wearing his welding goggles to protect his eyes from rock chips. This was fortunate, because brilliant purple light flooded out of slit-like openings in the upper part of the craft, and he would have been blinded otherwise.

Suddenly, a door opened in the side of the craft and he could see smaller lights shining out of the opening. Michalak warily approached to within 20 metres of the craft and was able to hear two human-like voices, one with a higher pitch than the other.

Convinced the craft was an American secret test vehicle, he brazenly walked up to it and called out, "Okay, Yankee boys, having trouble? Come on out and we'll see what we can do about it."

The voices stopped abruptly, but he, feeling brave enough now, walked closer to the craft, ending up directly in front of the open doorway. Poking his head through the opening, he saw a maze of lights on some sort of panel, and a group of lights flashing in a random sequence.

He stepped back from the craft, and noted the wall of the craft was about half a metre thick. Without warning, three panels slid over the opening in front of him, sealing it completely. He took this opportunity to examine the outside of the craft, and reached to touch it with his gloved hand. There were no signs of welding or joints; the surface was highly polished and looked like coloured glass.

Suddenly, the craft rotated and Michalak was now facing the grid of an exhaust vent of some kind. A blast of hot air hit him in the chest, setting his shirt and undershirt on fire. In a lot of pain, he tore them off and threw them to the ground. He looked up to see the craft rise and fly off, feeling a whoosh of air as it ascended.

Michalak noticed that some moss and leaves had been set on fire by the blast of hot gas, and so he stamped out the smouldering debris. When he went over to where the object had been, he immediately felt nauseated and his forehead throbbed from a headache. Piled up in a circle about three metres in diameter was a collection of pine needles, dirt, and leaves.

As he looked around, his headache became worse, and he decided to head back to the motel. By the time Michalak made it back to his motel, he was exhausted. In his own words:

I did not go inside the motel for fear of contaminating people around me ... I felt detached from the rest of the world ... The pain was unbearable ... the odour seemed to come from within me, and I could not escape it ... I was afraid that I had ruined my health and visualized the resulting hell should I have become disabled ... my mind centred on the possible consequences ... there had to be some way of getting medical attention ... I thought of the press. Things that happened to me were definitely news, if nothing else ... I did not want to alarm my wife, or cause a panic in the family. I phoned her as a last resort, telling her that I had been in an accident ...

Michalak felt that it was his duty to report the incident. At 4:00 p.m., he entered the motel coffee shop to inquire whether or not a doctor was available, as he was now in considerable pain. He decided to return to Winnipeg and took the next bus home. His son met him at the terminal and took him the Misericordia Hospital.

Investigations

Michalak called the *Winnipeg Tribune* late Saturday afternoon of the holiday long weekend, after returning home from the hospital. The next evening, May 21, reporter Heather Chisvin was the first one to talk to him about the experience, and her story must be considered as the first account uninfluenced by later documentation.

The first investigator on the scene, however, was Barrie Thompson, who had read the account in the newspaper and immediately contacted Michalak. Thompson's investigation, on behalf of APRO, began the series of civilian UFO investigations. Michalak noted that "after hearing my story, [Thompson] stated his belief that the craft was not an earthly creation."

UFO investigators took Michalak to get a body radiation count at the Whiteshell Nuclear Research Establishment (WNRE) and encouraged him to take other tests.

The RCAF investigations were under the direction of Squadron Leader P. Bissky, who was of the opinion that the case was a hoax. However, many relevant documents are contained in Department of National Defence files on the case and have been obtained by several ufologists. A rather carefully worded statement is in the National Research Council's Non-Meteoric Sightings File, DND 222, noting: "Neither the DND, nor the RCMP investigation teams were able to provide evidence which could dispute Mr. Michalak's story."

Further, RCMP analysis by its forensic lab was "unable to reach any conclusion as to what may have caused the burn damage" to Michalak's clothing.

The Site Near Falcon Lake

Investigators from the USAF and the University of Colorado Condon Committee pointed out that Michalak couldn't find the site while in the presence of officials. Michalak visited the site twice after recovering from his encounter before finding the site with a friend. Some writers point to this fact as a reason for labelling the case a hoax. However, locating the site presented several difficulties.

First, when the incident occurred, the trees and bushes were bare and without leaves. When brought back to the area, Michalak said he was disoriented because the foliage was lush and full, unlike when he was last there. This is a logical reason for experiencing difficulty in finding the site.

In addition, Michalak said that for the first expedition, he was transported to the area by helicopter and was told to find the site from the anonymous location where they landed. He found that very difficult. The second expedition began from where the RCMP thought Michalak came out of the bush after his encounter. It too was unsuccessful, due to the increased vegetation and Michalak's unsettled state of mind and body. Disorientation in the wilderness can definitely be a problem in the locating of specific sites.

Credit: Ufology Research.

The flat rock outcropping on which the UFO seen by Michalak landed.

However, the site can be located today using proper trailblazing. The usual method of finding the site is to head north from the Trans-Canada Highway and follow a creek around large rock outcroppings until the bare rock-face is seen.

The actual site is within direct view of a forest ranger's tower. However, the ranger on duty at the time of the incident said he did not observe the landing or flight of the UFOs, nor did he notice the smoke that resulted from the ignition of grass by the landed UFO.

Another problem the Condon Committee had was the direction in which the object departed. This was westward, which would have had the object fly away from most corroborating observers, but within sight of anyone playing on the local golf course. No golfers reported seeing the UFO. However, as Michalak stated, the object rose vertically before departing — this isn't impossible.

Radiation

Much was made of the finding of radioactive debris at the site. The story got around that Michalak was suffering from radiation poisoning.

The radiation detected was from soil samples brought back to Winnipeg by Michalak and an associate, after they had finally located the site on their own. An official from the Manitoba Department of Health and Welfare said the soil analysis "showed radiation." His report noted:

> One small area ... contaminated ... across the crown at the rock. There was a smear of contamination about 0.5 x 8.0 inches on one side of the crack. There was also some lichen and ground vegetation contaminated just beyond the smear. The whole contaminated area was no larger than 100 square inches.

The origin of this radiation is a mystery. Whatever its cause, it was enough for the federal Radiation Protection Division to consider "restricting entry to the forest area." However, after assessing the readings, it was decided that this was not necessary. Beyond the areas located by Hunt, there was no radiation above the normal background. A more detailed soil analysis showed a "significant" level of radium 226, for which there was no explanation. It was suggested that the radium had come from someone scraping a luminous watch dial and scattering the flakes around the site.

Analyses performed by the federal government's Whiteshell Nuclear Research Establishment showed that the radioactivity in the samples was that of "natural uranium ore." This was supported by a re-analysis carried out in June 1979 to check the soil samples taken 12 years earlier. The radiation levels were not of concern, and all the energies detected could be adequately explained by the decay of natural uranium.

This, of course, raises the question of why the Department of Health and Welfare would consider closing off the area from such radioactivity at all. The early test results from 1967 have not been located. These would be helpful, since it is possible that at that time there may have been different peaks detected from elements with short half-lives. It will be noted, though, that the Whiteshell results, done in 1968, showed nothing other than the 1979 run, so this may suggest that the early analysis yielded the same results.

Metal

The mysterious metal samples found at the site are curious. A year after his encounter, Michalak returned to the landing site with an associate. With a geiger counter, they found two "W-shaped" silver bars, 12 centimetres in length, and several other smaller chunks of the same material. All this was found five centimetres under some lichen in a crack in the rock, over which the UFO was said to hover.

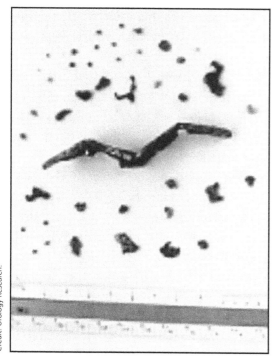

A metal bar and other bits of silver were found in the rock over which Michalak's UFO had landed.

Analysis showed that the silver was of high purity, but with small amounts of copper and cadmium. The University of Colorado noted that the composition was "similar to that found in commercially available sterling silver or sheet silver." This contradicted claims by UFO investigators that the silver concentration was "much higher than would normally be found in native silver or commercially produced silver such as sterling or coinage."

The metal showed signs of heating and bending, as if it was molded into its present shape. Support for the heating theory also comes from the fine quartz crystals that were found to be imbedded in the outer layer of the silver. The sand was similar to typical foundry sand, covering all of one bar and half of the other. But the strangest thing about the silver bars was their radioactivity. They were covered with small particles of radioactive pitchblende and held to the silver by a sticky substance that could be removed by washing the metal with alcohol and using a soft camel-hair brush. The problem is that the Department of Health and Welfare went to the site on more than one occasion, and checked the site thoroughly. Why was the silver never discovered by them?

Physiological Effects

Michalak was physically injured during his UFO encounter. When the object took off, Michalak was burned by a blast of heat or heated gas that came from the grill-like opening in front of him. Following this, he experienced cold sweats, vomiting, a headache, and strange red marks covering his abdomen and chest.

When he was examined at the Misericordia Hospital, he did not tell the examining physician what had happened, but instead that he had been burned by "exhaust coming out of an aeroplane." A few days later, Michalak's family physician examined him and decided the first-degree burns on his abdomen were not very serious. He prescribed 292s for the pain and seasickness tablets for the nausea.

Michalak then went to a radiologist who found no evidence of radiation exposure. A whole-body count taken a week later at the Whiteshell Nuclear Research Establishment also showed no radiation above normal background levels. The burns on Michalak's abdomen were caused by heat, not radiation as some people claimed.

Over the next few days, Michalak reported he lost about 10 kilograms from his normal weight of 82 kilograms. Since he couldn't hold food down, his weight loss in one week could very well have been considerable, as he claimed. However, his physician could not verify the weight loss, since he had not seen him for over a year. Also reported was a drop in Michalak's blood lymphocyte count, although it returned to normal after a month.

Radiation was also blamed for the "awful stench" that some people said seemed to "come from within" Michalak's body. It was suggested that a quick dose of gamma rays may have deteriorated the food he had just eaten for lunch, giving him a vile odour and causing him to vomit green bile. Individuals consulted on this, however, say that such a strong burst of gammas would have deteriorated *Michalak*, not just his digested food.

Another physiological effect was a rash that appeared on Michalak's upper body. The University of Colorado reported that the rash was "the result of insect bites and was not connected with the alleged UFO experience." An RCAF investigator reported that he had been bitten by black flies when he was with Michalak searching for the site.

A hematologist's report showed that Michalak's blood had "no abnormal physical findings," in contradiction to several published accounts which claimed that there were "impurities" in Michalak's blood.

The swelling of his body, however, strongly suggests an allergic reaction of some sort. After an apparent reoccurrence of his swelling while at work on September 21,

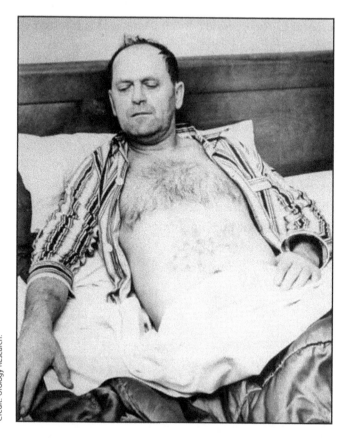

Credit: Ufology Research.

Stefan Michalak with the odd pattern of burns on his stomach.

1967, Michalak reported that doctors diagnosed his affliction as "the result of some allergy." The events leading up to this diagnosis were a burning sensation around his neck and chest. Then, there was a burning in his throat, his body turned violet, his hands swelled like a balloon, his vision failed, and he lapsed into unconsciousness.

Later, he described how sometimes his wrists swelled so much that they filled his shirt cuffs. What sort of allergy could Michalak have had?

The Mayo Clinic

In August, 1968, Michalak went to the famed Mayo Clinic in Rochester, Minnesota. The purpose of his visit was to undergo tests to determine exactly what was ailing him, as the doctors in Winnipeg appeared to be unhelpful. It is worthy of note that Michalak paid for the Mayo tests entirely on his own, as Canadian Medicare would not cover such a trip. He went and stayed at a hotel near the hospital, walking across the street each day and attending as an outpatient. He reported that he was given a thorough physical and psychological examination by various doctors, and then sent home.

Michalak had been found to be in good health but with neurodermatitis and fainting spells due to sudden cerebral blood pressure losses. This was suggested as having to do with hyperventilation or impaired cardiac output. This is interesting, as Michalak did indeed have heart problems later in his life.

The psychiatric section of the report showed no evidence of delusions, hallucinations, or other emotional disorders. Additionally, psychiatrists did not consider Michalak to be someone who would make up stories for notoriety or personal gain. It seems that there was nothing wrong with him. He had no ailment directly related to an encounter with a UFO.

It was claimed that Michalak had been to a clinical hypnotist and that he had been hypnotically regressed. While both statements are true, the clinical hypnotist had in fact only interviewed Michalak and not put him under. A tape of a hypnosis session with Michalak is in existence, but the session was conducted, apparently, by someone who was a reporter for the *Winnipeg Free Press* at the time.

Government Involvement

The Canadian Government seemed to refuse access to information on the Michalak case. On June 29, 1967, it was reported that MP Edward Schreyer asked about UFO investigations during a question period in the House of Commons.

The Speaker of the House "cut off the subject without government reply." Then, in response to requests by several cabinet members to obtain information on the incident, on November 6, 1967, Defence Minister Leo Cadieux stated that "it is not the intention of the Department of National Defence to make public the report of the alleged sighting."

On November 11, 1967, Schreyer formally placed a written question on the Commons order paper seeking information on UFOs.

This closed-mouth attitude of the government was not ignored by the press, which prompted several comments about it. About the case, one editor noted: "The attempt to keep it concealed can have only one effect — it will give the UFO legend another boost."

On October 14, 1968, House Leader Donald MacDonald refused MP Barry Mather access to reports on the Michalak case. However, on February 6, 1969, Mather was given permission by a member of the Privy Council to examine their file on UFOs "from which a few pages have simply been removed." It was reported that outright release of the file "would not be in the public interest, and might create a dangerous precedent that would not contribute to the good administration of the country's business."

Theories and Explanations

Would Michalak have gone to so much trouble to perpetrate a hoax? There is no question that he became seriously ill and had lasting effects from his experience. If we assume that Michalak burned himself while concocting his hoax, would he have then repeatedly pursued medical assistance and gone to the Mayo Clinic to make it "look good?"

One physics professor at a major post-secondary institution believed that Michalak was experimenting with toy rockets, which exploded due to mishandling. He also suggested that he was amateurishly trying to hit two chunks of uranium together to make a homemade bomb! The grid-like pattern of burns on his body was caused by the grill he was using as a support. This totally unfounded theory ignored most of the known facts of the case, yet was seriously proposed by a leading scientist.

An RCAF spokesman was convinced that Michalak was drunk and had fallen on a hot barbeque grill. One immediate objection to this is that such an act would give exactly the *reverse* impression of the burns actually found on Michalak's body.

Others suggested the case was a hoax because Michalak could not find the site when with the Condon investigators. Roy Craig, the Condon Committee's investigator, concluded that "if [Michalak's] reported experience were physically real, it would show the existence of alien flying vehicles in our environment." However, he noted "inconsistencies and incongruities," and said that even with some of the other evidence associated with the case, he would have to stick to his "initial conclusion," namely that "this case does not offer probative information regarding inconventional [sic] craft." Despite this apparently negative conclusion, the index of the Condon Report lists the case as an unexplained sighting.

Craig also found reason to question that the metal samples found by Michalak would have been missed by early investigators at the site. Stewart Hunt of the Department of Health and Welfare described his examination of the area as "a thorough survey," using three different radiation counters. It is definitely odd that the metal chunks were not found until a visit to the site a year later. Thompson remarked that the samples were deeply buried inside the crack in the rock, and that some effort was expended in getting them out. He also remarked that most of the radiation detected was inside the fissure. A close examination of soil samples showed that small silver particles were present in the mixture, suggesting that someone did not simply plant the silver bars. However, this is not conclusive as native silver particles occur naturally in the area in small amounts and their presence in the soil samples does not eliminate the possibility of planting.

There is no doubt that the metal bars are very suspicious. They even had an obvious seam, which suggested fabrication, as if someone moulded the silver in a definite shape. Did Michalak produce these himself? Or did someone *else* produce them and plant them at the site to make it look better? Even without the metal samples the case was a significant one, needing no support. In fact, the samples tend only to confuse the case. An amateur UFO buff would probably not have realized this, and thought only that the samples would enhance the case. Since the case attracted many such individuals, it would be difficult to determine whom this might have been.

Another theory involves the cover-up scenario, and has the government fabricating the samples themselves. However, this would be impossible to prove. If true, this would raise the question of why the government would deliberately enhance the case and then create an aura of secrecy, lending themselves to suspicion. Other hoax theories can be postulated, but all need the necessary proof, including a motive for their devices.

The fact that the site was eventually found by Michalak and a family friend suggests to skeptics that the site only existed after he had created it himself as part of a hoax. But would the RCMP and RCAF not have checked Michalak's movements previous to his finding the site, and tried to pin a public mischief charge on him if they were convinced he was having them on? The numerous searches must have cost a great deal of money at the time.

Furthermore, what could a hoaxer have been doing in the wilderness that would have resulted in a peculiar pattern of chemical and heat burns? Why go to the media with a story that couldn't have been supported? Why not just shut up about the whole thing?

So many aspects of the hoax theory don't add up. It raises more questions than it answers. In some ways, it's easier to believe that Michalak was burned by a flying saucer.

A host of explanations have been offered by writers on the subject. Journalist Yurko Bondarchuk suggested that Michalak was burned by "an intelligently guided craft of unconventional structure and of unknown origin." He also found evidence of government intervention in the case and noted that the publication of Michalak's book, which to some suggests a hoaxer's methods, was financially not a successful venture, and the experience proved to be costly to Michalak.

Palmiro Campagna is a historian about Canadian government and military projects. He is of the opinion that Michalak was burned by a secret American test vehicle, essentially a version of the AVRO "flying saucer" that had been in development and reportedly cancelled in the early 1960s.

In Their Own Words

Cape Hatteras, North Carolina
Summer 1986

I was standing lookout aboard the USS Edenton ATS 1 (currently decommissioned). The lookout watch, stood outside on top the bridge of the ship, and was responsible for reporting all contacts seen both in the water and sky. It was around eleven p.m. one clear night at sea, located about fifty miles off the coast of Cape Hatteras, NC.

During one of my scans of the night sky, out of know where, four red circular lights appeared. The lights where hundreds of yards apart from each other and formed a square. At first, I thought it was four separate air craft, such as, military helicopters because the lights were stationary; however, due to the distance from the ship, the lights where too large to be aircraft running lights.

There were also no other normal running lights like green and white, which make-up the normal outline of an aircraft seen at night. The lights where located about twenty degrees above the horizon and about a mile away from the ship. Again, these four red lights were each about the size of a small plane, which were very bright and visible in the night sky. The night sky was also clear, moon lit, and a moderate amount of stars were visible, which also aided in calculating the distance and size of these lights.

When I first saw these lights they were all stationary in the sky and appeared out of know where. Once I noticed that these were not normal lights, grouped in a square and not moving, I called down to the bridge over a salt and pepper line informing the conning officer of a possible UFO sighting. This brought laughter across the wire at first, but I relayed the contact again in a stern but excited voice, which succeeded in getting the bridge officers attention. After relaying the contact information a second time, the four lights, in a flash, darted towards the horizon amazingly fast. The lower two lights in the square went first, with the top two lights following directly behind them in a curved swooshing motion and there was no sound.

Then all four shot straight up into outer-space and out of sight, all within a split second. At this point, I felt very excited and shocked, and was personally praying someone on the bridge had seen what I just saw. Having been an avid watcher of the night sky, seen shooting stars and a believer in that life has to exist somewhere out there, I become even more excited because I knew, I just saw my first unidentified flying object(s).

To my amazement, when I returned to the bridge after my watch, I was very pleased to learn that the conning officer and everyone else on the bridge had seen this sighting and logged it into the ship's log as a UFO sighting.

A half hour later, the radiation detection system (gamma roentgen meter) on the bridge started making a loud clicking sound. At first, no one seemed to know what was making this sound then a very loud bell went off notifying us as to what was going on, we were being radiated.

When the instrument stopped clicking, it indicated we had taken a hit of 385 roentgens in the period of about one minute. At this point, the captain of the ship was awoken and called to the bridge, as well as the chief in charge of the radiation metering equipment onboard ship.

The captain was not impressed with an entry of a UFO sighting being placed in the ship's log, and at first, took the roentgen meter as being defective. However, the chief informed the captain that the meter had been serviced and calibrated the day before and that other like meters throughout the ship had just gone off indicating the same amount of roentgens received as the bridge.

The captain stated not to log the instance concerning the radiation exposure and left the bridge. During the rest of my watch duty that night, no officer or enlisted person spoke of what happened, and also acted liked nothing happened. This experience, however, was etched into my memory as if it happened yesterday and I have told this story to only a few people, people who I thought would believe me. This is also the first time I have documented the events of this night.

In conclusion, as an indication of the strength of gamma radiation, I and others received that night; all the personnel during the Project Trinity experiments conducted in 1945 at ground zero, only received between 1 and 6 total roentgens of gamma radiation. This leads me to believe, we traveled through the wake of radiation produced by the UFOs seen thirty minutes earlier.

Reported by Anonymous
Source: UFOCasebook.com

Conclusions

There is no question that something very unusual occurred on May 20, 1967, north of Falcon Lake. There is no question that Stefan Michalak came back from his prospecting trip badly burned and seriously ill, claiming that he had encountered a strange craft. But is the account true?

Can this case be effectively proved beyond a shadow of a doubt at all? The evidence includes the following:

- An eyewitness account of a vehicle behaving in ways not attributable to conventional craft.

- Physiological damage to the witness, the mechanism of which is not immediately obvious.

- A visible landing site, consisting of a ring of loose soil on a bare patch of rock, plus some unusual radioactive materials including relatively pure metal bars.

Does this prove that an alien craft landed near Falcon Lake? No. If we assume that Michalak's story is truthful (and we have no reason immediately obvious to suppose otherwise), then we have a solid report of a landed UFO, complete with physical and physiological effects. What could it have been?

Even with a healthy dose of skepticism, the Falcon Lake case is intriguing. If it is a hoax, it's got enough complications to make it one of the best on record. There is, of course, no proof that the object Michalak encountered was a flying saucer. It could have been a military test craft of some sort, which might explain the official interest in the case and why investigations seemed incomplete.

All we have is a record of actual injuries to a man who claimed he was burned by a close encounter with a strange craft in a sparsely populated part of the Canadian Shield. It's a single-witness case, yet it does come with some physical evidence. It may be inconclusive evidence, but it's there nevertheless.

Michalak's family supported him completely. Wouldn't they have grown tired of the whole charade after all these years and called him on it? They gained nothing and suffered greatly. With all the attention and the number of people involved in the case over the years, wouldn't an accomplice have finked on them at one point?

ALIEN FIREWORKS

A remarkable UFO case took place in the Soviet Union on August 13, 1967, near Yalta on the Black Sea. A fighter pilot was on a training flight at around 11:00 p.m., flying at 9,100 metres, when he looked up from his instrument panel to see an oval light to his left side, very close to his aircraft. He radioed his commander about the object and was told that there were no other planes in the area at the time. He banked and as he did so, the object's light dimmed considerably. Suddenly, a bright beam of light appeared in the sky ahead of him, and he tried to avoid it but could not change course in time and the beam impacted his plane's left wing. He was shocked to see the beam shatter into a collection of sparks like a fireworks display. When it did so, the plane shook and rattled, and his instrument panel malfunctioned. Soon, the light and its solid beam vanished. When the pilot returned to his air base, he noted that the surface of the plane's wing shone mysteriously, even several days later.

A SHAGGY UFO STORY?

The Shag Harbour UFO crash on October 4, 1967, is sometimes called "Canada's Roswell." Eyewitnesses, including pilots of a DC-8 airliner and several Royal Canadian Mounted Police Officers, observed a glowing object fall from the sky into the Atlantic Ocean off the coast of Nova Scotia. Witnesses on a ship off the coast had been seeing objects on radar and in the sky, and watched as a red light flew from its position on the horizon to directly over their vessel and headed out to sea. Rescue vessels found a bed of luminous green foam on the surface where it went down. It was also never satisfactorily explained.

Ufologists Don Ledger and Chris Styles uncovered a series of official government documents that show an investigation had taken place, and that an "underwater search" may have been conducted by American or Canadian navy teams. Rumours had been circulating in the area that military divers had been in the region for some time and that something was taken out of the water.

Was this a crashed UFO or a secret underwater Navy exercise to recover a spy satellite instrument-package that had fallen off course? Perhaps the Navy was in the sea off the Canadian coast laying sonar nets for submarine defence. Or, perhaps, something else entirely. Whatever fell from the sky, it was documented by the Royal Canadian Mounted Police and also the military.

UFOs and Aliens on TV

The comedy show *My Favorite Martian* ran from 1963 to 1966. It stared Ray Walston as Uncle Martin and Bill Bixby as Tim O'Hara. Tim is a reporter who sees a flying saucer crash near Los Angeles. He finds a Martian who is an anthropologist studying Earth, and who went off course during a foray into our atmosphere. Tim takes the Martian home and explains to his neighbours that he is his Uncle Martin. The alien stays on earth to repair his ship but ends up staying longer. He has two antennae that poke up from his head when he wants to use his powers such as levitation and super-speed. A *My Favorite Martian* movie was released in 1999 by Disney, also starring Walston.

It began in the early evening of October 4, 1967, when pilots of an Air Canada DC-8 over Quebec saw a large, bright, rectangular object, estimated to be around 3,700 metres in altitude. The object was trailing smaller flickering lights that were flying in parallel to it. They saw an explosion around the UFO and the smaller lights flickered erratically, then the entire group was lost to sight.

Half an hour later, people on the ground saw strange lights in the sky. Two people near Shearwater, Nova Scotia, saw lights moving from the northeast to the southwest. Around 9:00 p.m., the captain and crew of a fishing boat near Sambro, Nova Scotia, saw several red lights over the ocean and also detected an object on the ship's radar. They notified the RCMP, which asked the Captain to file a report upon returning to port.

Witnesses in Nova Scotia reported more UFO sightings at about 10:00 p.m. UFO investigator Chris Styles himself saw a disc-shaped object, glowing orange, drifting over Halifax harbour. He thought it was 15 metres in diameter, orange coloured, and hovering silently and slowly over the ocean.

Other witnesses reported seeing an orange ball in the southeast. Around 10:30 p.m., a photograph was taken of three lights over Lunenburg Village. And at about 11:00 p.m., southwest of Waymouth, a policeman and two game wardens observed a fireball. Less than half an hour later, five people saw an object falling into Shag Harbour. They could see an object of some kind floating in the water, about 60 metres from the shore. They called the RCMP, who sent officers to the area. The RCMP then contacted the air force, who assumed the object was a downed aircraft and notified the National Rescue Coordination Centre.

The officers on the scene saw a yellow light on the water and something that appeared to be a ring of foam around it. They approached some fishermen nearby and enlisted them to transport them to the site. Unfortunately, by the time they arrived at the spot, whatever had been on the surface had sunk beneath the waves. However, the unusual foam was still visible; it was about 10 centimetres thick and was now a trail 25 metres wide and at least 600 metres long. Bubbles kept coming to the surface and there was an odd odour hanging in the air.

Other boats joined the "rescue" mission, including the local Coast Guard. The group stayed for several hours, but by 4:00 a.m., it was decided that nothing was going to come to the surface and they gave up. The next morning, a navy team of four scuba divers was sent down to search for the object, but came up empty-handed.

According to an air force memo dated October 6, 1967, only two days after the event: "The Rescue Coordination Centre conducted preliminary investigation and discounted the possibilities that the sighting was produced by an aircraft, flares, floats, or any other known objects."

Although nothing had been found officially, there were rumours in the community that something had been recovered under cover of darkness and had been sent to a nearby naval base. One person even said he had seen divers bringing some metallic material up out of the water.

As if the story of a UFO crashing into the ocean wasn't enough, investigators learned of a second incident that occurred not in Shag Harbour but in Shelburne Harbour, only about 32 kilometres to the northeast. According to this version, both Canadian and American navy ships combed the area for at least a week. Investigators received information that NORAD had tracked an object around the globe and noted its fall into Shag Harbour, where navy vessels followed its underwater journey to Shelburne and a barge was brought in to take it away.

The official standpoint is that nothing was recovered from the ocean following the crash into Shag Harbour. The Condon Committee reviewed the evidence in the case in its final report and concluded: "No further investigation by the project was considered justifiable, particularly in view of the immediate and thorough search that had been carried out by the RCMP and the Maritime Command."

This, despite the fact that it also noted a naval watch officer with Naval Maritime Command "read a report from the RCMP indicating that at the time in question a 60 ft. object had been seen to explode upon impact with the water."

And yet for some reason, the Committee didn't feel a need to investigate or comment on the official report of an object exploding on the water, the many UFO sightings, or the glowing ring of foam observed by many people that night.

UFOs and Aliens in Literature

In *Dune* (1963), humans 20,000 years in the future encountered sandworms on the desert planet Arrakis.

In general, the case is dismissed as being due either to a satellite re-entry or a meteor. However, even if one of these explanations was correct, it is unusual that no extensive searches were conducted, especially in the former situation. A downed satellite would certainly have demanded a major recovery operation, and if it was a secret spy satellite of another country, it would of course have been an excellent reason for a clampdown on public access to information.

Today, there is a Shag Harbour Museum and yearly festival, complete with guest lectures by prominent UFO experts and tours are of the area.

DR. X

A French UFO case that involved a "beam of light" occurred on November 1, 1968, in the southern part of the country. The exact location is unknown because the identity of the witness has been kept secret, although we know that he was a physician who served in the Algerian war many years ago. In fact, relevant to this story, while serving in the war he had the misfortune of stepping on a land mine and had received serious wounds, becoming permanently disabled.

Three days before the UFO encounter, he had been chopping wood when his axe slipped and he cut his leg, severing a vein. Bedridden as a result of the accident, he was awakened early on the morning of November 1 by the crying of his infant son.

Top Five Reasons Why UFOs May be Alien Spacecraft

5. Reports of UFOs going back into ancient history show that aliens have been monitoring us for many years.
4. Many UFO sightings cannot be explained.
3. Government documents show that some high-ranking military officers consider UFOs as alien craft.
2. Intelligent extraterrestrial life likely exists in the universe.
1. The reported speed and maneuverability of UFOs is beyond any craft made on Earth.

Dr. X, as he has become known in ufology, struggled out of bed and went to the nursery to see what the baby was babbling about. When he entered the room, he saw the child pointing to the window, where he could see flashes of light coming through the shutters. Assuming the light to be from lightning, and hearing a sound like rushing wind outside and a rattling noise, he thought that a storm was brewing. He went into the kitchen to get a bottle of water for the baby and then walked into the living room, then upstairs past another window. He poked his head out but could not see what was causing the flashes of light, and it did not seem to be lightning. He went back downstairs and opened a set of patio doors leading outside that faced the countryside.

Dr. X was surprised to see two cigar-shaped objects hovering over a hill, with columns of bright white light radiating down to the ground. Each object had an antenna on the top and another sticking out the side. They were white on their upper surfaces and red on the lower. He saw that the flashes of light were coming from the top antenna of one of the objects and shooting to the other.

The strange objects slowly moved in the witness' direction, and when they were relatively close to the house they seemed to merge and form a single object! This lone craft moved closer and its beam fell on the house and doorway where Dr. X was standing. There was a loud bang and the object disappeared, leaving behind a white "thread" which flew upwards and vanished into the night sky.

Dr. X was astounded by what he had experienced and, being a scientific man, sat down in the kitchen to write an account of what had occurred. He went to wake his wife and told her the story, who was surprised but then pointed out to him that his leg seemed to be healed, because he was no longer limping. Sure enough, the swelling was gone and he could walk normally.

A week later, an odd triangular rash appeared on his body, centred on his navel, about six inches on a side. A similar mark appeared on the baby's body a few weeks later. The triangular rashes continued to appear and fade on a regular basis. Perhaps more remarkable is that Dr. X's war injuries seemed to have healed as well, and he was checked by other physicians who documented the recovery.

Dr. X and his family were interviewed at length by French ufologists Aimé Michel and Jacques Vallee. He has granted a few interviews to journalists but has insisted on anonymity, and has not sought any monetary gain from his story.

ASTRONAUTS AND UFOS

If some UFOs are alien spacecraft, it would make sense that NASA would be aware of their existence. And, if anyone has first-hand knowledge of what may be in space, it must be astronauts and cosmonauts. Have they seen UFOs while on their missions?

February 20, 1962

Mercury astronaut John Glenn reported seeing thousands of "little specks" that were "floating around outside the capsule." He thought that these "fireflies" were flying past his spacecraft as it flew over the Pacific. When he went into direct sunlight, these tiny objects vanished. It was very likely that they were ice crystals that had come off the side of his spacecraft, Friendship 7. Interestingly, on an episode of the TV series *Frasier*, John Glenn made a guest appearance, playing himself, and "admitted" that astronauts were not alone in space. Some conspiracy buffs have taken this as a confession that NASA is covering up the truth about UFOs, but … this was a comedy TV series, after all.

Credit: NASA.

On February 20, 1962, astronaut John Glenn was aboard his spacecraft Friendship 7 when he saw numerous "fireflies" outside his window.

May 24, 1962

Astronaut Scott Carpenter was piloting a Mercury capsule and also saw tiny "fireflies" around the spacecraft. He asked Mission Control to let John Glenn know that he had not been dreaming when he reported seeing them! Carpenter was able to photograph the miniscule lights. Later, he also took a photo of a larger object, but this was subsequently said to be a tracking balloon.

May 16, 1963

It was reported that Gordon Cooper had seen a green object with a red tail while he was over Australia in Mercury 9. It was also said that he notified a tracking station on the ground, and that they had it on their radar display. However, he denied that he ever saw a UFO in space and stated that the story about Mercury 9 is completely false. What Cooper did agree to is that, in 1951, he had been flying a jet on a training run over Germany when he saw several metallic, saucer-shaped objects. Convinced that UFOs were alien spacecraft, he has been quoted as saying that "extraterrestrial vehicles and their crews are visiting this planet."

June 3, 1965

One of the most noted astronaut UFO cases is that of James McDivitt, which took place while he was flying the Gemini 4 spacecraft over the Pacific Ocean. He saw an object shaped like a cylinder with some kind of antenna or arm sticking out of it, similar to a rocket booster. It was near enough that McDivitt could see the structure and it was not simply a light in the blackness of space. It seemed to have been approaching his craft, and he was concerned it might have come near enough to collide with him. However, as the capsule rotated, the object was lost in the glare of the sun and McDivitt was unable to see it anymore.

Debunkers have dismissed the sighting as simply the observation of a rocket booster; Philip Klass even sent McDivitt a photo of a Titan booster in space, asking him if that was what he saw. McDivitt, however, being an experienced astronaut, knew what was in the photo and stated his UFO was different. He always maintained that he had seen a UFO, but was consistently careful in calling it an unidentified object, not an alien spacecraft, for which there was no proof.

December 4, 1965

A few months after the McDivitt case, astronauts Frank Borman and James Lovell were on Gemini 7 when Lovell reported seeing a "bogey at 10 o'clock high." Mission Control responded by asking, "Is that the booster or is that an actual sighting?" The ground controllers thought that the astronauts had mistaken the first stage of the Titan booster rocket as something else. What was that "something else?" By asking if Lovell had an actual sighting, they were wanting to know if he was reporting a real bogey: a UFO. He replied, "We have several ... looks like debris up here. Actual sighting." He added: "We also have the booster in sight." Lovell noted he had definitely seen something in addition to the booster, but what it was, he had no idea.

Confusing the issue is that a tabloid newspaper printed a photo taken by Gemini 7, apparently showing lights near the spacecraft. Debunkers have dismissed the entire incident because this photo was allegedly the only proof the astronauts had seen something, but this was obviously not the case. What Lovell actually saw is uncertain.

July 18, 1966

Aboard Gemini 10, John Young and Mike Collins saw two lights moving with a tube-shaped object. NASA radar did not show anything near them, but Gemini 10 was out of range during this observation. It was assumed by skeptics that they had seen a booster rocket.

September 13, 1966

During their 16th orbit, Gemini 11 astronauts Pete Conrad and Richard Gordon saw an object that they couldn't identify. It was near enough that they could see it was not a starlike point of

> **UFOs AND ALIENS IN LITERATURE**
>
> Anne McCaffrey first published *Dragonrider* in 1968, set on a world where humans ride telepathic dragons.

light, but they could not determine what it was. Conrad noted: "We had a wingman flying wing with us going into sunset here off to my left. A large object that was tumbling at about 1 rev per second, and we flew ... we had him in sight, I say fairly close to us. I don't know. It could depend on how big he is and I guess he could have been anything from our extravehicular life support system to something else."

A photograph was taken, showing an irregular shape like a cylinder with bumps or bulbs. NORAD originally explained that the object was the Proton 3 satellite or its booster. However, it was 725 kilometres away at the time, and later analysis showed it could not have been seen as an extended object. The object is listed as *unidentified* by NASA, but debunkers note that the UFO may not have been Proton 3, but was certainly some other nearby debris or satellite.

Apollo 11

Several accounts have been published about UFOs that accompanied Apollo 11 on its way to the Moon, and some about alien craft that were waiting for them there. In fact, a transcript of a radio transmission from the astronauts supposedly recorded when they were on the Moon has them saying: "Oh my God! You wouldn't believe it! I'm telling you there are other spacecraft out there, lined up on the far side of the crater edge. They're on the Moon watching us!" Not surprisingly, such a comment does not appear in the official NASA version.

However, it is true that the crew of Apollo 11 did see unidentified objects while en route to the Moon, and some objects were seen from orbit. In fact, the likely origin of the much-publicized quote above may have been astronaut Michael Collins' orbital observation of something he saw while looking for the LEM on the surface of the Moon. He said: "I did see a suspiciously small white object ... right on the southwest end of a crater, but I think they would know if they were in such a location." In other words, he was looking down at the Moon, hoping to see the lunar lander, and saw a small object at the edge of a crater. It couldn't have been the LEM, because they were actually on a flat plain, but it was an "unidentified" object.

Another Apollo 11 incident that has been heralded as proof aliens were checking up on the astronauts is the photograph of a "snowman" that Buzz Aldrin took while still in lunar orbit. He saw the object moving from east to west, and as it did so he saw it was actually two objects, close enough to one another they seemed to be touching, and some kind of "halation" or diffuse trail was emanating from them.

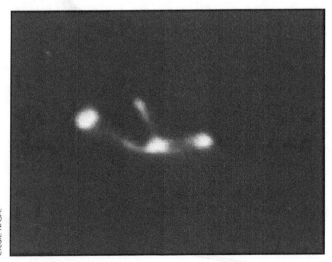

Credit: NASA.

In 1973, astronauts aboard Skylab 3 photographed an unusual object that has not been conclusively identified.

Stills from the film shot by the astronauts definitely show some kind of fuzzy lights, but without any real definition. However, as debunker James Oberg pointed out, an examination of the original film from that date resolves the puzzle. The astronauts were filming through the window and captured a series of reflections and glares, one of which was the series of "snowman" images. In the context of the entire film, the solution becomes more clear and less mysterious.

As for the UFO that was said to shadow Apollo 11 on its way to the Moon, Buzz Aldrin recently noted in an interview that the object was identified as a small linking panel that had attached the command module to the rocket booster. It had the same velocity and directional bump as the Apollo 11 command module, so it kept pace.

While not in the 60s, photographs of an odd UFO were taken by astronauts aboard Skylab 3 over the Indian Ocean on September 20, 1973. Alan Bean, Owen Garriott, and Jack Lousma said they observed a red object that seemed to be some kind of satellite, but which was not anything they could definitively identify. Furthermore, it was uncomfortably close to their spacecraft, "the closest and brightest one we've seen." The object was "reflecting in red light and oscillating at ... about ten seconds," and was "much brighter than Jupiter or any of the other planets."

When Skylab went into the Earth's shadow, the object passed into shadow about five seconds later, allowing them to calculate that it was "no more than 30 to 50 nautical miles" away from them.

Researchers Bruce Maccabee and Brad Sparks examined all available data and found there was no man-made satellite that could explain the sighting. They exhaustingly went over the flight data, the NASA transcripts of in-flight transmissions and later de-briefings. They checked the camera details, compared the UFO photos with others taken by the Skylab astronauts, calculated sun angles, orbital data, and image brightness. Ultimately, they concluded that the object was "truly anomalous." Debunker James Oberg simply noted the Skylab photo was that of a "passing satellite, distorted by some camera artifact."

So, have astronauts ever seen UFOs? The answer is yes, in that some have seen and photographed unidentified objects while in space. In none of these instances, however, is there evidence they have ever seen alien spacecraft. While it would seem reasonable that if there were any alien spaceships in orbit around the Earth that astronauts would have seen them, the argument actually makes little sense. Astronauts in space are flying in specific orbits, with limited views of space outside their spacecraft. Given specific tasks to do while on board, they are not looking for UFOs, although they are sometimes tasked with astronomical observations and observing of the Earth. While in a fixed orbit, they would not be able to see many objects at a distance from their shuttles or capsules. Many have observed known satellites in orbit that were within range, but most are simply too far away or too dim to see.

6

THE SEVENTIES

ROCKETS, ROBOTS, AND RHODESIA: A TIMELINE

August 13, 1970

At 11:00 p.m., in Hadersley, Denmark, a police officer was driving home when a bright light suddenly blocked his path. His car engine quit and the electrical system died. The light was so bright he had difficulty trying to find his radio, doing so by touch alone. As the light passed over his car he felt an intense heat that penetrated the vehicle. He could make out a large grey object on which the light was attached, but beyond that he couldn't see anything. He judged it to be about 10 metres in diameter, with two hemispheres on its underside. He got out of his car to watch the object; after five minutes, the light seemed to be pulled into the grey object and it sped away without making a sound. When it was gone, his car started and the radio was again operational. He reported his encounter to the police station, but they would not believe him at first. After considerable questioning, however, as he stood by his story, the other officers thought he must have been telling the truth. This did not sway the Air Force, who dismissed the observation of the lights as a T-33 jet trainer that had been in the area. The police officer countered by stating that he had also seen the aircraft several minutes later.

Sometime in 1970

The famed seagoing explorer Thor Heyerdahl wrote that early one morning in 1970, while in the middle of the Atlantic Ocean, he had seen a UFO fly along the horizon for several minutes. It disappeared in a "bright orange flash." Investigators believe the sighting may have been a U.S. Navy missile launch.

October 8, 1972

A security guard was on patrol in Oldham, England, during the evening when he heard an odd humming sound like a "swarm of bees." He looked up to see a strange object hovering about 60 metres over the side of his building. It was about 30 metres in diameter, and "almost seemed to completely fill the sky." It had a large window in its side, glowing with a blue-white light, not casting any shadows or shining any beams of light. Then, after about five minutes, as he watched, it "turned itself upon its edge" and he could see that it was a saucer with a large dome that was also lit up. It then shot into the air without warning, and was lost to sight, all the while making the same humming sound that did not change pitch.

10 Things Often Misidentified As UFOs

1. Stars
2. Planets
3. Airplanes
4. Balloons
5. Birds
6. Clouds
7. Fireballs
8. Spotlights
9. Laser Shows
10. Kites

Ufologist Jenny Randles noted that the object was not seen by anyone else in the area even though this was in a densely populated area and this was, according to the security guard, a very large object. Furthermore, the guard was paralyzed with fear and didn't scream or make any noise, which was unfortunate because another person was nearby and did not see or hear anything. However, the "factory cat" was terrified by the appearance of the object and hid for some time following the incident, presumably because animals are said to be more sensitive to such phenomena than humans.

June 1974

During an ill-fated Japanese military encounter with a UFO, an F-4 Phantom jet had its on-board weapons system lock on to an object that appeared to be approaching at high speed. The pilot and his weapons officer thought the object on their radar screen was a Soviet aircraft, which often would play cat-and-mouse with their own planes. But as it came in visual range, they saw it was a 40-foot-wide disc, with square openings on its side.

When the Japanese crew locked its weapons on the UFO, it increased speed and collided head-on with the jet's nose cone, forcing the crew to eject. Unfortunately, the weapons officer died as a result of the accident. According to one published source, the Japanese government never acknowledged the encounter with the UFO, only attributing the in-flight accident to "a collision with an unknown object at 30,000 feet."

February 1975

Near Kofu, Japan, two boys claimed they watched a UFO land and were brave enough to walk up to it, noting it had oriental characters on its side. As they watched, a ladder came out of the craft and a silver robot-like creature descended then headed towards them. Not surprisingly, the boys panicked and ran away to the safety of home, where one of their parents observed an object rising into the sky.

July 1975

In what was then Rhodesia, a flurry of UFO activity had many residents concerned. In Salisbury on July 4, a couple watched an odd orange light hover stationary near their home for six minutes, and two days later another couple saw a similar object. At 8:15 p.m. they were driving near Karoi and saw an orange object "with a jagged tail and pointed front." When they stopped the car to get a better look, the object stopped its movement as well. Although such behaviour is typical of a star or planet, the light in this case began moving downward rapidly and vanished below the trees in a matter of minutes, thus ruling out an astronomical body.

On July 26, near Macheke, a man was walking around the side of his house during the evening when a bright white beam of light struck him and threw him to the ground. It appeared to be coming from a source about 12 metres away and about the height of nearby power lines. He tried to get up and out of the beam but found that he was paralyzed. On the ground, he could see the light and the beam reflecting in a window. He blacked out, and when he came to the light and beam were gone and he could move again, although he was stiff and sore. He went inside his house and found that his fire had gone out, indicating he had been unconscious for more than an hour.

September 10, 1976

A British airliner was en route from Moscow to London at an altitude of 10,000 metres and was just inside Lithuania when the pilot saw a "blinding" stationary light off his starboard side. It was estimated to be 16 to 24 kilometres away and slightly below them at about 8,200 or 8,500 metres. The yellowish light was of constant intensity and too bright to look at for any length of time, reportedly illuminating a cloudbank below it. The pilot radioed Soviet air control about it but was told to "not ask questions" about the object. After 10 to 15 minutes, the British plane had progressed far enough that the object was no longer in sight.

October 17, 1976

As many as 50 people in Akita, Japan, reported seeing a gold-coloured, disc-shaped object early in the morning that hung in the sky for 10 minutes. Air traffic controllers at the airport advised approaching flights to avoid the area because of the unknown craft. Witnesses included Japanese media who had been filming a documentary at the airport, so the sighting attracted considerable attention.

February 18, 1977

In Uruguay, a dog died apparently as a result of a close encounter with a UFO. The dramatic incident occurred on a large ranch south of the city of Salto. A farm family and their ranch hands all had seen unusual moving lights throughout February, but on the 18th at around 4:00 a.m., something more sinister came by. As the farmers were milking the cows, all the lights on the farm suddenly went out and a bright glow appeared near the barn. The owner of the farm ran towards the source of the glow, thinking the barn might be on fire. His watchdog, a large black and brown police dog, was excited and ran with him to investigate.

The farmer saw a "fire disc," like two plates facing one another, moving with a rocking motion across the barnyard at about 20 metres above the trees, breaking some branches as it progressed. The livestock were greatly agitated, "going crazy, running everywhere." The strange craft finally came to a stop about six metres above the ground and next to a water tank, where it shone a bright light around the entire yard. The watchdog ran towards the object but stopped in its tracks, sat down, and began howling as if in pain. The farmer walked almost underneath the craft, and got a good look at it. It had beams of light like lightning or small wings on either side, and was radiating intense heat. The farmer felt electric shocks all over his body and he was unable to move. After several minutes, the object moved away and eventually headed over a forest and out of sight.

The electric generator started up again when the object was gone, but its wires were "burned out." The dog was lethargic throughout the next few days and on the third day it was found dead, laying in the yard. An autopsy report noted that the dog's blood vessels had ruptured and that he had been bleeding internally. The farmer's own arm became very red after the encounter and he was told by investigators that he may have been burned by radiation.

September 20, 1977

A series of objects were seen near Petrozavodsk, Russia. Soviet media carried many eyewitnesses' accounts of unusual moving lights and other objects in the early morning sky. A disc-shaped, glowing object was seen by pilots of an aircraft near Riga, who were said to have had to make drastic maneuvers to avoid collision. A cigar-shaped object flew alongside a ball of light that appeared to land in a forest, while a different ball of light was said to land near the Petrozavodsk–Leningrad highway. Other reports included sightings of an object with "exhaust pipes" that hovered over towns and villages such as Namayevo, and sightings of UFOs from Western Europe. Together, this all confirmed that something odd had occurred that night in northwestern Russia. Later investigations showed that this incident was likely caused by a rocket launch carrying Cosmos 955 into orbit.

October 1978

An aircraft disappeared in association with a UFO, over Bass Strait off the coast of Australia. The unfortunate pilot was Frederick Valentich, a young aviator who was

UFOs and Aliens
in Movies

Close Encounters of the Third Kind (1977) was a grand tour of ufology, with pre-*X-Files* government conspirators, UFO fanatics, and early abduction themes. Richard Dreyfuss is outstanding as an average guy whose UFO experience turns his life upside down. The railway crossing scene, where he gets burned by a close brush with a UFO, is very memorable and taken from actual witness' narratives of close encounter reports. The movie is also noted for its attention to detail from actual UFO sightings and the people who study them. The French scientist working with the American government is patterned after noted UFO researcher and author Jacques Vallee, while noted ufologist Dr. J. Allen Hynek, the person who created the term *close encounters* to describe an up-close sighting of a UFO, actually makes a cameo appearance during the climactic scene towards the end where the mother ship finally lands.

planning on picking up some friends at King Island. He dutifully filed a flight plan and checked the weather conditions at the Moorabbin airport office in preparation for the short night flight in his Cessna. His plane fully fueled, he took off at about 6:20 p.m. on what should have been less than a 90-minute trip. During his flight, he was in constant contact with Melbourne air traffic control.

About halfway across Bass Strait, he asked the tower if there was any other aircraft near him. He was told there was no known air traffic out there, and he replied that there was "a large aircraft below five thousand feet," above him. He told the air traffic controller that he could see what appeared to be four bright landing lights, like those of an aircraft, passing about 300 metres over him. He asked the tower about other aircraft again, this time wanting to know if there was any military activity in the area. Again, he was told there was nothing in his area.

At 7:09, he radioed: "It's approaching now from due east towards me ... he's playing some sort of game, he's flying over me two, three times at speeds I could not identify." Valentich was flying at an altitude of almost 1,400 metres and was becoming increasingly worried about the craft that was toying with him in midair.

When asked by the tower if he could identify the kind of aircraft, he replied, "it's not an aircraft, it is …" without finishing the sentence. Prodded by the tower again, he said that the object was a "long shape," with a green light and was "metallic like, it's all shiny on the outside."

As he talked to the tower he was telling them that the mysterious craft had become stationary and that his airplane was orbiting it, somehow. Suddenly, Valentich reported that the object had "just vanished." Looking around, he reported that the same or similar object was approaching his plane from the southwest, and now his airplane's engine was coughing and sputtering. He told the tower, "That strange aircraft is hovering on top of me again … It is hovering and it's not an aircraft." The shocked tower operator heard only a metallic sound, then the radio went dead. Valentich was never heard from again.

Despite an extensive search in the Bass Strait, no wreckage of the plane was ever found. Many theories for Valentich's disappearance have been proposed, including the possibility that he had become disoriented and was actually seeing the lights of his own aircraft reflecting in the ocean, and that he flew into the water by accident while flying upside down. Another idea was that he had decided to disappear and start his life anew, so he faked his death and is now living in Tasmania. Debunkers have even suggested that he was involved in drug running and had paid the ultimate price for his illegal activity.

December 31, 1978

Another UFO case from Australasia made news around the world, this one off the east coast of New Zealand in the early hours of the morning of New Year's Eve, 1978. There had been some UFO sightings off the coast of South Island on December 21, and the tale of Frederick Valentich was still a hot topic in the media. A television crew had been sent up in a plane to get some video of New Zealand from the air as the witnesses to the events of December 21 included pilots and radar operators.

The cargo plane had taken off late on December 30 from Wellington, heading for Christchurch, carrying newspapers and other goods between the two cities. Along for the ride with the pilot and copilot were reporter Quentin Fogarty, a cameraman, and a sound recording engineer. Just after midnight, the plane was flying northeast of South Island when the pilots saw an odd light in the sky. They checked with air traffic control to confirm the sighting, and were told that some intermittent radar echoes were detected. The plane was flying at 3,000 metres at the time.

Looking towards the ground, Fogarty saw a row of five bright lights that were pulsating and growing in size from a pinpoint to a "balloon." These lights seemed to be near the town of Kaikoura. As Fogarty was talking about these lights with the others on board, Wellington air traffic control notified the crew that they had picked up another radar target near the plane. The crew and passengers saw an object with a flashing light. A few minutes later, the tower told the pilots that yet another return was seen, this time directly behind the plane. During the rest of the trip, several other lights and radar returns were seen and detected. Throughout this time, the cameraman was recording all the various lights observed, although he was jostled by the others in the cabin and the plane made several turns and banks to see the objects better. The resulting video is very choppy and the images shake considerably.

At about 2:15 a.m., the plane and its crew headed back to Wellington on the same path. This time, a large radar target was detected by the plane's system only about 20 kilometres away. The camera caught images of a "spinning sphere" in a "sort of bell shape," with lines running around its middle. At about 2:50 a.m., two additional bright lights were seen, one of which dropped 300 metres before stopping its descent.

The film shot during this round-trip flight has been analyzed many times by believers and skeptics alike. Depending on which expert you believe, the lights seen by the pilots and news crew could have been Venus, Jupiter, meteors, secret American spy planes, and even the lights from Japanese squid fishing boats on the ocean.

May 22, 1979

A strange encounter took place in Piastów, Poland. Late in the evening a man was walking through a park when he saw three bright lights ahead of him. He looked up and saw that they were shining down from a circular object about three metres in diameter, hanging in the air above the grassy path. He walked closer, getting to within three metres of it and saw that its surface was becoming an array of geometrical shapes, and other lights were flashing on it. It suddenly gave off an intense blue light and the man felt as if he was being burned, so he ran away. The next morning, he had burns on his face and a bad headache, but had no idea what the object had been.

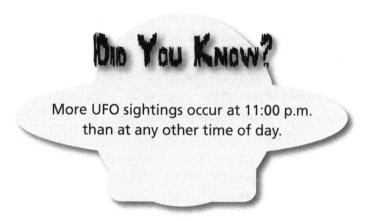

DID **Y**OU **K**NOW?

More UFO sightings occur at 11:00 p.m.
than at any other time of day.

ZAPPED!

On November 5, 1975, a logging crew was heading home after a long day of thinning new growth in the Apache-Sitgreaves National Forest in northern Arizona. Among the seven-member crew was 22-year-old Travis Walton, who shared duties cutting scrub with a chainsaw and gathering branches into piles. The foreman of the group was Mike Rogers, an experienced forester who had the contract with the U.S. Forest Service, but had been running behind and had already been given an extension. As a consequence, he had been working his crew hard, and they didn't finish until about 6:00 p.m., when it began to get dark.

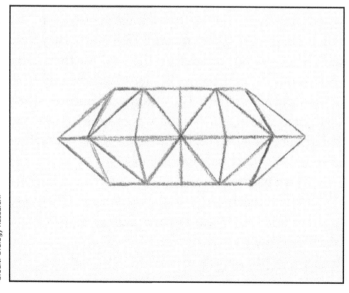

Credit: Ufology Research.

The faceted UFO that zapped Travis Walton in 1975.

The entire crew climbed into their pickup truck and drove off along a dirt track through the rocks and trees, with Rogers driving and Walton by the passenger door. As they turned a corner, they saw a glow that resolved into a blue, disc-shaped object hovering in the air over a clearing not far away from the track. The object was lit from inside, as if it were an opaque fluorescent light, and was covered in black lines dividing it onto "facets" like a diamond. Judging from its position in the clearing, it appeared to be about six metres wide and two and a half metres along a vertical axis.

On impulse, Walton suddenly opened the passenger door and jumped out. He had thought the object was going to zip away and wanted to get a really good look at it, so he ran towards it. He stopped nearly underneath it, gazing sharply upward at the strange craft. The object started to emit a pulsating rumble and tilted down slightly towards him, so he backed off and hid behind a log. But he was frightened now, so he rose and began to turn back towards his friends when he felt a shock, as if he had been electrocuted, and blacked out.

Walton's co-workers in the truck saw a brilliant flash of blue light hit him, raising him off the ground slightly and then throwing him about three metres away onto the ground like a rag doll. Spooked, Rogers put the truck in gear and sped away, not wanting to suffer the same fate. Eventually, he stopped the truck about half a kilometre down the road, and after some agitated discussion with his companions, he turned back and they went in search of Walton.

Walton and the UFO, however, had disappeared without a trace.

His co-workers contacted the police at about 7:30 p.m., when they made it back to town and called the sheriff's office from a shopping mall. The police who arrived were suspicious of the foresters' bizarre story but observed that all the men were highly emotional and some were even crying. The officers went back to the site with Rogers and some of his crew, searching the area with flashlights. They were becoming concerned because Walton was not dressed for the cool weather. Later that evening, Rogers and a police officer went to the home of Walton's mother, about 15 kilometres away, to break the news to her. The officer was surprised when Walton's mother didn't fall apart at the news that her son was missing; in fact, she was relatively unemotional. This observation led skeptics to later charge that Walton and his mother had conspired together to fake his disappearance.

During the next several days, search parties combed the area but did not find any trace of Travis Walton. Suspicion fell on Rogers and the rest of his crew, and they were eventually implicated in an apparent homicide. Each one was even given polygraph tests to see if they had killed Walton or knew where he was. (They all also passed the polygraph question asking whether they had actually seen a UFO that night.)

In Their Own Words

California
August 1994

I was backpacking in the Big Bear Wilderness Area in California last August. My friend Robin and I were hiking to a lake, which I think was called Bull Run Lake (or something close to that). It was a full moon and we were camped in a large meadow about 3 miles from the lake. The moon was so bright it was almost like daylight. We were sleeping outside of the tent, just in our sleeping bags under the stars. I think I must have been dozing off when Robin yelled to me to look at the sky.

I looked up and we saw a formation of lights moving across the sky. They were moving incredibly fast, much faster than an airplane or helicopter or anything like that. They were shooting across the sky. I could see four off-white lights. They flew completely around us one time and then stopped and hovered over an area near the lake we were hiking too. Two of the lights stopped at the lake and two continued on and disappeared behind some mountains. The two lights still in view began bouncing all over the sky. They shot straight up and straight down. They went at diagonal angles. And all of this was extremely fast. So much faster than any modern aircraft I have ever seen. One other strange thing was that there was absolutely no noise. We were in a valley and even small noises echoed loudly. But it was perfectly still.

While we were watching the lights, Robin told me that a moment earlier the lights had been doing the same thing and one light had stopped and actually hovered in place over the lake. Then a beam of light, colored red, yellow and white in sequence down the length of the beam, extended from the large light and went into the trees towards the lake. She said it was a thin beam, smaller than a spotlight. It stayed on the ground for a short time, less than a minute, and then retracted back into the larger, white light. Then the ships started flying around in circles and she had called my attention.

Robin and I were getting nervous. I was getting a tingly sensation in my neck. Robin suggested we leave the field. I thought it was kind of extreme, but as I thought about those lights, I got a little scared myself. The whole thing just felt wrong. So we took off back to the vehicle. It was only a 1/5 of a mile or so. But the walk seemed to take forever. We both felt kind of panicky by the time we reached the vehicle.

I slept poorly and had a dream of being chased by aliens. Now, I realize it is probably just a dream, but I will relay the details anyway. I don't remember much, but the strongest image I have is of a thin, bony, green arm reaching for me. I can see pale green fingers closing around my forearm. I have images of running through the woods in the dark in terror. It was a pretty disturbing dream.

The next day we returned to the field and grabbed our gear and did not ever hike to the lake. We both had very bad feelings about that idea.

Reported by Anonymous
Source: Ufology Research

Late in the evening on the fifth night after Walton vanished, one of his brother-in-laws received a phone call from someone claiming to be Travis, saying he was at a phone booth by a gas station in a town about 50 kilometres away. Initially leery because pranksters had been calling the entire Walton clan all week, he was eventually convinced that it was Travis and agreed to pick him up.

Travis Walton was found gaunt and exhausted in the phone booth, barely able to stand. As they drove, he talked about creatures with large eyes and how he had been very frightened. He asked to be taken to see a doctor, but did not want anyone else to know he was back.

While Walton was gone, his brother Duane had been approached by many ufologists once the strange story of the foresters had been made public through the police investigation. One of these was Bill Spaulding, representing a group called Ground Saucer Watch (GSW), who impressed Duane with his credentials and his claim that the group had many affiliated professionals, including doctors. So, when Travis asked to see a doctor, Duane took Spaulding up on his offer. Unfortunately, the doctor to whom the Waltons were referred turned out to not even have a licence to practice and was only a hypnotherapist without professional accreditation.

Fortunately, the Waltons soon were set up with licensed physicians by representatives from another UFO group, who came to their home to do an examination of Travis. Two odd things were found: a red mark on the inside of his elbow and the absence of acetone in his urine sample, which normally builds up when someone goes without food for several days.

Skeptics have noted that the urine sample was not actually produced by Walton at the time of the medical examination. In fact, the sample had allegedly been produced not long after Walton had come home after his ordeal, at the suggestion of Spaulding, and had been "preserved." Further, skeptics suggested that the mark on Walton's arm could have indicated he had injected himself with a hallucinogen, leading to his bizarre story.

And what a story! Walton said that after blacking out, he woke up on his back, fully clothed, in a small, sterile room, similar to a hospital. He was tired and thirsty, his body was sore and his vision was initially blurry, though slowly clearing. He seemed to be on a hard bed of some kind, with a curved piece of hard material around his chest, possibly as a restraint. He was shocked to see three strange creatures standing near him.

These beings were less than a metre and a half in height, with large hairless heads and no eyebrows, eyelashes, or beards. They had large, staring eyes and only slit-like mouths. They seemed to be delicate creatures, soft and fragile, with whitish skin and slight builds.

Walton realized they were not physically a threat to him, and because he was angry at his captors, he lashed out, hitting one into the others and watching them fall like dominoes. He grabbed a short rod off a ledge along a wall and waved it in their direction menacingly. They stopped advancing towards him and turned about, leaving the room.

He followed them out, warily, and found himself in a curved hallway. He progressed along it and came to another open doorway. Inside was an almost empty room, except for a single "captain's chair" with panels of buttons and switches. When he approached the chair, the lights dimmed and the ceiling and walls appeared to dissolve into a dome of stars like a planetarium. When he backed away, the room returned to normal.

Suddenly, another door opened and in walked a tall being with a bubble-like helmet on his head. This entity was obviously different from the smaller aliens, wearing a tight-fitting garment that showed he was very muscular and formidable. This being took the dazed Walton by the arm and led him out of the room, down the hallway, and into yet another room. This area was very large and they soon walked down a sloped ramp into what could only be described as a hangar. Walton saw that he was exiting a craft shaped like the one that had "zapped" him back in the forest. Other craft sat silently not far away.

Walton was led by the tall being across the hangar to a doorway that opened into a long, wide hallway. They continued walking along the corridor until they reached a set of doors that opened into a room where three other beings like his tall companion were sitting, all without helmets. They teamed up, forced Walton down onto a table and placed a device like an oxygen mask over his face. He passed out almost immediately.

He woke up lying on the highway near the gas station and looked up just in time to see the same craft, or another that was similar to the one he had first seen in the forest, hovering over the road. Suddenly, it shot vertically upward and out of sight without making any sound whatsoever. He immediately ran over to the payphones, trying three before finally getting one to connect, and called his brother-in-law.

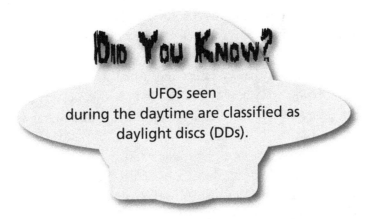

Did You Know?

UFOs seen
during the daytime are classified as
daylight discs (DDs).

The question of whether or not Walton had made up the entire story has been debated by skeptics and proponents since the case became known. As is usual in all abduction stories, there are elements that seem absurd and suspicious. Could the story just be a grand lie, orchestrated by Rogers because he knew he couldn't finish the contract on time? In theory, he could have coerced his workers to help with the scheme, but one wonders why the hoaxers had not simply admitted their ruse once the police investigation began to turn towards murder? What would have happened if Walton had not turned up?

The police investigation had also examined the phone booths for Walton's fingerprints but found none. Lie-detector tests on Walton, Rogers, and the other foresters were either passed or inconclusive. One psychiatrist stated that in his opinion, Walton only imagined the abduction experience, although he could not explain "five witnesses having the same basic story and passing lie detector tests about it." Could the entire forestry crew have collaborated in a conspiracy to defraud the government by fabricating an alien abduction?

FALCONBRIDGE

On November 13, 1975, the North American Aerospace Command (NORAD) issued a press release concerning an incident near Sudbury, Ontario. They reported:

> At 4:05 p.m., Nov. 11, the Canadian Forces radar site at Falconbridge, Ontario, reported a radar track of an unidentified flying object about 25–30 nautical miles south of the site, ranging in altitude from 25,000 to 72,000 feet. Persons at the site also saw the object and said it appeared as a bright star but much closer. Two F-106 aircraft of the U.S. Air Force Air National Guard's 171st Fighter Interceptor Squadron at Selfridge ANGB, Michigan, were scrambled, but the pilots reported no contact with the object.

By itself, the story was quite amazing, apparently involving a UFO tracked on radar, observed from the ground and causing enough concern that NORAD recommended interception by American jet fighters.

The Falconbridge incident took place in the context of a major North American wave of UFO reports. Arch-skeptic Phil Klass pointed out that on October 20, 1975, NBC had aired *The UFO Incident*, a recreation of the Betty and Barney Hill UFO abduction story, which he believed contributed to the public's heightened interest in UFOs. This had been followed by three weeks of "an abnormal number of reports of sightings of unidentified objects in the sky."

Klass noted that Jupiter was an evening star that month, and also that Venus was very bright, rising about 2:30 a.m. local time. He concluded that the visual sightings of UFOs were mostly probably one or the other of these astronomical objects.

The commander-in-charge of NORAD sent a message to all its units that night, noting:

> This morning, 11 Nov 1975, CFS Falconbridge reported search and height finder radar paints on an object up to 30 nautical miles south of the site ranging in altitude from 26,000 ft. to 72,000 ft. The site commander and other personnel say the object appeared as a bright star but much closer. With binoculars the object appeared as a 100 ft. diameter sphere and appeared to have craters around the outside.

The rather large difference in altitude is curious, as is the estimate of size if the object was really as far away as thought. One could hardly judge the diameter of a light source that was nearly 60 kilometres away and between 8,000 and 22,000 metres in altitude!

Another source with information about the observations comes from an ATC Log Book, classified as SECRET and released through the National Archives of Canada.

The relevant entry on November 11, 1975 reads:

> 1118   CFB Falconbridge [illegible] called re: UFO over the base and also rep of UFO over OPP bldg downtown Sudbury. Brilliant color - like looking at a large gem with colored lights all around it.

> 1123   North - Cape activity. Intel. Stand-by DO (Col. OECHSLG) Advised.

> 1147   Maj. Oliver fm. Falconbridge called re: UFOs. Report is as follows:

> Time 1115Z - 1129Z - sighted 2 UFO brilliant lights - one at 200E fm. CFB Falconbridge, the other at 180E but much further aways. Maj Oliver took 3 snapshots with Brownie camera (no results) as of this time. Other observers were Capt. Calson and Cpl. Lawelenceson of CFB Falconbridge - They observed the closest object through binoculars and

> object was rising vertically at tremendous speed - they had
> it on ht. finder at two cuts of 44,000' and again at 72,000'
> - object circular - well lighted and what appeared as two
> black spots in the centre.

Apart from the fact that trying to take a photograph of a distant light with a Brownie is quite ridiculous, it seems as though there were many witnesses of the UFO, including Ontario Provincial Police and some base personnel. In this document, however, the time of the report is given as 1118Z, or 0618 local, again differing from other records. Not only that, but the UFO was painted on radar at between "44,000 and 72,000 feet," whereas other altitudes are given as "26,000 and 36,000 feet." It is no wonder that airborne jets couldn't find anything when the object's location couldn't even be reckoned with any consistency or accuracy.

UFO Hotspot: Niagara-on-the-Lake, Ontario

On the south shore of Lake Ontario, a group called Orbwatch has been logging sightings of lights moving over the water.

A report in the *Winnipeg Tribune* on November 13, 1975, noted:

> Ontario police sight 4 UFOs
> Sudbury, Ont. (CP) - Police reports say unidentified flying
> objects were sighted over Sudbury and Halleybury, about 90 miles
> northeast of here.
> Reports on the sightings were compiled by regional police,
> provincial police and staff at Canadian Forces Base Falconbridge.
> Regional police constables Bob Whiteside and Alex Keable said

they saw three objects in the sky Tuesday, and later spotted a fourth.

Regional constable John Marsh said he saw lights in the sky to the southwest while on patrol on Highway 17 near Coniston, about five miles east of here.

He said the object moved in a jerking manner, had pulsating lights and "was different from what you would normally call a star."

Four persons at the Canadian Forces Base Falconbridge said they had sighted objects in the sky and on radar.

In total, seven members of the Sudbury detachment of the OPP observed UFOs that night. Constables Chrapchynski and Deighton reported that "4 objects were observed clearly in the sky. The brightest in the east remained in a stationary position. One on the southwest moved at times in a jerky motion. One in the northwest remained stationary. The one in the northeast was the dimmest, also stationary. They were still plainly visible after day break when all regular bright objects in the sky had disappeared. Seen intermittently for 1 hour."

Given that the stationary objects were probably stars, the only one in some doubt was the object in the southwest, which could very well have been Jupiter observed with some illusory autokinesis effects. Note also that they only observed "intermittently" (probably because they were also attending to more important police duties), so that it would have been easy to get confused over the objects' movements or lack thereof.

Constables Keables and Whiteside reported only one object, observed with binoculars:

"At times it appeared to be cylindrical with shafts of light bright enough to light up clouds in immediate area it appeared at times to travel in circles. At one point, it came quite close. It was still visible to the naked eye after the sun came up."

If this was Venus or Jupiter, it was certainly bright that night. But why did these two witnesses not see the other objects?

Meanwhile, at Falconbridge, Captain Carson, Master Corporal Kreutz, and Corporal Lawrenson had reported a "circular object, brilliantly lighted with two black spots in the centre, moving upwards at high speed from 42,000 to 72,000 ft. with no horizontal movement. This object was sighted visually and by radar bearing 210 magnetic at 30 nautical miles from CFS Falconbridge. A similar object was sighted by the same observers bearing 270 magnetic but at too great a distance to provide details."

A further note said that Major Oliver (who had been the one to take the photographs), Captain Carson, and Corporal Lauritsen saw an object that was "spherical shaped and appeared to be rotating." The object "appeared to have surface area similar to the Moon and was ascending and descending." They watched it for two hours, intermittently due to the cloud cover.

UFO researcher Brad Sparks thinks the evidence points to "a balloon that has been caught in the east-flowing jet stream, having been launched at about 6 a.m. apparently somewhere in the general Sudbury region."

Sparks also believes the OPP observations were likely stars and planets:

> Sunrise was at about 7:20 a.m. Venus would have been very bright in the SE sky before sunrise and for some time after, rising above the horizon almost due east at about 3:08 a.m. The first sightings with times reported were 'very low' over Sudbury Stadium from about 3:00 to 4:55 a.m, then apparently continued for some indefinite time afterward. Jupiter was very bright in the western sky and set beneath the horizon at about 4:30 a.m. Mars and Saturn were very high up in the SW and SE skies. The brightest star Sirius was high in the southern sky.

What about the radar targets, if the original visual observations were only of stars and planets? When the pilots were eventually dispatched six hours later to the area where the UFOs had been seen, Venus was long gone, as was any balloon which would have travelled at least 650 kilometres east and much higher than the planes were flying by that time. Klass reports that the pilots could only find "high-altitude clouds laden with ice crystals that reflected sunlight ... Such clouds would return radar energy and produce blips on the Falconbridge height-finder radar." This contradicts the balloon hypothesis, but does give us a second possible explanation for the radar observations.

Finally, if the visual observations were really of stars and planets, how do we explain the descriptions of the objects as having craters like the Moon, and two black dots? When binoculars are improperly focused, starlike objects will appear to be mottled spheres due to effects of the optics and the internal aqueous humor of the eye. And if binoculars are focused on Saturn, it can appear as an extended object, with the gap between the rings and planet visible as black areas, which can be interpreted in many ways if the observer does not know he is looking at a ringed planet.

This "classic" Falconbridge radar/visual UFO case appears to be much less mysterious than has been claimed. While there is no way to determine if all the objects seen that night were stars or planets, it seems as though many might have been misidentified. Why experienced radar operators would not be able to distinguish between clouds and truly anomalous tracks is somewhat odd, as is the reason why USAF fighters would be sent up to investigate potentially unknown targets after more than five or six hours had passed.

TEHRAN

On September 19, 1976, at 12:30 a.m., the Imperial Iranian Air Force was contacted by a civilian airport at Mehrabad, near Tehran, regarding calls they had received from citizens about UFOs seen over the capital. One person described an object as "a kind of bird," and another requested the airport to "tell this helicopter with a light on to get away from my house because I'm scared." According to the IIAF, there were no helicopters in the area at the time.

Brigadier General Yousefi, assistant deputy commander of operations at the base, contacted the Mehradbad tower operators and determined that the object that had been reported was not on any air defence radar screens. Going outside to look for himself, he saw a large, bright, starlike object that he considered unusual. He decided to order the scrambling of a F-4 jet fighter from Shahrokhi AFB, about 240 kilometres southwest of Tehran, to investigate the light.

The plane lifted off at about 1:30 a.m. local time and headed north towards the object, which seemed to be about 110 kilometres away. Even flying at Mach 1, the pilot was unable to close on the object very much. As he reached a point about 40 kilometres away from his target, he lost all communications with the base. Following procedure, he broke off his pursuit of the target and turned back towards the base, and eventually his communications came on line again.

On October 1, a transcript for the recording of the pilot's conversation with the control tower was released to the media. The operator had told the pilot, IIAF Lieutenant Jafari, to return home if he was unable to close on the target. When he turned to go back, he told the tower: "Something is coming at me from behind. It is 15 miles away ... now 10 miles ... now five miles ... It is level now. I think it is going to crash into me. It has just passed by, missing me narrowly ..." The tower then guided the agitated pilot back to base.

At 1:40 a.m. that night, a second F-4 was sent out. This time, the radar operator on the jet got a lock on the object, placing it at 50 kilometres away and at a 12 o'clock high, closing on it at 240 kilometres per hour. When the pilot had closed to within 40 kilometres, the object moved away at a pace that maintained the distance. Judging from the size of the radar return, the object was estimated to be comparable to a Boeing 707 tanker, but visually it was difficult to see, because the light was dazzling. It seemed to have flashing strobe lights in a rectangular pattern, alternating blue, green, orange, and red, sequencing so quickly that all colours could be seen at the same time.

As the jet continued pursuit, another bright object, described as large as half the size of the Moon, seemed to emerge from the first object and head straight towards the plane at a high speed. In response, the pilot tried to fire an infrared-guided missile at the rapidly approaching object, but his weapons control panel shut down and his communications system went dead as well.

The pilot then went into a turn and dived to evade what he believed was an enemy offensive manoeuvre, but the object followed his action and chased him at an estimated distance of five or six kilometres. The second UFO seemed to move into the inside of his turn, then moved away to join up with the first object.

Flying at an altitude of 8,000 metres, the pilot continued to watch his pursuers. A third object appeared, seeming to come out of the first one, this time shooting directly down to the Earth. It descended, then suddenly decelerated, illuminating the surrounding area and either gently stopping a short distance above the ground or hovering slightly above it. The pilot reduced his altitude and made a note of the landed object's location, then flew back to the air base. Curiously, the pilot and his crewman both had lost their night vision (probably from observing the bright objects) and had some difficulty vectoring in on the runway.

PEOPLE IN UFOLOGY

Josef Allen Hynek, known as the "Father of Ufology," was born in 1910 in Chicago. In 1935, he earned his Ph.D. in astronomy while working at Yerkes Observatory. He became professor of astronomy and director of McMillin Observatory at Ohio State University. There, in 1948, he was asked by the USAF to be a consultant on Project Sign, the first official government/military study on flying saucers. It was his job to examine reports of unidentified flying objects and evaluate them in terms of astronomical phenomena such as stars, fireballs, and meteors.

As they approached the airport, there was considerable interference with their communications, and when they turned, the onboard communications went out completely. A commercial aircraft that was in the area also reported electronic interference as well, but did not see any UFOs.

Finally on approach to the runway, the F-4 crew saw yet another UFO, this time cigar-shaped, with bright lights on each end and a flashing light in the middle. This object, as with the first, was not on the airport's own radar screens. The night scramble ended with no further incidents.

The next morning, the F-4 crew travelled by helicopter to the area where they believed the third object had landed, but found only a dry lake bed. However, just west of there they detected a signal on their radio that led them to a small house. Landing, they asked the residents if they had seen any unusual activity the night before, and were told about a loud noise and bright lights that had disturbed their sleep.

In January 1978, the tabloid *National Enquirer* announced that the Tehran UFO case was "the most scientifically valuable" of all the ones its "Blue Ribbon Panel" of experts had studied. They found the testimony of the pilots' observations, plus the jamming of the planes' electronics, to be very compelling evidence that something truly mysterious had occurred.

Arch-skeptic and aviation journalist Philip Klass disagreed. He pointed out many problems with the case in his book *UFOs: The Public Deceived*. He noted that, for a spectacular case that involved military confrontation with apparently extraterrestrial craft, the details of the case were, amazingly, unclassified. Klass noted there was no evidence that a follow-up investigation was conducted, and that the report was made available to the public fairly quickly, suggesting the U.S. government was not taking the case very seriously.

But researcher Martin Shough countered Klass' argument by observing that the absence of any evidence of a high-level investigation is not proof one did not occur. It's possible, he reasoned, that the USAF was very interested in the case and conducted its investigation at a level of secrecy far beyond the classification levels of anyone Klass interviewed.

Klass also quoted a Tehran newspaper as stating that the UFO was observed flying to the south of the city, clearly at odds with the statement of the first F-4 crew that had been north of Tehran. However, as noted by Shough, skeptics are critical of UFO proponents who use newspaper accounts as a basis for supporting the facts of a UFO case, yet Klass was guilty of the same. The newspaper version did not specify which UFO sighting was in the south, which would actually support the second crew's testimony. Similarly, without talking to the Iranian crew himself, Klass suggested that they reported the communications malfunction in error, but does not consider the possibility that the newspaper account or the statements provided to the USAF were somehow inaccurate.

One further misinterpretation comes directly from Klass' own version of the story. He noted a discrepancy in the statement by the pilot who reported the UFO coming at him "from behind," yet this was the pilot who had been chasing the UFO, which therefore must have been forward of him. While Klass used this contradiction as another reason to dismiss the case, a careful reading of the account shows that by the time the pilot noted the UFO was coming at him from behind, he had already turned his plane around and was heading home. The directional confusion does not actually exist.

Shough's remarkably detailed refutation of Klass' debunking of the Iran case addresses key points and suggests that there was something truly anomalous in the sky over Tehran that night.

This is not to say, however, that some elements of the sighting cannot be explained. Klass noted that about the same time, there were sightings of very bright fireballs far to the west along the coast of Africa, and reasoned that it was possible the Iranian pilots had seen another salvo of these. He further found evidence that the flight crews may not have had the high level of training as other pilots, although Shough disputed this as simply Klass' opinion and not based on documented evidence.

VAL JOHNSON'S UFO ENCOUNTER

In 1979, a police officer on routine patrol had "too close an encounter" with a UFO as he was travelling on a dark highway in Minnesota. The case had all the best features one would want in a UFO incident: a reliable witness, physical evidence, and immediate investigation by police officers. No other UFO sighting in the history of ufology has such a pedigree.

UFOROM investigator Guy Westcott visited the scene of the "accident" soon after it was reported in media. He managed to interview the police officer and hear what happened in his own words.

Johnson said that on August 27, 1979, at approximately 1:40 a.m., about 15 kilometres west of Stephen, Minnesota, he was on routine patrol when he looked south down State Highway 220 to check for traffic before turning. He noticed a very bright, brilliant light, 20 to 30 centimetres in diameter and about a metre off the ground. He thought perhaps at first that it could be an aircraft in trouble, as it looked similar to a landing light from an aircraft.

He drove south a little more than a kilometre and a half, then the light suddenly flew quickly towards him and hit his police car. The result was damage to a headlight, a dent in the hood, a broken windshield, and bent antennas on top of the vehicle.

UFOs AND ALIENS ON TV

On air from 1978 to 1982, *Mork & Mindy* was a spaced-out comedy show about an alien named Mork from the planet Ork. The show introduced Robin Williams, who played Mork, as an alien whose mission was to observe Earthlings' behaviour. The show was actually a spinoff from an episode of the popular series *Happy Days*, where Mork wanted to abduct Richie Cunningham but was stopped by Fonzie. (This episode aired several months after the infamous "jump the shark" episode of *Happy Days*.)

As for Johnson, he blacked out and was unconscious for 39 minutes, because the next thing he remembers is coming to his senses and finding that the car was almost 300 metres down the road, sideways across both lanes. Somehow, the police car had travelled in a straight line 260 metres, at which point the brakes were applied and left almost 30 metres of black skid marks on the pavement. Johnson, however, does not remember braking at all.

At 2:19 a.m., he radioed a 10-88 (Officer Needs Assistance) to his dispatcher. The police officer who came out assessed the situation as best he could and called for an ambulance to take Johnson to Warren Hospital for tests, X-rays, and observation.

When this officer arrived, Johnson was complaining that his eyes were sore. At Warren Hospital, he was diagnosed as having a mild case of "welder's burns," as if he had looked into a very intense light source. Finally, the officer noted that both the dashboard clock in Johnson's police car and Johnson's wristwatch were slow by exactly 14 minutes.

This fascinating, very close encounter was thoroughly investigated by police immediately after it had occurred. Westcott's interpretation was that the light had been ball lightning. He makes an interesting case, in that the previous evening had been hot and humid and could possibly have created a charge in the atmosphere the next day. Another supporting point is that Johnson estimated the object to have been five kilometres away, near some trees that just happen to be along a power line.

The bending of the antennas, in Westcott's opinion, was not due to an object travelling at high speed and striking the two aerials. Centre for UFO Studies investigator Allen Hendry was widely quoted as saying that the bends occurred from an impact with an object. Westcott suggested that the aerials bent after whipping forward when the brakes were applied and struck the red outside dome light on the roof. In support of this, Westcott noted two melted indentations in the rear of the dome light that could have been caused in that manner, and the bends were at appropriate heights in the antennas, each with discoloration of the metal. The aerials were taken to the Honeywell Labs in Minneapolis, which concluded that they were bent "by force" and "not heat." The magnetic pattern scan done on the car showed it was not subjected to a strong magnetic field.

When Val Johnson was found by Officer Everett Doolittle, he was slumped forward over the steering wheel and in mild shock. A bruise later appeared on Johnson's forehead, presumably caused by impact with the steering wheel. He was dazed, and said that "everything was in slow motion. " He had an excruciating pain in his eyes, and, having done some welding in his career, knew what welders' burn was like, comparing his pain to this.

"It was as if someone had hit me in the face with a 400 pound pillow, " he said of the sensation of his head. However, he stated repeatedly that the only pain he experienced was from his eyes. Later, a dentist found that Johnson's bridgework was broken at the gums, yet he had not complained of swelling or pain in his mouth.

Then, there was the other physical evidence. When Everett Doolittle arrived on the scene, Val Johnson's police car was front-end-first in the left-hand ditch, with the rear sticking out into the road. The impact point was determined by the location of the broken glass of the headlight on the road, 290 metres from where the car was found. From that point, yaw marks (described as faint skid marks caused by putting a car out of gear without applying the brakes) travelled in a straight line for 260 metres down the road. Here, these became dark skid marks to where the car stopped moving, going in a straight line for most of the remaining length, and turning abruptly at the end toward the ditch.

A right headlight was broken. There was a round dent, approximately two and a half centimetres in diameter, directly over the master brake cylinder, on the hood, as if someone had hit it with a hammer. The windshield of the car was cracked in the shape of a teardrop on the driver's side. Testing of the glass by the Ford Motor Company suggested that there were signs of both inward and outward motion of the windshield. The roof light had its glass knocked out. The police radio antenna on the centre of the roof was bent about 13 centimetres up from the roof, at about a 45 degree angle. The CB antenna on the trunk was bent near its tip, at an angle near 90 degrees, eight centimetres from the top.

After much debate, investigators eventually concluded that the incident was inconsistent with the theory of the car having been struck by an object of some sort, including ball lightning. The idea of hits by multiple objects was considered and found marginally tenable. However, there are 39 minutes to account for, a complex sequence of impacts by several objects, and some effects caused at a short distance that still need satisfactory explanations. Actions by unknown individuals can be included in the list of possibilities.

Something very unusual happened that morning. At the present time, there is no adequate explanation for the effects noted in the case, based on the proposed theories. Many questions still remain unanswered, and they may remain unanswered for some time to come. The Stephen, Minnesota, incident is listed in UFOROM files as *unknown*.

Did You Know?

One in 10 people
in North America have seen a UFO.

7

THE EIGHTIES

THE MOSCOW JELLYFISH, CHERNOBYL, AND THE BANANA CRAFT: A TIMELINE

June 14, 1980

The Moscow "jellyfish" is one of the best-known UFO cases to come of out of the Soviet Union. On June 14, 1980, an enormous object shaped like an upside-down U was seen over Kalinin, near Moscow. It had several strands of glowing gas that streamed downward, like tentacles. Hundreds of people, including many scientists, witnessed the spectacle. Some residents were so taken with the appearance of the jellyfish that they ran into the streets, convinced it was an American nuclear attack.

The sighting caused considerable controversy that persisted for years, and it was only after the Soviet policy on secrecy was loosened somewhat that an explanation was possible. We now know that the sighting of the jellyfish coincided with the launch of Cosmos 1188 from the then-secret cosmodrome at Plesetsk, north of Moscow. In fact, it is believed that many of the Soviet UFO reports are due to experimental launches from various secret facilities throughout the continent, and that a label of *UFO* was advantageous in covering up some classified activities.

August 1980

Many people reported unusual lights in the skies over Tientsin and Bo Hai in China in the August of 1980, but only a few months later, a UFO was tracked on radar near Tientsin on October 16. Chinese air traffic control was tracking routine air traffic when a return they assumed was an expected incoming flight appeared on the screen. The blip mysteriously disappeared and they contacted the pilot to see what had happened. To their surprise, they realized the airliner was not the return they had detected, but was not yet in range. When the airliner finally did come into view, the mysterious unknown blip appeared once again, crossing their screens in the opposite direction of the airliner. As another flight came by, the unknown object vanished then reappeared again. In addition, the air traffic control tower heard some radio interference, which caused some concern.

Shortly before this, on October 5, 1980, a schoolteacher in Tangshan was awakened by a bright light outside her window just prior to 4:00 a.m. She woke her husband and the two of them watched an illuminated, cigar-shaped object with a ring around its middle fly slowly across the sky, heading into the southeast. Investigators found four additional witnesses who had seen the same object while fishing on a beach.

January 1981

A compelling case for the physical existence of UFOs is that of Trans-en-Provence. This sighting was investigated by police as well as GEIPAN, France's official government department involved in studying reports of unidentified flying objects.

On January 8, at 5:00 p.m., Renato Niccolai was at home on sick leave from his work as a technician. He was outside his house when he heard a strange whistling sound and looked up to see a dull-grey, disc-shaped object with a ring around it descending from the sky. It eventually landed on a terrace beside his garden about 50 metres away. Niccolai walked closer to where he could get a better view of the object and saw that it was more like a "bulging disk like two plates glued to each other by the rim, with a central ring some 20 cm wide." The odd craft was relatively small, only about two and a half metres in diameter and one and a half in height, resting on some stubby legs that looked like upside-down buckets.

After just four seconds on the ground, the object rose into the air and flew away, disappearing into the east. The entire sighting lasted only about 30 seconds.

Niccolai then walked over to where the craft had rested on the ground and discovered two long "skid marks" in the soil. When his wife returned from work at about 9:00 p.m., he told her about what he had seen but she didn't believe him. This was mostly because he joked with her by saying, "Your cat is back. Extraterrestrials brought him home." It was the next day before she went and looked at the site and then told a neighbour, who reported the incident to the police.

Investigators took samples of plants from the affected and non-affected areas a day after the event, then 15 days later, and again 40 days later. However, critics have found that the samples were not gathered methodically and that errors in the sampling invalidated the process. Despite this, an analysis of the plants within the marks were said to show "the action of an energy field" or a "beam of pulsed microwaves."

A skeptical French ufologist proposed an explanation for the case that includes all of the reported details. Niccolai's neighbour is an ardent believer in UFOs, and so it was suggested that Niccolai concocted a simple hoax in which he made up the sighting and then claimed that the marks in the soil, likely from a terrestrial wheeled vehicle, were from the saucer.

July 24, 1981

At about 10:30 p.m., perhaps the most remarkable UFO sighting in China took place. Literally thousands of people in 12 provinces across China reported seeing a large, bright object shaped like a spiral flying through the night sky. Some witnesses in Guizhau likened it to a dragon while others called it a flying saucer, suggesting that some information from Western media had been making it to the Chinese population over the years.

Several students at Kunming Medical College in Yunnan Province watched the UFO with binoculars as it progressed rapidly through the sky. The object had at its core a disc or lens that had a row of windows on its upper part. The centre was bluish-green, and it was surrounded by a spiral of light, making the entire thing about four times as wide as the full Moon. A farmer had seen the object as a Moon-sized disc, from which sprouted a tail that made a spiral as it rotated. The New China News Agency published stories about the sighting throughout the next few months.

This 1981 incident was almost exactly like an event of December 9, 2009, when a very strange sight was observed over Scandinavia and parts of Russia. A large, blue spiral of light slowly wound its way across the sky as seen from Oslo, Norway, and many other places, including Trondelag and northern Sweden. The beautiful spiral display lasted for several minutes, changing shape and size as it progressed. Thousands of people saw the bizarre phenomenon, and speculation as to its cause ranged from an interdimensional portal opened up because of the testing of the Large Hadron Collider in Switzerland, to the end of the world.

Eventually, the phenomenon was found to be the result of a malfunctioning Russian ballistic missile which had a rocket valve stuck open during its flight. The spiral was the missile's gas jet shooting out at right angles to its flight, creating a spiral effect.

In Their Own Words

Spanish Fork City, Utah
December 15, 2005

At 3:30 a.m., my friend and I went on a little drive to see the UFO activity in Utah Valley. We focused our attention the night sky above Spanish Fork City and the Spanish Fork City Airport.

Both of us were absolutely astounded, to say the least — as we approached Spanish Fork City from the north — when we observed one of the biggest UFOs that I've ever seen. The diamond-shaped UFO was floating slowly, about 300 feet above this city, moving northbound.

We were fascinated with the camouflaging measures used by this sinister looking spaceship. Reproduced into this massive UFOs outer shell were high intensity discharge lamps of the city of "Woodland Hills" which is a few miles south.

Looking directly at this UFO, one may very well be inclined to believe that they are merely looking at some boring city lights, which we are all so familiar with. This, I believe, is exactly what the Aliens are counting on. In my opinion, it is an absolutely ingenious camouflaging measure.

As I gazed wide-eyed and open-mouthed at this colossal craft-which I estimated to be about three city-blocks wide and two blocks tall (please excuse my inarticulate and unscientific terminology) — I had an inexplicable and conclusive feeling that I was looking at an "airborne Alien nursery!"

Both of us were also very intrigued by the appearance of two "EYES," human looking in every way — about six-feet in diameter — which were placed into the sides of the UFOs outer shell. The technology which the spaceship exhibited in placing so many lights, of various sizes which matched all of the lights of Woodland Hills, revealed a high degree of intelligence — in my opinion — of those who possessed and piloted it!

At the Spanish Fork Airport at 5:30a.m. — as we sat parked — we observed a strange sight. Rolling slowly down the runway — escorted by a low-flying, egg-shaped UFO, was some type of wheeled unit — which appeared to be some type of "star projector." It was close in size to a typical "potato chip" truck. An astounding number of glistening lights — all of which had the appearance of "stars" — covered this mysterious contraption.

The "projector" looked to be rolling down the runway of the airport. I knew, however, that it could be somewhere else, perhaps far beyond our locale. I have been aware now, for some time, that the Aliens have the technology to mask the precise locations of their hardware and activities, by making their appearance seem always to be "distant" as one approaches those areas.

At 7:30 a.m., as we made our way home, I casually looked back towards Spanish Fork, and was amazed to see two "black helicopters" attending to a slow moving cloud-shaped precisely like the massive UFO which we had been observing with interest throughout the night! It crept slowly away, at the same speed as all of the clouds around it, until it rose up gracefully above the nearby mountains and disappeared.

Reported by T.C.
Source: UFOCasebook.com

October 1981

A Russian pilot on a routine mission encountered a UFO when a ball of light, estimated to be about five metres in diameter, suddenly appeared nearby his MiG jet. As he continued to fly, watching the object, his radio stopped working and his engine cut out. The object moved to a position behind the plane and an explosion was heard and felt in the tail section. The object vanished and the plane's engine started functioning again, likely to the relief of the pilot who was able to land safely. Investigators believed the effects were caused by highly charged plasma.

A year earlier, on June 14, 1980, a retired colonel in the Soviet army claimed that at his home in Russia one evening, he heard a strange "booming" noise and saw a spherical object hanging in the sky only 90 metres away from him. He ran towards it to investigate but found himself struggling to make progress as if he were wading through thick molasses. Finally, when he was within about 50 metres of the object, he found he could walk normally. He approached the object, which he could now see was hemispherical on its underside, and bulbous above. The booming sound was now accompanied by a whizzing noise like an aircraft engine and the object emitted three blasts of light towards the ground and ascended higher into the sky. It hovered in place for a few seconds, moved away a short distance, then completely vanished.

Looking around, the officer saw another strange, lighted object over some trees, and when he went inside his apartment building and looked out from an upper-floor window, he could see other objects as well. About 30 other people, including military personnel and scientists, had also observed these or similar UFOs that same night. Investigations revealed that two Soviet satellites had been launched that night, and it was suggested that this was what had been seen by the witnesses, although the Colonel's experiences seem to be something more than this.

March 13, 1982

Several teenagers were walking together during the evening in Messel, Germany. At 9:10 p.m., they saw three clusters of lights up in the sky, each with four lights flashing different colours. The first group moved slowly and then stopped in midair; the second group moved slowly through the sky; and the third group of lights flew quickly and disappeared. The other two did the same. At about 9:30 p.m., these teenagers were called to look at something else in the sky. A bright flash like a rotating spotlight was slowly moving through the air, and then a metallic blue, domed, disc-shaped object appeared over some trees about 300 metres from them. As it moved towards them, they could see it was about 12 metres wide, and its dome was segmented with different colours, while inside it a light rotated. Other coloured lights flashed around its rim, and there were four white steady lights on the disc's surface. After a while, the disc started to descend to the ground, alighted briefly, then took off and flew away out of sight. The witnesses called the police to report what they saw, but when the officers arrived the object of course was gone.

September 7, 1984

In January 1985, *Tass*, the Soviet news agency, made public some details of a strange UFO encounter near Minsk. On September 7, 1984, Aeroflot Flight 8352 was flying from Tbilisi to Tallinn at 4:10 a.m. when the pilot reported seeing a yellow, starlike object to the right and slightly above their heading. As he watched, a thin beam of light shot downwards from the light source, and the beam then opened up into a broad cone. The witness pointed it out to others on the flight deck and they watched as another cone of light appeared, this time not quite as bright as the original.

The first witness had time to make a sketch of what he was seeing, and he saw that on the ground, illuminated by the beam of light, he could clearly see houses, highways, and trees, despite the hour of night. The beam suddenly turned from the ground to the aircraft, and the crew were dazzled by the intense light now directed at them. The source of the light flared outward and became a green cloud, which appeared to be approaching the aircraft at high speed.

The pilot radioed air traffic control in Minsk and as he did so, the object stopped its approach then dropped below the altitude of the plane, maneuvered somewhat, and took up a position directly opposite them, pacing their progress. It maintained speed and position while the airliner was flying at 10,000 metres and 800 kilometres an hour. The crew could now see that there were individual lights within the "cloud" that seemed to be moving erratically and flashing off and on. As they watched, the cloud then appeared to take on solid form, first developing a tail then forming a square or rectangle out of its oval body.

A stewardess came into the flight deck to say that the passengers wanted to know what the green object flying beside the plane was. The pilot directed her to tell them it was simply a cloud, reflecting the northern lights. He then got confirmation from air traffic control that they could also see flashes of light near the plane, and word that another airliner was nearby but its pilot could not see anything at all. Only when the second airliner had approached to within about

15 kilometres did its pilot see the object, and was able to describe it exactly as the first crew detailed. In 1985, the prestigious and conservative Soviet Academy of Sciences itself issued a statement saying that after investigation, the case was deemed unusual and that the object was a true UFO.

July 22, 1985

At 5:45 p.m., two Zimbabwe Air Force jets were scrambled from Thornhill Air Base in response to UFO reports from Bulawayo and other towns in the western part of the country. The object was observed by airport personnel and also tracked on radar. It was described as a disc-shaped object with a cone on top, shining so brightly in the afternoon sun that it was difficult to look at directly.

"This was no ordinary UFO," an air marshal was recorded as saying. "It was no illusion, no deception, no imagination." When the jets arrived over the city, they found the UFO at an altitude of 2,100 metres, but it immediately shot upwards to 21,000 metres in only a minute. The jets pursued to about 9,100 metres then broke off their chase. The object was seen again briefly near the ground, and then it flew off across the horizon at high speed and was lost to sight. When asked to comment on the incident, the director general of air operations said, "We believe implicitly that the unexplained UFOs are from some civilization beyond our planet."

UFOs and Aliens in Movies

Uforia (1980) is an underrated story of a checkout clerk played by Cindy Williams, who thinks she's been chosen by aliens to carry their message of peace to the masses. She attracts quite a following, and there's lots of resemblance to *Elmer Gantry* when her boyfriend begins exploiting her as a contactee who is acting as the aliens' ambassador. But then it seems the government is taking her seriously for some reason ...

April, 1986

Amazingly, there is some speculation that UFOs were blamed for the Chernobyl nuclear accident on April 26, 1986. On that day, it was reported that technicians rushing to the scene of the fire in unit 4 at 4:15 a.m. saw a brass-coloured, spherical object hanging in the sky about 300 metres from the reactor. It was moving very slowly, and two red beams of light were shining from it onto the reactor building. After three minutes, the beams of light disappeared and the UFO moved off to the northwest. "Were UFOs to blame for the tragedy?" asked a sensational Russian tabloid.

September 27, 1989

The most bizarre Russian UFO case on record is certainly that which happened on September 27, 1989. It came during a rash of UFO sightings near Voronezh, about 320 kilometres south of Moscow. At 6:30 p.m., commuters and schoolchildren were in Western Park when they saw a pink haze in the sky, like a bonfire seen through mist. As they watched, a silver ball came out of the mist and came down to the Earth, bending treetops as it flew over them. As it came nearer, they saw the object was actually shaped like a banana. As the witnesses looked up, a door or portal opened in its side and a humanoid creature poked its head out, then popped back inside. The door closed, and the weird craft descended lower into the trees and extended landing gear into the soil. The door opened again and out came several creatures who scrambled down to the ground and walked towards the onlookers.

At this point, the story gets confusing, with many different details claimed by different witnesses. Some say that a robot came out of the craft and approached a boy, who was screaming in terror. The robot's eyes glowed and the boy was frozen, unable to move or make a sound. Another witness said he saw one of the entities aim a gun of some kind at a man walking away and hit him with a beam of light. The man simply disappeared and only appeared again after the UFO left, as if he had never been gone. Other aliens supposedly walked over to an electrical pole and climbed it, but did not expect the high voltage. They immediately caught fire and disappeared in a shower of sparks!

Investigators took soil samples, interviewed witnesses, and videotaped the area, looking for clues. They uncovered many other sightings that residents had been having for months in the same region. Many children had claimed to see a variety of alien beings and odd, lighted craft nearby. Soviet news agencies wrote about it for many weeks, carrying stories from a variety of perspectives. The incident as a whole has never been explained other than by attributing it to children's imaginations, although there were many adults who also reported UFOs in the area.

RENDLESHAM

It was just after midnight on the morning of Boxing Day, December 26, 1980. Near Suffolk, England, personnel stationed at Royal Air Force Woodbridge and RAF Bentwaters were enjoying a quiet time during the Christmas season. There were no planes in the air, none scheduled to land or take off, and only a skeleton crew was maintaining the bases.

Airman First Class John Burroughs was posted at RAF Woodbridge's back gate, called the East Gate. With him was Staff Sergeant Bud Steffens, a long-time member of the air force. As they talked to get through the monotony, Burroughs noticed some odd lights hovering low in the sky, near the edge of Rendlesham Forest not far from the base. The lights were flickering and flashing red, yellow, and green, dancing through the trees. Because they were certain they had not seen the lights before and they seemed close to the base, Burroughs and Steffens decided to investigate. They left their post and drove off the base, soon discovering that the lights were much closer than they had first thought. As they neared the area from where the lights seemed to originate, another light, this one very bright white, appeared and moved towards them. Nervous, they turned around and went back to the base to ask for some help.

Back at their post, they called Sergeant McCabe inside the base and excitedly took turns telling him what they had seen. McCabe thought that the lights may have been from a plane crash and contacted the main security control centre, who dispatched Staff Sergeant James Penniston, the flight chief on duty that night at RAF Woodbridge. When Penniston got to the East Gate and heard Burroughs and Steffens' story, he went to further investigate, taking with him Burroughs and another airman first class, Ed Cabansag. Steffens was too anxious to join them.

They drove along the edge of the base, following a logging road that quickly became impassable because of ruts and potholes. They decided to continue on foot, leaving Cabansag at the truck to remain in radio communication with the base. As they did, they received word that Woodbridge had heard from London's Heathrow airport that an unidentified object had been seen on radar near their area.

Penniston and Burroughs continued into the forest towards the lights, encountering many agitated animals that were fleeing the area. The men were getting uneasy, too. They realized that if the lights were from a burning plane, they would have seen evidence of a fire by this time, and the lights seemed to be more ordered and in a distinct group. For some reason the hair on their necks and hands was standing straight, as if they were near an electric field of some kind, and then their radios seemed to cut out. They became disoriented and felt as if they were having to struggle with every step, "like everything seemed slower than you were actually doing and stuff."

By this time, they were close to the object with the array of lights. It was about three metres tall and three metres wide at its base, but tapered to a cone, with blue lights around its middle. It was solidly standing upright, although no landing gear was visible. Penniston ventured close enough to touch it, noting its surface was smooth and hard, like glass.

On Boxing Day, 1980, military personnel at RAF Bentwaters and RAF Woodbridge investigated reports of a light in trees near the base. They found a cone shaped object moving through the forest.

Back at the truck, Cabansag saw an unusual object through the trees appear near where his colleagues had gone. Just to the side of the beacon of a lighthouse just off the coast, he saw an egg-shaped object with lights around its middle, flashing blue, white, and red. Despite suggestions to the contrary, he insisted that the object he saw was not the lighthouse.

UFO Hotspot: Stephenville, Texas

In 2008, UFOs began appearing in great numbers in and around this town, resulting in international attention. Sightings continue today.

Penniston leisurely examined the object, taking notes in his logbook and photographs with his camera. He described it as "triangular in shape ... at the left centre is a bluish light, and on the other side, red ... a small amount of white light peers out the bottom." Some symbols were etched or embossed upon the side of the object, and when he touched the lettering, the object's lights intensified, frightening the men. They moved back just as the object rose silently off the ground, then began to move erratically back and forth through the trees until it was about 30 metres away. It ascended over the trees, "and then literally with the blink of an eye it was gone."

The men found that with the departure of the object, their world and perception of it came back to normal. But they then saw another light moving in the forest an estimated 800 metres away, so they went towards it briefly before they realized they had been out too long already and turned back. When they reached the clearing, they found three triangular "landing gear marks" about three metres apart. They left the area, rejoined Cabansag, and travelled back to the base.

At the base, they were told to keep quiet about what they had seen, but were directed to go back into the forest and search for some physical evidence that would confirm and support their experience. So, they went out again, not knowing what they would find, but hoping it would be something that would affirm their story.

They found the three indentations, and also some nearby trees with scorched leaves. Plaster casts were made of the indentations, which seemed to be proof of their experiences. But when the local police investigated the area themselves, their report said only that lights had been seen and that marks like "rabbit scratchings" had been found, and nothing more.

Pennsiton and Burroughs seemed very shaken by their experience, and became reclusive, even seeking out transfers from the base.

Later that day, Lieutenant-Colonel Charles Halt, deputy base commander, returned from his short Christmas holiday and heard the story of what had transpired the night before. He interviewed Cabansag and was amazed at what had supposedly happened to the three men, but being a UFO skeptic, he doubted their story.

As it turned out, Halt was away from the base the following night, December 27, 1980, when more unusual events began unfolding outside the gate. This time, four men stationed there saw lights moving over the trees again that seemed to drop into the forest. They received permission to drive off the base and entered the forest, where they heard a deep humming sound and saw fog laying over a field. There were lights embedded in the fog, and they also felt some kind of electricity in the air.

Another patrol had heard about the lights and went to investigate as well. Eventually, one of them found Halt and told him that the lights had returned. Halt organized a detailed expedition, arming his men with Geiger counters, cameras, tape recorders, sampling materials, and portable lights. But when Halt and his team arrived at the edge of the forest, meeting the other personnel who had been sent to investigate, they encountered difficulties with the personnel carriers he had brought. Nevertheless, he found what appeared to be a landing site, with indentations on the ground and broken branches in the trees. The Geiger counter seemed to be registering radiation above the normal background levels, and the men noticed that animals in the area seemed very agitated.

Suddenly, they saw a bizarre object, only about 150 metres away. It looked like a large, glowing red eye, with a black pupil in its centre. It was giving off flashes of light and dancing through the trees, even appearing to wink at them. Halt later insisted to investigators that this eye was not the lighthouse, which he could see some distance away. The strange light disappeared, only to reappear again later, emitting sparks or smaller lights that fell towards the ground. The object exploded before their eyes and vanished, but they noticed three starlike lights low to the horizon in the north and south, which they believed were connected with the sighting. These lights remained in the sky, dancing about their positions and changing colours for several hours, sometimes shining what the men thought were beams of light to the ground, as if searching for something.

The third major night of sightings was said to have taken place on December 28, 1980. The main witness this time was Larry Warren, an airman stationed at RAF Bentwaters, another base near Woodbridge. He had joined the air force only a few months earlier in 1980 as a young, 18-year-old recruit. Around midnight on December 28, and in the early morning hours of December 29, Warren claims that he had his own series of encounters with a UFO and met its alien occupants. He also said that in his debriefing by his superiors on the base, he was told that aliens had a "permanent presence" on Earth. Warren's story, although very detailed and bolstered by transcripts of interviews with witnesses of the previous nights' events, remains unsupported by tangible evidence.

The Bentwaters case was leaked to UFO investigators only a few days after it occurred. Years of slow, careful investigation by researchers uncovered more and more details, and found reluctant military witnesses eventually willing to give their testimonies. An official USAF memo was obtained by researchers documenting what had occurred.

The audio recording made by Lieutenant-Colonel Halt on the second night of the incidents was made available to researchers as well, although much of the dialogue is unintelligible due to background and transcription noise. Nevertheless, it is a valuable piece of supportive evidence that bolsters the credibility of the case.

There is no question that something remarkable occurred outside RAF Bentwaters and Woodridge at Christmastime in 1980. There is enough evidence and testimony to indicate that a series of lighted objects was observed by civilian and military witnesses, though exactly what the lights were is a matter of conjecture.

Skeptics have often pointed to the fact that a Russian satellite was re-entering the atmosphere about the time of the UFO incidents, as well as to the existence of a lighthouse on the other side of the forest. Many people across Europe saw flaming satellite debris as it streaked across the sky on December 25 and 26, 1980. And on the ground, at least a few people misidentified the lighthouse as a UFO. However, neither explanation fits all the details of the witnesses' observations. The objects seen at close range certainly were not re-entering satellite debris, nor were they a distant light source. Furthermore, the duration of the sightings make a short-lived re-entry display unlikely, and some witnesses who were familiar with the area insist they saw the lighthouse in addition to the UFO. Similarly, the military witnesses were familiar with aircraft crash scenes, having investigated many in their tours of duty.

In one rigorous analysis of all the testimony, transcripts, site visits, and physical evidence, the series of Rendelsham events has been explained as a combination of misidentification of meteors, stars, and the lighthouse, and by possible electromagnetic experiments at Orford Ness, a nearby military research facility. The effects of experimentation at Orford Ness, according to this theory, could have affected the minds of the witnesses, inducing illusions that were then aggravated by the real light sources.

Of course, the testimony of Colonel Halt, who insists his observations were not of any astronomical objects or navigation lights, remains puzzling. Something happened in Rendlesham Forest that Christmas, but what?

In Their Own Words

San Rafael, California
June 19, 1995

At about 9:45 p.m., I was outside enjoying the beautiful clear and cool night sky. I saw, on a line 1/3 of the way to Mars from Jupiter was another object, just slightly larger than Jupiter and about twice as bright. It was stationary, as if hovering. I am fairly familiar with the night sky and immediately knew that the additional object between Jupiter and Mars was not normally there.

My guesstimate of the proximity of the object would place it no nearer than the Golden Gate Bridge or further South than the San Francisco Airport, relative to my viewpoint. After a 4 or 5 second hover, the object began to slowly move upward towards Jupiter. At this point, I called to a nearby associate to join me outside.

During the three seconds while I was waiting for my friend to arrive outside, the bright light/object continued to rise and accelerate at a 45 degree angle towards the South, which appeared as going directly away and up. By the time my friend had arrived the light had shrunk from slightly larger than Jupiter to a red dot about the size of Mars.

When it stopped climbing, it turned, without stopping, and I mean on a dime, to the East and continued to acceler-ate. At this point, it was traveling perhaps 4 or 5 times faster than any satellite I have ever watched.

The object continued East for about 4 or 5 seconds and then, again without stopping and on a dime, turned directly North and put the pedal to the metal. Total time elapsed for the sighting was about 30 seconds. It left no vapor trail. It just quickly went way up, over and away. Once it turned North, it took about 10 seconds to disappear in the Northern sky.

Reported by G.K.
Source: Ufology Research

THE BELGIAN WAVE

One of the most remarkable series of European UFO sightings in recent memory occurred in Belgium from 1989 to 1991. It involved multiple witnesses, military and government investigations, countrywide skywatches, and both photographs and video of something strange moving in the night sky. The number of reports is staggering — about 3,500 sightings, a quarter of which were investigated by ufologists. In surveys of ufologists asking them to rank the best cases of all time, the Belgian wave is often cited.

It began, unfortunately, with a multi-witness UFO sighting on November 25, 1989, near Limbourg, which was explained relatively easily. Many people reported seeing large disc-shaped patches of light that moved about the clouds and sometimes circled overhead, then darted away. Investigators quickly found that the owner of a popular nightclub had been using a strong spotlight projector to shine a rotating beam of light on the underside of the cloud cover. It was such a striking display that Belgian Air Force jets had been scrambled to intercept the intruder one night, eventually leading to officials pulling the plug on the searchlight.

The Belgian wave began again in earnest on November 29, 1989, at about 5:30 p.m. Two police officers were driving from Eupen to Kettenis, when they saw a bright light moving slowly over a field near the road. They decided to head it off by driving to where it seemed as if it would pass over the highway, and sure enough it did. They watched as the object noiselessly moved over the road, stopped, made a U-turn, and headed back from whence it came. The witnesses said it was a dark object in the shape of a triangle, with three bright lights, one at each corner, and a red flashing light "like a fire truck" in the centre.

The officers drove back to Eupen, and learned that there had not been any civilian or military aircraft scheduled in the area. At 6:30 p.m., they drove back out into the countryside to a vantage point that would afford a better view of the surrounding area. They reported seeing the object again, this time stationary and low over a lake, but it seemed to be more internally active, with beams of light shooting out, and fire balls that seemed to pop out of it occasionally.

Suddenly, they were surprised to see another group of lights rise into the air from behind some trees. It, too, looked like a dark triangle, this time with a greenish pallor, and it also appeared to have a row of windows on its side. It turned in flight, moved in a spiral path, and headed out of sight by about 8:30 p.m.

Other police officers who had been listening in on their radios as the sighting unfolded also reported seeing odd lights in the sky. One officer actually saw the

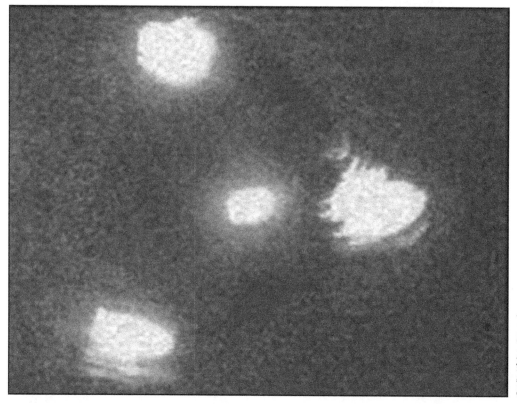

Credit: Ufology Research.

In 1989, many people in Belgium saw triangular formations of lights flying overhead. One photograph was taken by a man who continues to remain anonymous.

triangular object, its white lights and central red light, but also a turbine spinning at its trailing edge. Others heard the distinct sound of a generator or motor whirring. This has led some investigators to suggest that the triangular object may have simply been a blimp or ultralight aircraft maneuvering in the night, without a flight plan. As for the light that was stationary near the horizon and shooting out other beams of light, investigators noted that the planet Venus was in the exact direction that this object was seen, and that no witness reported seeing both the planet and the UFO.

The next major sighting was on December 1, 1989, when a Belgian Air Force meteorologist and his daughter saw a triangular object moving slowly in the sky over the town of Ans. Then, on December 11, many people in Liège and other cities saw several lights moving about in the night sky. One man said he even watched as an egg-shaped object made a loud humming noise while apparently stuck in a tree. It also had three bright white lights and a structure of some kind. After a short while, it freed itself and flew away. Investigators combed the area and examined the tree the next day, but had no explanation for what was seen, other than a possible nighttime blimp.

A remarkable press conference was held on December 12 in Brussels — a cooperative venture with the Belgian Air Force, the Eupen police, and the civilian UFO group Société Belge d'Etude des Phénomènes Spatiaux (SOBEPS). Media were told that an official investigation was underway, and that the origin of the UFOs was going to be found through in-depth investigations conducted by all groups involved. Hundreds of cases were soon under investigation, a unique partnership between government, military, and civilian organizations.

Things happened quite quickly. On December 21, 1989, the Belgian minister of defense released a statement about the investigations. He noted that the UFOs were not related to military activities, and were not radar patrols, American F-117A fighters, remote control drones, or ultralight aircraft. Some ufologists thought that the UFOs might have been secret military aircraft anyway, and the UFO story was just a cover. A statement was made, however, that should there be another reliable case of a triangular craft, the Belgian Air Force would scramble American F-16 fighters to investigate.

8

THE NINETIES

THE BELGIAN WAVE CONTINUES

Sightings continued in Belgium well into the 1990s, following the wave of 1989. Perhaps the most remarkable night of the entire UFO wave was the night of March 30–31, 1990. On that night, hundreds of people reported seeing UFOs in the skies over Belgium. Most were stationary lights, but some seemed to be moving about. At 10:50 p.m., a police officer in the village of Ramilles reported seeing a UFO, and police in Wavre confirmed his observation. They notified a Belgian Air Force radar station at Glons that three lights in a triangular formation were again flying nearby, and the NATO base at Semmerzake confirmed an unknown target.

The Belgian Air Force made good on their promise, and two F-16s were sent out. One pilot was told to videotape his radar screen, while the other was asked to record his field of view. No visual images were recorded, but the radar showed 13 separate lock-ons of unidentified targets. Some of these targets moved slowly, at about 270 kilometres per hour, before accelerating to 1,800. At times, the targets appeared to drop from an altitude of 2,700 metres to 1,500 in only a few seconds. One even crossed directly in front of the jets without being visually identified. The Belgian Air Force reported: "Each time the pilots were able to secure a lock on one of the targets for a few seconds, a drastic change in the behavior of the detected targets occurred."

The anomalous radar tapes were analyzed and explained to be the result of processing defects within the on-board computers. At least one of the lock-ons was one F-16 accidentally targeting the other! The other targets were nothing but ground clutter, and the lights in the sky were bright stars and planets.

These explanations did not satisfy the Belgian public or the international community, who were suspicious of official pronouncements about UFOs — especially since on March 31, the day after the radar case, a man in Brussels shot a video of the infamous triangular craft. It had all the earmarks of the classic Belgian triangle: three white lights, a red flashing light, and steady movement. But even SOBEPS had to concede that the video was simply of a plane taking off from an airport.

Throughout the entire Belgian UFO wave, only one photograph has held up to scrutiny, at least partially. It has been regarded as proof that something strange was occurring in the skies over Belgium. A member of a photography club near Petit-Rechain, near Liège, took a photo that clearly shows a dark, triangular object with three bright lights on its corners and a fourth red light in its centre. SOBEPS and other ufologists believe that this is an authentic photograph of the object that harangued Belgian townspeople for more than two years. The three corner lights themselves show some structure, perhaps being composed of a group of smaller lights. Yet even this evidence is problematic; the exact date of the sighting and photograph is unknown, and there are no reference points on the image that would indicate how large it is or how far away it is from the observer. Further, the authenticity of the photo is complicated by the story that it was supposedly put in a drawer and forgotten about for four months until the photographer (who remains anonymous) was questioned by a reporter about it.

Ultimately, as with all UFO waves, the large number of cases that compose the Belgian wave can be boiled down to a relatively small number of unexplained events once misidentifications of ordinary phenomena are excluded.

One of the more unusual cases took place on the night of October 21, 1990, near the town of Bastogne. Two people were driving home, when they were shocked to see two bright lights coming down from the sky, apparently heading for them. The lights disappeared behind some trees, but then as the car came around a hedge its occupants were confronted by a strange lighted object only about 15 metres away on their right side. They continued to drive, panicky, but the object kept with them until they finally stopped in fright. They could see

UFOs and Aliens in Movies

Probably the true forerunner of the *X-Files, Hangar 18* (1980), out-Roswelled the popular stories about a crashed UFO at Roswell, presenting a military base where a crashed saucer is under study. Another example of fiction meeting fact, Hangar 18 was a real location at Wright-Patterson Air Force Base in which debris from a crashed flying saucer from Roswell was (or is) allegedly housed. In the movie, when a saucer collides with a NASA vehicle, it's all quickly hushed up because it's election time. Can the heroic astronauts find the saucer in time? Aliens = good. Government = bad.

it was actually a dark craft, about 13 metres in diameter, with a ring of seven or eight lights on its underside. It continued to move, and rose swiftly into the air before vanishing from view.

By the middle of 1991, the Belgian UFO wave was over. Sightings had dwindled to a comparative trickle, and residents were left wondering what had really occurred during those frenetic few years.

In Their Own Words

Whitehorse, Yukon
December 25, 2005

I was watching UFO invasion: Rendlesham on TV and the description of the craft almost was exactly what I saw on Christmas Eve by my grandmas that is about 40 km outside Whitehorse.

We were driving on the road going out of my grandmas when my dad said he saw something and told my mom to stop the vehicle. We got out of the car and looked about 40 feet from us and 200 feet in the air and it was a UFO.

It couldn't have been anything else because it made absolutely no sound and it had three lights connected like a triangle and it had no other lights and it was completely black and it was extremely bright and it hovered as if it was watching us. Then it started to leave going slowly like it was studying the ground or something.

We followed it for about 7 minutes and then all of sudden it really really just shot out of the sky. We phoned the airport and asked if they were expecting flights tonight and they said they were no planes in the air tonight.

Reported by R.M.
Source: Ufology Research

TRANSFORMERS, SOLAR ECLIPSE, AND LITTLE MEN IN BLACK: A TIMELINE

March 1991

In 2007, a recording of an exchange between a Chinese air traffic controller and a pilot was played at a UFO seminar in Shanghai. The tape was made on March 18, 1991, when a pilot radioed an airport tower that he had seen a fast-moving object near his plane. The object was about three or five metres in length, red in colour, and "spraying fire-like gas and transforming into two objects, a ball and a cube." The object made several mid-air turns, first heading northeast, then southeast, then west, and finally north as it split into the two shapes. They then climbed higher and moved out of sight of the pilot, who was mystified by what he had seen.

July 11, 1991

A well-witnessed UFO over Mexico was seen during a total solar eclipse. To better observe the eclipse, astronomers from all over the world had flocked to the eclipse area stretching from Baja California through Mexico City and beyond. None of them reported seeing anything unusual, but hundreds of lay observers and members of the general public said that they saw a strange object near the obscured sun. Some even claimed to have taken photos and videos of this object. It was in view for only a matter of minutes before and after the depth of the eclipse, and videotapes showed only a bright object in the sky, in some cases leaving a trail as it moved jerkily. Reports claimed that the UFO was seen by people throughout Mexico City, although again it must be noted that no astronomer in the area saw the object, which according to some witnesses looked "metallic."

Astronomers pointed out that during the eclipse, both Jupiter and Venus were east of the Sun's disk and shone brightly during the short darkness. An examination of photos and videos taken of the UFO during the eclipse confirmed that the sources of light seen before, during, and after totality could have simply been planets that became visible because of the sun's brief disappearance.

Not everyone agrees. Abduction researcher Whitley Strieber, in his book *Confirmation*, argues that the objects videotaped could not have been Venus. From his recreations of the conditions of the time of the eclipse, Venus does not look like what is in the Mexican videos. Public opinion following the airing of the videos almost universally supported the view that the UFO observed was not a planet. Furthermore,

UFO sightings continued during the days and weeks following the eclipse. The entire state of Puebla was inundated with reports of strange flying lights in the night sky, some of which had flashed and remained in place for long periods of time, and others that zipped throughout the air.

July 15, 1993

On this day, the USS *Eisenhower*, an aircraft carrier, was north of Puerto Rico on a routine mission. Two seamen on watch at about 3:00 a.m. saw a bright ball of orange light, "big as the Moon," approach the ship from behind, bathing the flight deck and parked aircraft with an eerie glow. It was completely silent, and was only about 23 metres above the water as it flew past the ship. Once it passed the bow, it sped up and shot up into the sky until it was lost to sight.

September 16, 1994

One of the most bizarre African cases took place in Zimbabwe on this day. Teachers at the Ariel School in Ruwa (not far from Harare) were having a morning meeting while their 62 students, between the ages of five and 12, played in the schoolyard. A young boy ran into the school "tuck shop" (snack bar), where he told the adult there that something had landed in the schoolyard and that a "little man" was running around with the children. Since the adult thought that the boy was simply being mischievous, she did not go outside to look herself.

The children later explained to their teachers, parents, and the investigators that they had been playing games when they observed as many as five unusual craft flying through the sky and ducking in and around the power lines. Eventually, the craft landed in some brush next to the schoolyard, only about 100 metres away from the students. As the children watched, two small humanoid creatures dressed all in black appeared from one of the objects and walked towards them. The entities had long black hair, large staring eyes, no nose at all, but slit-like mouths, and they walked in a stilted manner.

The children said that the creatures "spoke" to them without using their mouths, through a kind of telepathy. Some children were given warnings about pollution, others that the Earth was going to be destroyed, and still others that humans were too technologically advanced. After a while, the creatures went back to the craft, and according to the children the objects "just went."

The headmaster of the school had all the children draw pictures of what they had seen, and the case was investigated locally by renowned ufologist Cynthia Hind. Later, abduction researcher Dr. John Mack travelled to Zimbabwe from America and spent several days interviewing and counselling the children.

November 4, 1999

In a case from Papua New Guinea, an object described as 200 metres long and 50 metres wide was observed by thousands of people in the Gazelle Peninsula of East New Britain. It made a soft puffing noise as it chugged slowly across the night sky. Members of a remote tribe called the Bainingo, who do not have television and other modern influences, claim they saw a large object, glowing like a "red hot stone" and with "lumps on the sides," moving over the mountain range.

Other people living near the St. George Channel saw a large object moving slowly over the water. Smaller lights seemed to circle the object, and it continued on its way until it reached the mountains of New Ireland, when it rose and passed over them.

At Rangulit, a family was sitting on the verandah of their home when they saw the same large object flying over their mango trees. It was moving slowly and "lit up like a shooting star and it had two very bright lights at the tail." The witnesses were certain it was not an aircraft, of which they are very familiar. As it puffed along, some people lit torches and chased it as it flew ponderously along before it flew out over the sea and was lost to sight.

THE GIANT YUKON SAUCER

The best-documented and most thoroughly investigated recent Canadian UFO case was a multiple-witness event in the Yukon on December 11, 1996. The lead investigator who took on the exhaustive case was ufologist Martin Jasek, who has devoted much effort and expense studying UFO phenomena in the North.

Around 7:00 p.m., four people were travelling north, nearing the town of Carmacks, when they saw a group of lights in the northwest above some nearby hills. They pulled off the highway to get a better look, where they saw the lights seemed to be on a larger unseen object moving across the sky. There were several large orange lights in an oval pattern, with dozens of smaller white lights on the main body. One witness saw only three large orange lights in a row with the other smaller lights to the right side. The object was very large, covering an estimated 60 to 90 degrees of sky, and moved ponderously across their view, vanishing suddenly after approximately 10 minutes.

At the same time, in the town of Carmacks, another family was at home watching television, all facing a large window with a view to the northeast. They saw a row of lights, which at first reminded them of a 747 jet airliner, slowly moving over trees to the northeast. Three young children believed that it was Santa Claus coming early. The silent object, estimated to be at least 30 metres across, had four large red and yellow lights in a row, with smaller orange and green lights trailing. Additionally, there seemed to be "white sparkles" dropping to the ground from the bottom of the object. As it made its way east, the lights went out one by one, as if the object was moving behind trees and was lost to sight after about five minutes.

People in Ufology

Before he died, as a parting shot to ufologists and UFO buffs, renowned debunker Philip J. Klass cast "the UFO Curse" upon all those who believe UFOs are real. It reads: "To ufologists who publicly criticize me, ... or who even think unkind thoughts about me in private, I do hereby leave and bequeath: THE UFO CURSE: No matter how long you live, you will never know any more about UFOs than you know today. You will never know any more about what UFOs really are, or where they come from. You will never know any more about what the U.S. Government really knows about UFOs than you know today. As you lie on your own death-bed you will be as mystified about UFOs as you are today. And you will remember this curse. Signed, Philip J. Klass."

Driving north along the Klondike Highway from Whitehorse to Carmacks, another witness saw a bright white light over the far end of Fox Lake. He watched it during his 16-kilometre trip along the lake, noting some cars parked at a campground halfway along. When he reached the northern end of the lake, he could see that the light seemed to be on a larger object, and was partly illuminating a curved surface. He lost sight of the object briefly, but then saw three rows of rectangular lights slowly moving over the crest of a hill on the east side of the highway away from the lake.

Around the same time as the Fox Lake sightings, a trapper was working his trapline about 15 kilometres east of Pelly Crossing. He was looking west, when he saw a row of lights moving over the hills in the distance. As they approached, he realized they were on an object so large, he had to turn his head from side to side to look at all of it. The object stopped about 3,000 metres away, blocking out the stars across a wide expanse of sky. He estimated the craft was just over a kilometre across and about 250 metres above the trees.

The trapper noted that the row of lights was comprised of as many as 100 individual, rectangular "windows," each approximately two by six metres in size. Above these and centred on the middle of the craft were seven white or yellow rectangular lights. A beam of white light was projected from the bottom of the object, playing upon the ground in front of him. The object made no discernable sound, and was in view for about four minutes before moving behind some trees to the east, where it abruptly vanished.

At about 8:30 p.m., four students were taking a break from classes at Yukon Community College in Pelly Crossing, when one of them noticed some odd lights in the sky. She called it to the others' attention and they all watched a horizontal row of lights in the northwest moving to the northeast. The yellowish lights appeared to be on an object travelling slowly, making no noise, and about the same size as a large aircraft. They all watched the object for about three minutes until it was lost to sight behind a hill in the north.

In total, Jasek interviewed 36 witnesses to this remarkable event, but also received second-hand information about many other witnesses across the Yukon and Northwest Territories that night. He sorted through the testimonies and calculated distances, directions, and a timeline in order to piece together what he believed happened that night. He checked with airports and military bases, but was told that there was no activity in the area at the time of the sightings.

Jasek considered a dozen possible explanations, ranging from hoaxes and hallucinations to satellite reentries and military aircraft. He rejected all of these, giving sensible and logical reasons for his judgment, showing that they "did not adequately explain the data." He concluded in his widely circulated report: "The sightings of a giant UFO in the Yukon Territory on December 11, 1996, by at least 31 people were most likely a product of non-human intelligence and a technology far beyond current scientific knowledge reported by mainstream science."

THE PHOENIX LIGHTS

The night of March 13, 1997, will be remembered for many years in Phoenix, Arizona. It was then that hundreds of people watched formations of lights moving over the city and the surrounding mountains, giving rise to the general belief that a huge, mile-wide aerial craft was manoeuvring over this balmy, populated area. And in the case of the Phoenix Lights, we not only have eyewitness testimony, but many photographs and video apparently showing the strange craft to be real.

Around 7:30 p.m., a cluster of six (or eight) amber-coloured lights was seen over the Superstition Mountains east of Phoenix, then a group of eight or nine additional lights was seen as well. Sightings continued throughout the evening.

At 7:50 p.m., five to seven blue-white lights in a V formation were seen leaving Nevada, entering Arizona airspace, and eventually passing over Prescott on their way south, where they were videotaped at 8:28 p.m. just north of Phoenix. Witnesses said the lights seemed to be getting in the way of aircraft flying in and out of Sky Harbour International Airport, although the airport radar was not detecting the formation. As it flew along I-10, the formation hovered over a car, the passengers of which reported that the lights were now reddish in colour. Then, as witnesses watched, the formation appeared to break into separate lights, each one flying off in a different direction, some over Phoenix.

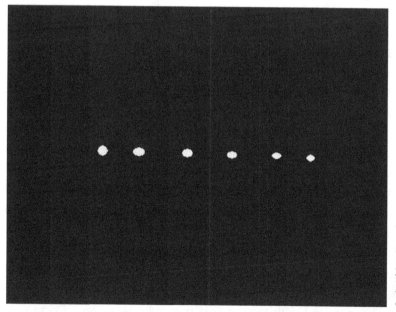

Credit: Ufology Research.

Hundreds of people in the area of Phoenix, Arizona, saw formations of lights flying over the city and desert.

At about 8:15 p.m., a V formation of five white lights flew slowly from the northwest towards Prescott, where witnesses said they could see that the lights were on a single, large, "chevron-shaped" object. It rotated in the air over a witness' house and the lights turned red, shifted to form an arc instead of a V, and zipped away at high speed. Some observers insisted the object was only 30 metres above them, flying at a relatively slow speed of about 15 or 25 kilometres per hour.

There are many reports on record from people who said they saw F-16 jets from the nearby Luke AFB take off to intercept the various objects or lights. Some stories have even surfaced from workers at the base who insist that jets were scrambled and that some gun-camera footage was taken. None of this, however, can be substantiated.

On March 14, 1997, at 3:20 a.m., a caller to the National UFO Reporting Center Hotline said that he was on staff at Luke AFB and watched two F-15C jet fighters get sent up to intercept a large triangular object flying at 5,500 metres over Phoenix. The object did not have any strobe lights as on military or commercial aircraft, and its lights dimmed all at the same time before they went out completely. The caller noted that the F-15Cs are part of the Air Force One Protection Group and are on standby when needed. He also claimed that the jets had gun-camera film of the object, but that their radar only showed "white noise." What were these mysterious lights and V-shaped craft?

Regarding the large object that was seen flying south over I-10 around 8:00 p.m., debunker Tim Printy located witnesses who said it was composed of several individual aircraft, and was not a single large craft. One witness, a pilot, saw the formation of lights and watched them with binoculars: "I saw 5 aircraft with [their] running lights (red and green) and the landing lights (white) on. They were also flying fairly slow and in the delta formation. As they went over me I could see stars going between the aircraft so it could not have been one large ship."

Other pilots also said they saw planes flying that night, which is something that proponents of the alien visitation theory don't usually mention. But wouldn't the airport radar pick up the planes as they flew overhead? An air traffic controller at the Phoenix airport confirmed that no radar returns were detected, but explained that in a formation of planes, only the lead plane would have its transponder on. And, if for some reason its transponder was malfunctioning or was turned off, none of the plane's information would be painted on the radarscope.

But, of course, that doesn't answer the question of who was flying in formation that night, or why. Despite all the publicity surrounding the case, no group of pilots has even come forward admitting it was they who were seen flying over Phoenix that night.

Another possibility is that the strings of lights were flares dropped from military aircraft during a training exercise. This theory is very popular among skeptics and seems to be very reasonable. Ufologist Lynne Kitei, who interviewed hundreds of witnesses and made many public comments about the lights, spoke with information officers at both Luke and Davis-Montham air force bases about the possibility of flares. She was told that aircraft out on nightly flying missions over Goldwater Range near Phoenix do drop flares, but that no planes were in the air that night and that they "never fly over populated areas."

However, on July 25, 1997, the *Arizona Republic* carried a story about how, while planes from the local air force bases were not flying over Phoenix on March 13, 1997, a "visiting" Maryland National Guard squadron was in the area, flying overhead and dropping flares as part of an exercise. Records were released which showed how several planes flew throughout the area during the period of 8:15 p.m. to 10:30 p.m. Later investigations showed that the planes actually landed by 8:30 p.m., so while they might explain some sightings, they could not explain all the reports.

In other words, the flares can explain some of the sightings, but certainly not all of them. Printy makes a good case that some of the other observations were flights of aircraft, although the identities of the planes remain a mystery. They certainly weren't part of an ordinary flight, because the sightings didn't repeat themselves over the next several months or years.

On June 19, 1997, Arizona governor Fife Symington III pulled a bizarre political stunt during a news conference in Phoenix. He appeared with his aide Jay Heller, who was dressed up as an alien in a metallic jumpsuit, sporting handcuffs and wearing a large rubber alien mask, and announced that he was ordering the Arizona Department of Public Safety to conduct an investigation into the Phoenix lights. He later admitted he did it all in fun because many Arizonians were in a frenzy over the UFO flap, stating that he "wanted people to lighten up and calm down," but he "never felt that the overall situation was a matter of ridicule."

However, in an interview in March 2007, 10 years later, Symington confessed that he, too, had seen the Phoenix lights, but had not wanted to go public at the time. His sighting was of a large triangular object with lights, "enormous and inexplicable," with "a geometric outline, a constant shape." He added: "And it couldn't have been flares because it was too symmetrical."

During a news conference in 2000, Senator John McCain, Republican candidate for president of the United States and a friend of Symington, commented on the

Phoenix lights by stating: "That has never been fully explained. But I have to tell you that I do not have any evidence whatsoever of aliens or UFOs."

UFO Hotspot: Rachel, Nevada

This tiny hamlet is near the famed Area 51, along the "UFO Highway," where many UFO enthusiasts have said they have seen odd lights flying over Groom Lake and the surrounding mountains.

9
THE 2000s

FRANKFURTERS AND THE TEXAS FLAP: A TIMELINE

January 31, 2000

The Egyptian newspaper *Al-Ahram* published an article by noted author Mohamed Salmawy about several UFOs that had been seen over Cairo. He wrote that on January 25, 2000, three witnesses were driving on the Mounib Bridge from Cairo to Giza and saw objects floating in the sky over the pyramids that were described as glowing, neon "frankfurters." Salmawy may have seen the same objects that same night, while his flight from Italy to Egypt was approaching Cairo. At around 11:30 p.m., he says he saw a light like a "big light bulb" that he could later make out as being on a "rectangular shape flying just above the ground."

June 9, 2002

At about midnight, an amateur astronomer in M'bour, Senegal, was observing the sky over the ocean, when he saw what he thought was a satellite, moving slowly and steadily from north to south, almost overhead. He watched the object for about 30 seconds as it

UFOs AND ALIENS IN MOVIES

The Brother From Another Planet (1984) is a low-key but sympathetic movie about an alien whose UFO crashes on Earth and finds himself on the streets of New York. The story follows the alien as he tries to grasp the intricacies of human society, but the movie is actually about our xenophobia when encountering unexpected things. *E.T.* had a similar theme, but this low-budget film was a more touching, powerful statement about our society.

went across the sky, stopped moving for a second, moved erratically, and then took off to the southwest. The witness noted that he spends much time observing the sky with binoculars and telescopes, and is familiar with astronomical phenomena and satellites, and was certain that the object he had just observed was unusual.

August 2002

Probably the strangest UFO story to come out of India is one that has several variations and is recounted from year to year, so it is difficult to verify. In August 2002, a mysterious object was said to be terrifying villagers in Uttar Pradesh by flying into their homes and causing injury and even death! One survivor said it looked "like a big soccer ball with sparkling lights." She added: "It burned my skin. I can't sleep because of pain." Near the village of Darra, seven people were reported killed, one with "his stomach ripped open," and many others scratched and burned. Doctors in Lucknow explained the effects as mass hysteria, while police in the Mirzapur District believed the culprit was a type of winged bug that is about nine centimetres long, and which leaves rashes and superficial wounds when it bites. So many people were afraid of being attacked in their beds that when police dismissed their terror, as many as 10,000 rallied and protested, requiring police to issue warning shots over their heads.

April 26, 2003

A tour group was staying at a hotel in Banos, Ecuador, when they all saw a strange procession of lights in the night sky over the city. At about 7:00 p.m., they looked out from their balcony and saw "two small balls in the sky," reddish-yellow in colour and looking like spheres of lava. They were each zipping independently about the night sky, bobbing and weaving. One descended at high speed down into a valley and then zoomed back up into the air.

Across the valley was a mountain that reflected the flash of something like sheet lightning. Then a third ball rose into the sky and began performing the same aerial maneuvers as the first two. There was a flash from behind the mountain, and a fourth ball of reddish light joined the antics. The first three balls then flew to one side and formed a triangle, where they remained in place.

A flash came again and a fifth light rose up into the air, but instead of dancing around the sky it flew directly across the valley, over the witnesses' hotel, and went behind another mountain out of sight. The group watched the lights' movements for 30 more minutes and then went off to a scheduled dinner at a restaurant. When they returned, the sky had clouded over and the lights were obscured from view.

March 5, 2004

Mexico has a long history of UFO sightings; many significant cases have occurred during the past few decades alone, including videos and photographs of strange flying objects. One of the most well-documented and popularized pieces of evidence was an infrared video taken over the state of Chiapas in southern Mexico. A military aircraft of SEDNA, the Mexican Secretariat of Defense, was flying at about 3,300 metres, patrolling the skies for drug smugglers through use of an infrared camera designed to detect illegal flights. But instead of drug smugglers, the video camera picked up a group of 11 objects that the pilots could not identify, and which were not seen in regular light. This isn't all that unusual, as brilliant glare in the sunlight can make distant objects very difficult to see, which exactly why the military planes are equipped with such devices.

"We are not alone! This is so weird," one pilot said while he and others of the crew were watching the objects on the infrared monitor. The radar operator said he had felt afraid, "because [they] were facing something that had never happened before."

The captain of the crew told an investigator: "I believe 'they' could feel we were pursuing them."

During the observation, the plane's radar detected two objects, although ground radar did not show anything in that area. Furthermore, the direction of the radar returns did not match where the infrared images were, and later investigation showed that the radar returns did line up with a highway underneath the plane, on which numerous trucks and other vehicles passed.

The Mexican government gave the video to Jaime Maussan, a popular Mexican broadcaster and ufologist who has frequently been in media regarding UFOs and other esoteric subjects. On May 11, 2004, he held a news conference during which he showed the video and had various experts discussing it. Almost immediately, debunkers leaped to the fore and offered a multitude of contradictory and nonsensical explanations, including weather balloons, high-altitude plasmas, meteors, and ball lightning. It was not until Mexican ufologist Alejandro Franz did a more thorough analysis of the video that the real explanation was made clear: the lights were actually flares on oil wells burning in the Gulf of Mexico, something that was verified by later flights. The flames on the oil wells seemed to be objects flying in the sky because of the angle of the camera, the passing of the clouds, and the movement of the aircraft itself. This explanation wasn't embraced immediately, but once the evidence was presented for everyone to examine and verify, ufologists agreed that in this case, a mystery was solved.

March 21, 2004

One remarkable example of an official UFO report from a pilot occurred on March 21, 2004. A brilliant fireball was seen by witnesses on the ground and in the air, including observers on the private jet carrying the Right Honourable Paul Martin, then prime minister of Canada. An unidentified bright object was reported to air traffic controllers in Edmonton while his official aircraft was flying near Canadian Forces Base Suffield at 7:56 p.m. local time. The report, made available to UFOROM through Transport Canada, noted that pilots of three aircraft, including two commercial airliners and the government jet, all reported seeing "a very bright light falling from the sky, with smoke trailing." In addition, pilots of several other aircraft flying near Westaskiwin, Alberta, also reported seeing the object. One of these pilots was said to have described it as the brightest fireball he'd ever seen. It is not known at this time if the prime minister was advised of the incident, or in fact was also a witness to the event, but it is at least significant that his personal pilot saw and officially reported the object, which likely was a piece of cometary debris impacting the Earth's atmosphere.

	UFO PROCEDURES	
1	Gather the Following info for UFO	

    a. Identification of reporting aircraft/Wing/Unit /person.
          █████████████ Edmonton Airport
    b. Brief description of sighting: A number of A/C reporting bright light falling from sky in the vicinity of Wetaskiwin, Alberta. 3 other A/C, including Prime Minister's A/C report very bright light falling from sky, in the vicinity of military range in Suffield Alberta with smoke trailing. .
      c. Number of objects: ONE (1)
      d. Date and time of sighting: 21 0256Z Mar 04
      e. Alt: Very high, falling to ground
      f. Direction: Downward to earth
      g. Speed: Very fast rate of speed
      h. Additional Comments: Nil

Credit: Ufology Research.

Official documents released by the Canadian government show that a UFO was seen on March 21, 2004. One of the pilots was taking the Prime Minister of Canada to a meeting in Alberta. Did the Prime Minister see the UFO too?

November 10, 2005

At 6:30 p.m., a man in Accra, Ghana, happened to look outside his window and see a bright, round, orange fireball at a high altitude, moving overhead. As he watched, it quickly changed shape to that of a cigar, and a bright emerald- or fluorescent-green light glowed from its sides. It flew off to the south towards the ocean, travelling out of sight within about five seconds, leaving no visible trail.

December 25, 2005

On Christmas, at 8:00 in the evening, as many as 100 miners were gathered in an open area near Taparko in Burkina Faso for a Christmas dinner. Suddenly, the mine manager looked up in the sky and saw a group of lights in a triangular formation. He pointed it out to the other miners and they all watched it for at least a minute. The object travelled not much faster than a jet airline, but its lights were not flashing and no noise was heard. The miners wondered what it was and one of them used a computer to check websites, discovering that many others around the world have reported seeing triangular formations of lights.

March 22, 2006

A 9:15 p.m., two witnesses at Port el Kantoui, Tunisia, reported seeing a rod-shaped object. They estimated it to be about one to two metres in length, with dim lights running along its underside. The object was thought to be only 18 to 24 metres in the air, just about the same height as a nearby hotel, and appeared to be travelling towards the observers at about 80 kilometres per hour without making a sound.

November 7, 2006

About 4:15 p.m., a total of 12 people working at Chicago O'Hare International Airport witnessed something strange in the sky. They reported to the FAA that they watched an odd, metallic, saucer-shaped craft that was stationary over United Airlines Gate C-17. The object was judged to be less than 600 metres above the airport. It was in sight for more than two minutes and witnesses included tarmac

UFO Hotspot: Hessdalen, Norway

An ongoing scientific project to observe nocturnal lights has been in operation here for decades.

workers, pilots, and supervisors. The object was visible long enough for witnesses to alert others, who watched it as well. It eventually shot straight up away from the airport and out of sight, leaving behind a hole in the cloud cover that persisted for about 15 minutes before filling in.

The official explanation given by the FAA is that the object seen in the sky was a rare weather phenomenon, and was not of official interest. This is a curious stance, since the witnesses included airline pilots who thought the object was something more exotic. Further, it could be argued that if it was a weather phenomenon, more details should have been released, because any similar phenomenon might affect air travel at other airports as well.

There is no question that something was seen. There were also some security and safety concerns, because if the object had been a weather balloon, it would have been in the path of incoming aircraft and likely have posed a flight hazard. Two office workers who heard about the UFO through the airport radio system went outside to look for themselves, and were amazed by what they saw. The object was well-witnessed by reliable observers, but their testimonies were given little weight by authorities. One commented that after 9/11, it was baffling that Homeland Security would be concerned about luggage left unattended in airports, but a UFO hanging over an airport, witnessed by a multitude of airport employees, was not taken seriously.

January 18, 2007

From the files of Ufology Research of Manitoba (UFOROM), we have the following report: On January 18, 2007, United Airlines Flight 829 departed Chicago for Hong Kong, travelling at high altitude over Canada's North. At a point beyond the 81st parallel, somewhere over the Arctic ice pack, the pilots saw "a flaming ball" pass their airliner on a shallow but flat trajectory. As it passed them, it "was dropping wreckage." The object dropped into the clouds and was lost to sight. It was likely a large meteor or a bolide, and somewhere on the ice there is a meteorite waiting to be found.

On March 7, 2007

At about 9:30 a.m., an air traffic control radar in Delhi detected two UFOs. The objects were slow-moving and were flying about 10 kilometres apart, both passing over Safdarjung before heading east and vanishing off the radar. Both the ATC and the air force tried to establish radio contact, but failed. This was of concern, because Safdarjung is only about three kilometres from the prime minister's residence, and UFOs flying over a secure area might indicate a security threat.

The Indian Air Force claimed it was informed about the UFOs only when the objects were within five miles of Safdarjung, and the objects vanished from the radar with five minutes, so there was no time to scramble jet fighters to the area. The Civil Aviation Ministry said there had not been any other reports of UFOs over Delhi. The air force conducted an inquiry into the incident, but could not produce an explanation.

Just two months later, at about 9:00 p.m. on May 28, 2007, a civilian witness and his brothers in Bangalore saw a bright, slow-moving group of lights in a triangular formation heading to the west-northwest. He reported it was "definitely not an aeroplane." They watched it for about half an hour and managed to take several photos of the object.

October 29, 2007

The manager of a company in Kolkata, India, got up at about 3:15 a.m. to get a drink of water. When he came back to bed, his wife told him to draw the curtains because a breeze was coming in their ninth-floor apartment window. As he was at the sill, he looked east and saw a bright starlike object about 30 degrees up in the sky. He was puzzled by the object, and took out his video camera and began filming it.

Through the viewfinder, and after zooming to maximum magnification, the object appeared as "a white ball with flaming sides which changed colour and shape." Then, it seemed to be "dotted with red bulbs but with a white patch in the middle." And after a while it looked like a "jaguar-shaped plane with a blue flame at the top and yellow and green in between." He continued watching and videoing the object until it became lost in the lightening dawn sky at about 6:20 a.m. He was convinced it was not an aircraft, which he regularly sees from their apartment window. The sighting was reported to Indian authorities, who verified that there was nothing on radar in that direction at the time. However, the sighting sounds very much like a star or planet scintillating through the hazy atmosphere, similar to cases recorded elsewhere in the world.

December 26, 2007

In late 2007 and early 2008, a video of a curious smoke trail was made public. The video, shot by a couple, shows an object falling obliquely through the sky over Prince Edward Island, Canada, spiralling and creating a black streak as it descends. Marie Quigley noted: "When it came out of the cloud, we shot it from there until it went out of sight. I didn't think it was a UFO, but thought it was a plane having some kind of trouble. But we saw it was going really slow, so that didn't make any sense. It took at least half an hour to make it across the sky."

The couple asked aviation authorities and the local weather office about it, showing them the video, but neither official institution could explain the object. All they could confirm was that it was not an aircraft in the process of crashing; there were no records of downed aircraft or chunks of satellites. They then sent the video to Ufology Research, which examined the images and concluded it could have one of several terrestrial explanations, including "a balloon experiment, satellite re-entry, or something atmospheric, perhaps. Not a celestial object or astronomical phenomenon, or a rocket or satellite fuel dump. We're definitely not sure what this object was; it's very puzzling." An astronomer whom the reporter also asked for an opinion pointed out: "A definite scientific opinion is hard without firm data." In that sense, he agreed with the view of Ufology Research — that there was no definitive explanation at the time.

January 2008

It was reported that Lake Erie was a "UFO hotspot," and some people expressed the belief that there was an underwater UFO base somewhere offshore. Similarly, some people living on the north shore of Lake Ontario report seeing orbs of light hovering over the water and dropping into the waves straight north of them — near the Toronto harbour airport. This has led some UFO buffs to also suggest an underwater alien base near there, too, although it's much more likely that people are simply seeing terrestrial craft, as their lights can be refracted and reflected off of the turbulent water and smog. A typical report reads: "Sunday, January 15, 2006. We saw a lot of 'orbs' in the sky. They appeared to be over or in front of the CN tower and the Toronto skyline as seen from Wilson, NY. We have never seen this before as we are only in that area from time to time. They are not aircraft because we saw airplanes also."

UFOs and Aliens on TV

Yet another comedy about aliens was *3rd Rock From the Sun*. An alien exploration team is sent to Earth to study us, disguised as ordinary humans. Of course, they are unfamiliar with Earth customs and the comedy comes from their many gaffes, awkward relationships, and misuse of language and technology. Dick Solomon is the commander of the expedition and gets a job teaching physics at a college, entering into a romantic relationship with an anthropology professor who is bewildered by Dick's strangeness. The aliens' true forms are "gelatinous purple tubes," so the human concepts of gender, race, and genetic variation are puzzling to them. The show ran from 1996 to 2001.

January 11, 2008

A major UFO flap occurred in the area near Stephenville, Texas, starting around this date. A witness was driving near Denton, Texas, on his way to work at about 6:50 a.m. As he turned east, he saw some bright lights approaching over a dam and thought they were on an aircraft. Having been in the navy, he was familiar with the appearance of aircraft and looked for this object's red and green running lights. He was surprised that no such lights were present, and further surprised that the object was coming in very low and slow, at only about 50 kilometres altitude and 27 to 45 metres away. The strange craft "seemed to be hugging the shoreline, flying at eye level." The witness slowed his car to a crawl and rolled down the window as it passed his position. He had a good, long look at the object, which was black and grey in color, delta-shaped, and no bigger than a sedan in size. Its rear section was rectangular in shape, and there were three large round openings on its side. It made no noise, and there was no visible exhaust. On it upper part was what looked like a metallic canopy. Underneath, there were three white lights that shone brightly and did not blink. He had no explanation for what he had seen. While many of the UFOs reported during the 2008 Texas flap may have had explanations, the Denton sighting seems not to be explainable as a star, meteor, atmospheric inversion, or stray airliner.

Contrast this report with a more typical sighting from the same flap, on January 14, 2008, elsewhere in Texas. Two witnesses looked up to see "a brilliant yellow light, like a star, getting closer to earth." The object was only in view a few seconds, as it seemed to speed up, spawning a "trail of several little yellow brilliant lights." The object then "appeared to just stop," and "burned out as falling stars may." This sighting has many characteristics of a large meteor, known as a bolide, so it may not be as mysterious as the latter case from Denton.

AND BEYOND

Most UFO reports, statistically, are simply lights in the night sky. The most dependable recurring *spooklight* in the world is that of Hessdalen, Norway. For more than 100 years, the area has been plagued by sightings of an odd bobbing light that moves through the mountainous valleys there. Many expeditions in the area have actually produced photographs of the "Hessdalen light."

As an example, one study involving complex instrumentation looked at three specific lights seen on August 6, 7, and 15, 2002. Part of the study involved an expedition team of astrophysicists and engineers, who examined the anomalous lights over the course of the project by using radiofrequency analyzers, photometric instruments, and visual observations. The project, called EMBLA, was coordinated by the Institute for Radio Astronomy in Bologna, Italy, and the Østfold University College in Sarpsborg, Norway. The team of researchers were able to use triangulation to determine that some of the lights seen were car headlights, whereas others had no explanation.

There is no question that the phenomenon is real, as over the years hundreds of people have witnessed lights appearing and disappearing over the valley. Rarely has anyone suggested that aliens are responsible, however. The general consensus among ufologists is that the lights are related to seismic activity, which frequently is felt in that part of the country. Some proponents of the "Earth Lights" theory believe the Hessdalen lights are manifestations of a type of terrestrial energy that is also responsible for UFO sightings elsewhere in the world.

Regardless of their cause, the Hessdalen lights are a strange and fascinating phenomenon that scientists are taking very seriously. Projects and programs involving as many as 100 people, including researchers and their graduate students, have focused on a methodical examination of the lights in order to determine their exact nature, and why they appear so often in the region. Scientific papers have been published in journals, offering theories as to the lights' origin and even detailed analysis of particular observations. Speculation centres on the lights being some kind of plasma, but a full explanation for the phenomenon remains elusive.

CONTACT: ABDUCTIONS, CREATURES, AND THE SEARCH FOR PROOF

1
CONTACTEES

UFO *contactees*, as opposed to *abductees*, believe that they have had a contact experience with aliens but also feel compelled to tell the world of their meeting. Often, contactees say they were instructed by the aliens to warn we Earthlings of the consequences of our ignorant habits, such as war, pollution, and secularity. In contrast, abductees generally do not have such missions, and in fact shy away from public exposure to the point where they request anonymity at all costs.

Unfortunately, the line between abductees and contactees has become very blurred in recent years. More and more, abductees come away from their experience with the belief they have been "chosen," or directed to make changes in their lives and "spread the word." Some, like Richard Dreyfuss in the movie *Close Encounters of the Third Kind*, become obsessed with the UFO phenomenon, spending an inordinate amount of time trying to discover more about aliens and UFOs, reading books, attending conferences, and proselytizing.

George King and the Aetherius Society

One well-known, spiritual contactee group was the Aetherius Society, founded in Britain by George King in March 1954. One day, King said that he heard a voice from heaven, telling him: "Prepare yourself; you are to become the voice of Interplanetary Parliament."

Eight days later, King said a man in white robes walked through a door into his room and delivered the aliens' message that mankind is spiritually unwell. King was advised he was to become the terrestrial representative of the Interplanetary Parliament, which meets regularly on Saturn. He was told to prepare himself for his important duties by practising yoga and leading a healthier lifestyle.

A few months later, King was contacted again, this time by the aliens' leader, Master Aetherius. Aetherius was from Venus, where an advanced civilization rules over the solar system. King's body was taken over and controlled by Aetherius, who then began proselytizing through the "primary terrestrial channel." His mission was, simply, to "alert the world."

King attracted a considerable number of followers. His meetings usually took the form of a public channelling display, where King went into a trance and began speaking as a "lesser agent," telling of upcoming natural disasters as well as happier occasions such as sightings and landings of flying saucers. Then, Aetherius himself would be channelled, and inform the gathered crowd about esoteric teachings, describing "cosmic energies" and the need for more "positive ions" in the world.

UFO Hotspot: Mount Shasta, California

Several New Age movements believe that this area is a spiritual centre where aliens and underground Lemurians live, and UFOs are often reported over the mountain.

Occasionally, another entity would be channelled, including such individuals as Jesus Christ. According to the Aetherius group, Jesus explained He had been born on Venus and had come to Earth in a flying saucer that was disguised as the Star of Bethlehem. Jesus is now on Mars, where He continues His teachings. A channelled Jesus recited from the New Testament and led the group in prayer.

King commanded that his followers needed to "charge" mountains in order to prevent cataclysms. He would often lead groups into various mountainous regions where they would pray in circles, thus charging "energy batteries" which could be used by the aliens to prevent disasters.

George Adamski

Another UFO contactee was George Adamski. His mission on Earth began on November 20, 1952, at 12:30 p.m., near the town of Parker in the California desert, when he and some friends apparently saw a UFO land nearby. He instructed his friends to remain with their car while he went to investigate.

Adamski said that he came face to face with a space being who had human features and long, light-coloured, shoulder-length hair. (Later, such aliens were called *blondes*.) Communicating in sign language, Adamski learned that the visitor was from Venus. Later, he was told that the Space Brothers were very displeased with human behaviour and had enlisted Adamski to carry their message of peace and goodwill to all mankind.

Adamski published three books describing his encounters with the aliens and their messages. They each were financial successes, allowing him to travel widely and attract a huge following. He referred to himself as "Professor George Adamski," and claimed that he lived and worked at Mount Palomar Observatory. In reality, he ran a small cafeteria halfway up the mountain road leading to the astronomical institution. He did have a small portable telescope, through which he took several photographs of aliens and their spaceships hovering nearby, all of which were out of focus or of dubious heritage. One widely published photograph, showing a close-up of a flying saucer with portholes and ball-like objects underneath, has been dismissed by skeptics as the top part of a vacuum cleaner, a bottle washer, or a chicken brooder.

Adamski's followers formed groups in many cities around the world, including Canada. Adamski died in 1965, but his groups continued meeting as recently as the late 1970s.

George Van Tassel and the College of Universal Wisdom

George Van Tassel founded the College of Universal Wisdom in 1953. He is best known as the organizer of the Giant Rock Flying Saucer Convention, which was held annually for nearly two decades on a desert airfield near Giant Rock, California.

During the night of August 24, 1953, Van Tassel was sleeping with his wife and woke up at about 2:00 a.m. to find a man standing at the foot of his bed. The manlike entity said that his name was "Sol-ganda" and insisted that Van Tassel come with him aboard his spaceship. Van Tassel noted that his wife was in a deep sleep, which Sol-ganda said was because of a spell. Outside, Van Tassel saw a bell-shaped craft that was powered by an "antigravity beam."

Van Tassel didn't receive any direct message from his alien contact, but simply was shown things that he interpreted as directions and information to pass on to others. For example, during one of his later contacts, he was visually shown the "true history" of the human race, as observed by aliens. Typically, Van Tassel would go into a trance at a meeting and channel information from Sol-ganda or other aliens.

Van Tassel was often attacked by skeptics, and one of the most memorable incidents was the action of a lawyer who set out to show that Van Tassel's stories were hoaxes. He sent Van Tassel faked UFO photos, which Van Tassel quickly adopted as true and proof of his own experiences. However, when both the lawyer and Van Tassel appeared together on a popular UFO-related radio talk show, the lawyer revealed the photos as his fakes.

Despite such damaging evidence, Van Tassel remained popular and his Giant Rock convention attracted many thousands of devotees and contactees annually. Near the convention site, he built the Integratron, a wooden dome-shaped temple, from plans he said were supplied by the Space Brothers and similar to Solomon's Temple from the Old Testament. The Integratron was designed for rejuvenation of the human body, through "omni-beams" directed from above.

Richard Shaver and Ray Palmer

In September 1944, *Amazing Stories* magazine editor Ray Palmer received a letter from a man named Richard Shaver. Shaver detailed how he had learned of an ancient alphabet from a lost race that had once thrived on Earth and had battled evil aliens. Palmer had his reservations, but in the interest of catering to his science fiction audience, he published the letter and was surprised to receive hundreds of requests for more information.

Shaver replied with a long story titled: "A Warning to Future Man," which Palmer edited and rewrote as "I Remember Lemuria." It was published in March 1945. The piece received an unprecedented response from the magazine's readership. More than 50,000 letters flowed in from people who praised the work but also added their own personal experiences that supported the story.

Basically, Shaver's story relied on "racial memories" about a race of subhuman creatures called deros (detrimental robots) living in underground cities within the Earth. The deros had once been slaves of an advanced civilization that had once existed on Lemuria, but had perished during the cataclysm that destroyed Atlantis.

Deros had control of the Lemurians' highly advanced technology, including mind-rays that they directed at humans on the surface of the Earth, causing mental, emotional, and physical problems. Other devices caused earthquakes, volcanoes, and droughts. Their sole pastime was to annoy and persecute the human race. Occasionally, they would kidnap humans and torture them, sometimes returning them to the surface, but most often hiding them forever, such as in the case of Jimmy Hoffa and Judge Crater.

Ray Palmer continued to publish the Shaver stories as fact, which eventually led to his firing from *Amazing Stories*, but he then began his own science fiction pulp magazine, called first *Other Worlds*, then *Flying Saucers from Other Worlds*, and then finally *Flying Saucers*. The stories continued being published until the 1970s.

Mark-Age

Mark-Age is a quasi-religious group that still exists today. Its basic set of beliefs is that mankind was once part of an interplanetary spiritual communications system, but has turned away from spiritual matters. Because of this, the Hierarchical Board of the Solar System "drew the veil" over our consciousness. However, some of the aliens, being benevolent, are trying to increase our spiritual consciousness, using mental communications with certain members of our society, projecting their own bodies or actually making themselves seen in their flying saucers.

Mark is the chief contact for Earth, and has been assigned to make mankind "space-conscious" and ready to meet other life forms. Mark-Age devotees believe that God is helping the United States space program because it was defined as "one nation under God." The Soviet Union was not given such help because it was, in their opinion, atheist.

Robert Barry

Robert Barry founded the 20th Century UFO Bureau in the late 1960s. He stressed that the public had been lied to by the government about the existence of UFOs and aliens on Earth — they were basically an anti–cover-up group. Barry also taught that UFOs were spaceships piloted by angels, although a few are controlled by Satan and his forces, and That these angel-piloted UFOs assisted the Israelis in their battles in the Holy Land. In the 1970s, Barry held public meetings in a number of cities and towns, promoting himself in "bible belt" areas such as Steinbach, Manitoba, and in Pennsylvania.

In Their Own Words

Huachuca Mountains, Palominas, Cochise County, Arizona
July 1, 1995

It was about 10:35 a.m. While backpacking between Miller Peak and Montezuma Pass, my family and I observed two delta-shaped objects flying 360's above Miller Peak, which is 9,466 feet high. We estimate that the objects were at 15,000 to 17,000 feet. We heard no noise that would be associated with any air-breather propulsion system.

The objects appeared to be working in tandem, about 800 to 1,000 feet apart from each other, at about the same altitude. We observed them doing 360's for about 20 minutes. The first one faded from view into some clouds. The second one was observed departing north at the same altitude. We watched the second one flying north for about three minutes before it disappeared. It did not disappear in the sense of 'gone,' it just was not observable with the naked eye.

Reported by Anonymous
Source: Ufology Research

2
ABDUCTEES

Although we now know that some people have extensive histories of abduction encounters dating back to their childhood, the abduction phenomenon began with the publication of several books in the 1980s, such as *Communion* by Whitley Strieber and *Intruders* by Budd Hopkins. After this time, alien abductions were accepted into ufology on a broader scale than ever before, and the general public became keenly interested in the concept of aliens invading peoples' bedrooms, snatching drivers from their vehicles on lonely patches of road, and having mystical knowledge imparted to them by omnipotent space beings.

Ufologists specializing in abductions began appearing on television talk shows discussing their theories, and *OMNI* magazine even conducted a readers' survey at the time to find out how many people had their own such experiences. The result seemed to indicate that a significant percentage of the population believed that they have had abduction experiences, with stories ranging from visitations in witnesses' homes to the actual transporting of witnesses to places that are literally "out of this world."

BETTY AND BARNEY HILL

The most celebrated (and disputed) UFO abduction case ever reported is that of Barney and Betty Hill, an American couple whose experience in 1961 is considered the archetypal alien abduction scenario. It has been the subject of books, movies, and countless magazine articles. Even after numerous recountings of their story, their testimony remained essentially unchanged: they encountered a strange aerial object that approached them and frightened them to the point where they began having nightmares and anxiety.

Do You Think You Have Been Abducted by Aliens?

Some abduction ufologists have compiled lists of attitudes, feelings, sensations, and memories that they believe indicate you have been abducted by aliens (and may be unaware of it!). These questions are very general, and could obviously apply to many people whether or not they have been abducted by aliens. The questions include:

- "Have you had missing or lost time of any length, especially one hour or more?"
- "Have you seen balls of light or flashes of light in your home or other locations?"
- "Do you have a memory of flying through the air which you do not feel was a dream?"
- "Have you had dreams of UFOs, beams of light, or alien beings?"
- "Have you had a UFO sighting or sightings in your life?"
- "Do you have a cosmic awareness, an interest in ecology, environment, vegetarianism or are very socially conscious?"
- "Do you have a strong sense of having a mission or important task to perform, without knowing where this compulsion came from?"
- "Have you ever awoken in the middle of the night, startled?"

Since nearly everyone can answer "yes" to some of these questions, the list is not useful in proving someone has had a UFO abduction experience. However, answering "yes" to all the indicators may mean that you are a person who strongly believes in UFOs or is predisposed to a belief in alien abductions.

Abductees

It all started on September 19, 1961, as the Hills were returning to New Hampshire after a vacation in Quebec. As they drove, they noticed a bright, starlike object that seemed to be descending and pacing their car. They believed it to be a meteor of some kind. It stopped its movement and appeared to hang in the southwest for a while, then seemed to rise again. Betty told Barney to stop the car so that she could get a better look, and when he did so, she watched it through binoculars, having difficulty following it as it bobbed, weaved, and then flew across the face of the Moon.

When she gave the binoculars to Barney, he saw it move erratically again and it seemed to be coming towards them, decreasing in altitude. He suggested to Betty that it was just an aircraft heading for Canada and got back into the car and resumed driving home. They stopped discussing the unusual object, which still was moving in the sky and seemed to be getting closer.

As he drove around a bend, they were startled when the object appeared almost right in front of them, motionless and about only 30 metres above the highway. It was close enough now they could see it to be a broad, disc-shaped craft. Barney stopped the car and got out, holding up the binoculars to get a close-up view of the weird sight. It suddenly moved again, taking up a position over a nearby field. Determined to figure out what the object was, Barney grabbed his handgun (just to be safe) and strode across the field towards it.

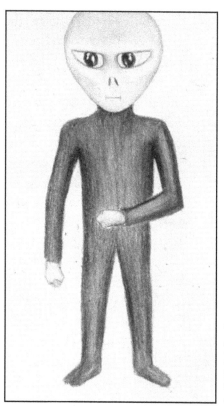

He had a good look at the craft, which he estimated was about 25 metres in diameter, with two rows of rectangular windows along its edge. In the windows, Barney could see strange creatures that were making odd gestures that somehow frightened him. Afraid for his life, he turned around and ran back to the car, hysterically telling Betty they needed to escape or they'd be captured by "them."

Barney drove off quickly but the craft followed them. The couple then heard some unusual buzzing noises that seemed to "bounce off" their car's trunk, and they felt a vibration. They continued to drive without making conversation and they later heard another series of buzzing sounds. Eventually, even though he was driving in a dazed state, they reached home.

Artist conception of an alien encountered by Betty and Barney Hill in New Hampshire, 1961.

Credit: Vladimir Simosko

(Most versions of the Hills' story note that when they reached home, they realized that they were much later in arriving than they had calculated, leaving them to conclude that hours of their journey were missing. However, this realization did not occur until months later, after discussing their experience with investigators.)

They both felt odd and were unsure why. When Barney unpacked the car, he noticed that the strap on his binoculars was broken, and Betty discovered a pinkish powder on her dress. They began to talk with one another about their drive, but they seemed unable to recall details of their trip. They both did have a vague memory of a large bright object sitting on the road ahead of their car, and they were both unnerved by it.

After a restless sleep, they began putting their clothes and other things away. Betty had a "feeling" that she had been exposed to radiation of some kind. When she told this to her sister, she was advised to perhaps run a compass over their car and if the needle deviated, it might be a sign the vehicle was now radioactive. (Note: This makes no scientific sense; furthermore, the metal on most cars will deflect a compass needle, regardless of the age or model of the vehicle.)

The next day, Betty phoned the local air force base to report their UFO encounter. She and Barney described the sighting, and their observation of the odd light and craft with windows was recorded. The air force investigators reached a conclusion of "insufficient data," and noted that the Hills' report contained inconsistencies that prevented an explanation, though it was suggested they may have seen Jupiter. However, the Hills had no knowledge of the air force's conclusion, as this was classified until recent years.

In fact, the Hills' case began to take on a life of its own. Betty was bothered by the UFO sighting and spoke with her sister and some close friends about her concerns. Betty began to have dreams about being escorted through the trees by several strange, grey-skinned men in air-force-like uniforms. In the dreams, Barney was walking near her, although he appeared dazed and did not respond to her calls to him. They both were led towards a large, disc-shaped craft and then onto a ramp inside. There, she and Barney were separated because their abductors wanted to do some tests on them.

The beings spoke English, although Betty noted they had odd accents of some kind. One being, whom Betty called a doctor, snipped some of her hair, looked inside her mouth and ears, and clipped her fingernails. He scraped her skin with a butter-knife-like object and then made her lie on a metal table while he used machines like X-rays to examine her more thoroughly. He then produced a long needle that he jabbed in her abdomen, telling her it was a pregnancy test. (This is particularly interesting, because it was not until several years later that amniocentesis tests became common among terrestrial physicians.)

In one dream, Betty realized that no one would believe her about meeting these creatures, so she asked one that seemed to be the leader if she could take something back home. Betty indicated a book that was on a table, and asked if she could have it. An argument among the creatures ensued, and it was taken away.

At one point, Betty asked the leader where he was from. In response, he went over to a wall and pulled a map out of it. Betty said it looked very odd, as if three-dimensional despite being a two-dimensional sheet. She noted it was a "sky map," with stars of varying sizes and colours, and lines connecting some of them. The leader explained that the lines represented expeditions. He then asked Betty if she knew where the Earth was on the map, and she naturally said no. He then said that because she did not know, there would be no reason to show her where he was from.

UFO Hotspot: Santa Rosa, Florida

The magazine *Popular Mechanics* did an analysis of UFO report trends in March 2009 and listed this region, near an airbase, as having more UFO sightings than other areas.

Even though the book had been taken away, Betty told the leader that she would remember their meeting. He retorted that it was unlikely, and even if she did remember, no one would believe her.

These consciously recalled images were brought out as nightmares from Betty's troubled mind. It's no wonder that she was having difficulty putting them in context. It was only weeks later, when being interviewed by UFO investigators from the National Investigations Committee on Aerial Phenomena (NICAP) that the Hills realized their drive home took at least two hours longer than normal. They tried to reconstruct the events of that night, but they still could not account for the missing hours. They began making trips back to the area to jog their memories, but to no avail.

Barney was also experiencing extreme anxiety for reasons he could not understand and began drinking heavily. The stress was getting to him and he sought the help of a psychiatrist. He told the psychiatrist about the UFO experience, among other things, and saw him for several months, without any significant easing of his anxiety.

Then, in September 1963, the Hills were talked into speaking about their UFO experience at a meeting of the Two State UFO Study Group of Massachusetts and Rhode Island. In front of 200 people, they told of their memories of seeing the object with windows and Betty's subsequent dreams. The overwhelmingly positive reception they received likely contributed to Barney's increasing anxiety, as he was more concerned by Betty's dreams with every telling. Finally, after continued suggestions to undergo hypnosis, supported by people who had been in the audience that evening and corresponded with the Hills, Barney asked his psychiatrist to set up an appointment with a clinical hypnotist.

In December, the Hills had their first meeting with Dr. Benjamin Simon, an expert on traumatic amnesia who was at that time in clinical practice in Boston. He outlined the limitations of hypnosis and tested their susceptibility over the next few months. Finally, in February 1964, Simon began regressive hypnosis with the Hills, working with each one separately in a soundproofed room and warning them not to discuss their sessions with one another. It was not until April 1964 that the sessions were completed and they could share their experiences.

Under hypnosis, Simon helped the Hills piece together a consistent narrative of their joint UFO abduction experience. Betty's dreams were nearly identical to her hypnotic recall, and Barney's involvement was related in considerably more detail, including his own physical examination at the hands of the aliens. It was this part of the experience that seemed to have been the source of much of Barney's anxiety. He had been rendered unable to protect his wife, and his treatment on board the UFO had been very demeaning to him.

Simon's therapy was ultimately successful. The Hills' lives and psychological states improved and they tried returning to normal as best they could, although still fielding requests for speaking engagements. Then, in 1965, a reporter who had known about the Hills' story through the UFO group broke the silence and filed a story that was syndicated worldwide. Eventually, the Hills' tale appeared many times in national magazines and was made into a TV movie in 1975. However, Barney never saw the film adaptation of his experience, as he died of a cerebral hemorrhage in 1969.

Simon's hypnotherapy has been criticized over the years by debunkers claiming that he only fostered their personal fears and fantasies, and that Barney's memories were simply contaminated by Betty's vivid nightmares. However, his outstanding record of working with amnesiacs and the extreme care he displayed in working with each of the Hills shows that there was no fault in his methodology. He himself did not ascribe to the belief that aliens were involved and thought that Barney was likely influenced by Betty's dreams somehow. One trouble with this view is that Barney began having anxiety, following the UFO encounter, weeks before Betty related her first nightmares to him. In a final report, Simon casually stated that the Hills' anxieties had been caused by a "harrowing experience."

UFOs and Aliens in Movies

The UFO Incident (TV) (1975) is a teleplay of John Fuller's book *The Interrupted Journey*, about the "real-life" UFO encounter and abduction of Betty and Barney Hill by aliens while driving through New Hampshire. The teleplay has wonderful, low-key, believable performances by Estelle Parsons and James Earl Jones as Betty and Barney Hill. A thoughtful portrayal of the "grandaddy" of all UFO abductions, this movie accurately conveys the confusion and angst felt by the Hills as they tried to come to terms with memories of their experience.

An interesting side note is that under hypnosis, when Betty was describing the star map shown by the alien leader, Simon told her to draw it, but she initially refused. She said she couldn't reproduce it accurately because it was so unusual. He then gave her a posthypnotic suggestion that she should draw it only when she felt she could do so with confidence. Eventually, she did so, producing an odd collection of dots and balls of varying sizes, some with connecting lines.

The map was published in a number of sources, and in 1968 amateur astronomer Marjorie Fish was curious about the map, so she decided to test the theory that it represented a real array of stars. Using data from available star catalogues that listed estimated distances and directions to known stars, she constructed a three-dimensional model of our local section of the Milky Way. Looking through the model from different angles, Fish searched for but was unable to find a match for the stars from the map. It was not until revised catalogues were published that she adapted her model accordingly and finally found a pattern that matched Betty's map.

The "home stars" on the map were Zeta 1 and Zeta 2 Reticuli, stars in a southern constellation that are much like our sun. All the other stars on the map joined by lines were also sun-like in their characteristics — in other words, they might have planets with life like Earth.

In later years, Betty became more and more involved with ufology. Other abductees sought her advice and experiential wisdom, and she became outspoken on the issue of contact with extraterrestrials. She had many other unusual experiences and seemed to be the target of odd phenomena, even of things like streetlights sputtering out as she walked by underneath, suggesting to her and others a supernatural or paranormal link.

Skeptics have argued that Betty's dreams were just that — dreams, and that Barney started having similar dreams after hearing about them from his wife. Other explanations have been with less merit; arch-skeptic Philip Klass at one time was certain that the Hills had encountered a very intense ball of plasma and were mesmerized by it.

In the end, there are only two possible explanations for the Hills' experience: either they hallucinated the entire series of events, triggered by unknown catalysts, or what they said actually happened as they described and recalled pre- and post-hypnosis.

PASCAGOULA

A strange, robot-like creature was encountered by two men near Pascagoula, Mississippi, in 1973. Charles Hickson and Calvin Parker were out fishing very late at night when they heard a buzzing noise and looked up to see glowing, egg-shaped object hovering about 12 metres over the river bank. The object was three metres wide and about two and a half metres high with blue lights on its front surface.

As they watched, riveted by what they were seeing, three things that looked like robots came out of a door in its side. These robots were about one and a half metres tall, with bullet-shaped heads that were attached right to their bodies without any sign of a neck. They had no eyes, and odd bumps or tubes sticking out of their heads where their noses and ears should have been. Although they had legs and arms, they didn't use them as they floated towards the two terrified men. They had wrinkled, grey skin, and instead of hands had claws like a crab or lobster.

Two of the creatures approached Hickson and grabbed his arms, while the third took hold of Parker. In their grasp, the men went limp like rag dolls and were floated over to the egg-shaped craft. Hickson recalls that he was taken into a room where a device like a large eye gave him a thorough medical examination. He was then taken back outside, where he was placed with Parker, who had apparently been subjected to a similar treatment.

The creatures went back into the craft, which then took off and flew out of sight. Because they realized their story would not be believed, they initially decided not to tell anyone about what had happened. However, they eventually contacted a nearby air force base because they thought the aliens were a danger to other people. The men were subjected to intense questioning and later, when the story came out in the press, extreme ridicule. However, both Parker and Hickson passed lie detector tests and at least one experienced UFO researcher, Dr. J. Allen Hynek of the Center for UFO Studies, believed their story.

VILLAS-BOAS

There are close encounters — and then there is what happened to Antonio Villas-Boas in 1957. He had what could be described as the *closest* encounter. You see, he didn't just see a UFO, he went inside one. And he didn't just get abducted, he was violated.

On October 5, 1957, 23-year-old farmer Villas-Boas was in his house getting ready for bed at about 11:00 p.m. He lived with his family near the town of Sao Francisco de Salles, in the state of Minas Gerais, Brazil. Looking out a window, he was surprised to see that the corral outside was illuminated from above by a strong light, although he could not see what was causing it. The source of the light seemed to play upon the ground and eventually moved across the yard and onto the house, peeking through cracks between boards before going out.

Just over a week later, on October 14, Antonio was ploughing a field with his oldest brother at about 9:30 p.m., when they saw a dazzlingly bright light appear at the opposite end of the field. It was about 90 metres in the air and seemed to be shining from an object that was hidden by the glare. Antonio bravely moved towards it to see what it was (his brother was too frightened), but as he did so, the object flew to the other end of the field. Again he went towards it, but it moved back. They played this game for several minutes before it suddenly disappeared.

The next night, Antonio was ploughing at the same location, and at about 1:00 a.m. noticed an odd, red-coloured star in the sky. It was moving towards him and getting perceptibly bigger as it approached. The object eventually took up a position about 45 metres over his head. It appeared to be an egg-shaped object and cast a very bright pinkish light around his tractor.

Antonio thought about running away, but the object had proven the night before that it could move faster than he could run. Besides, it was too late; the object dove from its position and landed about 10 metres in front of his tractor.

He could now see that the craft was oval-shaped with three spurs arranged as a tripod, on which it rested, and a lighted, rotating ring was on top. Completely "freaked out," he started the tractor and attempted to drive off, but its engine died. He then opened the door that was farthest from the craft and bolted outside, but a small creature in a strange uniform grabbed him from behind. He shoved the being away, tossing it metres away, but as soon as he made another dash for safety, he was accosted by three more creatures. They lifted him in the air and despite his struggles, managed to carry him to the craft and into a door in its side.

Once inside, Antonio saw that he was in a small room with shiny metal walls and ceiling, with what seemed to be fluorescent lighting along the wall. Five of the small but powerful creatures were restraining him and he was guided by them into another larger room through a doorway. This room had a support beam running from floor to ceiling, and also had a table and several small, one-legged stools. Antonio was held there by two of the creatures while all of the captors spoke to one another in dog-like grunts and growls.

The beings were similarly attired in seamless, one-piece "siren suits" that resembled skin-divers' outfits, grey in colour, that covered them from neck to feet. They wore helmets that were attached to their suits with metallic plates, and that had eye coverings that looked like goggles. The helmets were clearly designed for larger-than-human heads, and from the top stuck out three tubes that extended behind the creatures into their suits. Their leggings blended into their footwear, which had thick soles and odd turned-up toes, much like a jesters' shoes.

The creatures stopped talking, apparently having come to a decision, and began forcibly undressing their captive. Antonio fought them, but nevertheless ended up in his birthday suit. To make matters worse, one of the beings approached him with some kind of soft cloth and began giving him a sponge bath with a thick, clear, odourless liquid. He was then led towards a door over which there were red squiggly letters that Antonio did not recognize as any language he had ever seen. He was taken into the next room by two of the creatures.

In this room, the creatures produced two thick pipes that they applied to Antonio's body to suck out some of his blood, leaving painful scars. They then exited the room, leaving Antonio shivering in the cold metal prison, alone. Exploring the room, he walked over to a long, low table that he found to be a bed or cot, without legs or headboard. It was covered with a very soft and comfortable material that was very inviting, so he lay down. But he noticed an unpleasant smell in the room, and

UFO Hotspot: Surrey, British Columbia

The "Surrey Corridor" has had an abundance of UFO sightings since at least 1989.

when he got off the bed to investigate, he found that puffs of smoke or coloured gas were being pumped into the room from thin tubes along the top of the walls. His discomfort increased and he became very nauseated, eventually vomiting in a corner of the room.

Antonio lost track of time and may have also lost consciousness, for he was startled by the door opening suddenly. Looking up, he saw the unmistakable figure of a naked woman approaching him, with a curious expression on her face. She wasn't quite human, but she was beautiful in a way unlike an Earth woman. She had long, silver-blond hair that looked as if it had been bleached, parted in the centre. Her eyes were almond-shaped, and extended farther around the sides of her face than a human's. She had high cheekbones and an oval face with a small nose and a decidedly pointed chin. Her lips were thin and pale and her ears seemed "normal."

Her body was that of a well-developed human female, proportionately shorter than him by about 25 centimetres. Her skin was pale white, although she seemed to have many freckles on her arms and back. He also noticed that the hair in her armpits was red, instead of silver-blond like on her head.

This alien female moved towards Antonio, hugged him tightly, and rubbed her body against his, like a cat. Antonio said he became aroused by this. After more touching, the experience was over and the female alien left him. But as she exited, she turned back to him and pointed to her belly, then upwards, which he interpreted as meaning that she would return to take him with her to her home.

When she left, one of the creatures came into the room with his clothes, clearly indicating that he needed to get dressed. When he did so, he was led into another room where several of the creatures were sitting around a table. They appeared to be discussing the situation, and as they did so, Antonio realized he had no proof of what had happened to him. He noticed that on a table near them was something that resembled a clock, and he nonchalantly sidled over and made a grab for it. However, one of the creatures caught on to what he was doing and ran up and roughly shoved Antonio away.

Eventually Antonio was was taken back down the exit and ladder to the ground outside. Before long, the craft had sealed up once again, then it took off and rose into the air, spinning and making a loud noise. It ascended to about 30 metres and shot away like a bullet within a few seconds.

Credit: Susan Birdwise.

The alien female who enticed Vilas-Boas in Brazil, 1957.

Villas-Boas walked over to his tractor and tried to start it, but found it wouldn't turn over. He discovered that the battery leads had been disconnected, and he assumed that it had been done by the aliens because they didn't want him making an unexpected getaway if he had somehow escaped.

When he eventually got home, he found that he had been gone more than four hours, as it was now about 5:30 a.m. Exhausted, he slept the next day through and awoke at suppertime feeling refreshed. But he slept poorly or not at all during the next week, experiencing vivid nightmares about being captured by "them" again. During the next month, however, this trend reversed and he was excessively tired, even nodding off from time to time. When examined by doctors, he had some sores and purplish marks on his body, but was otherwise physically normal.

The case of Antonio Villas-Boas was brought to the attention of the Aerial Phenomena Research Organization (APRO), in the United States, in 1958 by Dr. Olavo Fontes of Rio de Janeiro. Fontes had examined Villas-Boas and was puzzled by his story and physiological condition. He was convinced that Antonio had not simply made up the story, because he had been reluctant to even come forward with the details. Furthermore, if it had been simply a sexual fantasy, surely he could have done better. The female alien didn't even have lips for kissing!

Villas-Boas kept to himself for many years, refusing all interviews. However, in 1978, he agreed to be interviewed on Brazilian TV, primarily to set the record straight about the many different versions and embellishments of his story over the intervening years. He was a learned man, having become a practising lawyer in Brasilia, and was married with several children. He had not discussed his experience in any detail, even with his family. Until his death, he maintained that his experience had been real and that he had not been making any of it up. He did not profit from his story and did not seek any fame or celebrity status, which were certainly in reach if he had tried.

Did You Know?

The most common colour of reported UFOs is white.

THE MANHATTAN ABDUCTION

In contrast to Antonio Villas-Boas, who refused interviews and went to great lengths to remain out of the limelight, the case of Linda Napolitano is one of notoriety and public attention. And rightly so, for many of the claims surrounding the case are fantastic and allegedly involve prominent individuals. The fact that it is said to have occurred in downtown Manhattan, in New York City, is also remarkable.

In May 1989, Linda Napolitano began corresponding with abduction researcher Budd Hopkins about some odd experiences she had that seemed to be related to aliens. But six months later, on November 30, she called Hopkins in great distress because of a very traumatic dreamlike memory she had of a bizarre encounter with "them" during the previous night. She said she remembered waking up at about

3:15 a.m. and finding small alien creatures around her bed. She tried to wake up her sleeping husband beside her, screaming at him, but he wouldn't stir. The aliens seemed to be telling her to be quiet, speaking in a strange language. Before she knew it, she was somehow floating outside her downtown Manhattan apartment in her nightgown, many stories above the ground, beneath a bright bluish-white light.

The light was revealed to be a large clam-shell-like object that opened up, and she was brought inside. Within the craft, her body was examined by small, large-headed creatures who poked and probed her with strange medical instruments, including a rod with a ball on its end that they put inside her nose. Eventually, the examination was over and she found herself back in her bed beside her snoring husband. The bedside clock showed that it was nearly 5:00 a.m.

As remarkable a story as it is, Linda's abduction experience by itself would hardly have merited much discourse, as literally hundreds of such cases are documented each year by abduction researchers around the world. Hopkins' files by themselves contain many, many abductees' accounts, in various stages of investigation, including regressive hypnosis, onsite investigations, and other therapy.

But in February 1991 Hopkins received a letter from someone describing himself as a police officer, who wrote of an amazing experience he and his partner had in November 1989. He said that very early one morning, they had been in a patrol car underneath the FDR Bridge in Manhattan when they suddenly noticed a bluish light near a tall apartment building in front of them. They were even more surprised to see the figure of a woman floating in the air underneath the light, accompanied by three odd-looking creatures that were also suspended in midair. They all entered the light, which had now been resolved to that of an oval object, and it then flew off behind the Brooklyn Bridge where the astonished officers watched it descend and enter the water, disappearing from sight.

This observation greatly unnerved the men. In fact, after their experience, they had been very troubled with guilt because they had been unable to do anything to prevent the woman from being abducted. The implications of what had transpired also gave the men extreme anxiety; aliens were indeed real, despite official denials of such things, and they had witnessed a close encounter over a populated area. The other man even had a nervous breakdown of sorts, taking time off his beat and spending many nights parked outside the building again, wondering what had happened to the woman.

Hopkins immediately realized the significance of this report. If true, it would be the first outsider eyewitness account of a UFO abduction, corroborating an abductee's memory of her experience. He told Napolitano about the letter from the police officers, and recommended that if the policemen contacted her, she was not to tell them any details of her experience, so that their testimony would not be contaminated by anything she said to them. Hopkins reasoned that they would eventually show up at her door and want to talk with her, and ideally, he wanted to talk with them first.

Sure enough, a few weeks later, a very agitated Napolitano contacted Hopkins with the news that the two men had shown up at her door. They had said they were not actually policemen but detectives named Richard and Dan. She said that Dan acted strangely during their visit but that Richard seemed genuinely concerned with her well-being. They were puzzled about how she had managed to float in mid-air outside her apartment building, and wanted to know "how she did it."

A few days later, Napolitano said she was at a bus stop when Richard showed up, wanting to talk with her. A few more days later he again confronted her, this time as she and her family were going into a church. She had been keeping Hopkins advised on each meeting, and he was telling her what to say and not to say, and had asked her to give the men instructions on contacting Hopkins with detailed answers to his questions. A few weeks later, Hopkins received an audiotape from Richard, describing what he had seen in detail that morning. Then he received a letter from Dan, who described how emotionally upsetting the experience was to him.

It was shortly thereafter that Hopkins received another letter, this time signed not only by Richard and Dan but also by a third person, whom Hopkins identified only as "Him." This time, the story had changed somewhat more: Richard and Dan were not police or detectives, but bodyguards whose job it was to protect and escort "an important political figure." This third man also saw the object and Linda's aerial abduction, even though Richard and Dan had made him lay down in the back seat of the vehicle, out of harm's way.

Speculation among other ufologists is that this third person was Javier Perez de Cuellar, former secretary-general of the United Nations. Hopkins refuses to reveal the third man's identity, although Cuellar himself has denied it was him. Another name bandied about is that of Canadian Prime Minister Brian Mulroney, who had apparently been in New York for a meeting at the United Nations, of which Cuellar had been a part. His being in the car with Richard and Dan has also not been verifiable.

The case began to take on still more strangeness as Linda and members of her family had chance (or prearranged) meetings with Richard or Dan throughout the next several months, with more letters and audiotapes coming to light. At no time did Hopkins himself ever meet Richard or Dan, leading some researchers to suggest that the entire thing was an elaborate hoax perpetrated by Napolitano herself.

Complicating the issue were events such as Linda's abduction in broad daylight on a street corner by none other than Richard and Dan themselves, after she had seen her son off at the school-bus stop. She claimed that they physically dragged her into a car on the street then drove off, in order to "interrogate" her about her experience. At one point, she says Dan accused her of being "one of them" — an alien hybrid half-human, having "alien blood" coursing through her veins. Her captors even examined her feet to see if she had toes (as they believed aliens do not).

On another occasion, Linda was abducted off the streets of New York by Dan, who was driving a red sports car, again in plain sight of many passers-by. (Perhaps such things are relatively commonplace in New York City, but Linda was challenged by skeptics about why she did not report the incident to police. Her reply was that because the kidnapping was done under the auspices of "national security," it was technically legal.) Dan drove her to a remote oceanfront location on Long Island, where he forced her to put on a nightgown similar to the one she had worn on the night of the alien abduction. He also attempted to have sexual relations with her, twisting her arm and overpowering her, then forcing her head under water when she resisted. (One can only imagine that if this was indeed the FBI or CIA at work, perhaps this was an early version of "waterboarding.")

Linda was saved by Richard, who appeared suddenly and in the nick of time. He brought Dan under control and protected Linda from further danger. Dan had been babbling incoherently and was clearly out of control. Richard drove her home, where she immediately contacted Hopkins for an emergency meeting, and he verified that she appeared dishevelled and with sand in her hair.

UFOs and Aliens in Literature

Nighteyes is a 1989 novel by Garfield Reeves-Stevens in which popular paranoid claims about UFOs are actually true. People really are being abducted from their bedrooms by sinister forces, and the government not only knows about it, but are aiding and abetting the abductors. The story focuses on Steve and Sarah Gilmour, whose child is mysteriously taken away and they frantically search for a solution. The answer is that aliens are here to help raise our consciousness and expand our minds. The novel is most interesting, however, because it parallels the "real" UFO abduction of Linda Napolitano from her Manhattan apartment on November 30, 1989, and her subsequent harassment by government agents.

Hopkins eventually received another letter from the mysterious political figure who was the "third man." In his letter, he advised that the aliens were directly involved in Earth's political process and that they were striving to achieve world peace in cooperation with terrestrial agents. He also warned that any attempt to contact him directly would seriously threaten the proceedings.

And, as if things weren't complicated enough, Hopkins received reports from additional witnesses to the UFO outside Napolitano's apartment.

Towards the end of 1991, Napolitano showed Hopkins an X-ray of her head that had been taken by a person whom she said was a doctor and a friend. She had been bothered by some discomfort in her nose, and the X-ray clearly showed a strange opaque object about one centimetre in length with a curly protrusion at one end. This has been interpreted as being an alien implant, used by the aliens for unknown purposes but possibly in the tracking and location of their subjects.

Debate has raged within the ufology community regarding this case. The credibility of Napolitano has been attacked, as has the objectivity of Hopkins. It has been suggested that he was the victim of an elaborate hoax perpetrated by a number of people in cahoots with one another. It has even been suggested that the case bears an uncanny resemblance to the plot of a science fiction novel, *Nighteyes*, written by Garfield Reeves-Stevens and published in April 1989, only months before Linda first contacted Hopkins.

TWO MORE CASES

Following a talk given by ufologist Stanton Friedman at a university on January 26, 1988, a shy man asked Friedman and another UFO researcher to meet later so he could talk about some UFO experiences he had. When they did meet, the man related a "classic" abduction experience or visitation by some sort of entity in his home. There was no physical evidence to support the experience he claims to have had, but he was sure that it did happen and he seemed to have a history of such experiences throughout his life. He rarely talked with his friends or family about the incidents, and was worried about their reactions should his story ever become public knowledge.

The most vivid of his memories is one that originated from a night in November, 1987. He was in his bedroom preparing to go to sleep, thinking about the day's events, and had been meditating. He got into bed with the lights out and lay on his back, starting to drift off. After a while, he became aware of a presence in his room that seemed to be in the vicinity of his closet. At almost the same time, he felt a peculiar tingling sensation in his body. He was surprised to find that he was paralyzed everywhere except for his eyes, which he was able to move. Somehow he felt that the presence was responsible and that it was approaching his bed.

Although he couldn't recall seeing the entity in its entirety, he did have the distinct recollection of seeing a face not more than a foot in front of his eyes. He drew this face for investigators without much difficulty, depicting a cherubic character with skin folds, slit-like eyes, and a thin mouth. The creature was also wearing some sort of tight-fitting helmet. He felt that something had touched his mind, and that images of things he had seen in his life were brought to the surface and taken from him. He remembers feeling or sensing that whatever was doing this to him was also reassuring him that it meant no harm, and that it only wanted certain things from his memory. After a while, the flashes of his past life ceased, the entity seemed to withdraw, and sensation once again returned to his body. He admitted he was extremely disturbed by this incident.

This had been only the most recent of a series of strange events throughout his life. He had experienced similar paralytic episodes before, each associated with some out-of-body flight, and on one occasion had seen a UFO radiating pulses of light as if it were signaling to him. Once, he felt as though he had been dragged out of his bedroom through a glass window one winter night, drawn physically into a UFO that had been hovering over a field.

In Australia on August 8, 1993, at about 5:00 p.m., Kelly Cahill and her family were driving from Melbourne to Monbulk. Near Belgrave, she saw a row of orange lights in a field. As the car passed the field, she had time to see that the lights were on a disc-shaped object, about 15 metres in diameter and resting near or just over the ground.

By the time she told her husband what she had seen, the object was already out of sight behind some trees, and he refused to believe it was anything other than an aircraft. They arrived at their destination feeling a bit odd, but they talked with others about the incident and laughed it off.

During the next few weeks, something began bothering Kelly and her husband. She began to vividly recall something much more unusual about their trip, and having nightmares in which she was visited in their bedroom by strange creatures, one of which was a "soul vampire." Her husband frequently became upset to hear her tell of such things. (Eventually, their marriage broke down entirely.) She had to be taken to the hospital twice during the next few weeks, once for intense stomach pain and the other for a uterine infection. She also had an odd triangular mark around her navel.

A counselor Kelly had been seeing to deal with the nightmares helped her relax to the point where she spontaneously recalled another part of their experience on the highway. They had been driving when a brilliant light appeared on the road ahead. She told her husband to stop, but he continued along, passing somehow through the object. The next conscious memory was of driving along several kilometres later, as if nothing had ever happened. Eventually Kelly remembered even more, and she was able to recall that their experience on the highway was more complex than they had originally remembered.

Her memory was now that she had convinced her husband to stop the car, and they got out to look at a huge object about 50 metres in diameter, which was glowing a soft blue and had orange lights around its upper rim. They walked towards it and saw another car parked there as well. When they got close to the craft, they encountered a seven-foot-tall creature, black and "void of colour." It had mesmerizing, glowing red eyes, and Kelly experienced great fear and dread when it approached. Soon, she saw several other identical creatures congregating in small groups. She screamed at them to leave her and the people from the other car alone, and she prayed to God to dispel these demonic beings. Suddenly, she and her husband were back in the car and they were heading for their original destination, but they were about an hour later than they had planned.

Credit: Ufology Research.

The face of a bedroom visitor, drawn by an abductee in 1987.

Had the story ended there, it would be a rather unique enough abduction account, but Kelly was determined to find out more about what had happened that night. She contacted a university for advice and found herself rebuffed and ridiculed. She then located a ufologist who listened to her story and placed an advertisement in a newspaper for witnesses to any event about the same time and date. The result was unexpected; another family, presumably the one from the other car Kelly had seen, came forward with descriptions of the exact same object and even drawings of the same tall, black creatures, although they did not have the large red eyes.

These two women and one man were driving near where Cahill and her family were encountering the UFO and aliens when they all heard an odd noise and fainted. The man who was driving lost control of the car and hit a pole, and after checking briefly for damage continued on. But the two women had conscious memory of being taken on board a strange craft and being subjected to a physical examination. Under hypnosis, the man was able to remember parts of his abduction as well. Their combined experiences have led ufologists to suggest that this was the first time independent witnesses were found to support the reality of an alien abduction.

People in Ufology

Donald Menzel was one of the foremost American astronomers who specialized in nebulae — remnants of exploded stars. However, in the context of UFOs, he is better known as having been one of the most vocal debunkers, insisting that flying saucers were nothing but fanciful notions of an uneducated public.

These were only a handful of the many cases that have been written up in books and magazines over the past few decades. In several volumes, Whitley Strieber described his own series of abduction experiences, and his work and that of others has served to popularize the phenomenon with an alarming effect on the populace.

WHAT DOES THIS ALL MEAN?

A scientific conference on alien abductions was held at MIT in June, 1992. The meeting laid the groundwork for investigation and research in this field, looking at diverse aspects of the phenomenon, including the use of hypnosis, case studies, and the development of clear and consistent methodology that would allow the scientific community to better appreciate the work that was being done. The conference was most noted, perhaps, for the discussion of a code of ethics for abduction investigators. This code was designed so that, in parallel with other psychosocial fields of research, practitioners would "Above all do no harm." In fact, not long after the conference, such a code was drafted and offered to ufologists, but few have formally endorsed the document. Other similar codes of behaviour among ufologists have been drafted, but without a formal regulating and monitoring body they are not enforceable. At the conference, Dr. Stuart Appelle of psychology at SUNY noted in unfortunate understatement that "many investigators in ufology are not acting professionally."

During the past few decades, hundreds of people have come forward with claims of their own abductions, and investigators are trying to deal with this new aspect of ufology as best they can. Although some psychologists are convinced that abductions are a psychological reaction to personal problems, others, especially those who have studied a large number of such cases, do not believe that the abduction phenomenon can be so easily resolved.

There is no consensus as to what really happens in abduction experiences. Some researchers insist that witnesses are actually encountering alien beings, while others suggest that the experiences are nothing more than vivid dreams. But even if they are dreams, the traumas associated with these experiences seem to indicate that the witnesses and victims are having particularly strange psychological reactions to something in their lives or their environment.

Some skeptics have argued that abductees have a kind of psychological condition that makes them fantasy-prone and causes them to think in abnormal ways. Studies of abductees given standard or specialized psychological testing, however, usually do not show such abnormalities. One example is that of an abductee who had been counselled by psychiatrist John Mack, and gave a presentation at the MIT conference. His psychological tests found him to be "highly functioning, alert, focused, intelligent, well-spoken and without visible anxiety." Mack also noted that "most significant is the absence of psychopathology," with no sign of "psychosis or major affective disorder." So, if most abductees are diagnosed as "normal" by psychologists, then what other process could be at work?

Regardless of the reality of abduction experiences, it is obvious that something unusual is being reported that should be studied in detail. A number of decades ago, UFO investigators would often ignore reports of creatures associated with sightings of flying saucers. This was because the observation of aliens was deemed too bizarre, even for UFO enthusiasts, who were already facing a negative image from biased news stories that poked fun at them. Over the years, however, the acceptance of various entities associated with UFOs has become the norm, and more attention is given to such cases.

Statistically, very few UFO reports have associated entities, although when considering the hundreds of thousands of UFO cases now on record, the number of entity cases is not insignificant. British ufologist Jenny Randles has suggested that "it is perfectly possible to consider that UFOs and abductions are two separate phenomena linked by an accident of social context."

Over the past few years, there has been a strong public interest in abduction stories, and some ufologists view them as perhaps the next step beyond mere contact with aliens. They reason that if we are under observation by extraterrestrials, then the infrequent examination as a guinea pig is a plausible scenario. Unfortunately, there has never been any incontestable physical evidence to support the claims of such contact, leading to the basic problem of the acceptance of UFOs by the scientific community.

Until such time as verifiable proof of alien visitation is found by the populace, we are left with a volume of cases that are simply suggestive of space entities in our midst, and with a fascinating body of stories that are said to be true tales of alien encounters. Skeptics insist that they are imaginary events, but to those who are witnesses or victims of the strange phenomena, they are as real as anything else in life.

THE PSYCHOLOGY OF ABDUCTIONS

Once some ufologists started to accept elaborate abduction stories as true, there was a need to effectively quantify the experiences. Some abductees remembered their alien encounters, while others did not until they were hypnotized to unlock their "missing time" episodes. Psychologists and psychiatrists gingerly began to get involved with abductees. Because abduction was still a generally taboo subject within the medical profession, only a few medical professionals ventured to offer their opinions on what was really happening.

One of the first people to openly study abductions was Leo Sprinkle, a clinical psychologist in Wyoming. He was a consultant to the famous Condon Report, advising the USAF/University of Colorado team on the psychology of UFO witnesses. Sprinkle's interest in the subject was related to a UFO sighting of his own in the early 1960s. His curiosity about the nature of the UFO phenomenon was heightened when he was called in to help investigate some early UFO abductions, particularly at Pascagoula in 1973 and in the case of Sandy Larson in 1975. In the 1980s, Sprinkle founded the Rocky Mountain UFO Conference, where abductees could find solace and support from each other and abduction therapists. The yearly event has a definite New-Age bias, and this is reflected in the personalities and beliefs of the abductees that attend. (Later, Sprinkle himself revealed that he was probably an abductee.)

Sandra Larson

Sandra Larson was driving with her boyfriend and her daughter to Bismarck, North Dakota, on August 26, 1975, at 4:00 a.m., when they had a weird abduction experience. They heard a rumbling noise, and then saw eight orange lights come down from the sky and approach their car. They then had a feeling of disorientation, and Sandra was suddenly in the back seat of the car instead of the front seat where she had been sitting next to her boyfriend. They continued driving and when they reached a gas station, they discovered that they had taken an hour longer than expected.

Later, under hypnosis, Sandra related the story of her abduction. Her captors had probed her in a medical procedure of some sort, and she vividly remembered the operating table where this had taken place. She felt as though her entire brain had been removed after an alien device was focused on her head. The aliens themselves were bizarre: their heads seemed to be wrapped in bandages, like mummies, and their arms were like the segmented metal rods found in a Meccano set.

UFO Hotspot: Warminster, England

Although the wave of UFO sightings here exploded in the 1960s, reports have continued intermittently since then.

The Larson case was remarkable in that it contained the incredible imagery typical of abduction cases in more recent years. When probed further by Sprinkle's hypnosis, Sandra also recalled being levitated through solid walls and having had a series of bedroom visitations earlier in her life. Moreover, her experience seemed to be entirely original. Neither the Hill case nor the Pascagoula case had the dreamlike qualities that Larson described.

In effect, the Larson case was the turning point in ufology. Because it had elements of both a nuts-and-bolts experience but also the dreamlike bedroom visitations, it was a forerunner of the cases that John Mack would study decades later. It brought together two disparate groups within ufology: those who approached the UFO phenomenon from a scientific perspective, and those who did not.

John Mack

John Mack was a Harvard psychiatrist who devoted his time to counselling — and studying — abductees. He risked his professional reputation by indulging in this particular subject, and indeed his status at Harvard was eventually challenged by a review committee concerned about his public support of abduction ufology. In the end, the committee found no reason to suspend Mack, and it appears as though academia grudgingly accepted the idiosyncrasy of one of its own.

Mack's book *Abduction*, published in 1994, details case after case of abductees and comes to the conclusion that something very unusual is happening to these people. In fact, he makes it clear he believes that none of the abductees' experiences can be attributable to mental illness.

Despite this, the case histories he presents show bizarre behaviour and incredible descriptive testimony that stretch belief. Furthermore, many of the case histories note that the abductees had been in abusive domestic situations, were leading difficult lives, or had other experiences suggesting that they may have been in need of psychological counselling. Some were deeply involved in New Age beliefs, and it could be that their abductions were a consequence of their desire to improve their personal well-being through an imagined experience. (One abductee told Mack he was "spiritually attached to deer" because it was his "totem animal.")

For example, in Mack's book, an abductee named Jerry is described as an ordinary housewife. Through Mack's counselling and therapy, she recalled an incredible series of medical procedures at the hands of aliens, who also gave her a gynaecological examination when she was only 13 years old. Since that time she had an aversion to sex. However, one must also consider how her parents were divorced when she was eight, and she married her first husband when she was 19 and pregnant. This marriage ended quickly, partly because she "never loved him" and because he "played sexual games" with the children.

Another abductee, named Joe, was himself a psychotherapist who worked with people to overcome their fears of the dark and other ailments. Under Mack's hypnosis, Joe remembered how aliens had experimented upon him and inserted a painful needle into his neck, behind his ear. But Joe came from a family who were dysfunctional and emotionally tight, and he wasn't hugged or kissed much as a child. As a teenager he experimented with LSD, and later in life he retreated into northern Maine, where he lived by himself for a year. He was on a "personal quest" and sought "spiritual understanding," even joining a spiritualist church. One of the memories unlocked through Mack's hypnosis was when an alien baptized Joe, who said the aliens told him they loved him. It's not hard to interpret Joe's lifelong spiritual quest as having something to do with his personal angst, and that the compassionate aliens filled a desperate need for acceptance and reassurance in his life.

In short, the cases presented by Mack show that while the abductees were not officially diagnosed with any mental illness, there are many signs that they had troubling lives, needed some positive reinforcement or affirmation that they were special, and were looking for some hope.

In his speculations as to why the aliens are abducting humans, Mack went as far to postulate that in cases where abductees did have a history of sexual abuse, the aliens were led to "intervene in a protective or healing manner." In other words, he felt abductees have alien encounters because the aliens are compassionate, not because the abductees are traumatized and are imagining the aliens as saviours.

Mack seemed to accept some very strange elements within the abductees' experiences. One woman said that after her abduction, she was returned to Earth wearing underwear that was not her own. The interpretation? Alien fallibility.

Mack dismissed his critics on various grounds and suggested that abductees' incredible experiences and memories "are experientially true but didn't factually happen in this reality." But what does *that* mean?

Mack believed that aliens are abducting humans for purposes unknown, and that it has been going on for many, many years. He interviewed hundreds of abductees at length over the course of his research. He debated skeptics on TV and at conferences, often gaining the upper hand because of his prowess at logical argument and his knowledge of ufology, something that most debunkers did not have.

Mack died in 2004 in a tragic accident, cutting short what would have been a decidedly interesting lifetime of publishing in this field.

In Their Own Words

Las Vegas, Nevada
January 22, 1995

It was a calm afternoon in Vegas on January 22nd and my neighbor decided we were going to go and try out some of his new hand guns he had gotten for Xmas so we loaded the truck and set off for a safe place to go shoot. We ended up about 10 miles outside of Beatty Nevada.

Unfortunately we had trouble with the guns and had to pack up early. We got done getting everything loaded into the truck for the trip back and were just doing some star gazing when we noticed 4 flashing lights in the sky right below Orion's belt. As they moved they stayed perfectly in line; the lights would blink one after the other: red, white, green and blue.

We had watched jets from the base do maneuvers over the desert all evening and these lights were traveling much faster then any jet we had seen in the sky that night or any night for that matter. (Might I add that my neighbor had previously worked for the Air Force for many years working on all of their top jets, F16, SR22, etc. He stated that he had not seen any of our planes move at the speed these lights were going: up, down, left, right and just at a hover in the sky.)

We watched for what seemed to be 45 min or so and the lights went behind the mountain. As they rose above the mountain crest about 20 min later they flashed a bright array of their colored lights and then faster than anything we had ever seen they shot off into the sky and disappeared so quickly if you weren't looking you would have never seen. We got the chills so we left.

The next day my neighbor told me that the time we had thought we got back in to town and the actual time we arrived were hours apart. His watch which had just been fitted with a new 5 year battery was hours ahead of actual time. Somewhere we had lost about 2 and a half hours. His watch was going and still is going ga-ga.

We have yet to go back to the site and look for more speeding lights but since the incident he and I have had recurring dreams about lights and objects. Some of our dreams have even been exactly the same.

Some say this is hard to believe but when truth is kept from so many for so long the only thing relevant is disbelief. Those that do accept the almost unacceptable are the awoken ones. Those that refuse to believe are the blind.

Reported by Kim H.
Source: Ufology Research

OTHER THEORIES ABOUT ABDUCTIONS

The trouble in disagreeing with Mack's findings is that very little unbiased and truly objective scientific research has been done on the abduction phenomenon to date, and one would need such data to refute his work. Vocal debunkers of abductions, such as Philip Klass, who called abduction therapy a "dangerous game," claim they don't have the time or resources to spend on the issue in order to produce a consistent rebuttal.

There is widespread disagreement among ufologists as to the nature of abductions. Some, like Mack was, are convinced of alien benevolence. Others such as David Jacobs, who writes of the threat of alien abductors in our midst, see a darker purpose. To Jacobs, the abduction phenomenon is due to the aliens' breeding of human/alien hybrids. They have now bred several generations of hybrids, who have human emotions but are second-class citizens on the aliens' spacecraft, performing menial labour and being oppressed. In fact, hybrids are the reason we know about the aliens' ultimate plan "to take over the world." The aliens have slowly been replacing us all with a hybrid population, and soon, within no more than a generation, the world will be theirs.

Perhaps the hybrids are bored and starting to rebel against their masters, to the point of telling abductees about the aliens' secrets. However, because the hybrids are not quite human, they feel no remorse for occasionally sexually abusing female abductees.

Jacobs feels that his "competent hypnosis" style is able to sort out the difference between fact and fiction in abductees' stories. Those who describe disparate details from his scenario are likely not understanding proper abduction research methodology.

3
MEMORIES AND MEMENTOS

HYPNOSIS

Common to many published accounts of alleged alien abduction is the hypnosis of abductees, whose memories are regressed to the time of the incident in order to uncover what might be suppressed or hidden. The kinds of experiences revealed include medical examinations aboard spacecraft, an imparting of spiritual guidance or wisdom, reassurance of life achievements, or trips into outer space with beings from other planets.

From a psychological standpoint, hypnotic regressions are sometimes useful as therapy to uncover suppressed feelings or remove mental blocks. Some ufologists use hypnotic regressions to penetrate the witnesses' memories of their experiences, which may have been deliberately clouded by their antagonists. Skeptics note that hypnosis cannot determine the truth of any memory, but instead allows a person's own beliefs to come through, whether they are true or not. That is, if a person believes he or she has been aboard a UFO, even if they were not, then they will still relate the false experience under hypnosis. Hypnosis, then, cannot be used to accurately distinguish between fact and fantasy.

Hypnosis focuses one's thoughts on a particular task or memory, blocking out other distracting thoughts or memories. Not everyone can be hypnotized, though; people who make good hypnotic subjects are those who can read a book while in a noisy or crowed room, pick out the flute playing in a symphony, or otherwise focus on a certain task while ignoring all other distractions. And, while hypnosis is itself not a science, it is a tool that can be used to produce repeatable results, which can then be used as scientific data.

Hypnosis was actually discovered after its inventor, Franz Mesmer, misunderstood what was causing certain reactions in his patients. Mesmer was a Bavarian scientist who, during the 18th century, thought that stroking a person's hands and feet with a magnet could affect our bodily fluids and thus cure disease. He found that some relief from headache could be achieved that way, but it later turned out that it was just as effective to talk quietly and have the patient imagine his or her aches were disappearing. Even soft music allowed patients to relax and feel better. (From his name we get the term *mesmerize*, which means to entrance or focus our attention.)

The term *hypnotism* comes from the name of the Greek god Hypnos, who ruled the realm of night and sleeping. It was thought in the 1800s that relaxed trance states were caused by being overtired, and that hypnosis made use of our tiredness. However, by the 1900s it was realized that trance states were something other than ordinary sleep, and that they were related to focusing one's attention in a particular way. It was quickly learned that people were highly suggestible to outside influence and ideas during these states.

Clinical hypnosis, which is different from stage hypnosis, can be used to induce a light trance that can be effective in altering problematic habits like smoking, eating disorders, and chronic anxiety. The degree to which hypnosis can be effective in treating such minor disorders is dependent on a person's suggestibility, the depth of their behavioural history, their age, and other factors.

Deeper hypnotic states are used clinically to treat amnesia, trauma, and other mental disorders. Again, although hypnosis can be used to recover lost or hidden memories, the images and content of the memories may not always be accurate. There could be other factors that influence a person's suppression of a particular memory, and the person guiding the hypnosis may inadvertently insert their own bias or impressions, which will alter the real memories.

This makes sense, since even our conscious memories are fluid and can be altered by external influences and competing memories. We will often forget details of certain events in our past and insert words, locations, people, and feelings into scenes where they were not originally present. Why would recovered memories be any more reliable?

A phenomenon called *false memory syndrome* is of real concern to those wishing

UFOs and Aliens in Literature

The Grays is a 2006 book by Whitley Strieber, about how humans are being contacted and abducted by aliens from other planets and dimensions. Secret government organizations and military units are dealing with the alien onslaught, including the actions of aliens who are up to no good in locations around the United States. The short-statured, large-headed, almond-eyed Grays are taking DNA samples from humans to make a clone that has emotions — something that the aliens lack.

to use hypnosis to recover lost or suppressed memories. As noted, memories regained through hypnosis may not always be accurate; a UFO witness' memory of being taken aboard a spacecraft by grey-skinned aliens may not actually reflect reality if recovered through hypnosis. However, some studies of recovered memories have shown that many of the images regained in this way are accurate — depending on the skill of the hypnotist and the way in which suggestion is used during the process.

The case of Sandra Larson (previously discussed) is particularly interesting in this regard. While Dr. Leo Sprinkle, the therapist who worked with her and performed the regressive hypnosis, was caring and deeply concerned with the psychological well-being of Larson and her daughter, he may have had some bias in his investigation.

Sprinkle is well-known within ufology, having been involved in many noted UFO cases, as well as cases involving other bizarre phenomena such as cattle mutilations and psychic events. Since Sprinkle believes he is an abductee, too, one can wonder if his experiences have influenced his treatment of abductees — or the other way around.

SLEEP PARALYSIS

Just after you lie down on your bed, turn off the TV, and switch off the light on your side table, something interesting happens to your brain. Your body begins to secrete certain hormones that tell your brain to stop sending signals to your arms and legs in preparation for sleep. This is primarily because when we are asleep, there is a possibility that we would move and act out our dreams, causing us to fall out of bed, trip over a table, and so on. People who have restless leg syndrome or twitch in their sleep (or even sleepwalk) are lacking in this particular set of hormones at nighttime.

The reverse occurs when we begin waking up: our body stops making the hormones and the brain starts sending signals again to our extremities that it's okay again to move around. However, if the hormone has not been absorbed correctly, we may wake up and still be unable to move. If so, we may feel as though we are paralyzed and panic. We may even be unable to cry out in fear or surprise.

This sensation of *sleep paralysis* can last several minutes and may be very frightening. Sometimes, since the entire body will not respond to the conscious brain's commands, even the chest and torso will not move. This feels as if something or someone is pressing down on your chest, making it difficult to breathe, even though the lungs are unaffected.

The feeling of paralysis together with the sensation of weight on the chest is sometimes called *old hag syndrome*. Fear and panic can cause the paralyzed person to have heightened sensory awareness, which leads to hearing odd sounds, seeing patterns in light and darkness, and believing that an entity is in the room. A feeling of being watched is common as well. The "hagging" part of it comes from the belief that a person experiencing this paralysis is under demonic attack by a succubus, an evil being, that is hovering over the bed and slowly strangling or asphyxiating the victim.

These feelings and sensations are classified as *hypnagogic* and *hypnopompic* experiences, the former occurring as sleep begins and the latter as we wake up. Hypnagogic phenomena are an attempt by the brain to make sense of sensory input while the nerves are being impaired or restricted by the hormones at work shutting down the body. Hypnopompic phenomena occur while the sleeping brain is receiving information from wide-awake senses but cannot process it effectively.

It is easy to see why sleep paralysis is of importance to UFO abductions. In many alien abduction stories, the witness describes being unable to move as the aliens appear to come through walls or doors, and while the witness is laying on a bed just before going to sleep. If there is a physical reason why people in bed can find themselves paralyzed, then it may explain some aspects of alien abduction accounts.

IMPLANTS

Is there any physical evidence of alien abductions? Some people would say yes, as there have been many claims regarding so-called alien implants being found in abductees.

It is true that some abductees *have* found small, unusual bits of metal or other substances within their bodies, and some people seem to have memories of aliens placing them there. These implants have been collected and examined by researchers, and reported in UFO literature. If the objects were in fact of alien origin, then there would be no question that clandestine examinations of humans were actually taking place.

The trouble is that the implants appear to be anything but devices for tracking or monitoring abductees. Each one is different, with different shapes and sizes, and is made from differing elements. They have been removed from behind ears, in wrists, noses, shoulders, and, in one celebrated case, a toe. Some of these implants are encased in organic membranes and display no sign of rejection by the body.

While abduction experts excitedly point to these artefacts as proof of alien intervention, others candidly note the assumption as baffling, since one would assume that the aliens who reportedly inserted these implants wouldn't use devices made of the same elements found on Earth. One such implant was found to be composed of aluminum, silicon, and titanium.

It was noted that this object "would be a transducer and can be used to transmit signals." But radiologists who had seen copies of one abductee's X-rays said they were similar to those of patients who had stepped on a needle or metal fragment that later migrated to another location, which then became encased in mineral deposits and tissue. Furthermore, what could be said about an alien tracking program with methodology varying from subject to subject? Wouldn't it at least make sense to put the implant in the same part of the body on each individual?

The main proponent of implant research is Derrel Sims, an investigator for the Houston UFO Network (HUFON). In 1995, he worked with Dr. Roger Leir, a podiatrist who has removed several implants, including three from a woman's toe and one from a man's hand. Sims is a former military police officer with no degree from any major accredited institution, but several from various hypnotherapy and personal growth institutes. His obsession with proving the extraterrestrial origin of implants has been shared with many others.

UFO Hotspot: Sagauche County

According to
the Computer UFO Network, this Colorado
county has the highest rate of UFO sightings in the U.S. —
almost 3,000 per 100,000 people.

Sims believes the recovery of implants is well-documented, and that the examination of these foreign bodies supports the theory that abductees are unwilling subjects of medical examinations or research. In some cases, this includes being surrogate hosts to embryo or fetal implants.

Virgil Priscu, an Israeli anaesthesiologist specializing in emergency room medicine, had an opportunity to meet and talk with Sims when the latter was giving a presentation to a group of believers. Priscu was not at all impressed. In a post to a UFO-related Internet mailing list, he noted: "I am afraid that all claims made by Mr. Sims or his associates have not been confirmed or underwent a peer review process. Therefore, I personally have serious doubts as to the veracity of these claims ..."

A physician familiar with foreign bodies found in patients, Priscu said:

> I know a thing or two about what we call "Foreign Bodies" (FBs) found quite often, especially in the feet of some unsuspecting patients by an incidental x-ray made for another purpose. They get there by various methods: walking or playing barefoot on the beach, grass, etc., and not noticing when the FB gets in.
>
> During a fall, running or getting hurt by some other bigger object from which a small splinter can get into one's foot and remain there for many, many years under the skin - until sometimes they are discovered by chance while some other physician or medical practitioner - like a podiatrist - is examining the patient for another, unrelated complaint - and sometimes x-ray their feet!
>
> If it is a substance that degrades slowly, after years only a small notch of "reaction" tissue remains in place of the former FB. It is composed of human tissue components. No mystery, no "implants."

However, Eve Frances Lorgen, another abduction expert and a profound believer in extraterrestrial intervention, said some implants removed were studied by two different pathologists, and then sent to various independent laboratories for extensive scientific analysis. The tests showed they were composed of aluminium, silicon, and titanium. And, because it was noted that these metals are used to manufacture transistors and semiconductors, and because they resist corrosion, conduct heat and electricity, "we can then extrapolate from that knowledge and form the obvious conclusion." Are implants are some kind of alien transponders? Medical experts argued that implants are only tissue that develops around any retained foreign matter in the body. In rebuttal, one interpretation offered by implant proponents is that the implanted objects are passive devices that must be scanned by alien sensors in order to be detected. However, it seems more reasonable to assume the implants are nothing more than what they appear: bits of glass, metal, and wood from old injuries long forgotten by abductees.

Nevertheless, the scientific testing of implants is a positive step towards verification of such phenomenon. To date, tests are done in relative secrecy and the methodology communicated only within a small circle of insiders. One reason for this is because mainstream science frowns on claims regarding alien implants, and would come down hard on a staff scientist who was openly interested in the subject, let alone using valuable research time and equipment for such an endeavour.

However, a few brave individuals arrange such testing as part of their professional development and personal curiosity. Canadian ufologist Nick Balaskas has assisted with several implant tests, with minimal results. Among the first things he looked at were X-rays of a UFO witness — they appeared to show an implant inside his head. Even though several other independent physicians and radiologists asked to examine the X-rays could not explain the mysterious object in the images, Balaskas' radiologist easily found that the object could be positively identified as an elastic hair band.

In Their Own Words

Riverside, California
March 4, 2010

On this particular night, I was parking my car after returning home from a friend's house. I generally look up at the night sky anyway, but on this particular night I heard a helicopter approaching from my right.

Thinking nothing much of it, I get out of the car and pan my head over in the direction of the helicopter. When I did this, I saw a very large object slowly approach overhead and it looked to me like it was being escorted by a helicopter.

The helicopter was flying directly adjacent to this very large triangular object. I'd say it was about 2–3 football fields in diameter. I saw the 3 bright lights making out the triangular shape, and noticed a very slow, pulsing red light in the bottom of the object.

Stunned at what I was seeing, I froze to look at the object in the middle of the street. It was about 6–700 feet above me, flying fairly low and extremely slow for an aircraft that large.

The curious thing about it was that it made absolutely no noise. All I heard the whole time was the sound of the helicopter and nothing else.

When the object went straight over my head, I felt a very eerie feeling — like I was being watched at that very moment. After it went overhead and beyond the horizon, it looked like it was heading toward (the direction of) March Air Force Base into the San Timoteo Canyon.

The total event only lasted a few minutes, and I thought it was very interesting that it looked like the helicopter was escorting it.

Reported by Anonymous
Source: UFOCasebook.com

GET THE SCOOP

The other seemingly tangible evidence of alien experimentation is the scoop marks found on abductees' following their experiences. Unfortunately, the history and date of creation of such marks often are frustratingly difficult to establish.

This is not, however, the way such physical scars are portrayed in popular UFO literature. Scoop marks are now an accepted part of standard abduction fare, and most pro-UFO writers mention them as factual components of many abduction experiences. Some abductees have memories of being subjected to painful experimentation at the hands of aliens, and small horseshoe, triangular, or bowl-shaped scars on various parts of their bodies are proof of their tortures. The assumption is that the aliens require some of our DNA or must take biopsies of humans in order to proceed with whatever programs they are undertaking at our expense.

A procedure known as a puncture biopsy is one way in which terrestrial physicians obtain tissue samples for study. However, hair strands can provide DNA, too, and are much less intrusive and painful to procure. Saliva can give alien researchers more microbial life forms than they can count on one tentacle. Puncture biopsies also don't make much sense if the aliens are really as omnipotent as is claimed. After all, if, as reported by abductees, the aliens can walk through walls, levitate cars, slow down time, and manipulate our memories, why should they need to perform such minor operations?

The scars are problematic in other ways, too. Abductees with scoop marks sometimes claim that the marks appeared overnight or that they had no recollection of ever being injured in that part of their bodies. Documented proof of such claims is elusive. How do we *know* that a particular scar on a knee was not present before an abduction, other than taking the abductee's word? Further, some marks vanish with time, too. Other abductees have reported being subjects of alien operations, immediately after which there were no scars whatsoever!

One case of this kind is that of the previously mentioned Sandy Larson, who was abducted with her daughter while driving from Fargo to Bismarck in North Dakota in August 1975. During hypnotic regression, Larson, one of the earliest reported abductees, seemed to have a memory of aliens actually opening up her skull and operating on her brain. She was stitched together again without any visible scarring.

In 1976, an article in a popular UFO magazine documented Leo Sprinkle's investigation and hypnotic regression of Larson. During one of his many sessions with Sandy and her daughter, Sprinkle may have accidentally helped along the conscious recall of Sandy's experience. She seemed to recall that on board the spacecraft, an alien, which looked like a six-foot-tall mummy with a miner's light on its head, had operated on her brain. One published transcript reads:

> SPRINKLE: Do you have a feeling of what kind of experiment it is?
> LARSON: I feel like I breathe different … It's like somebody took a knife and made the inside of my nose sore.
> SPRINKLE: Made the inside of your nose sore?
> LARSON: Scraped it.
> SPRINKLE: Did you see anybody touching your nose?
> LARSON: Uh huh.
> SPRINKLE: Could you see hands?
> LARSON: No.
> SPRINKLE: Could you see an instrument of some kind?

LARSON: Yeah.
SPRINKLE: Can you describe it?
LARSON: I would say like a little knife or like a cotton swab.
SPRINKLE: Not very big, but something that was placed inside your nose?

Here we see that, according to the published article, Sprinkle *himself* seems to have suggested that something was put inside Sandy's nose. In fact, since this article was published in 1976, this could be an original source of the popular abduction story element where an implant is placed in someone's nose. The point is it may have been the therapist and not the abductee who had suggested something being placed into the nose, even if it was simply an inaccurate quote.

The mystery seems to completely evaporate later in the article when it is noted:

Curiously enough, some time before, Sandy had undergone a very similar operation performed on her by a local physician, who was treating her for a sinus ailment. The operation proved quite painful and its effects lasted for more than a couple of months. Sandy was scheduled to undergo further treatment but, remembering the extreme discomfort, chose not to pursue the matter. Before long, her sinuses ran as freely as they ever had. She claims, however, that in the months since [her abduction], *she has had no trouble whatsoever.* [emphasis in original]

It seems more probable that Sandy's bad memories of her sinus operation spilled over into her dreams, creating the memory of the alien's sinus procedure, than the that the alien had been responsible for the cure.

As for her brain, she thought that it had been removed later in the operation.

SPRINKLE: Is there anything else you can recall about the examination?
LARSON: It feels like they're separating me ... Feels like they reached their hand on the top of my head and took the brain out and set it beside me.
SPRINKLE: Do you remember looking and seeing at that time?
LARSON: No.

The point here is that Sandy had no physical signs of brain surgery, let alone another sinus operation. So, if the aliens are capable of such advanced surgical techniques that they can perform brain surgery without leaving any physical indications, calling scoop marks on abductees' legs and forearms evidence of alien abduction seems rather problematic. It appears possible that both implants and scoop marks have their origins in UFO literature outside of actual cases.

A later case, in 1977, involved a Canadian woman whose encounters with aliens included being operated upon to remove a cancerous cyst inside her arm. She said that aliens possessed highly advanced technology, including interstellar drives, mind-reading devices, matter transporters, invisibility, and advanced surgical techniques.

When asked for proof of her claims, the woman explained how, while aboard their main ship high above the Earth, the aliens had used an amazing X-ray device on her that indicated she had a cancerous cyst within her arm, which had otherwise gone unnoticed by terrestrial physicians. She rolled up her sleeve to show that she did not have any trace of a scar from the aliens' operation, during which they removed all trace of the cyst and repaired her arm completely.

Why would some alien surgeries leave scars and others not? Perhaps some abductees' stories are false and others true. Perhaps the aliens have learned new techniques over time. Perhaps one race of aliens has perfected scarless surgery and has not shared the knowledge with their kin.

UFOs and Aliens on TV

The unsuccessful, humorous SF TV series *The Chronicle*, ran 2001–2002, just as the *X-Files* was winding down. Its premise was that a tabloid newspaper really did publish the truth: aliens, monsters, and Elvis all walk the Earth. It was itself a version of the well-conceived *Night Stalker* starring Darren McGavin, whose factual newspaper employer frowned on his consistently finding ghosts, monsters, demons, and aliens when out on routine news assignments, usually managing to save the world in the process.

4
ALIENS AND CREATURES

Despite what you may have observed in popular culture and newspaper tabloids, green-skinned aliens have rarely been reported by UFO witnesses. The grey-skinned variety is most common, although the blondes (or Nordics) are quite popular as well. In the 1950s, contactees almost exclusively described contacts with human-like aliens, most often with blonde hair. These aliens were usually benevolent, taking people on trips to Mars and Venus but also commissioning contactees as their intergalactic ambassadors. Their messages for mankind were often admonishments about our pollution of the environment or our inhumane treatment of one another. Chastising us for our nuclear tests was also high on their agenda.

Despite their superiority, aliens who have accosted contactees have so far been unable to give them a single clear photograph of their spaceships, or impart some useful knowledge such as a cure for any specific disease or a new kind of rocket fuel. Contactees, then and now, are resigned to spread the word through appearances at conventions and on lecture circuits throughout North America. Some early contactees became so popular that they went on speaking tours around the world.

VENUSIANS AND REPTILIANS

Some contactees claimed they were themselves aliens incarnated in human form so as to live and work among us. Contactee Howard Menger not only received communication from aliens, but he even married a Venusian female who took on the appearance of a beautiful human woman. Menger revealed that he was actually from Saturn, and that he had entered his human body when it was only one year old.

Venus appears to be a very popular alien destination and origin. T. Lobsang Rampa, the British mystic who was born Cyril Henry Hoskin, wrote extensively about Tibetan culture and ancient knowledge until it was revealed he did not speak Tibetan or Chinese and had never visited Asia. However, he wrote a book titled *My Visit to Venus*, in which he described how he and other monks were taken up in a flying saucer by two wise aliens and given a tour of Venus' "fairy cities" and a "beautiful sparkling sea." Aetherius, the alien channelled by George King, was said to live on Venus, as did Jesus. L. Ron Hubbard, founder of Scientology, who is said to have described visiting a thetan "Implant Station" on Venus in one of his religious documents.

On December 3, 1967, police officer Herb Schirmer was on patrol near Ashland, Nebraska, at about 2:30 a.m. He noticed some lights ahead of him on the highway, and as he drove towards them his headlights illuminated an object shaped like two saucers, rim to rim, hovering about two metres above the road. The craft had a shiny, metallic surface and blinking red lights spaced along its upper surface.

As he watched in amazement, the craft began making a loud whining noise and rose higher into the air, then flames came out of its underside. The object moved over the police car and then shot away, vanishing into the distance.

Schirmer got out of his car and walked to the spot over which the craft had been hovering, examining the road with his flashlight. He then drove back to the police station, where he wrote in his logbook that he saw a flying saucer but noted it was 3:00 a.m., half an hour later than he had estimated it to be. Later that shift, he started feeling sick and nervous, had a bad headache, heard a buzzing sound in his head, and found an odd red mark on his neck behind his ear.

The case was investigated by the noted Condon Committee, which received full cooperation from Schirmer and his commanding officer. The sheriff believed his story and attested that Schirmer was a dependable and reliable officer. Schirmer was given a polygraph test, which he passed. He was then hypnotized by a psychologist to retrieve "otherwise inaccessible information" about the UFO.

Under hypnosis, Schirmer recalled approaching what he had assumed was a truck with blinking red lights. A white object came from inside the "truck" and had "mental communication" with him.

Another hypnosis session with a different therapist revealed that Schirmer had been taken from his police car by humanlike beings dressed in tight-fitting grey uniforms. The creatures, reminiscent of lizards, had slanted, black eyes that never blinked, grey skin, flat noses, and mouths like slits. On each one's uniform was the insignia of a winged dragon.

The reptilian aliens, who were about one and a half metres, a bit shorter than

Schirmer, told him that they were space travelers and had bases on Venus. They meant him no harm, although he did admit that they had given him a medical examination while on board the craft.

The Condon Committee, however, said that because of the lack of physical evidence and because there was no way to prove Schirmer's fantastic story, they had "no confidence" that his experience was real.

Among reports of green-skinned or reptilian aliens, the most remarkable claims are those made by conspiracy theorist David Icke. In a collection of books, audiotapes, and videos, he has laid out his thesis that lizard-like aliens have infiltrated the population of Earth. He believes that alien reptiles from the constellation Draco live inside the Earth and "manipulate humanity from another dimension by 'possessing' human bodies." His oddest claim is that the British Royal Family are all members of the "reptilian Brotherhood" and are controlling much of the free world through corruption and manipulation of governments.

Did You Know?

Dozens of UFO sightings are reported each year on Australia's east coast, just north of Sydney.

This last idea may have originated with a science-fiction television mini-series that later spawned a large following. In *V* (1983), enormous flying saucers appear over most major cities on Earth. They are controlled by a race of aliens that look identical to humans and claim that they come in peace, only seeking friendly cooperation and exchange of ideas. As the Visitors possess superior technology and weaponry, terrestrial governments and military powers quickly agree to co-operate with these apparently benevolent beings. However, journalist Mike Donovan and medical student Julie Parrish discover the real intentions and disguised reptile appearance of the aliens, and organize a resistance movement against what are really hostile invaders.

Icke says he is on a mission to warn everyone on Earth about the global conspiracy between reptilian aliens and terrestrial governments. His claims skirt paranoia, and his anti-government stance has made him a very controversial figure indeed. He goes far beyond where early contactees of the 1950s ventured, stringing together ancient astronauts, UFOs, conspiracies, aliens, and radical fundamentalism.

NORDIC ALIENS: THE BLONDES

Before Whitley Strieber's book *Communion* popularized greys as alien visitors, the most common alien encountered by UFO witnesses looked very similar to a human. They were often described as beautiful, with pale skin, blue eyes, thin build, and long yellow or blonde hair.

These Nordics (because they appeared Scandinavian) were first reported by contactees in the United States, but were supplanted by the greys in recent years. They are now more commonly reported in Europe or South America.

Contactee George Adamski first described contact with Nordic aliens in 1952 in Arizona, when he claimed to have met and conversed with Orthon from Venus. Orthon was a strikingly attractive humanlike alien, who piloted a flying saucer and took Adamski for a ride. Orthon naturally told Adamski that his mission to Earth was peaceful and benevolent.

In 1956, Howard Menger said he took photographs of a flying saucer in New Jersey, then had encounters with its Nordic occupants. He even married a female Nordic alien, with whom he was wed for more than 50 years. His aliens, in addition to being benevolent, also wanted to impart practical knowledge to humans, such as how to appreciate life and live longer through proper diets.

More recently, Billy Meier, considered by some to be a hoaxer, claimed that starting in the 1970s and continuing for decades, he had been contacted by several Nordic-appearing aliens. They allowed him to take photographs of their "beam ships" and invited him aboard for trips to other planets, and even back in time to photograph dinosaurs.

GREYS

When the word *alien* is mentioned in the context of extraterrestrial visitors, the most common image that comes to mind for most people is that of a small, grey-skinned alien with large, almond-shaped eyes. This is a recent phenomenon, as the most common image of an alien used to be that of a "little green man."

The 1977 film *Close Encounters of the Third Kind* ended with the appearance of small, spindly, pale-skinned creatures that were forerunners of what would be the standard grey aliens.

The aliens described as greys rose to prominence in 1987 following the publication of the book *Communion* by Whitley Strieber, who wrote about how he was being watched and stalked by small, malevolent beings from outer space. However, pasty-skinned alien creatures had been described in science fiction stories and in UFO reports before that date.

In H.G. Wells' *War of the Worlds*, the Martian that emerges from its spacecraft is a "big grayish rounded bulk" with "two large dark-coloured eyes." It had tentacles instead of arms, but the impression was that of a sickly, menacing creature intent on causing harm. And the leader of the aliens that abducted Betty and Barney Hill in 1961 was grey-skinned, with a large, bulbous forehead, and large, dark, "wrap-around eyes."

Even this latter connection is controversial; debunkers point out that an alien with a similar appearance was featured in an episode of the *Outer Limits* that aired in 1964, just a week or so before Barney was hypnotically regressed. The alien, from the episode "The Bellero Shield," is pale-skinned, with no hair and relatively small eyes, but is quite benevolent. Ultimately the alien is killed by humans, even though it gives us advanced technology. The assumption is that Barney saw the TV alien and it stuck with him, contaminating his memory. However, there is no evidence that he actually saw the show, as he worked nights. He also had consciously recalled a being with "compelling eyes" long before the show or the hypnosis.

The greys are said to be the creatures whose flying saucer crashed near Roswell in 1947. Various claims have the greys' bodies found in the wreckage, while others assert that some survived and have been working with the American government in clandestine operations. This was a major theme in the TV series *The X-Files*, in which the aliens are being assisted (or are they assisting?) in genetic experiments on humans.

In another TV series, *Stargate SG-1*, the American government eventually meets an advanced race of greys called the Asgard, who had been visiting Earth since ancient times as Norse gods. (But oddly enough were not Nordic aliens.)

Since the mid-1980s, greys have been the predominant archetype of a visiting extraterrestrial, appearing in many TV series and video games.

According to UFO mythology, greys are said to be less friendly than the Nordic blondes, having a manipulative streak that extends to coldness when dealing with humans. This is said to be because they are emotionless, perhaps from a genetic flaw or evolution beyond recognizable humanity.

ALIEN HYBRIDS

What, exactly, would aliens want with humans, anyway? One explanation given by some UFO researchers is that the greys are conducting breeding experiments with humans. Many abductees have said that while aboard the aliens' spacecraft, they were shown transparent tubes or tanks filled with unidentified liquids. Floating in these receptacles, in some stories at least, are small, humanoid bodies, often with tubes or wires attached. These abductees report that the aliens are cloning or otherwise manufacturing alien-human hybrids, combining our genetic material with theirs.

Some female abductees claim that, following a series of abduction experiences, they have become pregnant, carrying for a few months and then either miscarrying or suddenly finding themselves not pregnant, as if the baby vanished from their womb. Their interpretation is that during another abduction, the aliens somehow took the fetus from them to raise elsewhere.

Another scenario is that the aliens take ova from human females and sperm from males during medical examinations aboard their spacecraft. This idea can be traced back to the abduction case of Betty and Barney Hill in 1961. During their experience, Betty said she was examined on a operating table. Among other things, the alien doctor inserted a long needle into Betty's belly button. When she asked about it, Betty was told by the alien that it was a "pregnancy test." In 1961, amniocentesis was not widely practiced but was used to check for fetal

UFOs and Aliens in Movies

Independence Day (1996) is a movie about the arrival of giant alien saucer-shaped spacecraft, which use energy beams to destroy many major centres. An attack on a saucer by Earthly military jet fighters results in retaliation by an alien fleet that decimates the humans' best efforts. However, one alien tactical craft is shot down and the alien inside is captured by a USAF pilot and taken to Area 51, where it is learned an alien had crashed in Roswell in 1947. Information gleaned from the craft and the captive alien lead to the development of a computer virus counter-weapon that the jet pilot manages to fly into the aliens' mothership undetected. Just before the aliens launch a final attack on Earth, the human countermeasure works and the Earth is saved, on July 4th, the American Independence Day.

abnormalities, so the pregnancy test explanation was consistent with what was known, even at that time.

In addition, some abductees say that during further abductions they have been introduced to odd-looking humanoid creatures that appear half-human and half-grey. These are said to have pale skin, large heads with big eyes, wisps of blonde hair, and are slightly less frail than the aliens. These alien hybrid children sometimes interact with their human mothers, and may talk with them about things like human emotions and Earth culture. The premise is that emotions such as love, compassion, and forgiveness are impossible for greys, and they are looking to breed them back into their race through this kind of genetic manipulation.

This has certain limitations in reality, however. Such genetic tinkering through breeding would only be possible if the aliens were somehow genetically similar to humans. The only way that would be possible is if they were humans from the far-distant future, or were responsible for our own evolution in the distant past, perhaps sharing a common ancestor.

According to some writers, hybrid children are too fragile to survive on Earth and so must remain aboard the aliens' mothership. It's reasonable to speculate, however, that some might have been bred to the point where they could live on Earth and do so today.

LITTLE GREEN MEN

Although most recent abductees and contactees tend to describe aliens with grey or pale skin, a different colour has become part of the common language surrounding aliens. The term *little green men* is synonymous with *aliens from space*. In older cartoons, Fred Flintstone's alien nemesis was a green fellow called The Great Gazoo. While Marvin the Martian wasn't green, his companions, including an alien dog, were. And Spock, the Vulcan from *Star Trek*, had green blood that made him the focus of sarcastic comments from Dr. McCoy.

The suggestion that aliens from outer space are green has been thought to originate in several science fiction stories and pulp magazines. One in particular was *Amazing Stories*, which published a story titled "The Green Man" in October 1946, just before the age of flying saucers began. In the story by Harold Sherman, a green-skinned alien visits Earth. He is incredibly powerful, using a ray gun to stop cars, and his usual transportation is a flying saucer.

Some researchers have pointed out that the image of a small green creature as a strange visitor dates back many years, long before flying saucers were part of our culture. Fairies and sprites were green in colour according to several different folklores. It's possible that our mythological treatment of small visitors was updated when flying saucers were seen in the 1940s. However, very few actual reports of aliens associated with flying saucers and UFOs mention green skin. How the connection to UFOs became so firm is a cultural mystery.

If You Met An Alien

Let's suppose that *they* are here, and have decided to make themselves known. If you were an alien, where would you land first? To which individual or group of people would you announce your presence? Would you break in on our television broadcast bands on all channels and frequencies and bring greetings? In what language? How would you be able to convey your intentions? (And let's be blunt: what if the aliens' intentions are not benevolent and they actually are here to conquer us and enslave us?)

"Take Me To Your Leader!"
To whom would you take the alien that landed its UFO and came out and spoke to you?
- The President of the United States
- The Prime Minister of Canada
- The Prime Minister of Britain
- The Prime Minister of Russia
- The President of China
- The Queen of England
- The Dalai Lama
- Pope Benedict
- Oprah
- Anderson Cooper
- Your local air force/army base
- Your spouse or boyfriend/girlfriend
- Your parents (they seem to always know just what to do)
- The author of The Big Book of UFOs
- No one (I'll tell the alien that I just happen to be the person in charge of the planet)

5
Other Topics

CROP CIRCLES

In the summer of 1990, news about mysterious crop circles discovered in England was being carried by most media in North America. In addition to the major networks and magazines in Britain, UFO publications were giving a lot of attention to the phenomenon, and it was implied that aliens were definitely responsible for the strange formations.

Ufologists had been keeping track of the British reports through correspondence and media monitoring. There was media interest across the Atlantic in the possibility that there might be North American cases, and researchers had pointed out some historical cases such as those at Rossburn, Manitoba, in 1977 and Langenburg, Sakskatchewan, in 1974. Some British researchers were convinced that crop circles were a uniquely English phenomenon, although the fact that there were earlier North American precedents made it clear that the phenomenon did not "start" in England in about 1980, as some claimed.

Crop circles, as such, were not really a new phenomenon. The North American Institute for Crop Circle Research (NAICCR) was formed as a sister group of Ufology Research of Manitoba in 1990, in response to requests from British cerealogists wanting information about crop circles in North America. It had been realized that, although there were a number of people in North America who were independently investigating cropcircles, there was no comprehensive gathering of data underway. Furthermore, like most UFO or Fortean groups, UFOROM members had been studying crop circles for decades, long before they were popularized in Britain.

In the U.S., many years before the crop circle phenomenon had begun, UFO trace expert Ted Phillips had created a catalogue of physical traces that included many such swirled circles in grass and other plants, long before the 20th century. These unusual ground markings (UGMs) had been "cropping up" from time to time in North America, sometimes with associated UFO sightings.

Investigator Chris Rutkowski standing in a crop circle discovered near St. Francois Xavier, Manitoba.

Path leading to one of the Strathclair crop circles discovered in 1992.

NAICCR began investigating Canadian crop circles and soliciting information on American cases from other investigators and groups. With the co-operation of several researchers, NAICCR published reports and an annual review of North American UGMs, something that British crop circle experts were slow in generating.

In August 1992, a group of crop circles were discovered near Strathclair, Manitoba, about 275 kilometres northwest of Winnipeg, Canada. There were said to be seven separate sites plus a handful of UFO sightings. Since the circles had been found, at least two or three hundred people had visited the formations. Unfortunately, this meant that some evidence, such as tracks and other markings that might have offered a clue as to how the crop circles had formed, was destroyed. Nevertheless, NAICCR investigators made the four-hour trek to the site to get a better look at what had been reported. Another motivating factor in attempting an investigation was that media had been heralding the crop circles in Strathclair as mysterious and baffling, so an objective investigation seemed prudent.

Researchers Roy Bauer, Guy Westcott, and Chris Rutkowski made the journey to Strathclair and began by making casual inquiries in local businesses about the crop circles. Everyone had at least heard of the circles, and some people admitted visiting the sites.

At the RCMP detachment office, the commanding officer barely contained his amusement and joked that he had the aliens in a jail cell. He did admit, though, that the RCMP had also received some calls about some bright lights that weekend. This would have been important in establishing a connection between crop circles and UFOs, something that was considered a foregone conclusion in England.

The investigators went to the local newspaper office where a reporter met them and was able to guide them to a patch of field halfway between Shoal Lake and Strathclair, just outside a hamlet named Ipswich. Once led in on the well-trodden path, the shape of the formation became quite clear.

The formation was an ellipse, 8 by 7.5 metres. And, on a northeasterly heading of 65 degrees, the shape of an arrow protruded away from the crop circle, giving the effect of the symbol for Mars, or male. The wheat was just over a metre tall outside the formation, and was neatly bent and swirled counterclockwise inside the circle.

The wheat was bent away from the circle inside the arrow, toward its end points. The width of the arrow corridor was about 70 centimetres. While investigators measured, took samples and photos, two truckloads of visitors arrived, trampling the neatly woven grain and adding to the disturbed state of the site.

The site was only 12 metres away from the nearest access road and about

PEOPLE IN UFOLOGY

Since 1967, Stanton Friedman, the original civilian investigator of the infamous Roswell crash, has lectured on UFOs at more than 600 colleges and post-secondary institutions in all 50 U.S. states, all Canadian provinces, and in more than a dozen other countries around the globe. His talks, usually titled "Flying Saucers Are Real!", describe in detail how the United States Air Force lied about UFO reports being not of scientific or military interest, and why he believes it is possible and practical to travel between the stars. And, of course, why he believes that someone — or something — is doing just that: visiting Earth from a planet far away.

30 metres from the highway. It had been found on Saturday, August 16, 1992, by the owner of the land, and reported to the media the following day. By that time, word had spread anyway. Once news of the circle had spread, a woman reported that she had seen a UFO over the field on Friday evening. She had been driving from Shoal Lake to Ipswich, and had been passing the field, when she observed a dark object with two headlights and a flashing taillight. The UFO moved slowly over the field at an estimated height of a telephone pole, and about 75 metres away from the witness. After a minute or so, it moved out of sight behind some trees. Two other people driving along the highway also glimpsed the object before it disappeared.

The group of investigators were then led to the next site, nearer Strathclair. This formation was also visible from the highway, and situated on a slight hill so that it was visible to eastbound travelers. It, too, looked like a Mars symbol. This time, the main circle was perfectly circular, about seven metres in diameter. This arrow was thicker than the one at Ipswich and pointed on a bearing of 120 degrees, away from the highway.

Investigators considered how one would go about making such a formation, and the reporter was surprised they did not assume aliens were responsible. He told the investigation team that one of the first people on the scene had found a dinosaur footprint at the point of the arrow. It had been suggested that the arrow could have been made by a ramp extended from the landed, circular UFO. Unfortunately, the numerous visitors to the site had eradicated any sign of the print, so there was no way to verify the claim.

On impulse, the investigators decided to try and duplicate the formation using nothing more than the simple tools in their kits. Noting the wheat was planted in neat rows about 10 centimetres apart, one of the team walked about nine metres away from the site, carefully stepping between two rows. Seeing there was no visible sign of entry, he began walking in what he thought was a circle, met his own path and began spiralling inward. Another person joined in, performing a *triticale pas de deux*, crushing the wheat in a circle six metres in diameter.

In five minutes they had made a fair copy of the original circle. Stems stuck up here and there where they had missed stepping on them, so they did some touch-ups. All were surprised to find that the effort had created an almost perfect circle. Compared with the original site, the new one was declared a reasonable facsimile.

Examining the newly trampled wheat, the team was greatly surprised to find that virtually none was broken. Somehow, the stems were neatly bent over in a counterclockwise direction, swirled into the centre, and showing no evidence of having been trodden upon.

This was interesting because one of the primary points of contention in debates over real and hoaxed British circles is that wheat stems in real circles are bent, not broken. When one crushes wheat underfoot in a field, it is assumed that the wheat stems will show numerous kinks and breakage. However, in creating the fake crop circle, it appeared that this assumption was not always valid.

It was never the intention to show that hoaxers had made the formation this way. Indeed, it was expected that if this were so, there would have been some tools used instead of one's own feet, such as rope, planks, wooden poles, and tape measures. But the original formation had been made a few days after a full Moon, meaning that there would have been significant light available for carrying out the task. Also, the wheat was tall enough to afford cover if a car had chanced to pass on the highway, so any hoaxer could have simply ducked down out of sight when the occasional vehicle came by, and the formation likely would not have been noticed at night.

There were still a few other questions about the formation, however. What was the motive? How was it done, really? Why would anyone bother? And what about the UFO sightings?

Investigators headed for the other sites, which were all approximately five kilometres south of the main highway, along a farming road. Two were directly across a road from one another. As they drove up, they saw that some enterprising young boys were standing in front of one of the formations, wielding a hand-painted sign that read: A LOONIE A LOOK. (*Loonie* is a Canadian slang term for a dollar coin, because of the image of a swimming loon on one side.)

The boys turned out to be a gold mine of information. Contrary to what had been claimed earlier, this particular formation (another arrowed circle) had appeared over a week before the one that had attracted the attention of the media. Further, the one across the road had appeared first, a week before that. After the second had been found, the boys had the insight to make a ring-like path around the whole formation, so that visitors could examine the site without disturbing it. Unfortunately, their idea didn't completely work, as many people had strayed off their path to get a better look. What's more, the ring had been assumed by later visitors to be part of the original formation.

The arrow from this circle pointed on a bearing of 260 degrees. When later plotted on a map, it was disappointing to discover that the directions indicated by all the various arrows did not converge. Furthermore, none of the arrows pointed toward a significant local feature such as a native midden, burial mound, mountain, or new age mystic site.

The fifth site examined was clearly *lodging* — a crushing of grass or wheat caused by a strong downdraft of wind combined with heavy rain, flattening the crop. However, because it was only about a kilometre and a half from the two nearest formations, many people had visited it, thinking it was an additional example of a crop circle.

While it was being examined, more visitors came by and were asked about other sites. The investigation team was given directions to other fields where formations were said to have been found, but were unable to verify any others that day.

It was learned that a TV special on British crop circles had been aired on the Friday night that the Ipswich circle was probably made. It was speculated that someone in the area got the idea to hoax a circle from that show. However, investigation revealed that two circles were found before the show was aired. Other than that program, there had been very little local media attention given to crop circles. There was no national or international coverage of the North American circles during the summer, and the American media were not covering the British formations.

As part of the investigations into the crop formations, both VHF and AM/FM radios were used. No interference was heard at the sites. A compass was not deflected by any magnetic anomaly. A tape recorder worked fine, and there were no beepings or strange signals left on the tape. Animals were not wary to enter the sites (several dogs accompanied the investigators in the fields), and there was no lack of insects. None of us felt any "bad vibes" inside the formations, unlike the experiences claimed by some circle investigators at other formations. All of these effects were checked because some crop circle experts (cerealogists) insist that anomalous phenomena plague crop formations.

Wheat samples collected from crop circles are often sent to researchers for testing. Cerealogists originally believed that *spagyrical analysis* showed changes in the crystalline structure of the plant cells in samples taken from crop circles,

Top 15 Recorded Songs about Aliens or UFOs

"I saw Elvis in a UFO" — Ray Stevens
"UFO" — Sun Ra
"Calling Occupants of Interstellar Craft" — Klaatu
"Pink UFO" — Calm
"I saw a UFO Last Night" — Paul Barfoot
"The Flying Saucer" — Buchanan and Goodman
"Purple People Eater" — Sheb Wooley
"Mr. Spaceman" — The Byrds
"Little Green Men" — Steve Vai
"I've Seen the Saucers" — Elton John
"Zero Zero UFO" — The Ramones
"Hangar 18" — Megadeth
"Aliens Exist" — Blink 182
"UFOs Over Leytonstone" — Squarepusher
"Flying Saucers" — Nina Hagen

whereas samples from outside the formations did not. As well, it had been claimed that some crop formations were radioactive, although that was disproved in the late 1980s and early 1990s, the radiation readings found to be simply glitches in the data.

Other anomalous effects associated with crop circles are the growth studies done by Dr. W. Levengood at the Pinelandia Biophysical Laboratory. He claimed that wheat from crop circles will grow more readily than control samples. This was easy enough to check with the Strathclair samples, but the claim could not be confirmed.

BRITISH CROP FORMATIONS

A series of programs were implemented in the late 1980s and early 1990s to systematically investigate crop formations in Britain. These included Projects White Crow and Blackbird in 1989, Project Blue Hill in 1991, and then Project Argus in 1992. These relatively scientific studies used electron microscopy to examine the plant samples from inside crop circles, but also employed electromagnetic field detectors, rain gauges, and radar. This was in addition the large number of observers who maintained a watch on British fields in hope of catching a crop circle in the making.

Although the crop circle phenomenon didn't begin in England, it seems as though it has taken up residence there. There have been many formations in North America, for example, but the numbers of these have dwindled almost to nothing, whereas each year more interesting and more elaborate formations have been found in Britain. Why does Britain have so many crop circles, and why do they look as they do?

By the end of the 20th century, cerealogists were conceding that between 50 and 75 percent of all British formations were suspected to be hoaxes. It's likely that the actual fraction is much higher. Either way, there is no question that the British data was badly contaminated with hoaxed formations.

Despite this, crop circle experts speculated about mystical philosophy and Gaiean premonitions without first sorting out the good data from the bad data, whatever the two sets may be. By the mid-1990s, Paul Fuller, editor of *The Crop Watcher*, a British publication about crop circles, noted that expert cerealogists had grudgingly begun considering the fact that most, if not all, crop circle formations are likely hoaxes. He noted:

> ... in reality the awful truth has dawned on cerealogists everywhere — that most modern crop circles really are man-made hoaxes and that if there ever was a 'genuine' phenomenon in the first place it has now been utterly swamped by a smokescreen of wishful thinking and media-inspired mythology.

Typically, during the 1990s, fewer than two dozen North American crop circles were reported each year, compared with hundreds per year in Britain.

Cerealogy attracts at least as many hardcore believers as ufology. It's likely the fascination with crop circles is another sociological phenomenon, perhaps a reaction to our confused technological age. Part of the reason why crop circles attract such mysticism is because the British formations are located not far from ancient mystical sites. These include Stonehenge, prehistoric barrows, Silbury Hill, and other areas with so-called paranormal energy that follow ley lines across the British countryside.

Some crop circle researchers were convinced that some formations were caused by anomalous meteorological phenomena. But in the 1990s, Terence Meaden, the theory's main proponent, stated that "anything other than a simple circle is definitely a hoax, " and he lowered his estimate of the number of "genuine circles" to "fewer than a dozen a year."

In North America, it was known that some debunkers made crop circles in Alberta, to "prove a point," and in Manitoba, a farmhand admitted to UFO investigators that he had made at least one formation. In addition, at least one set of hoaxers admitted to some circles in the American midwest.

ARE CROP CIRCLES REAL?

Is there any physical evidence for crop circles? When the discovery of radiation within crop circles was announced in the 1990s, researchers were very surprised. Crop circle experts were convinced that these readings were correct, and that there was something abnormal about the creation mechanism for crop formations that resulted in bizarre nuclear reactions. They listed radioactive elements that they believed might have been created: rare elements such as yttrium, protactinium, and tellurium, among others.

However, this list was suspicious. In order to create such elements, the proposed mechanism (a neutron beam directed downward by a UFO) would have had to make other elements as well: some that would created as byproducts and others into which the primary elements quickly decayed. However, these were not detected, meaning that the findings were probably spurious. There had rarely been any detectable radiation associated with circular, swirled impressions previous to the age of crop circles, so it was odd that these new versions of UGMs (unusual ground markings) were suddenly littered with unstable elements.

For those researchers insistent that crop circles were something other than the traces catalogued by Ted Phillips, the radiation discoveries were proof that the crop circles were abnormal, and a new phenomenon altogether. For those who considered the British crop circles as only a new twist on an old phenomenon, the radionuclides were only red herrings.

What about the unusual characteristics of the circles? What about the woven nature of the wheat and the claims that the stalks were bent, not broken? One obvious caution is that expert cerealogists were fooled on more than one occasion by hoaxers imitating real crop circle characteristics. This suggested that these characteristics were not as cut-and-dry as one would like. And, as the experiment at the Strathclair site indicated, wheat stalks can be bent by manual or mechanical means in ways that would not necessarily leave breakage. To complicate matters, the quality of the wheat affects this characteristic. The diameter of the stalk, the moisture content, the weather, the soil nutrients, and a host of other factors will all affect the bending and breakage.

One oft-repeated mystery is the abnormal crystalline structure of wheat stalk sections, as discovered by a British laboratory. Micrographic photos of these sections were reproduced in a number of cerealogy books and websites as proof of a mysterious force at work in the circles. But as soon as the photos were published, some researchers became suspicious. What, exactly, was the procedure which generated the crystalline analyses? What devices were used?

It was reported in some publications that questions about the analyses were rebuffed by the reporters of the information. It was only through continued requests that it became known that the procedure was actually *spagyrical analysis*, a technique developed by an alchemist hundreds of years ago and without much scientific credibility. Even Colin Andrews, a prominent crop circle researcher, conceded in 1992 that the analyses were not acceptable as scientific methodology and that the results were suspect.

Finally, there is the appearance and abnormal growth of wheat seeds taken from within crop circles. Reported originally by crop circle researchers in the 1990s, the seed tests were performed on samples obtained from circle sites in Canada, the U.S., and England. Microscopic examination showed that the outer seed shells were irregular in shape, with many pits. When grown in a laboratory, the seeds from inside crop circles grew better than control samples.

It was therefore concluded that some mysterious force had caused an alteration in the genetic structure of the wheat. However, since it has been acknowledged that most sites called crop circles or crop formations have been hoaxes, it would seem odd to have changes in the seeds in these samples. The likely case is that the researchers found effects and changes in their samples because they believed the formations were caused by anomalous forces and therefore that the grain must have been affected in some way — confirmation bias.

Did You Know?

In 2008, more than 1,000 UFO reports were recorded in Canada — the highest number on record for any year.

Another claim often hawked about crop formations is their similarity to ancient hieroglyphics. The implication is that aliens must have created the complex shapes, had been visiting Earth for millennia, and were sending messages to humans based on ancient languages. Some cerealogists translated crop formations and discovered warnings from space beings, communications from Sumerian priests, and diatonic ratios.

The most scientific of these interpretations was published in *Science News*, in an article written by a noted archaeologist. He made the observation that whatever was creating the crop formations in England had a knowledge of geometrical theorems. Four mathematical theorems seemed to be proven through the appearance of some sites, while a fifth theorem was postulated. It was argued that random hoaxers could not possibly possess such abilities.

If most crop formations are hoaxes, then *any* discussion about translating the formations' text is pointless. Aside from a few definite Arabic lettering examples at sites (and one reply to the aliens/Sumerians), reading obscure alphabets into crop formations led only to confusion over whether the circle creators were Hebrew, Sumerian, Egyptian, or alien. Of course, if the circle creators knew enough about terrestrial alphabets to begin with, one would think that a better medium could have been selected. Also, if they were really advanced, they would know that modern Helvetica would be more properly used to communicate with humans, rather than archaic script. Since the identification of circle formations with old alphabets involves some liberal artistic licence, advanced circle creators should make their attempts at communication more precise and open to less interpretation.

All this is hair-splitting compared with the real problem of why crop circles seem to be most prevalent in southern England. More than 3,000 circles were discovered in Britain during the late 80s and 90s, yet the numbers and complexity of the formations were not evident in other areas of the world.

A curious aspect of the UFO phenomenon is its presence around the globe at all, with cases in Asia as well as America. Associated ground traces with UFOs were found in virtually all corners of the globe. But complex crop formations are really only in England. Why, if there is a UFO connection? Was this an indication of a profound, new kind of physical phenomenon, as some cerealogists insisted?

Probably not. As the ratio of suspected crop circle hoaxes to real circles climbed higher with each new evaluation, the British crop circle wave boiled down to a level comparable with worldwide activity. There may have been a new phenomenon at work in southern England, but the data so far presented does not bear this out. Even a suggestion that crop formations tended to be found in places where strong or variable winds existed some of the year (which would swirl and make the circles) seemed flawed, because it used lists of crop circles with no consideration that many were hoaxes, and the wind vortex theory was unnecessary.

There is no definitive evidence that suggests there is a real crop circle phenomenon at work in Britain. Physical evidence is debatable, expert opinions are questionable, and proposed theories are not supported by known physical mechanisms.

But who, then, was (or is) responsible? In 1991, Doug Bower and Dave Chorley of Southampton came forward to announce that they had created the first series of crop formations in the late 1970s as a lark. They had seen a news report about the Tully saucer nests in Australia in 1966 and thought it would amusing to make their own version.

They really didn't come into their own until 1991, after they made a large complex formation in 1981 in Matterley Bowl in Hampshire, near the pub where they had planned their hoaxes. Using planks, ropes, and wire, they were able to make small circles in a matter of minutes and larger formations in a half an hour. They continued to make formations after their admission, and even after Chorley died in 1996, Bower continued making circles into the 2000s.

Since so many crop circles were found, it's not surprising that other hoaxers were responsible, too. Other crop formation creators were Matt Ridley and Matthew Williams, the latter a British paranormal researcher who wanted to show that formations could be made discreetly at night, proving that aliens were not involved. Several people have even been prosecuted for making crop circles in private or commercial fields, having trespassed and causing the destruction of valuable crops.

The amazingly complex and intricate formations found in the late 1990s and 2000s certainly give pause for wonder. As beautiful artwork, some showing detailed geometric shapes such as Mandelbrot sets, the crop formations are testament to the ingenuity of humans and their engineering feats. This is especially true since the majority of formations were said to have appeared overnight, the fields in which they were found being untouched only a matter of hours before the intricate designs were discovered. Were these caused by aliens, or were clever humans the culprits?

As for the possibility that aliens were responsible, that remains intact — as a possibility. The extraterrestrial hypothesis is almost always invoked when a UGM is discovered, with or without a UFO sighting. Admittedly, there are some videos of lights bobbing about British fields around crop circle sites, and at least a few disputed videos of small probe daylight discs flitting across British fields. In rebuttal, vortex theorists produce eyewitness testimony of winds creating flattened circles. Can both sides be right?

There is an overwhelming amount of published comments and literature that do not seem to have addressed the core of the cerealogy problem. Instead, there have been coffee-table books of marvelous photographs and exciting speculation about the messages from the alien scribes or the new atmospheric mechanism responsible. But in very few cases have the Emperor's New Clothes been examined very closely.

Debunkers quickly pointed out the absurdity of such claims, but cerealogy refused to listen. This was one of the causes of the embarrassment faced by cerealogists during the days of the hoax expose. Researchers were too keen to expound upon the circles' mystery without taking a tip from ufology: try a conventional explanation first.

Despite convincing scientific evidence for a paranormal phenomenon, experts on crop circles will continue to talk about mysterious energies at work inside circles, invisible alien scout craft with rotating landing gear, secret military aerial microwave beam platforms, ancient Sumerian hieroglyphics, witnesses of perfectly circular wind vortices and, of course, the infamous mating dance of hedgehogs.

In Their Own Words

Lake Morena Village, California
April, 1998

It was around 4:00 a.m., and I had just left my house on a short walk to Lake Morena to do some early morning fishing. While walking down the street, I noticed what I first assumed was the moon between some nearby tree tops. It was very big, as the moon often appears here high in the mountains.

As I looked, I noticed it had an odd shape to it. Intrigued, I left the road and climbed a small hill with a rock pile atop it to get a better look. What I saw was a well defined craft. It was V-shaped and was luminous, the same color as the moon.

It was the most immense thing I have ever seen. I am guessing its distance at 20 miles and its height at 10,000 feet, and was in roughly the same flight path as that used by the commercial airlines that fly past. Comparing it to the commercial airliners, I am guessing it was as thick as 5 airliners stacked atop each other, and AT LEAST 1000 feet long.

Aside from being luminous, it had what appeared to be a luminous mist of some kind which surrounded it and tapered to a point maybe a half mile below it. It was like a classic tornado shape, which didn't trail behind it, but moved along with the craft (very strange).

It moved very slowly from the west to the east, towards Arizona. It took about 20 minutes to cross the horizon, and was quite a sight to behold.

If it ever came down to it, I would be more than willing to take a lie-detector test. The next chance I get, I will be sending another report on a very close encounter I had in the same area in 1997.

Thank you for your time, and God bless.

Reported by Anonymous
Source: UFOCasebook.com

THE FACE ON MARS

On July 25, 1976, The Viking 1 spacecraft was routinely taking photographs of the surface of Mars when it captured an image of the Cydonian plateau that would create more controversy than likely any other NASA photograph. This was the famous (or infamous) Face on Mars, a Martian mesa with hills and rilles that give the appearance of a humanlike face when seen under indirect sunlight. Additional images, taken under slightly different lighting conditions, were taken 35 orbits later.

Since the photos were released, there has been considerable debate about its origin, at least among ufologists and conspiracy buffs. NASA photo analysts quickly said that it was simply an optical illusion and a "trick of light and shadow."

Some paranormal researchers, such as Richard Hoagland, believe that the Face is proof that aliens have visited (or are visiting) Earth, and that they created the sculpted mountain. The aliens' intent was apparently to have us find it when we had achieved space travel and enough of a technological level that we can join them in conversation. Alternatively, the Face is a remnant of a long-dead Martian civilization.

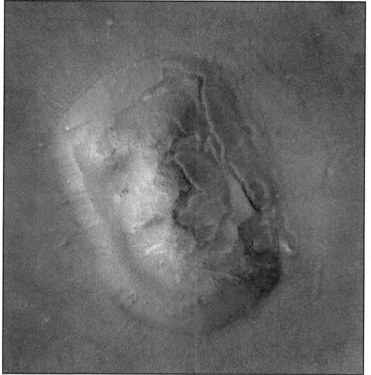

Credit: NASA.

Photograph of the infamous face on Mars, taken from orbit.

Since the discovery of the Face photos, diligent researchers have found other unusual formations on Mars, such as pyramids, tunnels, and buildings. Most of these structures cannot be seen easily and are hidden to untrained eyes. Some people are convinced they can make out roads, domes, and other features as well, indications of a *current* civilization on the red planet.

In the late 1990s, other spacecraft sent to Mars have photographed the Face again, with much greater resolution. Using multiple photographs, it has even been possible to create a 3-D image of the Face, showing its hills and valleys in much better definition. On April 8, 2001, a high resolution view was taken, including laser altimetry data that showed the Face to be only an irregular, eroded low mountain. But because the photo was not released immediately and instead processed during the next two months before giving to media, conspiracy theorists accused NASA of covering up the truth: that the Face is not natural.

While it is reasonable to think that the Face on Mars is an optical illusion, many people fervently believe that it is an alien artefact. The Face has taken on a life of its own, with books and articles written about it, and discussions peppering the Internet. In the movie *Mission to Mars* (2000), the Face turns out to be an alien spacecraft that has been waiting for astronauts to enter it and learn the secrets of the universe.

At least, the Face on Mars spurs us to consider the possibility of extraterrestrial life, firing our imaginations. It may simply be a low, naturally sculpted Martian feature, but it does focus our interest on planetary exploration. The issue will hopefully be resolved some day when humans finally set foot on the surface of Mars.

CATTLE MUTILATIONS

One of the most persistent issues regarding UFOs and alien contact is that of cattle mutilations. Even though most reported cattle mutilations have no associated UFO activity, many people believe that aliens (or perhaps a clandestine government agency) are involved in the killing and vivisection of cows and bulls across North America.

In the early 1970s, ranchers in the American midwest reported that cattle were mysteriously dying in growing numbers. Supposedly, there was never any obvious cause of death, but most strangely, certain organs on the animals seemed to have been removed with surgical precision. Teats, rectal areas, sex organs, lips, and tongues were often missing when the cows were discovered, leading ranchers to believe that someone or some group of people were deliberately killing and mutilating cattle for nefarious purposes.

In most cases, however, mutilations were not examined by reputable veterinary pathologists but by amateur investigators, including UFO buffs. The UFO connection arose because of a number of UFO cases in which animals disappeared or were otherwise reported killed. In 1970, for example, a book on UFOs and cattle mutilations noted (without a reference): "In Barcelos, Brazil, 15 children, seven pigs and two cows vanished from a farm during a UFO flap." In March 1977, UFOs described as white lights were seen to hover and land on the ground near Everett, Washington. The same night they were seen, a steer was found mutilated, leading a veterinarian to state "it was not predators" and that he "could not duplicate the mutilation with any instruments."

A more typical case was that which occurred on a small farm near Elsberry, Missouri, in 1978. Six cows were discovered dead on the property, with their eyes, ears, tongues, and sex organs cut out as if with a sharp knife. No blood could be found around the animals, either, suggesting it had all been drained away by whomever had perpetrated the atrocity. Each animal was discovered inside a fenced pasture and police could not find any evidence of intruders. According to farmers, coyotes and buzzards, normally attracted to carcasses, would not go near the dead cattle.

On June 8, 1978, Elsberry farmer Forrest Gladney had found a dead, mutilated calf on his farm, and on the following night had witnessed a large, glowing, orange UFO "as big as the Moon" over the same field. On June 16, a bright red light was observed flying soundlessly in an arc over another farm, and the next day a mutilated calf was discovered in that field.

Police sometimes found evidence suggesting Satanist cults or individuals were connected with the mutilations, including stone altars and the bodies of smaller animals such as rabbits and weasels, all drained of blood. Some laboratory analysis did detect unusual drugs in the bodies of some mutilated cattle, leading some investigators to believe a complex, secret nationwide mutilation project was underway. However, investigators could find no hard evidence of a large conspiracy, satanic or otherwise.

Officials within the government both encouraged and stymied investigations of mutilations. Because of a growing public outcry from ranchers about the perceived epidemic of *mutes* in Colorado, in August 1975 Senator Floyd Haskell sent a letter to the FBI asking them to investigate. He noted "ranchers are arming themselves to protect their livestock, as well as their families and themselves ... Clearly something must be done before someone gets hurt."

Surprisingly, the FBI said no. A letter in reply to Haskell came from none other than Clarence M. Kelley, the director of the FBI, who told Haskell: "The information set forth in your letter regarding the mutilation of cattle in Colorado and several other western states and the reported use of an unidentified helicopter by those individuals responsible has been carefully reviewed. I regret to inform you that these actions do not constitute a violation of Federal law coming within the FBI's investigative jurisdiction."

Many people found it odd that the FBI would not find any reason to investigate or act on an official request from an elected official regarding suspicious activity and the reported arming of civilian vigilante groups. This led some to believe that there was an official cover-up in effect, and possibly even some secret activities on the part of the FBI itself. This approach only served to spread paranoia and rumours throughout the United States, leading to a widespread belief that the government was using black helicopters to snatch cattle from farms for secret experiments and operations. This may have been a catalyst for science fiction stories and movies such as the *X-Files*.

A cattle mutilation case in Canada took place in the late 1970s near Teulon, Manitoba, and involved a cow that had been found in a field after being missing for several days. A bright light had been seen near the field about the time it went missing. When investigators visited the farm and were shown the carcass, it was already badly decomposed. The farmer thought that predators "had been at it," but he did not think they were the cause of death. Not having experience in veterinary pathology, investigators sought out a regional agricultural representative who said they would be investigating the case but were under the impression that dogs, wolves, or coyotes were responsible.

Another Manitoba case in 1980 was somewhat more curious, although it had no direct link to UFOs. Investigators had been told about it simply because of the alleged connection between UFOs and mutes, according to sensational tabloids. A dead male calf was found on June 10, 1980, in an alfalfa field along with the rest of its herd. The left ear, scrotum, testicles, anus, and tail had been cut and removed. There were also two cuts or incisions on its left flank. There were no marks on the ground to indicate how any perpetrator may have done the mutilation.

A veterinary pathologist with the provincial department of agriculture said he had performed an autopsy on the animal soon after it had been brought into his laboratory by the farmer. He determined that the calf had died of peritonitis and that the mutilations had been done after its death.

As for the mutilations, a regional veterinarian explained that the parts removed were "an unusual collection of coincidences" and that predators seemed an unlikely explanation. The mutilation occurred in a very conservative farming community and there had not been any publicity or media reports about mutes, which might encourage pranksters. Nevertheless, he noted there were many predators in the area, including coyotes, foxes, cougars, and even the occasional bear.

A year earlier, the RCMP had responded to a farmer's report of a mutilated calf

UFOs and Aliens in Literature

Majestic, published in 1991, is Whitley Streiber's fictionalization of the popular view that government and military officials have been covering up knowledge of alien intervention in human history. In the story, a former government agent acts as a "Deep Throat" and gives secret papers documenting the UFO cover-up to a reporter, who digs deep into the conspiracy, finding evidence of crashed saucers and bodies of aliens found on his property. It was found at the end of September, 1979, near Tofield, Alberta. In this case, the veterinarian had performed a post-mortem exam of the animal at the farm, *in situ*. This calf had much more extensive injuries. While its anus and scrotal area had been excised like other mutes, the pathologist found "massive contusions" on its body, broken ribs, large bruising, cervical dislocation, and other damage, including the odd fact that the bladder was missing. He noted "some scavenger damage in the pelvis was present but was not extensive."

After his examination, the veterinarian made the following statement: "In my opinion this animal was struck on the right side by a large object, probably a vehicle, with sufficient force that the animal's neck was dislocated at the level of cervical vertebra C5 or C6, resulting in its death. The removal of the anal area and scrotum and section of penis was done with a sharp instrument, probably a knife. Since the urinary bladder is [difficult to locate within a large animal], it is my opinion that whoever removed it must have some knowledge of the anatomy. In my opinion, the removal of the portions described previously was definitely done by human hands immediately after the death of the animal, using, I believe, a knife."

In other words, evidence was found to suggest humans were behind the mutilation, as in many other cases throughout North America. But why? One science fiction scenario has government mutilators killing cows as part of a program to monitor how certain toxic chemicals have been absorbed into Earth flora and fauna. In effect, it's part of an experiment upon living tissue in the environment, perhaps (according to conspiracy theorists) biological warfare agents.

Contradictory and more cautious views have been offered by other veterinary experts, however. A major paper published in the *Canadian Veterinary Journal* in 1989, for example, insisted that mutes were only caused by predators. A provincial veterinary pathologist examined several animals whose owners believed they were mutes. His conclusion was that in all cases, "the parts reported missing from mutilated cattle are the same as those known to be removed by scavengers, primarily coyotes and birds, in the early stages of scavenging a carcass. Jagged edges and tooth marks were found in all laboratory-examined animals."

To this day, the debate rages on. One of the foremost experts on mutes is Fern Belzil, an Alberta rancher who has been travelling throughout North America talking with farmers, examining mutilated cattle for himself and trying to solve the mystery. In his opinion, predators cannot be held responsible for the mutes. Some kind of human intervention is involved, whether it is by satanic cultists, government agents or something more benign.

Recently, Saskatchewan researcher Barb Campbell has taken up the mantle of mutilation investigation in Western Canada

2012

According to some researchers, the end of the world is approaching. Its exact date is known: December 21, 2012, and it will be such a cataclysm that our planet will never be the same again.

The UFO connection is that contactees who have received channelled messages from aliens claim they were told the "Space Brothers" have issued warnings that 2012 will be the year the Earth is destroyed. Alternatively, it will mark the time when the aliens will make their presence known to us, thus creating a great upheaval throughout the globe.

Another UFO connection is through the writings of Whitley Strieber, the abduction researcher who is himself an abductee but is also a horror novelist. His book *2012* concerns the actions of aliens who want to travel between dimensions but can only do so by mutilating humans. The recent film *2012* is loosely based on the book, but involves the destruction of the Earth and the survival of a handful of people who will go on to repopulate a new planet.

Where did the idea come from that 2012 will be the year of global disaster? The ancient Mayans of Central America had a calendar known as the Long Count that kept track of the number of days since the time of creation. The Mayans flourished between 250 to 1000 A.D., although by about 850 A.D. they were on the decline. The Long Count calendar was actually invented by the much older Olmec civilization, but the Mayans adopted it for their own use, setting the date of creation as 11 August, 3114 B.C.

The Long Count calendar was made up of five units, the largest of which was a *b'ak'tun*, which is made up of 144,000 days. The Mayans noted 13 *b'ak'tuns* between creation and the end of the Long Count calendar, which calculations show will be about December 21, 2012. Some Mayan scholars believe there is evidence that the ancient peoples thought that the end of the world would occur on the final day of the 13th *b'ak'tun*.

Other scholars, of course, disagree. Their own calculations and understanding of the Mayan culture are such that the 13th *b'ak'tun* was not an end, but a beginning, or at least the cause for a celebration. Some have even examined the Long Count calendar inscriptions closely and concluded that it goes far beyond 13 *b'ak'tuns* into the future.

Although present-day Mayans don't believe that the world will end on the last day of the 13th *b'ak'tun*, one Mayan inscription can be translated to forebode a significant event that day. The Tortuguero monument in southern Mexico apparently says that on that day, "Black will occur," and a god called *Bolon Yookte' K'uh* will descend from the heavens. Unfortunately, hardly anything is known about this Mayan god, although he is associated with war or death.

Apart from the Mayans, some New Age practitioners believe that 2012 will be the time of a shift in human consciousness. Others have used the term "harmonic convergence" to describe this raising of our spiritual awareness and an abrupt end to human selfishness. We will become peaceful and more focused on emotional issues rather than the materialism in which we now revel.

Some UFO and New Age writers believe that 2012 is when the Earth will be in collision with a "rogue planet" called Niburu. This object, also called Planet X, was originally predicted to hit Earth in 2003 but then when it didn't happen, recalculations were made and its new arrival year of 2012 is more convenient as a disaster is supposed to occur then anyway. The information that Niburu is on its way comes from contactees who received channelled messages via spiritual communication.

If Niburu was actually heading towards us, astronomers would have some knowledge of its approach, as even asteroids only a mile or so in diameter can be tracked easily by Earth telescopes. Claims of where precisely Niburu is in the sky right now vary from contactee to contactee, so no reliable and accurate information can be used to verify any of the claims.

Still other researchers, such as Richard Hoagland (better known for his claims about the Face on Mars) have predicted that 2012 will be when major cataclysms raze the Earth, destroying cities and killing millions of people. The year 2012 seems to be a focus for much speculation, just as the millennial change of the year 2000 (or Y2K) was heralded as a year of major destruction.

UFOs and Aliens in Movies

Mars Attacks (1996), was a parody of science fiction movies involving UFOs and alien invasion, the perfect foil to Independence Day. Martians surround the Earth with scores of saucers and announce they want to negotiate peace with the humans. They are lying, however, and they annihilate dignitaries and politicians on a mass campaign of destruction around the globe. Nothing seems to be able to stop the Martians until it is discovered that they are vulnerable to a particular sound: country and western yodeling.

RELIGION AND CULTS

Fanatical belief in aliens and UFOs can be considered anti-science in nature: a rejection that science is doing a good job of describing the universe as we see it. It replaces the scientific evaluation and rational explanation for UFOs in favour of a mystical and religious view.

Such a belief progresses to the next level of cult when believers become closed to any explanation of UFOs as ordinary phenomena. Fanatical UFO believers can alienate themselves from other UFO buffs who are interested in a search for the truth, but not the truth of the cult followers.

Spiritual UFO cults believe that UFOs are controlled by powerful beings known as the "Space Brothers," closely akin to deities. They are always much more advanced than humans, and their levels of advancement are such that they almost always have magical or mystical powers, often including ESP and other psychic abilities. In some cases, they are also more "spiritually-attuned" than humans.

The Space Brothers are extraterrestrial in the same sense that God is "not of this world," and they come from distant planets. Each sub-cult names a different planet of origin for their alien brothers and sisters, including Clarion, Korendar, and Zanthar. In UFO cult mythology, for example, Clarion is said to exist "on the other side of the Sun." Some groups select planets within our solar system as their aliens' homes, including Mars, Jupiter, Saturn, and Venus, although some have located their aliens on or inside the Earth.

Belief-based cults, on the other hand, usually have no spiritual relationship with the Space Brothers, but simply believe that extraterrestrials are visiting Earth. They reject scientists' explanations of UFOs and often insist that there is some sort of grand cover-up of the knowledge that aliens are among us.

Rael

On December 13, 1973, French journalist Claude Vorhilon encountered a small, olive-skinned humanoid with long dark hair and almond-shaped eyes. The alien told Vorhilon that spacemen like himself created life on Earth through a series of genetic experiments. The aliens were mistaken for gods and our Bible is a record of their activities. Vorhilon was told to take the name Rael, and the alien directed him to spread the word of the true origins of mankind and establish an interplanetary embassy in Jerusalem in preparation for the aliens' "second coming."

Rael has claimed he was taken by a UFO to their planet, where he met advanced beings such as Jesus and John F. Kennedy. While there, Rael was given explicit instruction in sexuality, which is an integral part of the aliens' master plan. He was also taught the secrets of cloning, which is one of the advanced scientific methods aliens used in their development of our race.

The Raelian movement has attracted a significant following around the world, including many scientists and learned individuals people. Rael announced that a team of scientists working at a Quebec laboratory had successfully cloned a human and that the first baby created in this manner was born on December 26, 2002. However, despite repeated requests, the proof of the cloning was never provided, and the baby "Eve" has never been publicly introduced. Rael has stated that his CLONAID program is a way in which humans can become more like their alien ancestors.

Rael claims that he was spiritually directed to go to an extinct volcano near Puy de Lassolas in France, where he met the aliens. While there, he discovered a spacecraft left by the aliens for his examination. He has built a replica of this spaceship and put it on display in Centre UFOland, an amusement and theme park that his followers have built near Valcourt, Quebec, about 90 minutes northeast of Montreal.

Raelians believe that all of the miracles and visitations recorded in the Bible were performed or caused by aliens and their UFOs. They have about 10,000 members worldwide, based in France but with satellite groups in other countries including the U.S. and Canada.

Urantia

Urantia is the name of Earth according to revelations given to psychiatrist William Sadler in 1932. One of his patients, allegedly Wilfred Kellogg, a relative of the founders of the famous Battle Creek Sanatarium, claimed to have received divine revelations from space beings. *The Urantia Book* is a huge volume of more than 2,000 pages, describing in great detail the hundreds of planets in the universe, and how we were created by an omnipotent alien being named Michael, better known as Jesus.

The Urantia Book has information on Havona, a planet that is what we call Heaven, and various other worlds populated by spiritual beings in "superuniverses" beyond time and space. Urantia is apparently world number 606 of a planetary system called Satania, within which there are many more planets harbouring developing civilizations under the watchful eyes of alien Seraphim and their lesser ministers. *The Urantia Book* is densely packed with channelled information about minutiae regarding the unseen reality of alien administration. For example, Gabriel is the name of "the chief officer of execution for superuniverse mandates relating to non-personal affairs in the local universe."

The recurring themes present in most of these groups are that 1) Mankind's spiritual awareness is missing or weak; 2) Space Brothers are trying to coax us back onto the path of spiritual understanding; but that 3) Salvation is possible through adherence to the teachings of the terrestrial leader or appointee. For the most part, UFO religious cults and groups are all concerned with the welfare of the human race, spreading the teachings of their masters in hope that mankind will be saved from itself. From a religious standpoint, they simply replace God with a physical being or beings from another planet. As a side effect, UFO cults reject science's dismissal of UFO reports, and therefore adopt an anti-science and sometimes anti-establishment or anti-government attitude that can make their followers outspoken against normal society.

HEAVEN'S GATE AND OTHERS

In the 1970s, a man named Marshall Applewhite had a mental breakdown. While recovering, he met a woman named Bonnie Nettles, who helped nurse him back to health. During his recuperation in Houston, Texas, he believed he had a revelation that he and Nettles were the "two witnesses" mentioned in the biblical Book of Revelation. They would be the prophets of the coming New Age.

In 1972, Applewhite and Nettles founded the Christian Arts Center in Houston where they gave lectures and taught courses in music and other art forms to help people realize their spiritual potential. By 1975, they were holding religious meetings at which they were trying to attract followers to their cause, warning of the coming end-time and preaching salvation by joining their group. At this point, they were calling themselves "The Two" or "Bo and Peep" or "Do and Ti."

New adherents were encouraged to leave their materialistic ways, selling or giving away their worldly possessions and going with The Two to a private wilderness location. As time went on, people began telling family and friends that they were approached by recruiters from the group, which was now promising "salvation in a UFO." The group, now obviously a cult, was said to be preparing their devotees for leaving this physical realm for a high plane of existence where they would join with an advanced race of extraterrestrial beings.

ALIENS: PLEASE LAND HERE!

The world's first UFO landing pad was opened in St. Paul, Alberta, on June 3, 1967, when Paul Hellyer, the Canadian Minister of Defence, officially declared it so at a special ceremony to mark the 100th birthday of Canada.

Recruitment meetings were held through the southern Midwest of the United States. They were calling themselves Human Individual Metamorphosis (HIM) and gave compelling presentations about how much better their lives were now that they had renounced many human foibles. (It was learned later, however, that although Bo and Peep preached celibacy among couples, women were encouraged to offer Bo "spiritual pleasure.")

While the group was originally unknown to the general public, some sociologists and at least several ufologists had been made aware of the group because of its devotion to UFOs. Author Jacques Vallee wrote about the group in his book *Messengers of Deception*, published in 1979, in which he described meetings with them and interviews with some close to the group. His worries about the dangerous nature of the cult and other contactees would not be brought to light until March 26, 1997.

On that day, police in San Diego, California, were called to a well-appointed residence in a quiet neighbourhood where they found the bodies of 39 members of the group. Each was wearing black shirts and sweat pants, new Nike running shoes, and had pieces of purple cloth covering their faces and upper bodies. They all had armbands with the words "Heaven's Gate Away Team." They also had plastic bags affixed over their heads, causing asphyxiation. Applewhite and Nettles both died with their followers.

Investigation revealed that the group had taken an overdose of barbiturates by eating it with applesauce. They had all voluntarily ingested the drugs in preparation for leaving Earth (spiritually, not literally) to join aliens who had travelled to Earth orbit in a spaceship that was hidden near Comet Hale-Bopp, which was in the sky at the time. (Which begs the question, if the aliens had a spaceship that was material, why didn't the cult join them as physical entities?)

One member of the group had left the house just previous to the mass suicide and did not die; his job was to ensure the group continued to gain members for future events. It is not known how many people had been members of the cult, from its inception in the 1970s until the suicides in 1997. It is known, however, that many people left their homes and families to join the cult, and were never heard from again.

The group may still be operating in remote areas of the American Midwest.

Olive

The experiences of a contactee named Olive are most interesting with regard to religious interpretations of UFOs. She was born in 1933 in Fredericton, New Brunswick. According to her biography, when she came out of her mother's womb, she had a caul on her face, considered a lucky or fortunate omen. She claimed that at age seven, she died from pneumonia, but "rose again on the third day" after sulfa drugs were administered to her. At age 10, she walked into another dimension and began having visions.

In 1968, space creatures took her in their craft to other planets, and even inside the Earth. During one of her journeys, they used an X-ray device to look inside her body. They found several tumours and operated on her with such advanced surgical techniques that they left no scars.

Olive says she was chosen by beings from the fourth dimension to carry their message of peace and sanity to the world. She was directed to help convince mankind to stop pollution, cease atomic testing, and repent to God. She was interested in educating children in the aliens' message through UFO comic books and TV shows.

In 1975, a "scout craft" burned a cross into a field in New Brunswick. No snow stayed on the cross, which remained warm to the touch all winter. In spring, no grass grew. A spring nearby turned reddish, then cleared, but Olive began holding religious ceremonies at the site. She claimed that people could be healed by water from the spring, and her services were attended by many devotees who were healed of ailments such as arthritis, lameness, and blindness.

However, some local residents who were skeptical of the activities attempted to put an end to them by hiring a bulldozer to plow the cross over. Olive and her group made a public demonstration of solidarity by laying in front of the bulldozer and stopping the plan. But, as Olive noted, the bodies of those who wanted to plow over the cross were found soon after at the bottom of a lake, with many bones broken. She said that this showed how bad things would happen to those who got in the way of the plans of Space Brothers.

Olive also said she could sense vibrations emanating from the UFOs flying overhead, and also from radiation left behind after they took off from their landing sites.

The Society of Unarius

The Society of Unarius was directed by Ruth Norman (Archangel Uriel) for several decades until her death in the 1990s. The group owns dozens of acres in California, where each year they await the mass landings of spaceships that will save selected spiritually attuned individuals. They believe that Earth needs to become the 33rd member planet of the Interplanetary Confederation. Jesus, Mohammed, and Einstein were channelled by Norman, giving further teachings to the Society's followers. The Society holds parades and meetings for which members dress up in costumes representative of other planets in the Confederation.

Recurring Themes in Most Religious UFO Cults:

1. Mankind's spiritual awareness is missing or weak.
2. "Space Brothers" are trying to guide us back onto the path of spiritual understanding.
3. There will be a Second Coming.
4. Salvation is possible.

For the most part, religious UFO cults and groups are all concerned with the welfare of the human race. They are trying to spread the teachings of their masters in the hope that mankind will be saved from itself.

Therefore, they are basically normal religious groups that simply replace God with a physical being from another planet. They reject science's dismissal of UFO reports, and in doing so, adopt an anti-science attitude that is impressed on their followers.

(However, the Heavens Gate cult used technology itself to spread and interpret spiritual and mystical teachings, an interesting combination of beliefs.)

These groups usually receive instructions directly from their masters, usually through channelled missives. Unfortunately, this sometimes led to many unauthorized readings and messages by individual members, since there was no control over the depth to which members could become immersed in the particular group's ideology. This sometimes led to their own contacts with the alien masters, distorting the original teachings. Since individual members could themselves become in tune with the aliens, they could obtain their own ego-enhancing, spiritual high.

However, as we have seen from the Heavens Gate incident, there are personal dangers from becoming too involved in one's faith. In November 1982, major news outlets carried the story of two people who waited in their car for more than a month in North Dakota. They spent the entire time in their car, waiting for a spaceship to arrive. They said they were drawn by a higher power as they sat in below-freezing temperatures, snowbound in their vehicle. Eventually one of them died of a combination of hypothermia, dehydration, and starvation, which spurred the other to seek help.

Some UFO-based religious groups' concepts probably reflect anxieties about our present society and more specifically, the possibility of nuclear war or the general angst felt by those oppressed or otherwise left out. Other themes are the role of religion in a technological society, the need for peaceful international relations, and the possibility of extraterrestrial visitation.

According to most groups, the Space Brothers come from planets free from war, poverty, and need. They also have achieved immortality through an emphasis on spiritual matters. In short, they exist in a idyllic paradises much removed from terrestrial problems. The Space Brothers also have come to Earth to stop arms proliferation and to prevent further war. Many early religious UFO cults were anticommunist but were paradoxically socialist in their structure. Both the FBI and CIA monitored the groups because they were deemed dangerous, often infiltrating the groups in order to keep watch on them.

Cult members' fear of death is lessened or eliminated by the belief that the aliens will prolong their lives or reincarnate them on another planet. The groups often made Jesus a spaceman, but still defined him as a true messenger who died trying to teach us truth and love.

Since Earth was not ready yet, the groups had to have human leaders to act as go-betweens. All groups shared their mission to educate mankind in order to save us from destruction. Hence, they sought public exposure in order to transmit their leaders' messages.

Furthermore, it should be noted that UFO cults almost always promulgate a Christian philosophy of love, peace, and reconciliation. Most have taught that we should be kind to one another, respecting all life and caring for the Earth. Many have strong environmental convictions.

However, by shifting their omnipotent deity from a spiritual God to a more technological entity, UFO cults place humans at par with their saviours. If only we knew enough science, we could be like the aliens. This path to enlightenment is one that is much easier than spiritual development, which requires somewhat more complicated practices, such as honest introspection, altruism, and love for all.

ALTERNATE DIMENSIONS

Sometimes, UFO authors say that aliens are visiting us from another dimension. This is said to explain why we can only see their UFOs at certain times, as portals between dimensions only allow passage at particular times and under specific conditions.

Scientifically, this is complete nonsense. No theories in physics have included such concepts as travel between dimensions. Although there have been many proposals concerning higher dimensions of mathematics and physics, the actual manifestation of these concepts is not easily imagined.

All that can be said about other dimensions, scientifically, is that they probably exist. What they are and where they are is something that we, as three-dimensional beings, cannot conceive. The concepts of alternate or higher dimensions and alternate or parallel universes are generally used interchangeably by writers, although the two are not necessarily identical. A parallel or alternate universe could exist alongside ours without our being aware of it. There has been some speculation that the Big Bang created our universe and also a multitude of other universes, but we exist in only one of them.

Practically speaking, we live in four dimensions but perceive three of them. These three are length, height, and width, and all the objects in our world can be described using these three values. The fourth dimension is usually considered time, in that objects in three-dimensional space move along through time, which we cannot perceive ourselves.

Higher dimensions are described by physicists and mathematicians, however, as a matter of course. One oft-cited theory describes our universe as actually existing in 11 dimensions, although we can only see a handful. The others, as the theory says, are folded up and are unseen. Needless to say, this is difficult for us humans to imagine.

Something that may help visualize higher dimensions is a novel titled *Flatland: A Romance of Many Dimensions*, by Edwin Abbott, published in 1884. Abbott was a teacher who wanted his students to be better able to understand mathematical dimensions, so he wrote a fictional story about a two-dimensional creature called "Square."

In the story, Square is visited by a three-dimensional creature known as "Sphere," and is perplexed by what he sees and hears. First of all, Square lives on a flat plane and is unaware of anything existing off the flat surface. When Sphere calls to him, he has no idea where the voice is coming from. Then, when Sphere enters the plane, Square is mystified. All Square sees is a point that gets bigger and bigger as Sphere passes through. Then, just as quickly as he appeared, Sphere steps out of the plane, and to Square, his visitor simply vanishes.

The book describes Flatland in great detail, cleverly creating buildings, creatures, and other parts of a two-dimensional civilization. Later, the Sphere is himself flummoxed by the concept of a tesseract, a four dimensional object. A sequel by Dionys Burger was published in 1965, titled *Sphereland*. An animated movie titled *Flatland: The Movie* (starring Martin Sheen) was released in 2007.

This kind of thought experiment can help us understand what contact with other dimensions might be like. In analogy to Square's predicament, if we were to encounter a fourth-dimensional intruder, it might seem to appear and vanish suddenly. It could communicate with us without our being able to ascertain where the speaker could be.

Some have suggested this is exactly what is happening with UFOs and aliens. It is claimed that a UFO is able to appear and disappear and move blindingly fast because it is entering its own higher dimension, unseen to us.

Of course, this is all mere speculation. We have no way of really knowing what a higher-dimension entity might be like. Would it be flesh-and-blood? If so, would the physical laws of circulation, breathing, and motion apply in the same was as it would to our three-dimensional bodies?

We can only leave it to science fiction authors to explore the answers to this question.

In Their Own Words

Arizona
March 3, 2010

While driving from my house heading west I noticed what at first appeared to be a satellite in the night skies.

But when I saw it was moving up and down in a split second, and its orange/red color I changed my mind. After that I came to a stop sign and change my direction to the North and the object also accelerated to the North with great speed.

By then I was driving in the middle of the road because I could not belief my eyes. Then, I came to a street light and changed my direction to the East and guess what?

The object changed direction to the East, by that time I was a little nervous.

But still I was thinking there's another explanation for what I was seeing. All my windows were down, so there was no reflection of any lights.

Again I stopped at a street light and focused my vision on a light pole to confirm that the object was moving, and sure enough it was.

It almost seemed to me that it had the same heading and speed as my car — stopping and going like my car was. Scary stuff!

Finally, I changed directions to the north, and of course the object did the same, by that time it seemed to be almost on top of central Tucson and finally it disappeared.

It was like the object dimmed its light.

Reported by Anonymous
Source: UFOCasebook.com

UFOS AND SOCIETY

1
GOVERNMENT AND UFOs

W hat does the government really know about UFOs?

A CNN poll in 1997, on the 50th anniversary of the Roswell crash, found that 80 percent of Americans thought their government is engaged in a cover-up, "hiding knowledge of the existence of extraterrestrial life forms." Supposedly, the government has been secretly studying the situation for decades, knowing full well that the aliens are here. Some conspiracy theorists are certain that the government is even in possession of crashed flying saucers (debris or intact) and their alien pilots as well, whether dead or alive. Ufologist Stanton Friedman calls this cover-up a "Cosmic Watergate."

Suspicion of government is not a new phenomenon, but the degree to which this is pervasive in society is alarming. UFOs are perhaps the ultimate government conspiracy, and the TV series *The X-Files* played into the relevant fears and suspicions well. Writers for the show admitted that they got many of their ideas for episodes from stories about UFOs in the news and in magazines, so the show reflected much of what the public believed about official interest in the subject.

CAN SECRETS BE KEPT?

A cynic could point out that a conspiracy as complex and long-lasting as the cover-up of a crashed alien flying saucer could only be done by a polished, resourceful, efficient, and competent organization, none of which are adjectives that are used by the general public in describing their government. The reality is that many secrets have been covered up successfully by government officials, including the Manhattan Project and the Corona program. The former involved the creation of the first nuclear bomb under the noses of students at Columbia University and in downtown New York City, employing a total of more than 100,000 people, while the latter was a spy satellite which regularly dropped its package of film to Earth for retrieval by military aircraft.

It is also known that the United States Congress each year passes billion-dollar budgets for so-called "black projects," for which there is no paper trail, detailed listing, or accountability. In 2009, *Wired* magazine discovered that the 2010 black budget in the U.S. is more than $50 billion, the largest amount ever allocated for completely secret operations. This implies that there are many things about which the public is blissfully ignorant. UFOs currently may or may not be one of them.

In the U.S., official investigations began immediately following Kenneth Arnold's sighting of a group of flying saucers over Mr. Rainer in 1947. Army Air Force Intelligence and the FBI co-operated to look into selected cases that they thought were deserving of attention, under two premises: the objects seen were astronomical bodies, or the objects were enemy aircraft — after all, this was only a few years after the end of the war. After only a few weeks of study, they concluded that flying saucers were not imaginary and that "something is really flying around."

Another study, this time by Air Materiel Command, also found that reported flying saucers were not imaginary and that apparently physical objects were being seen by reputable observers. This led to a recommendation that an official Air Force Project be set up in 1947 to investigate reports, called Project Sign. It was established at Wright-Patterson Air Force Base in Ohio and ran until February 1949 when it was renamed Project Grudge. In 1952, Project Grudge became Project Blue Book, which continued until government UFO investigations were officially terminated in 1970.

PROJECT SIGN

Officially, Project Sign reached no definitive conclusion regarding flying saucer reports, although it considered the possibility that they were alien spacecraft. Among the reasons it eventually dismissed the idea was that at the time, all the flying saucer reports it studied were from the United States, and it did not seem reasonable that aliens would single out one country.

A document known as the "Estimate of the Situation," described as an interim analysis of reports studied under Sign, was allegedly released in late 1948, concluding that flying saucers were extraterrestrial. However, when this analysis reached the Pentagon, it was supposedly rejected and destroyed so that we have only anecdotal evidence of its conclusions. Sign did, however, recommend further investigations and collection of data, so although Sign itself ceased to exist, it was renamed Project

Grudge and continued on, although its name reflected the attitude under which it was now operating. Ufologist Barry Greenwood notes that when the project name was changed, "former Sign personnel who favored UFOs were reassigned to other duties and replaced with more critical staffers."

PROJECT GRUDGE

Grudge operated for several years, at the end of which its final report concluded that UFOs were a combination of misinterpretations, mass hysteria, hoaxes, and hallucinations. An examination of the Grudge data shows that about 32 percent of reports were astronomical objects, 33 percent were hoaxes or had insufficient information for analysis, and 12 percent were weather balloons. But the remaining 23 percent were listed as *Unknown*, not hallucinations or mass hysteria, so one wonders what these cases might have been.

One case from the Grudge collection took place on November 16, 1949, near the University of Mississippi. At 9:15 a.m., a cigar-shaped object estimated to be about 15 metres long was seen by five witnesses travelling between Oxford and Batesville, Mississippi. The object was flying at about 60 metres through the clear blue sky, at a leisurely pace of only about 50 kilometres per hour. All five witnesses agreed on the shape and size of the object, and said that it looked like "a beam of light that stayed level" as it flew. As it passed by, the object "gave off an exhaust that had the appearance of phosphorus." Investigations did not explain the object as an aircraft or weather balloon. Since the object certainly wasn't any astronomical object, nor a weather balloon, that left the Grudge category of hoax, which seems unlikely given the number of witnesses.

UFOs AND ALIENS IN MOVIES

Communion (1989) is a very strange film, less of a UFO movie than it is a character study of horror writer and abduction researcher Whitley Strieber. Christopher Walken goes over the top to portray dissociation and paranoia in Strieber when aliens seem to be haunting Strieber's life. The ultimate message seems to be that aliens are in complete control and that they will show us only what they want. The movie does convey many elements of abductees' experiences well, especially the multi-layered memories and confusion that are part of some stories.

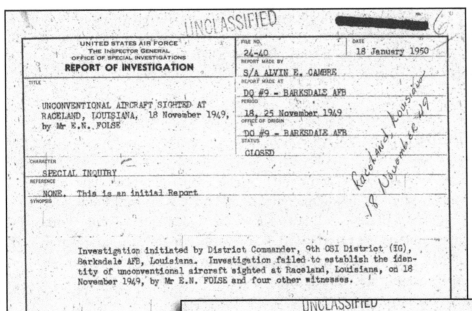

UNCLASSIFIED

| UNITED STATES AIR FORCE | FILE NO. | DATE |
| THE INSPECTOR GENERAL | 24-40 | 18 January 1950 |

REPORT OF INVESTIGATION

REPORT MADE BY
S/A ALVIN E. CAMBRE

TITLE
UNCONVENTIONAL AIRCRAFT SIGHTED AT RACELAND, LOUISIANA, 18 November 1949, by Mr E.N. FOLSE

REPORT MADE AT
DO #9 — BARKSDALE AFB

PERIOD
18, 25 November 1949

OFFICE OF ORIGIN
DO #9 — BARKSDALE AFB

STATUS
CLOSED

CHARACTER
SPECIAL INQUIRY

REFERENCE
NONE. This is an initial Report

SYNOPSIS

Investigation initiated by District Commander, 9th OSI District (IG), Barksdale AFB, Louisiana. Investigation failed to establish the identity of unconventional aircraft sighted at Raceland, Louisiana, on 18 November 1949, by Mr E.N. FOLSE and four other witnesses.

Project Sign investigated many unusual reports of flying saucers in the 1940s. An example of the cases investigated is an unconventional aircraft seen in Louisiana in 1949.

UNCLASSIFIED

DETAILS:

1. This investigation was initiated by the District Commander, 9th OSI District (IG), Barksdale AFB, La., upon receipt of clipping from the Times-Picayune newspaper, New Orleans, La., indicating that Mr E.N. FOLSE had sighted an unconventional aircraft in the vicinity of Raceland, La., on 18 November 1949.

AT RACELAND, LOUISIANA:

2. Mr E.N. FOLSE, a retired insurance agent of Raceland, La., advised during an interview that at approximately 0930 hours, 18 November 1949, he had observed an object in the skies from a point approximately one mile south of Raceland, La. The "Essential Elements of Information" obtained from Mr FOLSE are included in Paragraph #3.

3. ESSENTIAL ELEMENTS OF INFORMATION:

  a. Date of sighting: Friday, 18 November 1949
  b. Time of sighting: 0930 hours
  c. Where sighted: The object was sighted in the air from a point on the ground approximately one (1) mile south of Raceland, Louisiana.
  d. Number of objects: One (1)
  e. Distance of object from observer: Observer was unable to determine or estimate, due to lack of experience in such matters
    (1) Angle of elevation from horizon: Observer unable to determine or estimate due to lack of experience in such matters
  f. Time in sight: Approximately thirty (30) minutes
  g. Appearance of object:
    (1) Color: Shiny, aluminum type appearance
    (2) Shape: Similar to fuselage of aircraft, without protruding appendages of any type. (See attached sketch, labeled Exhibit "A".) Observer insisted object was not a blimp or dirigible.
    (3) Apparent construction: Unable to establish though appeared to be similar to aircraft.
    (4) Size: Estimated larger than large cargo type aircraft.
  h. Direction of flight: Southwest when first observed, executed 90 degree turn to Northwest, then another 90 degree turn to Northeast and proceeded in that direction until disappearance.
  i. Tactics or maneuvers: Object proceeded on level plane except when executing turning maneuver. Tail section seemed to be split when object entered turning maneuver. (See attached sketch.)
  j. Evidence of exhaust: No exhaust was observed.
  k. Effect on clouds: No clouds were in the area at the time of sighting.
  l. Lights: No lights were visible. Object was observed in daylight hours.
  m. Support: No wings or any other type of support were discernible.

2

UNCLASSIFIED

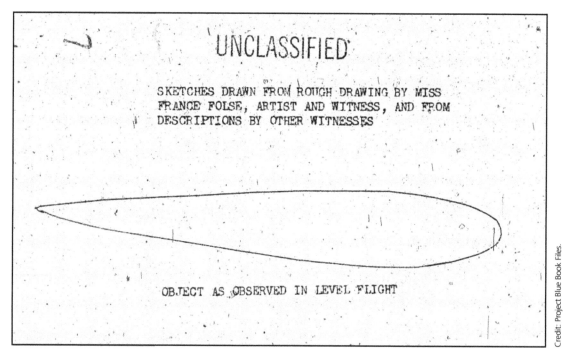

Sketch of object drawn by witness.

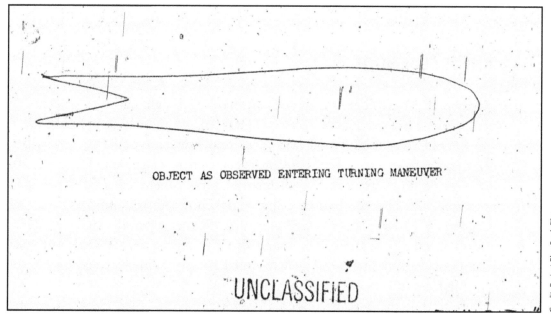

Second sketch of object drawn by witness.

A clearer case in which a very similar object was seen and also unexplained took place only two days later, on November 18, 1949, at Raceland, Louisiana. At 9:30 a.m., five different witnesses observed a shiny, aluminum-like object "similar to [the] fuselage of aircraft, without protruding appendages of any type." It was thought to be larger than a cargo aircraft, and did not seem to be a dirigible or blimp. It flew straight until it made two successive 90-degree turns before heading towards the northwest out of sight. The Grudge report on the case noted: "Investigation failed to establish the identity of unconventional aircraft sighted at Raceland, Louisiana." This sounds like the case was unexplained, rather than a misidentification or hoax.

According to USAF Captain Edward Ruppelt, who was the first director of Project Blue Book, the Grudge investigations were incomplete and inadequate. However, Edward Condon, director of the USAF-sponsored Condon Committee that studied Blue Book cases in detail, said the Grudge reports were "too vague for interpretation and that if anything, the Air Force investigators gave them more attention than they deserved."

Yet, the two cases cited here do not seem vague at all, and one wonders what criteria were used to make the judgments by Ruppelt and Condon. In any event, Project Grudge was suspended in December 1949, but flying saucer reports continued to be investigated by the Air Technical Intelligence Center (ATIC) "as part of regular intelligence activities."

PROJECT BLUE BOOK

In October 1951, Grudge was dusted off following a sighting of an unidentified object over a military base in New Jersey and was renamed Blue Book in March 1952, under Ruppelt's direction. It continued under various directors until December 1969, when an order to shut it down resulted in its complete termination in January 1970.

A contributing factor in its closure was the conclusion of the Condon Committee, which noted "nothing has come from the study of UFOs ... that has added to scientific knowledge" and that "further extensive study of UFOs probably cannot be justified." It found that, in general, all UFO reports had conventional explanations, and that the media were themselves responsible for distorting facts and encouraging the public's whimsy.

Despite this, the actual Condon Committee report raises many interesting questions. In fact, one contributed chapter on psychological aspects of UFO reports actually concludes by stating it "raises more questions than it answers." Its author asked, "Why do some persons who see an UFO regard it as simply an unidentified aerial phenomenon, while others are sure it is a 'space vehicle?'" He added: "The answers to such questions must await future research." However, the larger report concluded that there should be *no* further research.

During its operation between 1952 and 1969, Project Blue Book collected a total of 12,618 UFO reports. Of these, 701 were unexplained, comprising just over 5 percent of the total. It is important to note that these unknowns were not a "residue" as they have been labelled by some researchers, as there was also a Blue Book category of *Insufficient Data*. In fact, the unknowns were labelled *Unidentified* if they could not explained as a myriad of other things, including *Astronomical Objects such as Meteors, Stars and Planets, Aircraft, Balloons, Satellites, Hoaxes, Missiles, Rockets, Reflections, Flares, Fireworks, Mirages, Inversions, Searchlights, Clouds, Contrails, Radar Chaff,* or *Birds*. This list of possible misidentified objects seems quite exhaustive, and if there were sufficient data to rule out one of these, then one wonders what else could have been observed.

THE CONDON REPORT

Many people, notably scientists, accept the conclusions of the Condon Committee and Project Blue Book — that there is nothing worthwhile in the collection of UFO reports. One mandate of Blue Book was to assess whether or not UFOs posed any threat to national security, which it concluded they do not. The Condon Report was endorsed by the National Academy of Sciences, and the scientific community has accepted the study as the definitive answer to the UFO question.

Critics of the Condon Committee have charged that it only looked at 56 cases, after all, and that some of these cases were not explained as much as they were dismissed out of hand. Critics of Blue Book have said it was little more than a public relations exercise and that the really good cases were not sent to Blue Book investigators at all. And even when cases were sent in, they were not handled well. According to a Condon Committee investigator who visited the office of Project Blue Book, "public reports of UFO sightings were not investigated seriously by a great number of the 'UFO Officers,' one officer being so designated at each air base."

If the officers' bias wasn't a big enough problem, the way in which the public was informed about official UFO investigations also was a concern. Air Force Regulation 200-2, released in August 1954, set the tone for dealing with the public on the subject: "In response to local inquiries, it is permissible to inform news media representatives on [UFOs] when the object is positively identified as a familiar object ... For those objects which are not explainable, only the fact that

ATIC will analyze the data is worthy of release." In other words, if a sighting was explained the news media would be told, but any unexplained objects would not be described.

This approach makes perfect sense, since it would be embarrassing and awkward if the USAF admitted it could not explain UFOs seen by American citizens. It also makes sense that such a policy continues in some form today, and that it is this closed attitude which causes confusion when Air Force spokespersons are asked to comment on a particular UFO case, sometimes making the government appear foolish. The question is whether the government is covering up the truth or is simply at a loss to explain what is really going on.

Curiously, in parallel to the United States' official study of UFO reports, the Soviet Academy of Sciences also prepared an official report on sightings within its country. In 1979, its Institute of Space Research released a study on UFO cases in the U.S.S.R., although it was mostly a statistical analysis. About the UFOs observed, it concluded: "Some of them possibly can be due to atmospheric optics effects. However, in the overwhelming majority of cases, they evidently are of a completely different nature." As for them being satellites and terrestrial craft, "... the kinematic characteristics exclude the possibility of such an explanation for at least one third of the cases." They noted: "Obviously, the question of the nature of the anomalous phenomena still should be considered open."

WILBERT B. SMITH

Another insight into how UFOs were being viewed within the U.S. government and military came about through, of all things, a Canadian electrical engineering project. Wilbert Brockhouse Smith was a prominent electrical engineer with the Canadian Department of Transport. During the Second World War, he was involved in Canada's wartime monitoring service. Postwar, he was responsible for the creation of a chain of ionospheric measurement stations in Canada.

Smith's expertise was in radio wave propagation and geomagnetism. He became convinced that the Earth's magnetic field could be harnessed and used as some form of propulsion system. In the 1950s, he chanced upon some books about flying saucers and how they were speculated to fly using some kind of magnetic propulsion. His curiosity led him to investigate some flying saucer sightings, and he wanted to find out more about them. Through his contacts within the Canadian government, he was able to ask questions directly about flying saucer research through the Canadian embassy in Washington D.C.

Did You Know?

In France and Quebec, UFOs are called *les OVNIs —* *Objets Volants Non Identifiés* (flying objects that cannot be identified).

Smith met with Dr. Robert Sarbacher, former dean of Georgia Tech's graduate school and a consultant to the U.S. Government. Smith asked him directly if flying saucers were real. Sarbacher replied, "Yes, they exist," and that "it's pretty certain they didn't originate on the earth." Furthermore, Sarbacher told Smith that UFOs were "classified two points higher even than the H-bomb."

Sarbacher did not offer any proof that this was so, but Smith was convinced that the information was correct. In November 1950, Smith sent a memo to the Controller of Telecommunications at the Department of Transport, informing him that "the existence of a different technology is borne out by the investigations which are being carried out at the present time in relation to flying saucers." He also passed along the Sarbacher information about UFOs by noting that "flying saucers exist," and that "the entire matter is considered by the United States authorities to be of tremendous significance."

Ufologists later found documents that supported Sarbacher's credentials and claims. In fact, some diligent researchers found documents that seem to show that there exists a mysterious group known as MJ-12 (or Majestic Twelve) within the United States government. This group of scientists and military personnel may be responsible for the cover-up of everything from UFO case investigations to the actual crash of a saucer at Roswell in 1947.

Another possibility is that the story of a UFO crash is just a subterfuge, and that the U.S. military is using the public's fascination with UFOs as a way to conceal their secret aircraft experiments. Since many people still ridicule UFO witnesses and the scientific community generally scoffs at UFO reports, the experiments could even be conducted in the open, without fear of exposure.

In Their Own Words

Paris, France
January 28, 1994

I was commander of flight Air France 3532 on January 28, 1994, flying from Nice to London, with copilot Valerie Chauffour, and 24 passengers on board.

We were above the Paris area at an altitude of 11,700 meters, the visibility was of more than 300 km (150 Nm) and the cloud cover consisted of altocumulus. The flight encountered no air shakes. The navigation was under excellent weather conditions, in spite of the facing wind of almost 130 km/h (70 kts). That gave us a ground speed of 650 km/h (350 kts). The takeoff hour in Nice was 00h56PM UT and the arrival hour in London 02:13PM UT.

It was a particularly calm flight, without particular problem. We arrived above Coulommiers when a steward who was in the cockpit noticed an object which he thought could be a weather balloon. This object was then seen by the copilot and myself a few moments afterwards.

According to their description it seemed to have a variable form and to come very quickly across our road. I first identified it like an aircraft facing us, at approximately 45 km (25 Nm), at an altitude of approximately 10,500 meters (25 Nm) and at an angle close to 45°. I found this slope absolutely abnormal because aircraft are not inclined at this altitude beyond 30 degrees without risking to fall down. This object seemed to us then absolutely abnormal by its size which seemed immense, its dark red color and of the fuzzy edges. I had the impression to observe a gigantic lens in evolution. It did not resemble anything we had seen in our flying careers.

This object, this phenomenon, remained motionless while we left it on our left side, still at an approximate distance of 45 km. We observed it during a good minute, conscious that we were seeing something utterly anomalous. We continued to observe it when it gradually merged with the environment. We saw it becoming translucent, transparent, diluted in space. That was absolutely amazing.

After some interrogations we contacted the control center of Rheims to announce this unidentified object to them, as we are required by air transportation regulation.

I did not submit a written report to avoid being ridiculed. Three years later, I read an article in Paris Match which described how a UFO has been detected above Paris. I made the connection between this UFO and that what I had seen.

I then submitted a report to the Gendarmerie Nationale (French police, having an SOP for collection of UFO reports).

My report was transmitted by the Gendarmerie to the SEPRA, and the UFO Committee, was created within the framework of the Association of the Former Auditors of the Institute for the High Studies of National Defense (IHEDN). I was heard during nearly one hour and half by the group chaired by General Denis Letty. After discussing about the observation, we concluded that the object was approximately 300 meters in diameter.

I took note of the radar recordings by the CODED (Operational Center of Air Defense). There is a very curious characteristic for the trajectory of the UFO, as it shows that it would have almost collided with us. The minimal distance on the recording is less than 1 Nm, that is to say 10 seconds of flight.

Reported by J-C. D.
Source: UFOCasebook.com

OTHER GOVERNMENTS AND UFOS

Governments in many countries other than the U.S. have also investigated UFO reports to one degree or another over the past several decades, including Canada, Great Britain, France, Belgium, Sweden, Brazil, Mexico, Spain, and the Soviet Union (and now Russia) have all done some studies on the subject.

Although the policies and procedures have varied, most governments of larger countries around the world have conducted at least some simple studies of UFOs. Their conclusions are, with some exceptions, classified information, but many files are slowly being released to the public under Freedom of Information or Access to Information requests. For the most part, the official conclusions follow that of the United States government: studies of UFO reports have found that most are simple explanations and that the few that are unexplained aren't worth the bother.

Most countries have policies to refer UFO witnesses and inquiries to local police or authorities, but it is not government policy to waste valuable budgetary resources on UFO investigations. With wars, global warming, energy crises, and domestic problems, spending even a small amount of a departmental budget on UFOs would be viewed by opposition parties as foolish and would be very politically incorrect.

France

In France, the French Space Agency CNES created a unit in 1977 to investigate unidentified aerospace phenomena (UAP). Originally called GEPAN (Groupe d'Étude des Phénomènes Aérospatiaux Non-identifiés), it was later called SEPRA (Service d'Expertise des Phénomènes de Rentrée Atmosphérique, then Service d'Expertise des Phénomènes Rares Aérospatiaux) and finally in 2005 was renamed GEIPAN (Groupe d'Études et d'Informations sur les Phénomènes Aérospatiaux Non-identifiés).

The French Gendarmerie is directed to send information on UFO reports it receives to GEIPAN, which maintains a large database of cases. GEIPAN can also use the technical expertise and resources of CNES to investigate any physical trace cases. In March 2007, GEIPAN made its UFO archives available online. The quality of their investigations has been heavily criticized by French skeptics.

COMETA was a French non-profit UFO investigation organization made up of officers and officials from the armed forces and aerospace industry, mostly former members of IHEDN, a high-level French defence think-tank. In 1999, it produced the COMETA Report on UFOs and their possible implications for defense in France, but was not actually endorsed by the French government. The report drew largely on the research of GEIPAN and SEPRA.

United Kingdom

In the United Kingdom, the Air Ministry was involved in the investigation of UFO reports by the early 1950s, similar to the Americans. However, it has always claimed that its UFO files prior to the mid-1960s were destroyed because it did not take the cases very seriously.

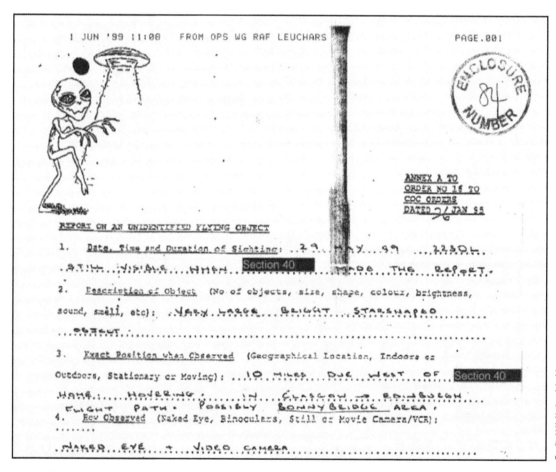

In 2010, the British Ministry of Defence released thousands of documents about UFO reports from British citizens. There is evidence they may not have taken the reports seriously, however. Some official UFO reporting forms included images of cartoon-like aliens.

Credit: U.K. National Archives.

	REPORT OF AN UNEXPLAINED AERIAL SIGHTING		32
1.	**Date and time of sighting.** (Duration of sighting.)	Everyday.	
2.	**Description of object.** (No of objects, size, shape, colour, brightness, noise.)	Vague description. Objects, Lucifer like things.	
12.	**Remarks.**	Wants these objects that look like Lucifer moved away. She knows it would be expensive, but they are an absolute nuisance to people, "holding people in their homes, so they are frightened to go out and getting people out of their beds, in to the air to listen to it".	

Credit: U.K. National Archives.

Another report from the British Ministry of Defence recorded one witness describing UFOs shaped like Lucifer, which were "an absolute nuisance."

Had been camping on Shell Island all week-end
Went out to do his job.
at 4am and saw something
cool. Thought it was an UFO
His wife thinks he has gone mental

Credit: U.K. National Archives.

Another report from the British Ministry of Defence recorded that one wife's opinion of her husband's UFO sighting was less than enthusiastic.

Timothy Good, in his detailed work *Above Top Secret* has found evidence that investigations were conducted and that interest actually existed at the highest levels. But when Sir Winston Churchill asked his staff about the various reports of flying saucers he had heard of in the news, even he was told that there wasn't anything to them at all. However, in the early 1950s, the Deputy Directorate of Intelligence of the Air Ministry noted that as many as 10 percent of all the flying saucer reports they investigated were from qualified observers, and that the reports "carried conviction" and were unexplained.

Former intelligence officers in the British Armed Forces have since gone on record to state that yes, indeed, secret UFO investigations were done within the Ministry in secure sites such as Room 801, which supposedly had a file on more than 10,000 cases. Later, the Ministry of Defence took over the responsibility for UFO sightings, although it also denied that they had found any evidence of a phenomenon that merited concern. Ufologist Nick Pope, the former "UFO Desk" officer in the Secretariat (Air Staff) for the Ministry of Defence in the early 1990s, documented how reports were handled within the office. His conclusion, after working there for several years, was that "some UFO sightings are probably extraterrestrial in origin."

In 2006, the Ministry of Defence released details of a UFO study called Project Condign, a secret investigation of UFO cases briefly conducted within the Ministry. It concluded that many sightings could be explained as glowing plasma, a natural but poorly understood natural phenomenon. Condign has been greatly maligned because its conclusion was at odds with so many other similar studies, but it did show that the British government had been taking the subject seriously for some time, enough to have at least one officer spend time studying cases in detail.

Credit: U.K. National Archives.

Included among the British Ministry of Defence UFO records are several photographs, including this one taken near Hack Green, a former underground military base.

In 2009, the British Ministry of Defence officially closed its UFO Desk and stopped accepting UFO reports and inquiries from the public. It has been releasing thousands of previously classified files to the public, mostly to avoid having to deal with the hundreds of inquiries it was receiving every year from citizens wanting information about UFOs.

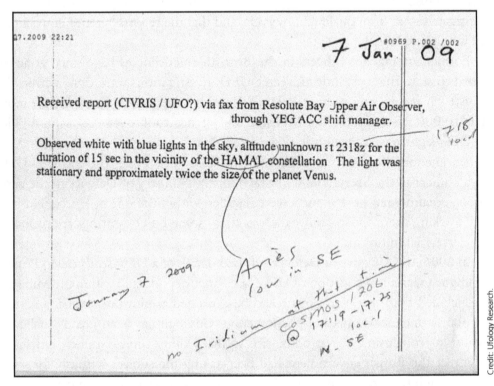

A brief UFO report in official Canadian Government files describes a stationary UFO twice the observed size of the planet Venus, seen in the high Arctic.

Canada

Canada's official UFO files have been much more accessible than those of the United Kingdom. Canadian government UFO files have been routinely declassified every calendar year, with UFO reports being transferred from agencies such as the Royal Canadian Mounted Police and the Department of National Defence to the National Archives. Once in the Archives, the UFO files can be examined at leisure by researchers.

The reports found in the Archives are very much like those eventually released by the British government. Most reports are simple lights in the sky seen by citizens, although there are notable exceptions. Names and contact information have been deleted for privacy, but the case files are otherwise intact.

UFO reports were investigated originally by the Royal Canadian Air Force, then by the RCMP. Until 1995, the RCMP investigations were in cooperation with the Herzberg Institute of Astrophysics in Ottawa, where astronomers were studying meteors and required prompt response to reports of fireballs in order to recover meteorites. Since many UFO reports were of meteors and fireballs, the scientists enlisted the aid and investigative skills of the RCMP whenever a UFO report was filed. This meant that police were investigating all UFO sightings reported in Canada for many years. However, when the meteoritical studies at the Institute were terminated, so too were the RCMP investigations.

After his investigation of the amazing case of the giant UFO seen over the Yukon in 1996, investigator Martin Jasek sent his report to a host of officials, including his local Member of Parliament. He asked them to consider the subject of UFOs more seriously, and in particular, to take note of this particular case. He called upon the Canadian government to initiate an inquiry into the matter and suggested several things that could be done to put an end to what is perceived as an "atmosphere of witness ridicule and government silence on the UFO topic." These were:

1. Ask the Government of Canada to assess what was likely the cause of the sighting of a giant (at least 0.88 km long) UFO on December 11, 1996 at Fox Lake, Carmacks, Pelly Crossing and Mayo, Yukon. Most importantly, they should make their conclusions public.

2. Ask the Government of Canada what conclusions they have reached about the large quantity of other UFO data that they have collected and specifically the reports that are highly suggestive of non-human intelligence.

3. Ask the Government of Canada what actions citizens should take if they are confronted with intelligently controlled vehicles of apparent non-human intelligence.

4. Ask the Government of Canada to educate the public and civil

servants about the potential seriousness of UFO sightings to encourage witnesses to report their sightings as well as feel free to discuss them openly.

5. Explicitly list "Ridicule of Witnesses" as a form of discrimination.

6. Encourage scientific study of the phenomena by sharing data that the Government of Canada has collected and conclusions (past and recent) it may have reached.

7. Ask the Government of Canada to encourage and support Universities and Colleges to study the UFO issue/topic much the same way they support other scientific programs.

8. Ask the Government of Canada to establish a government-sanctioned UFO study committee including both military and civilian investigators such as has been done by the Government of Chile.

The last point, making reference to Chile, was in reference to a news report that the Chilean air force had announced it had set up a special committee to investigate UFO reports. It had been noted that "reputable sources such as pilots and air traffic controllers had sometimes reported seeing objects for which there was no immediate explanation."

Whether or not Jasek's recommendations were embraced by any department within the Government of Canada, his noble effort to bring the subject of UFOs to the attention of politicians and Parliament is commendable. Jasek's outstanding and thorough investigation of a well-witnessed, well-documented UFO flap stands head and shoulders above many other UFO investigations.

Since the year 2000, reports of UFOs made to agencies such as Transport Canada and the Canadian Forces have been made available to Ufology Research, an independent civilian research organization.

Australia

In Australia, UFOs are known officially as Unidentified Aerials Sightings (UAS) and the Royal Australian Air Force was used to investigate sightings. This was terminated "after careful examination of the factual data" showed it "did not warrant the continued allocation of resources by the RAAF." Current Australian policy is to refer UFO witnesses to local police or to civilian UFO organizations.

Spain

In January 1992, the Spanish government started declassifying UFO files after having sealed its records following a leak in the 1970s of information regarding its official investigation of UFOs. In 1976, based on this information, journalist J.J. Benitez published a Spanish-language book about secret Spanish UFO investigations by the government. Following the clampdown, it took years of lobbying by ufologists Vicente-Juan Ballester Olmos and Joan Plata to get the release of more official documents. The Spanish Air Force seems now to be cooperating with ufologists by releasing files about more cases.

UFOs and Aliens in TV

The *X-Files* was a sweeping homage to conspiracy theories, touching on many other paranormal concepts such as telepathy, mind control, spirit possession, and voodooism. Its secret to success was including parallel story ideas about scientific concepts under discussion by media and taken directly from the news and pop culture, such as genetic mutations, Big Brother, implanted tracking devices, advanced weaponry and, of course, UFOs from outer space.

Japan

In 1991, at an International UFO Symposium held in Hakui City, Japanese prime minister Toshiki Kaifu expressed an opinion that it was "time to take the UFO situation seriously." Earlier, in advance of the symposium, he had been quoted as saying:

> As an underdeveloped country with regards to the UFO problem, Japan [has] to take into account what should be done about the UFO question, and that we had to spend more time on these matters ... to

solve the UFO problem with far reaching vision at the same time ... I believe it is a reasonable time to take the UFO problem seriously as a reality ... I hope that this Symposium will contribute to peace on Earth from the point of view of outer space, and take the first step toward the international cooperation in the field of UFOs.

This was in a letter to Mayor Shiotani of Hakui City, dated June 24, 1990, endorsing the upcoming space and UFO symposium.

CIRVIS REPORTS

When pilots or air traffic controllers or military personnel report seeing unusual aerial craft, their testimony should be taken seriously. In fact, such reports are mandatory, as dictated by government and military directives. One such directive is found within the Canadian Department of National Defence regarding the actions of all pilots in Canadian airspace. In documents relating to CIRVIS (Communications Instructions for Reporting Vital Intelligence Sightings), both civilians and military personnel are instructed that:

> CIRVIS reports should be made immediately upon a vital intelligence sighting of any airborne, waterborne and ground objects or activities which appear to be hostile, suspicious, unidentified or engaged in illegal smuggling activity.

> Examples of events requiring CIRVIS reports are:

> –unidentified flying objects;
> –submarines or warships which are not Canadian or American;
> –violent explosions; and
> –unexplained or unusual activity in Polar regions, abandoned airstrips or other remote, sparsely populated areas.

> (DND Flight Information Publication - GPH 204. Flight Planning and Procedures, Canada and North Atlantic, Issue No. 57, Effective 0901Z 20 May 1999)

In other words, it is considered in the best interests of everyone to report UFO sightings, and certainly of interest to the Department of National Defence. Similar directives exist for the United States, and there is no reason to believe that such policies are not in effect in other countries around the world.

2
COVER-UP?

Is there a UFO cover-up? Does the government know more about UFOs than it is letting on?

These and other questions have been asked about the subject of UFOs for decades. On the surface, the answer seems simple: yes. It should be obvious that military and government officials must, as a matter of course, withhold some information from the general public. Such information could include covert military operations in other countries to monitor activity of concern, or details on the sophistication of weaponry developed for use in a field of battle. Clearly, if the public knew such details, then the enemy would as well, and that wouldn't do anybody much good.

Other things that might be classified are personal details about citizens, such as medical histories, job performance, income tax forms, and so forth. Privacy is also a major issue when it comes to protecting human rights and maintaining secrecy for the sake of trust and integrity.

But are details about UFO sightings a matter of national security? Should they be?

Simple reports of UFO sightings by civilians might be justifiably classified in some situations. Obviously, not everyone wants the world to know that he or she has seen a UFO, because of the negative social stigma that exists about "seeing flying saucers." Therefore, making the identities of UFO witnesses a secret in official government UFO files makes sense, similar to withholding names of those who contributed to a particular political party. Other details in these UFO reports, such as dates, times, locations, and the descriptions of the objects seen, should probably be made available.

This is, essentially, what we have seen in the UFO files released by various governments in recent years. The British Ministry of Defence UFO files available from its National Archives show exactly such details, with the names and contact information blocked out. Canadian UFO files from the National Archives are identical, as are files from other countries.

UFOs and Aliens in Movies

A good example of the collision between science fiction and ufology is the latest entry in the Indiana Jones saga. In *Indiana Jones and the Crystal Skull* (2008), our hero finds himself facing off against government agents covering up activities at Roswell. What makes the movie work is not only the swashbuckling character of Jones (despite his aging considerably since the last episode) but the fact that the movie audience believes Roswell is a secret government base where aliens and UFOs are supposedly stashed, whether true or not.

What about UFO sightings by military personnel while on duty? It is reasonable that such reports would be classified higher that those by civilians. The sighting of an unidentified flying object by an army officer while on patrol in Iraq might have significant security implications, so it would be logical that this information might be classified secret or above.

The location of the sighting makes a big difference. A UFO seen over Kandahar airbase in Afghanistan is one thing, but one seen over a Walmart in Kentucky is another. But what about a UFO seen over a military base in California? Shouldn't that be classified as well? Surely details of a military operation or exercise that is witnessed by civilians might be kept from the public for one reason or another.

Following the Second World War, military bases throughout North America, particularly those in southern states, were home to major post-war operations. Operation Paperclip, in which German scientists were transplanted to the United States, is one example of a clandestine project that needed extra security.

During the war, tests of jet aircraft needed to be performed in secrecy, and one place where this was done was the Groom Lake facility in Nevada, better known as Area 51. The U-2 sky plane was tested here, as was the A-12 reconnaissance aircraft and later, the SR-71 Blackbird. Since experimental aircraft are developed at the facility, it makes sense that it has a wide security perimeter and civilians are not permitted anywhere near the base. But since the aircraft fly out of the base, unidentified lights are frequently seen moving across nearby mountains and then reported as UFOs by ardent watchers. Some people even drive to the base's extended boundaries to get a closer view, and are met by security personnel who issue threats and prevent further intrusion.

Classifying military operations, therefore, is reasonable and needs no real justification. However, some researchers believe that there is a special cover-up in play regarding information about contact with extraterrestrials.

MAJESTIC-12

Many UFO experts believe that the government not only knows more about UFOs than they are letting on, but that there is a deliberate disinformation campaign in place to hide the truth about alien contact. This stems from the belief that an alien flying saucer did crash in the United States in the 1940s (or 1950s) and that the incident was effectively covered up.

There are many variations to the story, but the basic premise has become part of traditional folklore. In some versions, alien bodies were found in the wreckage; in others, at least one alien survived. In the latter, the alien either died soon after it was found or is still alive, being kept in a secret underground base in either Nevada or New Mexico. Some stories have the alien (or aliens) entering into a partnership with the United States government, assisting with the development of new technology, or negotiating a peace treaty — or takeover.

It would make perfect sense to keep such information from the general public. The revelation that aliens are not only real but in cahoots with the government would be almost earth-shattering. Contact with aliens is thought to be the one stage in the development of the human race that would cause the most extreme change in society, considering it will be occurring during a time when the population exceeds six billion souls.

The possibility of contact with aliens is of such importance, even those not involved in the study of UFOs are concerned. According to cosmologist Paul Davies, the International Academy of Astronautics, a world body of astronomers and other scientists, has created the SETI Post-Detection Taskgroup specifically for the purposes of mediating the announcement of alien contact to the world. Not surprisingly, this group believes it should be chosen to speak on behalf of Earth to the extraterrestrials.

But would that necessarily be the case? In 1984, the first of a series of documents were released that supposedly show that the United States government was dealing with extraterrestrial contact as early as 1947. This document noted:

> Operation Majestic-12 is a top secret Research and Development
> Intelligence operation responsible directly and only to the President

of the United States. Operations of the project are carried out under control of the Majestic-12 (Majic-12) Group which was established by special classified executive order of President Truman on 24 September, 1947, upon recommendation by Dr. Vannevar Bush and Secretary of Defense James Forrestal.

According to the set of papers known as the Majestic-12 Briefing Documents, the group was convened to decide what to do about the flying saucer phenomenon, especially in light of the discovery of a crashed flying saucer with dead occupants in New Mexico.

Included in these documents is a list of people who were said to be members of the group. Out of the 12 people listed, there were six civilians and six military personnel, two from each of the three branches of military service. Five were scientists, each outstanding in a particular field of study, and one was Forrestal, the secretary of defense. As noted ufologist Stanton Friedman pointed out: "It was truly an all-star cast." In other words, this particular set of individuals would have been an ideal panel to review and assess information about a recovered alien artefact, long before the SETI group had even been considered.

The trouble is that the provenance of this set of documents is somewhat cloudy. In December 1984, a roll of undeveloped black-and-white 35 mm camera film arrived in the mail at the home of Jaime Shandera in California, with no return address and simply postmarked from Albuquerque. Shandera, together with Stanton Friedman and Bill Moore, another researcher, had been working on uncovering details of the Roswell crash story after Friedman had been tipped off in 1978 to some military involvement in a UFO crash in New Mexico. Friedman had shared his information with Moore, who had later become friends with Shandera, a movie producer.

The film contained images of these documents, obviously flat-copied from a set removed from a three-ring binder of some kind. Where did it come from? A select few people knew that these three had been investigating the crash story, so it did make some sense that the film with photographic reproductions of the documents would be sent to one of the three. Later, Moore and Shandera also received other strange things in the mail, like postcards with enigmatic comments, from peculiar locations such as Addis Ababa in Ethiopia.

Not long after, while searching through military archives for evidence of UFO information, they discovered, almost quite by accident, a copy of a secret memo between Robert Cutler to General Nathan Twining. Cutler was an assistant for national security under Dwight Eisenhower in 1954. This memo, which was discovered slipped between two files in a box of carefully organized documents, casually described a briefing concerning MJ-12. This was hailed as proof that MJ-12 really existed.

Although the FBI considers the all of these documents forgeries, many UFO researchers believe they are either real or at least have some elements of veracity. There have been protracted debates over the wording in the documents, and even the style in which the date appears typed on them has been the subject of arguments. There was also a bet that cost UFO skeptic and debunker Philip Klass $1,000 dollars. He had offered his opinion that the typeface in the Cutler memo was an anomaly and that all others were in a different typeface, therefore it must have been forged. He challenged Friedman, who believed the memo may have been legitimate, to find other memos on the disputed typeface, at $100 per memo up to a total of $1,000. Friedman found 20 other documents. All this proved, however, was that UFO researchers knew their stuff, and were more diligent than debunkers often suggest they are.

Since the original set of Majestic-12 documents appeared, and the Cutler-Twining memo, literally hundreds of other secret documents have been discovered, leaked, or otherwise found and promoted as evidence that the government really is covering up evidence of alien contact. Unfortunately, all of these documents are disputed, and many have been shown to be outright hoaxes, some of them pathetic.

Some of these documents give details of underground bases where alien technology is being analyzed. Some show that scientists such as Albert Einstein were consulted. Some even document interviews with aliens in which they describe their home planet and their society. But since none of these documents can be proven legitimate, they cannot be considered as proof that there is a cover-up about UFOs or alien intervention.

Having said that, there is some curious and possible supporting evidence for the MJ-12 group. The information obtained in 1950 by Canadian scientist Wilbert B. Smith about American investigations into flying saucers was written in a memo which has never been called

People in Ufology

One of the most successful talk radio programs of all time has been *Coast to Coast AM*, a syndicated show that began in 1989 with host Art Bell. The program originally was broadcast from a small 50,000-watt station in Las Vegas, and was a political talk show called *West Coast AM*. In the 1990s, he realized there were far too many political talk shows and changed his format to focus on paranormal and offbeat subjects.

into question. Smith noted that in discussion with American authorities regarding flying saucers, he learned that, among other things, a "concentrated effort is being made by a small group headed by Doctor Vannevar Bush."

While not called MJ-12, this group sounds very much like it, especially since Bush was one of the members of MJ-12 listed in the original documents obtained by Shandera, Moore, and Friedman. Bush was the chair of the U.S. Office of Scientific Research and Development during the Second World War, then the Research and Development Board following the war. Later, he was president of the Carnegie Institute in Washington, D.C. In short, he would have been an ideal candidate for membership in an elite team studying evidence of contact with aliens.

So, if astronomers and SETI proponents have plans in place in the event of alien contact, it would make sense that military and government organizations would have such plans prepared as well. Is this what MJ-12 was designed for?

MEN IN BLACK

Popularized by the movies of the same name, Men In Black (MIB) have been part of the UFO mythos for many decades. On the big screen, MIB are protectors of Earth, running a super-secret organization that protects Earth from evil aliens. To UFO witnesses who have encountered them, MIB are odd, threatening individuals who stalk and intimidate their victims.

The story of the MIB can be traced back to the report of a flying saucer on June 21, 1947, near Maury Island, Washington. A harbour man named Harold Dahl, his son, and two other workers reported to investigators that they were on the water when they saw six unusual objects flying in the sky. They were shaped like giant doughnuts and were moving in a curious path in the sky, five circling the sixth that was slowly dropping towards the water.

When this object was directly over the men's boat, it suddenly spewed pieces of metal onto them. One chunk was even said to have broken Dahl's son's arm. The next day, Dahl said he received a visit from a man in a dark suit who seemed to know precise details about the incident. He warned Dahl not to tell anyone about what had happened, and then left.

Although this case is sometimes noted as the first MIB incident, it should be pointed out that it was a complete hoax. Dahl was not a harbour man and the pieces of mysterious metal they showed to investigators were nothing more than foundry slag. There was no man in a dark suit.

The next time MIB appeared in UFO literature it was in a book by Gray Barker titled *They Knew Too Much About Flying Saucers*, published in 1956. In the book, Barker describes the experiences of Albert K. Bender, who in 1952 had formed a group called the International Flying Saucer Bureau. He had placed an ad in a science fiction magazine, inviting membership in his group, which was formed to solve the mystery of flying saucers. Barker had joined the group and was corresponding with him from time to time. The group was dynamic, growing in size and seemed like it would become a major force in civilian saucer research.

But in 1953, Bender began closing down the group and in 1954 withdrew from the saucer scene completely, writing a farewell note that said he no longer felt that case investigations would amount to much. Barker revealed the reason for this: in September 1953, Bender had received a visit from three men in black suits who seemed to be from the U.S. government. They said they had come to him because of his work on the flying saucer problem and wanted to tell him the truth about the mysterious craft. After they did, they warned him not to tell anyone about it or else he would be sent to jail.

There has been some speculation that Bender really did receive a visit from government officials, since it is known that civilian groups interested in flying saucers were targets of clandestine observation by the USAF in the 1950s and 1960s. However, the likelihood that government agents would have told Bender about state secrets is unlikely.

After the Bender incident, MIB were occasionally reported by witnesses and investigators. Usually, MIB appeared to warn or scare people following a UFO incident, sometimes in person, sometimes over the telephone, and in other instances, only their large black car was seen parked outside witnesses' homes for hours before slowly rumbling away.

The assumption has been that MIB are part of a major conspiracy to prevent the truth about UFOs from ever becoming public. It has been suggested that the United States Air Force is behind the sinister events, although others have speculated that the FBI, CIA, or NSA are more likely the organizations in charge.

3
UFO Organizations and Groups

Ufologists are people who investigate or conduct research on reports of UFO sightings. They do not actually study UFOs because, of course, the UFOs were seen by the witnesses and are no longer around to be studied directly. Ufologists use various techniques to try and explain or understand what the witness has seen based on his or her testimony. In this sense, ufologists are more like private investigators or part of an expert *CSI: UFO* team.

Through studies of case reports and investigations, ufologists have demonstrated that few UFO reports can be said to have no explanation. Many sightings of what witnesses believe to be unusual objects in the sky are found to have reasonable causes, such as flights of military aircraft, advertising lights, brilliant meteors, scintillating stars, and fast-moving satellites. Only a small fraction of all UFO reports evade explanation while still being sufficiently documented, well-investigated, and detailed enough by cooperative witnesses. Even then, this does not mean the UFOs in question were alien spacecraft — that would be an explanation, too! We can only state that there was no explanation for what was seen, and shrug our shoulders. This may not be satisfying, and may not be as sensational as tabloid TV depicts, but it is the reality of ufology.

Canadian UFO Survey

In Canada, there are a handful of dedicated UFO investigators scattered across the country, interviewing witnesses and collecting information about cases. Almost all co-operate in a national study called the Canadian UFO Survey which compiles case data and publishes an annual analysis of UFO sightings reported officially in Canada.

In Their Own Words

Santa Clarita Valley, California
July, 13, 1979

It was one warm summer Friday around 10:00 p.m. I was brushing the swimming pool, standing on a high platform next to and overlooking the pool and about 4 feet over the rest of the pool area. As I reached to upper end of pole, I saw a craft approaching the house from about 1–2 blocks away and from the West and heading South East.

I knew right away that it was not a helicopter or plane. It seemed flatter and wider and with lights in a circumference of the main frontal area. I ran towards the house and called my family to see it. Only my wife came out. By that time it was directly over our house and pool.

It was approximately 75–100 feet above us. We stood along side of the pool deck. It made no sound whatsoever, and it was at a complete stopped over us for about 40 seconds. The only motion was a slight wobble and when it moved and tilted downwards at an angle. I took this as some form of acknowledgment. During the entire time, we were frozen in disbelief. It is a strange sensation knowing that what you are seeing is not supposed and very foreign. It was like seeing a Greyhound Bus floating over your house!

The craft was about 75–100 feet in diameter. It had small porthole and lights around it in the upper dome section, it was solid, metallic and shiny. There was a dome in the upper section attached to the body with no visible separation, as if it were molded as one solid craft. The under section was concave towards the center and had two rectangular shapes along side each other and the length of the concave undersection.

The rectangular shapes were about 7–10 feet in width and as along as the craft's concave underside center. I also noticed ski like devices on the front and on each side of the front leading edge window.

What caught my attention was that the devices were not in the center or the "center of gravity" for the craft's length and design but very forward. The skis were S shaped with the top of the S facing forward but a design I could not replicate.

Upon the craft leaning in a downward motion we could see a window or cockpit like glass that was situated in the underside, it was on the front lower edge of the round craft. The rectangular window was approximately 4 feet in height and possibly 12–15 feet in length. There was a glow of soft orange and blue lights from the inside but we could not see anyone or any controls.

It remained at a forward and downward angle for about 10 seconds. We both had the sensation of being watched. As it was angled, I noticed that light was emanating from the upper section that was not facing the swimming pool lights. Thus, it seemed to generate light through skin of the craft as the lights that first attracted me faced forward and were much lower than the upper section of the craft.

My wife and I did not say anything to each other during the experience but she kept saying "oh my God" over and over again. The craft then left slowly at 30–40 MPH. I jumped on a wall around our property to continue seeing for at least 7 miles.

My background include Group Propulsion Systems and later as an executive with several major computer companies. What we saw was close, real, solid, and a beautiful designed craft. I know from my aeronautical engineering background that mankind has no such technology.

Reported by Ed T.
Source: UFOCasebook.com

China

Hundreds if not thousands of Chinese are now members of various UFO groups in China, attesting to the intercultural fascination with the phenomenon. In 2005, a World UFO Conference was held in Dalian, a port city in Northeast China's Liaoning Province. It attracted a large crowd, even more than the 400 plus people who were reported to be members of the Dalian UFO Society, most of whom had college degrees. The Beijing UFO Research Association at that time had 110 members, "mainly from official organizations and research institutes." Ufologist Stanton Friedman, who attended the Dalian conference as an American representative, was impressed with the conference proceedings and discussions.

Japan

Compared with other Asian countries, less information about UFO sightings is available for Japan, despite its high population. Still, interest is said to be high. OUR-J was a Japanese UFO group that was formed in 2000 and by 2003 had several hundred members, but as of 2008, its website was closed and no information was available.

When it was active, however, OUR-J held periodic skywatches for UFOs and published newsletters. During one such skywatch on October 11, 1999, as many as 60 transparent, luminous rings appeared in the sky over Meiji Jingu shrine in Harajuku, Japan. They were witnessed and photographed by OUR-J founder Junichi Kato and many of his group, who "just gasped" at the extraordinary sight. An analysis of the OUR-J data indicated that the most common shape of UFO seen in Japan looks very much like a pachinko ball, with other shapes being ovals and lemons.

MUFON

The largest UFO group at the present time is the Mutual UFO Network (MUFON). It was formed in 1969 by Walt Andrus, as the Midwest UFO Network. Andrus had been a member of the Aerial Phenomena Research Organization and had been concerned that APRO's centralization of case investigations out of its office in Arizona was hindering onsite investigations by local teams elsewhere in the country. Frustrated, he called a meeting of UFO investigators in the American Midwest and formed his own group that he believed would be more efficient and able to react more quickly to reports of sightings.

MUFON was formed with a pyramidal structure, with a host of local investigators reporting to section directors, who in turn reported to state directors, who made up the board of directors, who then worked closely with the national MUFON director. MUFON also sought many scientific consultants to advise and recommend actions for the group.

Even in its first year of operation, the need for bringing MUFON investigators together to discuss findings and disseminate current research was realized. The first national MUFON conference was held in 1970 and featured guest speakers from a variety of areas, including physical trace expert Ted Phillips and astronomer J. Allen Hynek. (Phillips presented at a recent MUFON conference in 2009 in Denver, too.)

MUFON also saw the need for consistent methodology in UFO investigation, so it was one of the first to publish a Field Investigator's Manual in 1971. Its mission statement is simple: "The scientific investigation of UFOs for the benefit of humanity." MUFON's newsletter, called *Skylook*, has been continually published since 1967, although its title is now *MUFON UFO Journal*.

As of 2010, MUFON has more than 3,000 members worldwide.

MUFON has had only a few directors during its more than 40-year history. John Schuessler took over the reins after Andrus retired in 2000, and James Carrion assumed the role in 2006. In 2010, Colorado businessman Clifford Clift became the new director of MUFON.

NICAP

The National Investigations Committee on Aerial Phenomena (NICAP) grew out of a series of small meetings about flying saucers in Washington, D.C. The group had been getting together in the early 1950s to discuss the popular subject and was attracting the interest of people from diverse backgrounds. One member was T. Townsend Brown, an inventor who was fascinated with the possibility of interplanetary travel and antigravity machines. Thinking that UFOs were a clue to this development, he formed NICAP in 1956 as an official UFO investigative body, based in Washington as an indication of its importance.

NICAP's early board of directors was impressive. It included retired military personnel, such as Major Donald Keyhoe, Major Dewey Fournet, Rear Admiral Delmer Fahrney, and radio personality Frank Edwards. Soon, Vice Admiral Roscoe

Hillenkoetter joined the board, an interesting development since he was the first director of the CIA. (There were later charges that NICAP was "infiltrated" by government spies. Official air force documents that were later unclassified showed that it was concerned about NICAP's investigation of UFO reports.)

NICAP's position was that UFOs were almost certainly extraterrestrial in nature. Shortly after its formation, spokesmen for the group, including Fahrney, gave statements to the media proclaiming that UFOs were vehicles not of this Earth. Coming from an apparent position of authority, the press widely quoted the opinions and the popular UFO movement was given a tremendous boost.

UFOs and Aliens on TV

The real Project Blue Book itself was the topic of a major network television series, *Project UFO*, which ran in 1978 and 1979. The series played up the ability of the Air Force to solve all the UFO cases it was given in spectacular and sensational fashions, although it was done in a *Dragnet*-style approach, underlining that hard facts and cool heads can solve any mystery. (Jack Webb did, in fact, produce the show.)

Both Keyhoe and Edwards were authors of several popular books on UFOs that thrust the subject into the spotlight and raised awareness of flying saucers among the general population. Keyhoe's 1950 book *The Flying Saucers Are Real* was a huge best seller and its title was adopted 20 years later by Stanton Friedman for his public presentations on UFOs. Frank Edwards wrote about many kinds of paranormal phenomena including ghosts, monsters, and UFOs. His most popular book on UFOs was *Flying Saucers — Serious Business*, published in 1966, in which he recounted conversations with pilots, military officers, and scientists about UFO sightings around the world. His light and readable style made his books influential in the field of ufology.

NICAP published the newsletter *The UFO Investigator* beginning in 1957, which continued until 1980. NICAP's membership peaked at about 14,000 in 1966, but by 1969 had fallen to only 5,000. This was due partly to the closure of the USAF Project Blue Book in 1969 but also because the number of reports had been declining over time.

During the course of the group's history, it also managed to publish some important reviews of the subject, notably *The UFO Evidence* in 1964 and *UFOs: A New Look* in 1969. These remain some of the most informative books about UFOs and UFO case investigations ever published.

In 1980, NICAP folded and its collection of UFO reports and other files were given to the Center for UFO Studies.

CUFOS

The Center for UFO Studies (CUFOS) was formed in 1973, curiously just as membership in other UFO organizations was waning. It was created by Dr. J. Allen Hynek, an astronomer at Northwestern University in Illinois, a former consultant to the USAF's Project Blue Book. After Blue Book closed in 1969, he began talking with scientific colleagues and discussing the possibility of forming an organization that would examine the subject seriously and scientifically. The result of those discussions was CUFOS. Hynek described it as the first UFO organization founded by a scientist with the goal of scientific study and analysis.

Hynek's credentials made it an attractive organization to join through membership, and its serious and scientific approach was reflected in its newsletters and other publications. The *International UFO Reporter* was first published in 1976 and is still published today. A sister publication, the *Investigators' Quarterly*, was sent to active CUFOS field officers and the *Associates Newsletter* was published as well.

CUFOS' most notable publication is the refereed *Journal of UFO Studies*, which has been published in two series, the first beginning in 1979 and the second in 1989, continuing until 2006. CUFOS has also made available its UFOCAT, a huge database of more than 150,000 entries about UFO cases and related data.

During its most active period, in the 1970s, CUFOS had thousands of subscribers. It also had an excellent reputation among law enforcement agencies, which were given stickers with the CUFOS logo and telephone number to place on their switchboards. Many sheriffs and police officers contacted CUFOS directly with their sightings or passed on information about citizens' reports. It was an effective and efficient UFO investigation system.

After Hynek passed away in 1986, CUFOS was renamed the J. Allen Hynek Center for UFO Studies. The new director, Dr. Mark Rodeghier, is a sociologist and an astrophysicist, carrying on the scientific tradition.

Although membership in CUFOS, like all other UFO organizations, is declining, it continues to function as a major repository for information about UFOs, still publishes the *International UFO Reporter*, and is still involved in UFO investigations.

APRO

The Aerial Phenomena Research Organization (APRO) was formed in 1952 by Jim and Coral Lorenzen, a married couple with a passion for the subject. The group, which was based in Arizona, remained active until 1988 after the deaths of its founders.

APRO's mission statement was more explicit than MUFON; its purpose was to enlighten the world with regard to flying saucers, stating that "they are in fact interplanetary vehicles" and that contact with the aliens should be attempted.

Coral Lorenzen explained that the purpose of the group was to counter the air force's "stupid explanations for incidents that were really unexplainable."

While clearly sympathetic to the belief that UFOs were extraterrestrial in origin, APRO was not indiscriminate about its approach. APRO did not accept the contactee movement, for example, and instead considered itself as having a more scientific approach. This may have been true to a certain extent, although the reality is that APRO, being a membership organization, allowed a very diverse set of viewpoints. There were many members who were scientific in approach, but because it was popular with the public, some of its members got carried away with enthusiasm that in some instances proved embarrassing.

APRO accepted UFO reports of close encounters of the third kind — in which alien beings are seen — unlike another major UFO group in operation during the same time period, NICAP, which downplayed such reports when possible. APRO was the largest and most influential UFO group until Walt Andrus orchestrated a split in the ranks, forming MUFON in 1969. After that point, there was a three-way rift between APRO, MUFON, and NICAP, fracturing ufology and creating bad blood between factions.

The *APRO Bulletin* was published from 1952 until the group was dissolved in 1988. Among the most noted cases written up in its pages was that of Travis Walton, who was an early UFO abductee. APRO's involvement in the case was depicted in the Hollywood movie *Fire in the Sky*, based on the true events surrounding the incident.

Jim and Carol Lorenzen died in 1986 and 1988, respectively. As there were no clear instructions on what to do with the massive files of UFO reports and the infrastructure of the organization in the Lorenzens' wills, the APRO executive decided to cease operations of the group.

After some deliberation, the Lorenzens' estate decided that the APRO UFO files should stay in Arizona rather than be transferred to CUFOS or another UFO group. A small and independent UFO group called the International Center for UFO Research (ICUFOR) was given all of APRO's files, but unfortunately have not allowed any outside organization or researchers to have access to the more than 15,000 reports in the APRO collection. None of the contents have been made available in print or online. It is not known what has happened to the APRO files at this time, more than 20 years after the organization folded.

FUFOR

The Fund for UFO Research (FUFOR) grew out of the dissolution of NICAP. Many of the original members wanted to continue to pursue serious UFO research, which they realized was underfunded (or, more accurately, unfunded). In 1979, a meeting was convened in Maryland where the foundation for the organization was laid. Its purpose was defined as the support "all reasonable and scientific efforts" to study the UFO phenomenon, and benefactors assisted in the creation of a fund from which grants could be made.

The Fund's first grant was in support of research by Dr. Bruce Maccabee on the case of a UFO filmed from an aircraft over New Zealand in 1978. The research was published as a paper in a scientific peer-reviewed journal, calling the attention of scientists to a serious study of a UFO case.

Since then, donations to the Fund have allowed the support of many other UFO-related studies. It was able to purchase a complete set of the Project Blue Book microfilms in 1981, a valuable resource for ufology research. In total, about $700,000 was raised by the Fund for UFO research.

In recent years, the Fund has been less active, but still lists a board of directors that is composed of many notable figures in the field of ufology.

BUFORA

Since UFOs are a global phenomenon, it is not surprising that there are UFO groups and organizations throughout the world. One of the largest and oldest is the British UFO Research Association (BUFORA). It began in 1959 as the London UFO Research Association, one of several such groups in England that were consolidated to form BUFORA in 1964 as public interest grew.

BUFORA's focus, like much of non-American ufology, goes somewhat further than other groups. While interested in the scientific investigation of UFOs, it also states its concern with "related paranormal/parapsychological phenomena." It is therefore also involved in cases that might include such things as ghost lights and reality shifts, probably beyond the mandate of American groups such as NICAP and CUFOS.

BUFORA was originally conceived to allow regional investigators to consult with one another and share information about UFO cases. A primary way of disseminating the information was through the *BUFORA Journal*, which was continually published (through several incarnations, formats, and titles) from 1965 until 2005. BUFORA now maintains a website as a primary method of communication, and there is no longer membership in the organization. However, it is still quite active, holds public meetings and electronically publishes information on case investigations and discussions about the UFO phenomenon.

BUFORA is currently sponsoring several research projects, including studies on vehicle interference by UFOs, sightings by pilots, the relationship between UFOs and folklore, and the experimental production of UFO phenomena. The latter involved volunteers visualizing a UFO experience at a specific location and recording their feelings or thoughts.

4

Skeptics and Debunkers

What constitutes proof of alien visitation? Isn't eyewitness testimony enough?

When it comes to the subject of UFOs, the general population seems to be very polarized. Some people accept the possibility that aliens are visiting Earth, and others simply refuse to even consider it. The words used to reject the possibility of UFOs being alien spacecraft show the topic is infused with extreme passion: "Balderdash!" "Preposterous!" Or even "Dangerous!" This in itself is strange, because normally calm, objective people can become agitated and vehement when the subject is broached.

Scientists are particularly prone to polarization on this topic. Whereas they are usually meticulous and exact when it comes to laboratory measurements and reserved when it comes to speaking about advances in their field of interest, the topic of UFOs often finds scientists making statements out of character.

Most zoologists wouldn't think of offering a scientific opinion about a cosmological theory. A physicist wouldn't be able to comment on the reasons why certain bird species are waning in the Subarctic. If it's not in your area of interest, you obviously haven't studied the data in enough detail to comment on advances in another field. But ask about UFOs and a scientist from any discipline will give his or her opinion. Usually, it will be one of skepticism and probably debunking.

Scientific methodology forbids jumping to conclusions without detailed study of the facts, yet this is what happens in the battle between science and ufology. Scientists who know better make pronouncements about the non-existence of UFOs without having read any books or journals about the subject.

This is usually because in the process of becoming scientists, scholars learn ways in which to reason and assess knowledge. In effect, they learn how to learn. Through this approach, they acquire a way of looking at the world that is critical and analytical. Technically, they are in a good position to judge the merit of any theory or proposal, in any discipline.

However, scientists are not immune to biases. Scientists are people just like anyone else, with predilection and prejudices, laudable talents as well as character flaws. Some are even prideful.

UFOs pose a serious problem to scientists. Ufology, despite efforts to quantify UFO research, does not qualify as a science by itself. Certainly, one can use scientific methodology to study the subject of UFOs, but ufology is no more a science than is a study of beat poetry, of matchbook covers, or of weblogs.

CSI

Not the *CSI* of television, but the Committee for Skeptical Inquiry. This is an organization of skeptics who "encourage the critical investigation of paranormal and fringe-science claims." The CSI was founded in 1976 as the Committee for the Scientific Investigation of Claims of the Paranormal (CSICOP), but changed its name in 2006 to make a more "media-friendly" title that focused on critical thinking rather than on paranormal issues in particular.

In the 1970s, a group of scientists had met during a meeting of the American Humanist Association in Buffalo and decided that too many people in the world were not thinking rationally about absurd claims such as contact with aliens and psychic abilities. That year, they formed CSICOP with the intent to counter media acceptance of occult phenomena and pseudoscience, including UFOs, voodoo, astrology, channelling, faith healing, and homeopathy. Their methods included the outright debunking of claims regarding these phenomena, showing them to be false or at the very least misleading. Among the original founders were Paul Kurtz, Martin Gardner, James Randi, Marcello Truzzi, Carl Sagan, Isaac Asimov, and Philip Klass.

One of the catchphrases of CSI is "extraordinary claims require extraordinary proof," said by Truzzi, copied by

PEOPLE IN UFOLOGY

By far, the pinnacle of Carl Sagan's career was the successful television series *Cosmos*, accompanied by a book of the same name. In the series, Sagan waxed poetically on virtually all aspects of science and even commented on our culture and society, weaving a picture of how life on Earth has evolved, changed, and flourished.

Sagan, but originating much earlier with philosophers such as Laplace and Hume. CSI says that no paranormal claim has stood up to scientific scrutiny.

SCIENCE AND THE FAIRY RING

Scientists are often called upon to give opinions on UFO reports or some aspect of the phenomenon, but because they generally have not done much (or any) research or study on the subject, their answers can be trite, scoffing, and usually ill-informed.

In 1975, a lecture was given at a teachers' conference in Manitoba by a scientist from the National Research Council of Canada (NRC), a government-funded body that oversaw and generated much of the scientific research in the country. At that time, the NRC was known to be accepting UFO reports from the public for study, although its official position was that there was nothing of interest in the reports. During his presentation, the scientist responded to questions regarding a then-current UFO case, the Langenburg incident. In that case, several silver bowl-shaped objects were seen to take off from a farmer's field, leaving behind swirled patches in the long grass.

This scientist, who had made his views on UFOs abundantly clear to media and to the conference attendees (that UFOs were nonsense), implied that the formations in the grass were caused by fairy-ring mushrooms. In illustration, he showed several slides of fairy rings caused by such mushrooms to the teachers attending the conference, who readily agreed with and supported his view. This was many years before crop circles became a popular topic of sensationalist tabloids, and the formations in the field were then considered "landing traces" by UFO buffs.

What was most remarkable about the scientist's presentation was that it was completely wrong. It was shocking. Such a learned individual with self-professed expertise in the UFO phenomenon must have known that fairy rings could not possibly be an explanation in this case. What's more, he admitted that he had not investigated the report, nor visited the location firsthand.

The problem with the fairy ring explanation is that such formations do not appear overnight. In fact, mycologists know they take years and many seasons of growth to achieve a size comparable to the swirled patches found in the field. They are created when a spore from a mushroom lands on a patch of grass, usually a lawn. The mushroom sprouts, grows, and then releases its own spores in a burst that sends them out in a circle. These take root, grow, and continue the growth of the circular patch of dead grass until it is a couple metres in diameter. Some get to be quite large.

But this wasn't in a lawn. This was in very tall grass, which wasn't killed off; it was laid down in a large patch a few metres in diameter. Mycologists consulted on other cases have agreed that fairy rings simply couldn't form in such a field. Yet an expert UFO debunker, a scientist whose credentials would otherwise have qualified him to give presentations to scientific panels on a variety of subjects, gave completely wrong information to a roomful of people, who laughed along with him as he pooh-poohed the entire notion of UFOs. It was exactly what they wanted to hear.

ARE YOU A SKEPTIC OR A BELIEVER?

Sometimes, a belief about UFOs is divided into two opposing camps: the believers and the skeptics. Even the question, "Do you believe?" requires a yes or no answer that puts you on one side or another.

But is it really that simple? As we learned from asking the question, "Are UFOs real?" there are many ways to interpret what is meant.

To be skeptical means simply, "to doubt." A skeptic therefore doubts that aliens are visiting Earth or doubts that there are any reliable and well-documented UFO cases.

A believer thinks aliens are visiting Earth or is sure that there are good UFO cases on record.

However, a person who is closed-minded and refuses to consider someone else's view is a denier or a disbeliever, not a skeptic. A true skeptic, when asked whether some UFOs are alien spaceships, would answer, "I don't know," or "I doubt that the data so far proves that."

Also, one can believe that there are extraterrestrials in our galaxy, but that there is no proof they are visiting earth.

It's all in the way you phrase it.

Believe or disbelieve?

Skeptic or uncritical?

Can one be an "open-minded skeptic?"

It is best to have an open mind, but not so open that your brains fall out. And I've seen a lot of grey matter on the sidewalks, from both believers and skeptics.

DEBUNKING

Debunk means to present evidence showing the foolishness of someone or something. Curiously, although most debunkers are scientists, debunking is not a scientific procedure. Rational argument is the normal way for scientists to disagree and present differing theories, usually through a series of papers published in peer-reviewed journals. Name-calling and character assassination are not found in the pages of scientific journals, as a rule. (There have been notable exceptions, however, where very unprofessional conduct by scientists has been observed on certain issues. These have included debates on continental drift, cold fusion, N-rays, and most recently, global warming.)

The subject of UFOs has been categorized as *paranormal* by debunkers, placing it in the same group with astrology, ESP, ghosts, Bigfoot, the Loch Ness Monster, cattle mutilations, and faith healing. The term *paranormal* means something that is outside the range of normal human experience and explanation, and can be applied to "anything that comes within the range of human imagination and is thought to be 'incredible.'" And we might add: "... by mainstream science."

Prominent skeptic Paul Kurtz, a profound disbeliever in UFOs, pointed out that since "the boundaries of human knowledge are constantly expanding ... what was unknowable yesterday may become scientifically explicable the next ..." He noted that the DNA helix, black holes, and quarks could not have been considered paranormal, implying that they were somehow different from other things skeptics consider to be in that category. Yet 100 years ago, the idea of a black hole was complete nonsense and would have been considered paranormal. Two hundred years ago, seeing the image of a distant person on a small box would have been paranormal, as would laser pointers, cell phones, and iPods. Why, these would have all been considered some kind of magic, and certainly inappropriate for scientists to consider. Galileo was put to death for heresy.

The subject of UFOs can elicit such highly emotional debate from both debunkers and believers. Few people seem capable of holding a middle ground; most either believe or disbelieve, two opposing views that do not actually mean anything, as we have seen. Why is this so?

The reason UFOs are such a contentious issue is that there's a lot riding on it. If aliens really are visiting Earth, then the scientific community has been totally wrong and all world government has probably been lying to their citizens. The amount of evidence needed to create an overwhelming upset of this kind would be enormous, and only the proverbial landing on the White House lawn would be enough to tip the scales. It's such an all-or-nothing long shot that it is no wonder it arouses such passion.

Debunking is a completely expected response by science to such an important issue, especially one that attracts many people unversed in science. Many scientists advocate on behalf of ufology, but they are in the minority; the majority of those in the scientific community do not hold ufology in high regard.

Science continues to develop news ways of looking at, dealing with, and understanding our world. Its methodologies have helped achieve the high level of civilization we have today. We depend upon it for energy, food, and survival.

Debunking isn't part of typical scientific procedure, but over-analyzing and dissecting controversial topics may assist in the scientific process.

HOAXES

Throughout the history of ufology, many hoaxes have been uncovered, although not as many as you might think. Out of the 8,500 Canadian UFO reports studied during 1989 to 2009 by the Canadian UFO Survey, only a handful were found to be hoaxes.

Gian Monguzzi

One historical UFO hoax originally took place on July 31, 1952. At about 9:15 a.m., Gian Monguzzi and his wife were hiking over the Italian Alps near Scerscen Glacier when they noticed that all the sound around them had been dampened; even their voices could not be heard. Suddenly, a disc-shaped craft landed on the glacier, only about 230 metres away. It was about 10 metres in diameter, three metres in height, and had an antenna on its top. Monguzzi pulled out his camera and took some photos. This was especially fortunate, as a robot-like creature soon appeared beside the saucer, walking around it as if checking it out. Monguzzi continued to take photos until after a few minutes the being moved behind the craft and the object took off over the mountains.

Moguzzi went to Italian newspaper offices with his story and the photographs, asking millions of *lire* for the images. His story was printed in many papers and magazines and soon was being republished around the world, accompanied by photos of the saucer and "little man" framed against the mountains. Investigators eventually determined that Monguzzi had created the entire hoax in a field next to his house, and that he had spun the tale in revenge for being unable to get a job with the newspapers.

It must be emphasized that hoaxes are relatively rare in ufology. Most UFO reports are simply honest misidentifications, but there are still many good unresolved cases on record.

E-Hoax

In March 2005, hoaxers sent out email messages to thousands of recipients, encouraging them to all report an identical fake UFO sighting to official reporting agencies and UFO groups:

> Posted: Thu Mar 03, 2005
> Subject: Ssshhh! What I am about to tell you is a secret. Do not tell anyone.
> On Saturday, March 19, many people on the internet will hoax the world with the biggest mass UFO sighting in years. The craft will zoom around the United States and the world. What will they see?
> A craft with 4 lights, 2 of which blinked several colors. They will then report their sighting as happening at APPROXIMATELY (not exactly) the appropriate time, and that's it....
> Report the sighting to the National UFO Reporting center [the phone number was given in the original email].
> Do not post this information online. Only share it with 'real life' friends.

Sure enough, reports were made to the National UFO Reporting Center in the United States from people throughout North America. Cases were also reported to investigative groups in Canada, and Ufology Research received a handful of reports. Not having heard about the planned hoax beforehand, it was considered out of the ordinary to receive cases that seemed to confirm or support one another. They were also scattered across the country, in different time zones, but the local times were very similar.

When follow-up emails were sent out, no one replied, and it soon became evident that something fishy was going on. The hoax was uncovered in a short time and ufologists began sorting through the phony reports. In retrospect, it was an interesting experiment in viral communication. What *did not* happen, to the possible chagrin of skeptics, is the reports being accepted as real by investigators and lauded as a major new UFO wave. Looked at individually, each separate hoax UFO

UFOs and Aliens in Movies

Fire in the Sky (1993) was panned by some UFO researchers when it first came out, largely because of the end sequences in which abductee Travis Walton is encased in goo similar to scenes in the *Matrix* or *Invasion of the Body Snatchers*. Those images were not part of Walton's story, which was fantastic enough without Hollywood embellishment. Leading up to the final scenes, however, the film accurately portrays how UFO case investigations are conducted, and the difficulty in unravelling witnesses' testimony in complicated cases. James Garner did a fine job of playing the role of a confused but patient police officer trying to unravel the mystery of what happened to Walton during the several days he was supposedly off Earth and aboard a saucer.

report could have been added to a UFO sightings list or database, and assigned an *insufficient information* label, but might have been considered a valid UFO report. Ironically, it was the fact that so many nearly identical reports were made that alerted UFO investigators to the prank.

The Carp Case

In late 1989, UFO investigators and researchers in Canada and the United States received a package of documents through the mail from a mysterious "Deep Throat." These papers described the crash of a UFO that had occurred near the town of Carp, a dozen kilometres from Ottawa, Canada, and included a photocopied photograph of an alien standing in some shrubbery.

The absurdity of the information contained in the material made it particularly easy to dismiss it as nonsense. It included snippets of rumours about secret government and military operations, splicing together stories about the crash of a flying saucer, underground bases, clandestine laboratories, and technologically advanced weaponry, all within a few dozen kilometres of the capital of Canada. The text was mostly paranoid "New World Order" ramblings, like those disseminated by civilian militia groups and semi-terrorist operations.

Canadian investigators, although certain the papers were hoaxes, nevertheless decided to trace their origin in the hope that light could be shed on the perpetrators. With some detective work, one researcher was able to locate the crash site and even some apparent witnesses.

A witness claimed that on November 4, 1989, she saw an intense, bright light pass overhead, heading south toward a swamp at the far end of the field behind her home. Another woman had been scared by a very bright light that shone through her bathroom window, and she heard the sound of helicopters overhead. A few talked of dogs and cattle being disturbed. But with these few exceptions, most people in the region could not recall anything unusual happening that night.

Investigators examined the field and swamp indicated on the map but could not find any sign of a massive recovery effort with heavy equipment to retrieve the crashed saucer. Other UFO investigators visited the area, too, and all concluded that the whole affair was likely a hoax.

Then, almost two years later, the Carp case resurfaced with even more bizarre twists. In 1991, more secret documents were sent to several ufologists, all postmarked in Ottawa. There were partially censored documents that appeared to be similar to blacked-out UFO-related government papers uncovered by retrieval experts such as Stanton Friedman, who has documented an apparent government cover-up of information about UFOs. These Carp documents described

Credit: Ufology Research

In 1991, sets of hoaxed materials, including photographs and documents were sent to several UFO researchers in North America. Included in these materials was a photograph supposedly of an alien.

how China was preparing for war against the United States, assisted by aliens for some undetermined reason. The documents boasted: "America will be crippled; power grids, tanks, missiles, cars, antennas, phone lines will stop," but that the "ELITE will survive WW3" in "installations under mile-thick Canadian-shield granite." The documents went on to say that there were large underground installations built by the American government in the Carp area, where secret research was being done.

The package of materials, with cryptic notes signed by someone calling himself "Guardian," also included a map and sketch of alien activity near Ottawa between 1970–1991, with Masonic symbols and identification guides for different alien craft. There was also a black-and-white photograph of an alien standing in some tall grass and a Polaroid photograph of a UFO hovering over a road. Some packages contained a VHS videotape that showed what was alleged to be an alien craft on the ground. Although the packages of materials had the earmarks of an elaborate hoax, some UFO investigators thought there might have been a genuine UFO landing.

In May 1992, a group of ufologists met in Carlton, Ontario, on an expedition to examine the landing area identified on the Guardian's map. They were able to quickly find a location where something unusual had been occurring. There was an abandoned farmhouse with signs reading DO NOT ENTER and DND KILLING FIELDS,

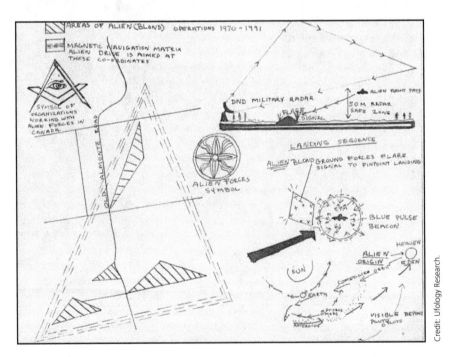

One of the Carp documents showing alien maneuvers in the area.

Credit: Ufology Research.

with drawings of tanks, helicopters and weapons on it. It was also riddled with bullet holes. (DND is the acronym for the Canadian Department of National Defense.) It was thought that the area was being used for war games.

They located a witness who told them of many strange UFO sightings over the years and suspicious military activity in the area. One of the sketches of the UFOs she drew exactly matched one of the UFOs on the "alien craft spotting chart" that

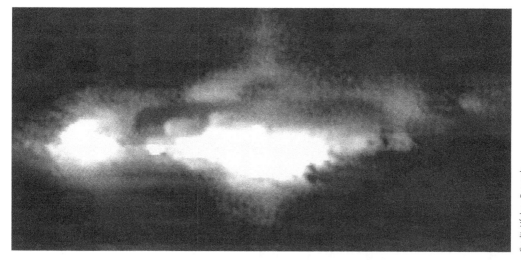

Included in the Carp materials was a video of a UFO with bright lights that seemed to be moving around the sky. Investigations showed the UFO was actually a truck on the ground, surrounded by bright lights, and that the camera itself was being jostled.

The photograph of the Carp UFO with the truck drawn in to help see the illusion.

Guardian had sent to the ufologists. The witness' story and account did not seem believable to the investigators because of some inconsistencies. They also discovered that a local man was a UFO buff and sometimes referred to himself as "Guardian."

Finally, some burned patches and a burned-out vehicle were found in a nearby field, leading the investigators to conclude that flares and fireworks had been videotaped in such a way as to so make a pickup truck look as if it was a hovering craft. Despite the investigators' publication of their detailed report and conclusions, the Carp case has continued to be debated and discussed, and the video has been promoted and shown on TV programs as "one of the best" UFO videos of a hovering saucer.

An exposé of the hoax was posted on a major UFO discussion list at *www. virtuallystrange.net/ufo/updates/1999/oct/m11-018.shtml.* (Retrieved September 16, 2007.)

Sawmill Bay

Another historical UFO case that was shown to have been completely fabricated supposedly occurred on July 2, 1950, in Sawmill Bay on Steep Rock Lake in Northwestern Ontario, Canada, according to an anonymous writer who sent a letter to a small local newspaper. The story was that an amorous couple was having a picnic when "the air seemed to vibrate as if from shock waves." They looked down at the lake and saw a large object floating on the water, looking like "two saucers, one upside down on top of the other." On its upper deck was an open hatch and walking around on top were several small creatures wearing some kind of metallic uniform.

While the creatures went about their business (whatever that was), the witnesses crouched behind a large rock and watched, noticing a large hoop-shaped antenna rotating slowly on top of the craft, making sure that the coast was clear. At one point a deer walked by the shore near the couple, and the antenna stopped rotating, focusing on the animal. The creatures froze in their tracks but as soon as the all-clear was commanded somehow, they once again began their work.

As the couple watched in amazement, they saw that one of the creatures was holding a green hose that hung down into the lake. A loud humming noise could be heard, and they assumed it meant that the craft was taking on a supply of water. After a while, the couple watched the saucer take off with a blast of air and disappear. Unfortunately, the story was later found to be a hoax after interviews with newspaper staff and local residents.

The Skeptics

On January 5, 2009, two men in Morristown, New Jersey, decided they would create a UFO hoax to show how unreliable UFO witnesses can be, and also to show that UFO investigators were unprofessional and gullible. They formed this plan because they were avid readers of *Skeptic* magazine and wanted to help other skeptics prove that there was nothing to the UFO phenomenon.

Around 8:15 p.m. that night, they tied flares to large helium balloons and sent five of the contraptions aloft over a field. They filmed their hoax so as to document their experiment.

Sure enough, many people saw the balloons but described them as mysterious lights. One experienced pilot was interviewed and featured on several news networks describing how the UFOs he saw were truly unusual. Also, when the host of a TV show about UFOs investigated, he stated that the UFOs were definitely not balloons or flares. Some ufologists even suggested that the UFOs were formations of alien craft.

The men repeated their balloon hoax experiment four more times throughout January and February, each time adding to the UFO frenzy. However, authorities became concerned that the UFOs, whatever they were, were hazards to air traffic. They were certain the objects were balloons, and wanted to catch the culprits.

The two men felt they had succeeded in showing that UFO investigators were charlatans and could be easily manipulated. They argued that if ufologists could be fooled on this case, then all UFO cases were suspect. They announced their ruse on April 1, 2009, after the case had received a great deal of coverage by news media and commentary by UFO experts. When their expose was published by *Skeptic* magazine, it seemed as though they were completely vindicated.

However, several things make the hoax less successful than has been claimed. First of all, not all UFO investigators and researchers thought the UFOs were alien spaceships. In fact, relatively few did; it appears that media sought out ufologists who would go on record to support the extraterrestrial explanation. Others felt the UFOs were odd but were unsure what they were. Peter Davenport, director of the National UFO Reporting Center in the USA, explained simply that the UFOs were likely not aircraft because of their observed characteristics, which was quite true.

The other point to note is that witnesses reported the UFOs quite accurately. That is, they reported seeing several lights, each having about the same red colour, with slow movement. Witnesses did not describe large, structured flying saucers or disc-shaped objects. Nor did they report seeing any aliens or other entities. Their descriptions of what they saw matched the balloon-flares more or less accurately.

It was simply the interpretation and the witnesses' own beliefs that clouded their statements about what was seen.

In other words, the hoaxers did not prove that UFO reports are of no consequence. If a witness sees and reports a light, there was likely a light to be seen. If he or she sees and reports a disc- or triangular-shaped craft, what was actually in the sky?

How to Report a UFO

First of all, don't panic!

Take it easy. Think about what made you think whatever it is you're looking at is a UFO. Why isn't it just an airplane? A star? A satellite? Try to find someone else to see it with you. Call them on your cellphone if you have to; maybe they can see it across town.

To make a report of a UFO that will be useful to investigators, you'll need some fairly basic information. Here's a simple checklist:

1. What's the date you saw the UFO(s)?
2. Where were you when you saw the UFO(s)? Not "your kitchen," but what city, town, or neighbourhood? Your province or state?
3. What is the time you first saw the UFO(s)?
4. How long did you watch it (them) before it (they) went out of sight or you stopped watching it (them)?
5. Was someone watching it (them) with you? Who?
6. What shape was (were) the UFO(s)? If it (they) looked like (a) bright light(s), say that.
7. What colour was (were) the UFO(s)?
8. What direction were you looking when you first saw the UFO(s)?
9. What direction were you looking when you last saw the UFO(s)?
10. What was the weather like at the time?
11. How did the UFO(s) move, if at all?
12. Describe what the UFO(s) looked like.
13. In your own words, tell the story of what happened. Describe how you saw the UFO(s) and what happened next, until your UFO sighting was over.
14. Finally, think about what you saw and why you think it was a UFO. Why do you think this was a UFO and not something else, like a plane, star, or balloon?

It would be really helpful to investigators if you could draw your impression of what the UFO(s) looked like. Give it a try!

Send this information in an email to *canadianuforeport@hotmail.com*. Or in an old-fashioned letter to:

Ufology Research, Box 204, Winnipeg, Manitoba, Canada R3V 1L6.

Information about UFOs, including details of sightings both old and new, can be found in many places on the Internet, so why not do some surfing for UFOs? The Ufology Research blog can be found at *http://uforum.blogspot.com*.

Bibliography

Some of the material presented in this book has come from my other works, including the following.

Rutkowski, Chris A.

- *Abductions and Aliens: What's Really Going On?* Toronto: Dundurn, 1999.
- *I Saw It Too!* Toronto: Dundurn, 2009.
- *Unnatural History.* Winnipeg: Chameleon Press, 1993.
- *A World of UFOs.* Toronto: Dundurn, 2008.

Rutkowski, Chris A., and Geoff Dittman.

- *The Canadian UFO Report: The Best Cases Revealed.* Toronto: Dundurn, 2006.

Particular Books of Interest

Clark, Jerome, ed. *The UFO Encyclopedia.* Detroit: Omnigraphics, 1992.

Evans, Hilary, and Dennis Stacy, eds. *UFOs 1947–1997.* London: John Brown, 1997.

Friedman, Stanton. *Flying Saucers and Science.* Franklin Lakes, NJ: New Page, 2008.

Friedman, Stanton, and Don Berliner. *Crash at Corona: The U.S. Military Retrieval and Cover-Up of a UFO.* New York: Paragon, 1992.

Friedman, Stanton, and Kathleen Marden. *Captured! The Betty and Barney Hill UFO Experience*. Franklin Lakes, NJ: New Page Books, 2007.

Fuller, John. *The Interrupted Journey*. New York: Dial Press, 1966.

Good, Timothy. *Above Top Secret*. Toronto: Macmillan, 1988.

Hynek, J. Allen. *The UFO Experience: A Scientific Inquiry*. Chicago: Henry Regnery, 1972.

Klass, Philip. *UFOs Explained*. New York: Vintage Books, 1976.

Randles, Jenny. *From Out of the Blue*. New York: Berkley, 1993.

Randle, Kevin, and Don Schmitt. *UFO Crash at Roswell*. New York: Avon Books, 1991.

Story, Ronald. *UFOs and the Limits of Science*. New York: William Morrow, 1981.

Vallee, Jacques. *Passport to Magonia*. Chicago: Henry Regnery, 1969.

ALSO BY CHRIS A. RUTKOWSKI

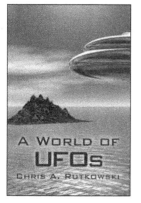

A World of UFOs
978-1-55002-833-1 / $24.99

UFOs and UFO encounters are truly global phenomena. What are some of the most interesting cases? Which ones seem most mysterious? From a floating platform watched by dozens in Indonesia, to a Saturn-shaped object that flew over a ship off the coast of Brazil, to a landing Down Under, UFOs have been baffling witnesses and making headlines around the world.

I Saw It Too!
Real UFO Sightings
978-1-55488-448-3 / $14.99

Although many adults believe they have had encounters with strange creatures from alien spaceships, not everyone has actually reported their experiences to official investigators. But if you're a young person it's even less likely that people will believe you and more likely that your story will never be officially recorded. After all, who would believe a kid?

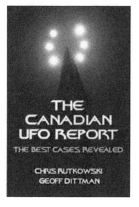

The Canadian UFO Report
The Best Cases Revealed
with Geoff Dittman
978-1-55002-621-4 / $24.99

This popular history of the UFO phenomenon in Canada is drawn from government documents and civilian case files — many previously unpublished. The book includes a chronological overview of the best Canadian UFO cases, from the very first sighting of "fiery serpents" over Montreal in 1662 to reports in the twenty-first century. There are chapters on the government's involvement with UFOs, UFO landing pads, media interest, and even UFO abductions.

Available at your favourite bookseller.

DUNDURN PRESS
www.dundurn.com

What did you think of this book?
Visit **www.dundurn.com** for reviews, videos, updates, and more!